ue ore the last date s

DATABASE MANAGEMENT
Developing Application Systems Using ORACLE

Ralph B. Bisland, Jr.

The University of Southern Mississippi

PRENTICE HALL, Englewood Cliffs, New Jersey 07632

Library of Congress Cataloging-in-Publication Data

Bisland, Ralph B., [date]
    Database management: developing application systems using ORACLE
    Ralph B. Bisland, Jr.
      p. cm.

    Includes index.
    ISBN 0-13-198052-1
    1. Database management.   2. ORACLE (Computer system)
3. Relational databases.   I. Title.
QA76.9.D3B53 1989
005.74-dc19
                                              88-30592
                                                  CIP

Editorial/production supervision: *Edith Riker*
Cover design: *Wanda Lubelska Design*
Manufacturing buyer: *Mary Noonan*

© 1989 by Prentice-Hall, Inc.
A Division of Simon & Schuster
Englewood Cliffs, New Jersey 07632

Printed in the United States of America
10   9   8   7   6   5   4   3   2

ISBN   0-13-198052-1

Prentice-Hall International (UK) Limited, *London*
Prentice-Hall of Australia Pty. Limited, *Sydney*
Prentice-Hall Canada Inc., *Toronto*
Prentice-Hall Hispanoamericana, S.A., *Mexico*
Prentice-Hall of India Private Limited, *New Delhi*
Prentice-Hall of Japan, Inc., *Tokyo*
Simon & Schuster Asia Pte. Ltd., *Singapore*
Editora Prentice-Hall do Brasil, Ltda., *Rio de Janeiro*

To Dottie, Wendy, and Amy

Contents

Preface

This book is designed as an applications-oriented text for teaching relational database management systems. The book is composed of two basic parts. Chapters 1 through 4 contain the necessary theory material that the reader needs to digest, for comprehension of how relational databases work. The remainder of the book is dedicated to illustrating how the relational theory can be implemented through a commercially available database called ORACLE.

ORACLE was chosen as the illustrative database for several reasons. First, it is a popular relational database used by virtually all types of industries. Second, it utilizes the SQL (ˆuSˆrˆtructured ˆuˆQˆrˆuery ˆuˆLˆrˆanguage) interface language that has become the industry standard for relational database access. Third, the ORACLE Corporation made the ORACLE package available to qualified colleges and universities free of charge during the 1986 year.

The book assumes some prerequisite computing knowledge. These concepts include a basic knowledge of data structures, COBOL Programming, and file structures. COBOL was selected because it is the most used host language to interface industrial database management systems. Knowledge of any higher level language will suffice.

The organization of the book is as follows. The first chapter contains an introduction to what databases are and what they are used for. It contains some elementary definitions and examples of databases. The second chapter contains an overview of the relational model. Chapter 3 consists of a discussion of relational algebra, which is a theoretical language used to retrieve and manage data in a relational database. It is important that the student understand the basic relational algebra commands, for they are referred to throughout the remainder of the text. The fourth chapter is dedicated to a discussion of relational calculus. Some instructors of relational databases feel that this material can be skipped without loss of continuity. Therefore, this book is designed so that Chapter 4 can be omitted without loss of continuity.

Chapters 5 through 14 are utilized to illustrate an implementation of the relational theory. These chapters cover the ORACLE implementation of the relational model through the on-line interface language SQL. Various concepts, such as data retrieval, data maintenance, formatting of data, concurrent processing, journalizing, import and export of files and so on, are integrated into the discussion of the SQL commands.

Chapter 15 is devoted to relational database design. This chapter could have been placed after Chapter 4, so that database design could be covered before the ORACLE syntax. It is debatable whether to discuss database design and then syntax, or vice versa. I have tried to teach it both ways, and the successful method for me is to illustrate the syntax first. If this organization does not please you, simply branch to Chapter 15 after Chapter 4 (or Chapter 3 if you plan to omit Chapter 4) has been completed. There are a few references to SQL commands in Chapter 15, but they should be very easy to understand.

All examples of Oracle code have been run on version 4.2.2 of Oracle on a Harris H800 computer system.

Ralph B. Bisland, Jr.
Hattiesburg, MS

Acknowledgments

This book was great fun to write, especially when I received the help and encouragement that I did. I would like to thank some very special people for assisting me in this 3-year project.

Janet Ponder: Janet was my undergraduate and later graduate assistant when I was developing this project. She did all of the preliminary editing and testing of the SQL commands. Her help with my students provided me with enough free time to concentrate on this work. Her assistance was invaluable to the completion of this project.

Karen Trest Sokatch: Karen is one of my former students who is now an ORACLE database administrator for E-Systems in Dallas, Texas. Karen reviewed almost all the material for technical correctness and made suggestions on improving the presentation of the material. Her critiques of the chapters were very helpful to me.

Dottie, Wendy, and Amy Bisland: These are my wife and daughters. I would like to thank them for providing me with encouragement and a reason for completing this project.

Ken Jacobs: Ken is Product Manager for ORACLE at the ORACLE Corporation. Ken is my contact person at ORACLE. Whenever I had a question or needed something, Ken was always ready and willing to assist me in any way that he could. His help was greatly appreciated.

Valerie Ashton: Valerie is the Acquisitions Editor at Prentice Hall with whom I was fortunate enough to work. I would like to thank her for all the help and encouragement that she has given me on this project. She has patience and understanding which made her easy and fun to work with.

Edie Riker: Edie is the Production Editor at Prentice Hall with whom I was also very fortunate enough to work. I would like to thank her for all the help that she has given me to improve the presentation of the material in this text.

All the students in CSS481/581: This is the course (Relational Database Management Systems) at the University of Southern Mississippi for which this book was developed. These students provided some excellent comments and suggestions that contributed to the final project. Special thanks goes to Sandy Gunter and Glenda Marks for their editing assistance.

The "Lunch Bunch" Hearts Group: This is a group of colleagues who get together to play Hearts every day for "relaxation." This group includes Mary Dayne Gregg, Glenn Oehms, Mike Rodgers, and Phil Richards. Their encouragement and help contributed immensely to the completion of this project.

Bob Wales: Bob is my golfing buddy who said that if I did not mention his name in my book, he would stop giving me 2 shots a side.

Introduction to Database Management Systems

PURPOSE: This chapter is designed to introduce you to database terminology, structure, operations, and access methods. An example database is given to illustrate the concepts covered in the chapter.

The Information Age is upon us. In today's complex world vast amounts of data must be stored, modified, and retrieved for an institution to survive. (By institution we mean any entity, i.e., business, school, government agency, or even an individual who utilizes any type of data.) Because of this overflow of data that institutions must utilize, it is obvious that computers must be involved in the manipulation of this data. There must be efficient methods developed for rapid storage and retrieval of large volumes of data. These methods must involve the use of computers. The most popular technique currently used to manage vast amounts of data is the database management system.

COMMONLY USED DATABASE TERMS

Before we can begin to explore databases we must understand a set of commonly used terms in the database vernacular. We would expect you to be familiar with some of these terms, and we will define the remaining ones for you. These are not all the concepts that are needed to understand database management systems completely, but they will get us started.

Terms That You Should Be Familiar With

The terms that you should already know are

1. File
2. Record
3. Data item or data field
4. Direct access storage device
5. Random access files
6. Keyed file organization
7. Compilers
8. Programming languages, specifically COBOL
9. Operating systems

Definitions of Some Commonly Used Database Terms

The following terms are defined for you so that we may have a common knowledge base to explore database management systems. Some of the terms will be considered in pairs due to their relationships.

Database   A database is a collection of interrelated data and everything that is needed to maintain and use it. A database does not have to be computerized. A recipe box of your favorite recipes could be considered a database. However when we use the term database, we will usually be referring to a computerized database.

Database management system   A collection of software required to store, delete, modify, and retrieve data that is stored in a data base. The term database management system is commonly abbreviated DBMS.

Data/Information   Data is a set of characters that have no meaning on their own. Data, for purposes of this book, will refer to characters that are stored on secondary storage devices (since we are referring to computerized databases). Information is data that means something to someone and is used in a context.

To illustrate the difference between these two terms, let us utilize an example. Consider the following six digits: 100945. At this point these digits mean absolutely nothing to you. However, if we told you that the first two digits represented a month, the next two represented a day of the month, and the last two digits of a year forming a date, and this date was the birthdate of a local college professor, it would now be information. The difference between the two is that data is just symbols and information has meaning to the user.

The same data can have different meaning(s) to different users. This implies that the characters are stored on secondary storage devices so that they can be used by multiple users. Each user determines what the data means to them—the meaning is not stored, only the raw facts. This is the reason we use the term databases and not information bases.

Type/occurrence   Type is a generic term used to identify a data component of a database. For example, we may have a data item type, a record type, and a file type. An occurrence identifies a specific value of a type. Type is a general term, whereas occurrence is a specific term.

Here are some examples of types and occurrences.

```
TYPE                    OCCURRENCE
STUDENT-NAME            RAY WILSON
AGE                     20
GENDER                  MALE
MAJOR                   COMPUTER SCIENCE

STUDENT-RECORD
STUDENT-NAME            ART JOHNSON
ADDRESS                 125 MAPLE AVE., HOUMA, LA 70364
MAJOR                   BUSINESS INFORMATION SYSTEMS
GENDER                  MALE
PHONE                   BR549
```

Note that for each type, there can be many occurrences.

Master-file   This is a file that contains all the up-to-date data that pertains to a given topic. This file is fairly permanent in that the data is usually kept for a relatively long period of time. An example of a master file would be the student master file of a university that should contain an up-to-date list of all the active students at a local university. This file may contain such data as the student's name, address, major, gender, current grade point average, total hours completed, and so on.

Transaction   This is an action that causes the master file to be brought up-to-date. These transactions can be grouped together and processed at the same time (i.e., the end of the day) in a batch (called batch processing) or processed as they occur. Transactions cause changes to be made in the master file. The types of changes that can be made are discussed later in this chapter.

Data integrity   Data integrity is concerned with the degree of correctness, timeliness, and relevance of the data within the database. We want the data in the database to be as correct as we possibly can make it. This can be accomplished by performing certain edit checks any time a new record occurrence is added to the database or a data item(s) is modified. An example of an integrity check would be to test a student's grade point average to ensure that it falls between

0.000 and 4.000 (assuming a 0.000 is the minimum and 4.000 is the maximum grade point average).

Database key   The database key refers to the address of a record occurrence stored in a database. The database key is usually composed of some type of file identifier, such as, the file name or file number, concatenated with the page number within the file that the record is stored on, concatenated with the line number within the page where the data for the record begins.

File-Name	Page-Number	Line-Number

By using the database key to retrieve records, the DBMS does not have to utilize a hashing algorithm or step through any type indexed structure to retrieve records. This makes using the database key the fastest method of retrieving records, for the DBMS can go "directly" to the record that it needs. This method of retrieval of records is sometimes referred to as direct retrieval. The database key of the record is generated by the DBMS when the record is initially stored in the systems' data files.

AN EXAMPLE DATABASE

To illustrate the various concepts of database management systems, we will introduce a sample database. This database will be used throughout the text. We have selected a student database for our example because we feel that the concepts, variables, keys, underlying assumptions, and so on, will be understood by more readers than will any other database application area.

Let us assume that a certain university has a data processing department as part of its organization structure. It is their function to keep track of students, faculty, and the courses that the faculty teaches and the courses that the students take. Let us further assume that the University Information System (it's always nice to have a fancy title for a bunch of computer programs) was not developed all at the same time—it was developed piecemeal fashion over many years.

The Student Records System

The first part of the system, the Student Records System (Figure 1.1), was developed in 1968, and the programmer who developed the system wrote all the necessary

Figure 1.1   Part I, The Student Records System

* This is a technical database term meaning "a lot" or "mucho."

Figure 1.2   Part II, The Student Record/Faculty Records System

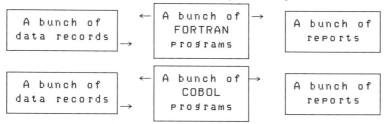

programs in FORTRAN because that is the only language that the programmer knew. The Student Master File, contains such data as the student's identification number, name, address, major, gender, grade point average, number of hours completed, and classification. All the programs are written in FORTRAN, and therefore, data is stored and retrieved by 32-bit words.

The Faculty Records System

The second part of the system, the Faculty Records System (Figure 1.2) was developed in 1972, and the programmer who developed the system wrote all the necessary programs in COBOL because that was the only language that the programmer knew; besides the programmer said, ''All business systems should be written in COBOL anyway.'' The Faculty Master File contains such data as the faculty members identification number, name, department(s) assigned to, salaries, genders, highest degrees earned, and so on. Since all the programs were written in COBOL, all the data files contain text-formatted data (either EBCDIC or ASCII).

The Class Records System

The final part of the system, the Class Records System (Figure 1.3), was developed in 1979, and the programmer who developed the system wrote all the necessary

Figure 1.3   Part III, The University Information System (note the name change)

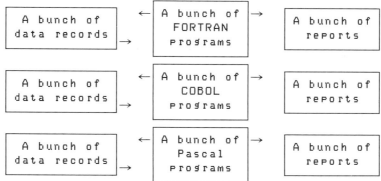

programs in Pascal because he had just graduated from a computer science program where he learned Pascal and he was "just dying to use it for something." The Class Record Master File contains such data as the course identification number, course title, section number, and room number where the course is meeting and the names of all of the students in the class. Since all the programs were written in Pascal, this means that the data files were formatted free-field (at least the numeric data was).

A Hypothetical Scenario

Over the years, this system, even though it has had its problems, has functioned very well for the university. However, one day the university president gets a phone call from a member of the board of trustees and says that he needs a list of all the female students currently being taught by female instructors and the list is to be placed in alphabetical order. The board member says that if the president can get this information back to him in two hours the university can receive the prestigious "Friends of Venus" society's annual donation of $68,854,965,218.04.

The frantic university president calls the director of computing services and gives him the request for information. The director thinks about the request, calls the president back, and tries to explain to him the reasons why the request cannot be filled.

His tale of woe begins by informing the president that even though the data that is needed to respond to this inquiry is stored in the University Information System, it cannot be retrieved in such a short time. He tries to explain to the president that some of the data files are formatted by words, some by character data, and some in free-field format. He then explains that the systems are three distinct entities and are not linked together. He mentions something about data structures and pointers, which goes right over the president's head. By now the president is furious and says, "Look, we bought the big expensive computer, and you tell me that my information is in the computer but you can't get it out?" The director sheepishly agrees, resigns and becomes a shrimp boat captain off the coast of Antarctica. The president, in his frustration, resigns his job as president and becomes a left shoe salesman (he sells only to pirates) at a department store in Little Rabbit, Australia.

Now that the president and director of data processing have left the university, some department heads begin to request to have their "own" copies of the various master files because "our needs are different from those of other departments." Hence, the registrar gets a copy of the master file to keep track of students who enter, leave, and graduate from the university. The registrar perceives that he has to keep track of additional data from what is currently kept in the Student Master File on each student. The Data Processing department is contacted concerning this problem and the registrar's master file is expanded to include such data fields as high school graduated from, high school grade point average, high school counselor's name that recruited the student.

The director of financial aid also requests to have his "own" copy of the Student Master File. He, in turn, requests additional data fields to be added to "his" master file. The data fields added include amount and date of amount borrowed, finance percentage applied to the loan, other loans outstanding, other financial aid received. The director can see no use for keeping track of the student's grade point average and number of hours passed, so he wants those fields deleted from "his" Student Master File record.

The bursars office also requests their "own" copy of the Student Master File. You guessed it, they want to add data fields to the Student Master record, too. They want fields such as what part of tuition was paid at registration, what meal plan did the student select, has she paid her parking sticker fee, has she checked out a refrigerator for her room. The bursar's office does not utilize the student's grade point average, hours passed, or the student's home address. In lieu of the letters "M" or "F" for gender, the bursar wants "MALE" or "FEMALE" displayed for gender.

What about the library? You had better believe that the director of the library wants his copy of the master file. The data fields he wants are total fines accumulated, books currently checked out, previous books checked out. The library does not need the data fields gender, grade point average, or hours passed, but they would like the fields in the record in a different order from the other users of the data. They would like to have the student's name as the first field in the record, followed by the student's address, home address, ID, fines, books checked out, and previous books.

We now have the following master files being used at the university (see Figure 1.4). **Boldface** indicates changes made to the original master file.

As you can see, each of these four departments has its "own" copy of the Student Master File because "its needs are different from other departments." Can you begin to see problems in updating the Student Master File by four different departments. What chance do you think there is for all four files to agree in content? There are two chances —slim and none.

What We Have Learned

This example should illustrate three very important problems in managing data. By exploring these problems further, we can illustrate the goals of a database management system.

The first problem is that if you have stored data in your file system, you should be able to retrieve it in any manner that you wish. Even though in the example we have a somewhat farfetched type query (Get the names of the female students who are taught by female instructors and display the list in alphabetical order) it should illustrate the fact that *ad hoc* inquiries (or queries as they are sometimes called) need to be satisfied, and sometimes within a very short period of time.

Figure 1.4 Current Student Master Files

ORIGINAL STUDENT MASTER FILE FORMAT

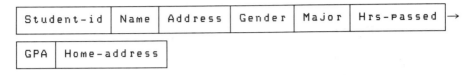

REGISTRAR'S FORMAT

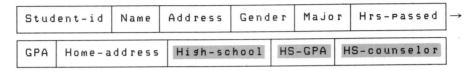

FINANCIAL AID'S FORMAT

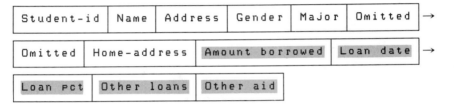

BURSAR'S FORMAT

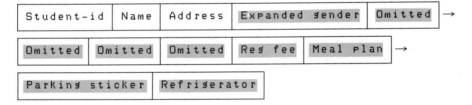

LIBRARY'S FORMAT

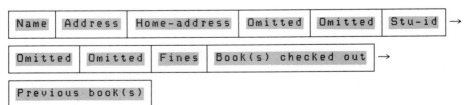

Obviously, the one way that this query could have been satisfied would be to search the Faculty File

```
FACULTY-FILE (FAC-ID, FACULTY-NAME, DEPARTMENT, GENDER, SALARY)
```

to find the faculty identifiers of all the female faculty members. (Note that FACULTY-FILE consists of the data items FAC-ID, FACULTY-NAME, DEPARTMENT and GENDER.) We could then place these faculty identifiers into a temporary list that we will call FAC-WOMEN. The following is a generic command to perform this operation:

```
FAC-WOMEN = FAC-ID OF FACULTY-FILE WHERE GENDER = 'FEMALE'
```

FAC-WOMEN is now a temporary list consisting of the faculty identifiers from the FACULTY-FILE, where GENDER is equal to 'FEMALE'.

Next we would have to use this list to determine which students were in the classes taught by the members of FAC-WOMEN. This would involve a matching of the identifiers stored in FAC-WOMEN to the faculty identifiers stored in the Course Master File.

```
COURSE-FILE (COURSE-ID, COURSE-TITLE, SECTION, FAC-ID, STU-ID)
```

We would extract the student ID numbers of the students that were in these classes, and we could place these numbers into a list called STU-LIST (making sure to delete duplicate numbers if the same student took a class under two separate female instructors). The following is a generic command to perform this operation:

```
STU-LIST = MATCH FAC-ID OF FAC-WOMEN TO FAC-ID OF COURSE-FILE
           IF A MATCH OCCURS EXTRACT UNIQUE STU-ID
```

Next, the values in STU-LIST would have to be matched with the values of the Student Master File.

```
STUDENT-FILE (STU-ID, STUDENT-NAME, ADDRESS, BIRTHDATE, GENDER)
```

The names associated with the student identifiers that match would be placed in an additional list which we will call RESULTS.

```
RESULTS = MATCH STU-ID OF STU-LIST TO STU-ID OF STUDENT-FILE
          IF A MATCH OCCURS EXTRACT UNIQUE STUDENT-NAME
```

Finally the names in RESULTS would have to be sorted to put them in alphabetical order, and then the list could be printed.

```
PRINT RESULTS SORTED BY STUDENT-NAME ASCENDING
```

Having all the data files in different formats (for they were created using different programming languages) compounds the problem. Some of the record formats had to be rearranged to fit the user's wants. Some data fields had to be redesigned (e.g.s changing "M" and "F" to "MALE" and "FEMALE"). Another major problem concerned the library's format. Notice that a student was allowed to check out more than one book. Also the student might have checked out more than one book in the past. To implement this data representation, a variable field length would have to be inserted into each record occurrence. (Think of it as a variable length array with each position holding the name of a book.) Obviously this is not a very intelligent method of implementing this desired feature of the system. We will discuss a much better method of implementing this feature later on in the text. **Flexible accessibility is one of the desired goals of database management systems.**

The second problem that was illustrated in our example was the problem of data integrity. If we have the same data stored in multiple master files, the chances of all the files being mirror images of each other is almost zero. As you can see, the reason for multiple copies of master files are necessary because users feel that they have different uses for the data from those of their fellow users. They also want to reconfigure the format of the master file. There should be only one working copy of the master file (excluding backup copies that are used for data protection), but each user should be able to view it his way. They should only have access to the data fields in the records that pertain to their function. **Reduction of data duplication and the elimination of "personal master files" is another goal of database management systems.**

A third problem is that if a programmer wants to write programs in FORTRAN, COBOL, or Pascal, for example, she should not have to concern herself with what language programs originally created the files that she wants to access. It should be up to the DBMS to convert the stored data into a form that could be used in whatever language the programmer desires to use. **This goal is called data independence—the data is insulated from the programming language, operating system, processing environment (batch or on-line).**

In summary, the goals of a database management system are as follows:

1. Since all of the institution's data will be stored in the database, the user should have a great deal of retrieval flexibility. It should be relatively easy to link data from various files together. The user really does not care how data is stored, only how it is available.

2. Since the database will be used by multiple users, it must allow for the reformatting of the same master files for the various users so that there is a reduction of data duplication. This also increases the level of data integrity in the database.

3. Since not every user will want to access the data in the same manner, there must be a high level of data independence.

4. All these goals should be achieved while the DBMS is operating in real-time mode.

Obviously we would not be describing these problems if we could not propose a reasonable solution. The solution that has been implemented by thousands of institutions is to manage data via database management systems.

PROCESSING OF DATA

When data is being processed two basic operations are performed: retrieval and maintenance.

Retrieval of Data

Retrieval refers to reading data from files so that it can be used for whatever purpose the user has. Uses may include displaying data on a video display unit (VDU) screen, writing data on a line printer, or retrieving data for use in some type of computation. More complex retrieval may also involve reading records from one file and linking them to records from other files as seen by the example just given (print the names of the female students who are taught by female instructors).

Maintenance of Data

Maintenance refers to changing the data in your master file(s) in some manner. Maintenance operations include three basic operations:

1. Adding new records
2. Deleting currently existing records
3. Modifying values stored in currently existing records.

Adding new records to the database.   Adding records results from some type of activity in the system, which we will call a **transaction**. An example of this might be that a new student enrolls at our university. To make sure that our enrollment statistics are accurate, we must insert a new record occurrence into the Student Master File. This record naturally contains whatever data we keep on our students, for example name, address, major, age, and gender.

Deleting records.   **Deleting records** also results from some type of activity in the system. A student might withdraw from the school, in which case we would delete the student's record occurrence from the Student Master File. (In actuality we might simply mark the student as inactive and/or transfer his record to another file, such as the inactive students file). Deleting students might involve retrieval of data before the deletion is done. We might want to delete all the students who are older than 35 years (any person over 35 reading this, please do not get excited—this is only an example). To accomplish this, we would have to retrieve all the records in the master file and decide whether this person is over 35 or not—if so, delete the record, if not, allow it to stay in the file.

Modifying data.   **Modifying values** might come about in either of two ways. First, a value might be stored incorrectly in a file. For example, a student's address might be stored incorrectly in the university's student master file. When this error is detected it must, it should be changed. Second, a value might be changed as the result of a system transaction. For example, when a student completes a semester of class work, his student record is updated (the number of hours completed is recomputed, the courses completed are added to his transcript, and the student's grade point average is recomputed).

There are also two types of modifications: assigned and computed. In *assigned modification*, the new value is simply assigned into the data field. For example, if a student changes addresses, the new address is assigned into the address field of the student's master file record. The old value is replaced with the new. *Computed modifications* consist of retrieving a currently existing value, doing some type of computation with it, and restoring the value. Computed modifications involve some type of data retrieval before the data item(s) can be changed. For example, a student completes a semester of class work, and his SEMESTER-HOURS-COMPLETED field must be updated. The student's current value of SEMESTER-HOURS-COMPLETED is retrieved from the student's master file record, the NUMBER-OF-SEMESTER-HOURS-PASSED is added to the current value of SEMESTER-HOURS-COMPLETED, and the new value is restored back into the student's master file record.

Table 1.1 summarizes the types of modifications possible when processing data. Remember that no matter how sophisticated your system is, there are only two operations that can be performed on your data: retrieval and maintenance.

Retrieval is the most important function of a database management system. Being able to retrieve data the way the user desires is the basic reason for constructing the database in the first place. Accessibility to data is paramount to users of the database. Maintenance is a subsidiary, but very necessary, function to maintain the integrity level of the database.

TABLE 1.1   MODIFICATIONS POSSIBLE WHEN PROCESSING DATA

Reason to make change	Type of Modification	
	Assigned	Computed
To correct an error	Student's address listed incorrectly	Student's gpa computed incorrectly
Result of a transaction	Student changes academic majors	Student completes a semester of class work

THE ROLE OF A DBMS IN PROCESSING DATA

The DBMS acts as an interface between the user and the data files:

USER ↔ | DBMS | ↔ DATA

The DBMS interprets the request from the user and decides how to retrieve or maintain the desired data and then passes this information on to the operating system, which, in turn, executes the request. The operating system, through the various device controllers, interacts with the data files:

USER ↔ | DBMS | ↔ | O/S | ↔ | Data files |

Most of the interfacing shown in the diagram is transparent to the user. If the request is for data retrieval, the raw data is usually brought into storage areas called *system buffers*. At this point the data is reformatted, if necessary, to the user's specifications. It is then passed on to the user. If the request calls for some type data maintenance, the maintenance is done in the system buffer(s) and then written to the actual data files.

TYPES OF USERS IN A DBMS ENVIRONMENT

Up to this point we have used the rather nebulous term "user" to refer to any user of a database management system. In reality there are two basic types of users of database management system.

The first is called an **end user**. This is a person who directly uses the information extracted from the database. This person generally has limited knowledge of computers and databases. She needs the information produced by the database to perform her function in the institution. This person does not care about all the intricacies of storage of data, integrity checks, or efficiency of retrieval. All she wants is information to perform her job effectively. End users may be managers, accountants, marketing researchers, auditors, or statisticians.

The second type user is the **database specialist user.** This person is usually very knowledgeable in database concepts. A database specialist can have any of the following job titles: database programmer, database designer, database analyst, database administrator (to be described at the end of this chapter), or systems analyst.

The database specialist user and the end user have different interactions with the database. The specialist user usually has the job of designing the database, writing programs to interface with the database, or maintaining the database. The end user uses either programs written by the specialist or special high-level languages called query languages to interface to the database. These interface methods are further explained later in this chapter.

IMPLEMENTATION OF A DBMS

From an implementation viewpoint, there are two methods of constructing a database: a tailored DBMS and a general-purpose DBMS.

Tailored DBMS

The first method consists of the database specialist user writing a program or a series of programs in whatever language she wishes (COBOL, C, Pascal, etc.) to retrieve and maintain the data that she needs. This approach to constructing databases is referred to as a **tailored data base management system**, for the user tailors the programs specifically to her application. As long as the user is getting the information that she needs from this method, it is a good method of implementation. However, problems usually arise when the user wants to make changes to either the access methods or the structure of the data. This usually involves extensive rewriting, or patching of applications programs.

Generalized DBMS

The **generalized method** involves utilizing a large prewritten piece of software (the DBMS) that acts as the interface between the data files and the user. The interface can consist of either or both of the following: either utilizing a series of "calls" embedded in a conventional language or a series of macro-type commands executed directly by the user. (Both these techniques will be explained in detail later in the text.)

One of the obvious advantages of this technique is that the computer programmer will not have to generate nearly as much code or manipulate the data structures to allow the user to access the data stored in the database.

An advantage of the tailored DBMS is that since the user does not have to worry about every possible access method to her data, she can write her code much more efficiently and have it execute faster. Specific methods of database access are described later in this chapter.

In general, a generalized DBMS is more flexible than is a tailored DBMS for it is designed to handle basically any type data ranging from the biological to accounting to sports data. Tailored DBMSs are also usually faster and more efficient, for they are tailored to a specific application. Generalized DBMSs are available from computer vendors or software houses, whereas tailored DBMSs are written as an in-house product or purchased from a software development firm.

For the remainder of this text when we refer to a database management system we will be referring to a generalized database management system.

STRUCTURE OF DATABASE MANAGEMENT SYSTEMS

Database management systems can be categorized by the method that they use to structure their data internally. Remember that we defined a database as a collection of interrelated data. For purposes of this text this definition precludes single-file systems. DBMS generally fall into one of four categories:

1. Hierarchical DBMS
2. Network DBMS
3. Inverted list DBMS
4. Relational DBMS

These structures are often called **models of data** for they represent a model of the structure of the data.

The Concept of a Set

Essential to both hierarchical and network DBMS is the two-level relationship between record types. The term set was used by the developers of network-type systems to describe this relationship. Developers of hierarchical type systems referred to the relationship as a parent-child relationship. The difference in the two is how they are implemented. Network sets are implemented with various pointer schemes, and parent-child relationships are implemented with physical adjacency.

A set is a two-level structure between two different record types. It is designed to represent a $1:n$ relationship between record types. For example, a department within a university has n faculty members on its staff. Let us further assume that a faculty member cannot be associated with more than one department.

There are two record types involved in this relationship: the Department record and the Faculty record. The data fields associated with the two records are as follows:

DEPARTMENT:	FACULTY:
DEPARTMENT-NAME	FACULTY-ID
DEPT-CHAIR-NAME	FACULTY-NAME
LOCATION	BIRTHDATE
PHONE-NUMBER	SALARY
BUDGET	RANK

To represent this $1:n$ relationship between department and faculty we will use a set. In a set, one record type is designated as the owner record type (the 1 in the $1:n$ relationship) and one record type is designated as the member record type (the n in the $1:n$ relationship). In our example, Department will be the owner record, and Faculty will be the member record. Figure 1.5 represents this relationship.

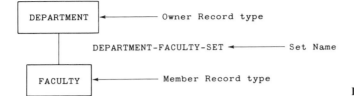

Figure 1.5   A Set Type

If this were a hierarchy, the Department record would be considered the parent, and the Faculty record would be considered the child record.

Network sets are implemented with pointers. Using the example, suppose that we had a Department named Accounting that had the following faculty members:

FACULTY-ID	FACULTY-NAME	BIRTHDATE	SALARY	RANK
S01	Sue Smith	10/25/60	46000	Professor
J01	Henry Jones	12/21/55	45000	Professor
J02	Dottie Johnson	1/05/57	42500	Associate Professor
W01	Bob Wilson	2/03/68	35000	Assistant Professor
S02	Joe Smith	4/01/63	32000	Assistant Professor

This set occurrence could be implemented as shown in Figure 1.6.

Each FACULTY-ID value (S01, J01, J02, W01, and S02) in a block represents a member record occurrence containing all the data fields in the Faculty records. (For example, S01 really represents. "S01, Sue Smith, 10/25/60, 46000, Professor".) The box with ACCOUNTING in it represents an owner record occurrence. For example, we will assume that the box with ACCOUNTING represents the record occurrence with

```
DEPARTMENT: DEPARTMENT-NAME: Accounting
            DEPT-CHAIR-NAME: Wendy Wilson
            LOCATION      : 225 Smith Hall
            PHONE-NUMBER  : 555-1234
            BUDGET        : $100,000
```

Please be aware that this is only one set occurrence. There will be a separate set occurrence for each Department-Faculty relationship in our database. For example, there will be a set occurrence for the History Department, one for the Mathematics Department, one for the Management Department, and so on.

In this implementation there is usually a NEXT pointer automatically implemented in the set (shown with the solid lines), a PRIOR or backward pointer (shown with broken lines), and an OWNER pointer from each member to its associated owner record (shown with double lines). In most network-type systems, PRIOR and OWNER pointers are optional.

Parent-child relationships of hierarchical structured DBMS are implemented

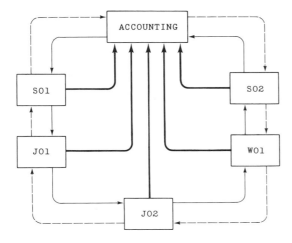

Figure 1.6   A Set Occurrence

with physical adjacency. This means that the record occurrences are physically adjacent to each other. Utilizing our same example of the Accounting Department having five faculty members, our storage would look as follows.

ACCOUNTING	S01	J01	J02	W01	S02

Again note that the values in the above diagram represent record occurrences. Note how these occurrences are stored in sequential order. Think about what would have to be done if faculty member J02 accepted a job at another university. The entire file would have to be compressed to eliminate physically the J02 record occurrence. Another method of implementation would be to mark (by turning a logically deleted switch on) the deleted record. The only problem with this technique is that in a volatile system (one with many adds and deletes), our storage area becomes filled with logically deleted records that would use up valuable secondary storage. Sooner or later, these logically deleted records must be physically deleted. This is usually done by some type utility program periodically executed by the database administrator.

One final note on sets: set relationships are determined by the database designer. They are developed based on her perception of data relationships and what information is to be derived from the data.

Hierarchical-Structured DBMSs

Hierarchical databases are constructed by combining multiple parent child relationships. For example, suppose that we were constructing a database for our state department of education.

We will assume that each university in the state had *n* departments, each department had *m* majors (different degree plans could be offered in a department),

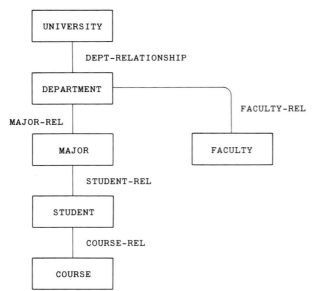

Figure 1.7   A Hierarchy Type

each major had o students, each student took p classes, and each department had q faculty members. The database structure for this example would look something like the structure in Figure 1.7.

The basic problem with hierarchical DBMSs is that a member record cannot have more than one owner record linked to it. Another way of stating this is that a record can only be a member of one set. For example, consider one of our previous examples of sets:

1. The $1:n$ relationship between Student and Course. A student can take n courses in a term.
2. The $1:n$ relationship between Course and Student. A course can contain n students.

If we wanted to generate a report listing the names of the courses that a particular student was taking, we could use the first relationship. If we wanted to generate another report listing the names of the student that was taking a particular course, we could use the second relationship. These two relationships could not be represented very readily in a hierarchically structured database without redundant data.

We could use a different structure to represent these relationships. This structure is shown in Figure 1.8.

Note that we have added another record type called GRADE, which contains

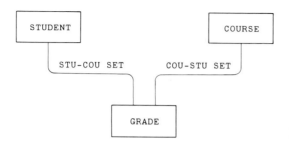

Figure 1.8   An *n:m* Relationship

the student's grade for a particular course. Further note that the GRADE record is a member record of two different sets. This is generally referred to as a **link record** because it links the two owner records together.

This structure is needed to represent the relationship just described, above but *it is not allowed in a hierarchical-structured DBMS*.

The relationship that is represented here is a very significant relationship in database design/implementation. This relationship is called an *n:m* relationship.

There is only one major commercial implementation of a hierarchical-structured DBMS: IBM's Information Management System, frequently referred to as IMS. Some authors consider System 2000/80 a hierarchical-structured system, and some consider it an inverted list-structured system.

Hierarchical-structured DBMSs are sometimes referred to as tree-structured DBMSs, for as the data records spread out under the main record (or root node), it resembles roots spreading out under a tree.

Network Structured DBMS

The structure of a network DBMS is essentially the same as that of a hierarchical DBMS except that a member (child) record can belong to more than one set. The database configurations that were just discussed that were not legal (the *n:m* relationship) in hierarchical structured DBMSs are legal in network structured DBMSs.

Network DBMSs are more flexible than hierarchical DBMSs. Note that a network can be a hierarchy, but a hierarchy can not be a network.

Network DBMSs were initially developed in the late 1960s and have become somewhat standardized in the past 20 years. Perhaps the best known standards were developed in the late 1960s and early 1970's by the CODASYL (**C**onference **O**n **DA**ta **SY**stems **L**anguages) Committee. A subgroup of the committee called the Data Base Task Group (DBTG) did most of the pioneering work on standardizing database management systems. Network databases are sometimes referred to as CODASYL databases. Since commercially available databases began being implemented in the 1960s and 1970s, the majority of database vendors implemented some subset of CODASYL-based DBMSs (IMS being the major exception).

Some commercially available DBMSs that are network structured are VAX-11/DBMS, IDMS (Integrated Database Management System) and IDS (Integrated Data Store).

Inverted List Structured DBMS

Inverted list DBMSs do not utilize the concept of sets to organize data. (Again the possible exception to this would be System 2000/80.) They use inverted lists (hence the clever name) to relate or link data together.

Data inversion involves constructing a list of keys, usually database keys, of records that have certain characteristics. These keys are usually kept in a separate file. To illustrate this concept, let's use our STUDENT record. You will remember the STUDENT record was composed of the following data fields:

STUDENT

STUDENT-ID
STUDENT-NAME
ADDRESS
BIRTHDATE
GENDER

Let us further assume that we want to retrieve records based on gender. We will assume that there are only two values of gender in our records: Male and Female. We will tell the database management system that we want to "invert" on Gender (we will discuss how this is done at a later point in this chapter). The system will automatically begin to keep a list of keys of all records where the Gender is Male and a second list where gender is Female. These lists are generally automatically updated for the user by the DBMS every time a new record is stored in the database or the value of gender is modified. The inverted list itself is transparent to the user, although she may use it to retrieve records whenever she wishes. Here is an example of an inverted list:

GENDER value	Database Keys of Records with That Value
FEMALE	R1, R3, R4, R6, R8*
MALE	R2, R5, R7, R9, R10

* We are using R1, R2, . . . to represent the generic database keys of the records. The actual value of the key would depend on how the DBMS vendor implemented database keys.

ACTUAL RECORDS

DBKEY	STUDENT-ID	STUDENT-NAME	ADDRESS	BIRTHDATE	GENDER
R1	S001	WENDY JONES	125 MAPLE AVE	10/25/65	FEMALE
R2	S002	SAM WALES	3006 NAVAJO CL	1/10/60	MALE
R3	S003	CATHY SMITH	1600 PENN AVE	2/22/22	FEMALE
R4	S004	DOTTIE STACY	10 DOWNING ST	3/31/67	FEMALE
R5	S005	JAY LANGER	GOLF COURSE RD	4/19/65	MALE
R6	S006	AMY LOPEZ	123 SUN RAY RD	5/10/64	FEMALE
R7	S007	SAM WATSON	225 TEST DRIVE	6/09/63	MALE
R8	S008	TAMMY REDD	113 MANCHESTER	7/01/60	FEMALE
R9	S009	TOMMY WADKINS	APPLE TREE DR	8/24/67	MALE
R10	S010	BEN TREVINO	BOWLING ALLEY	9/30/66	MALE

If we wished to access all the female students, we would only have to access the records with the keys R1, R3, R4, R6, and R8.

Inverted list DBMS are generally very fast and efficient for retrieving data but very slow (in database terms) when data maintenance is done. The reason that data maintenance is slow is that every time a record is added, deleted, or modified each participating inverted list must be updated. Some of the commercially available inverted list systems are System 2000/80 and ADABAS.

Some DBMS such as XEROX's EDMS (Extended Data Management System) utilized the network structure but also allowed data inversion.

Relational-Structured DBMS

The user of a relational database management system (RDBMS) perceives data as a series of two-dimensional tables. There is no concept of a set (although the word set is used in conjunction with relational systems, it has a different meaning from the two level hierarchy that we have just presented) utilized in RDBMS. The system may use any structure to *implement* RDBMS, but the underlying structure is transparent to the user. Using our example of the student database, our relational table types might be structured as follows:

```
STUDENT (STU-ID, STUDENT-NAME, ADDRESS, BIRTHDATE, GENDER)
COURSE  (COURSE-ID, COURSE-TITLE, SECTION-NO, STU-ID, FAC-ID)
FACULTY (FAC-ID, FACULTY-NAME, DEPARTMENT, GENDER, SALARY)
```

The notation used describes three tables (STUDENT, COURSE, and FACULTY) and lists the data items associated with each table. This notation is further defined in the following chapter.

Table occurrences might be as follows:

TABLE NAME: STUDENT

STU-ID	STUDENT-NAME	ADDRESS	BIRTHDATE	GENDER
S001	WENDY JONES	125 MAPLE AVE	10/25/65	FEMALE
S002	SAM WALES	3006 NAVAJO CL	1/10/60	MALE
S003	CATHY SMITH	1600 PENN AVE	2/22/22	FEMALE
S004	DOTTIE STACY	10 DOWNING ST	3/31/67	FEMALE
S005	JAY LANGER	4 GOLF COURSE RD	4/19/65	MALE
S006	AMY LOPEZ	123 SUN RAY RD	5/10/64	FEMALE
S007	SAM WATSON	225 TEST DRIVE	6/09/63	MALE
S008	TAMMY REDD	113 MANCHESTER	7/01/60	FEMALE
S009	TOMMY WADKINS	3 APPLE TREE DR	8/24/67	MALE
S010	BEN TREVINO	300 BOWLING ALLEY	9/30/66	MALE

TABLE NAME: COURSE

COURSE-ID	COURSE-TITLE	SECTION	STU-ID	FAC-ID
CSC100	INTRODUCTION TO COMPUTING	1	S001	J01
CSC100	INTRODUCTION TO COMPUTING	2	S002	S01
CSC200	PASCAL PROGRAMMING	1	S001	D01
CSC200	PASCAL PROGRAMMING	2	S003	S01
ACC200	PRINCIPLES OF ACCOUNTING I	1	S001	J02
ACC201	PRINCIPLES OF ACCOUNTING II	1	S004	J02
HIS200	HISTORY OF PIROGUES	1	S005	N01

TABLE NAME: FACULTY

FAC-ID	FACULTY-NAME	DEPARTMENT	GENDER	SALARY
J01	RAYMOND J. JOHNSON	COMP SCI	MALE	40,000
S01	WENDY SWIMMER	COMP SCI	FEMALE	45,000
D01	AMY DANCER	COMP SCI	FEMALE	34,500
J01	BOB JONES	ACCOUNTING	MALE	35,000
N01	JACK NELSON	HISTORY	MALE	28,000

The relational approach was developed by Dr. E. F. "Ted" Codd of IBM. The approach is based on set theory and logic. Dr. Codd's first article concerning the relational approach, "A Relational Model of Data for Large Shared Data Banks," can be found in the June 1970 issue of the *Communications of the ACM*.

Some commercial database implementations that claim to be relational are ORACLE, DB2, INGRES, Query-by-Example (QBE), dBASE II & III, and Knowledgeman. There is a criterion that has been established to determine if a database management system is truly relational. This criterion is described in Chapter 3 of this text.

Since the primary focus of this text is the implementation of the relational approach through ORACLE, we will defer further discussion of the relational model until later in the text.

KNOWLEDGEBASES

A powerful extension of a database is the knowledge base. The difference between a database and a knowledgebase is that in addition to containing basic data, knowledgebases contain rules that can be used to infer additional pieces of information that are not directly stored in the basic data. To illustrate this let us consider some common family relationships. Let us assume that we know the following parental relationships.

1. Ralph is the father of Wendy and Amy.
2. Ralph Sr. is the father of Ralph.

We could represent these facts in a simple relational table called PARENT.

TABLE NAME: PARENT

Parent-name	Child
Ralph Sr.	Ralph
Ralph	Wendy
Ralph	Amy

By using this basic data we could define what a grandfather is. A grandfather is a father whose child is also a parent. This relationship could be represented in the following notation.

```
grandfather (Grandfather-name, Child-name)
if parent (Grandfather-name, X) and parent (X, Child-name)
```

This rule is interpreted as follows: find all the instances where a child is also a parent. Note the use of the variables Grandfather-name, X, and Child-name. The knowledge base would select the first record and substitute Ralph Sr. for grandfather-name and Ralph for X. It would now advance to the next record and try to match the value of X (which is Ralph) with the value of parent-name. Since the two values of X match, it knows that Ralph Sr. is the grandfather of Wendy. These two values would be displayed on the output device. It moves to the third record and attempts to find a match for the value of X again. It finds a match for X and it knows that Ralph Sr. is also the grandfather of Amy. This procedure continues until all the grandfathers are found.

The language that is most utilized to represent these knowledge bases is PROLOG (which stands for PROgramming in LOGic). The LISP (which stands for LISt Processing) language can also be used to represent these relationships. Utilizing PROLOG notation to represent the parental relationships we would produce.

```
parent (ralph_sr, ralph)    /* Ralph Sr is the parent of Ralph */
parent (ralph, wendy)       /* Ralph is the parent of Wendy  */
parent (ralph, amy)         /* Ralph is the parent of Amy    */
grandfather (Gf,Gc) if parent (Gf, X) and parent (X, Gc)
```

Note that facts (basic data) are specified in lowercase and PROLOG variables are specified in uppercase (only the first letter need be in uppercase). We can now use the data and rules to retrieve data (basic and implied) from the knowledge base. This is a different method of representing relational database relations. Some examples of inquires into the knowledge base are the following:

1. Desired information: Is Ralph, Sr. the grandfather of Wendy?

```
PROLOG command: grandfather (ralph_sr, wendy)
PROLOG response: True
```

2. Desired information: Who is Amy's grandfather?

```
PROLOG command: grandfather (X, amy)   /* note the variable X */
PROLOG response: X=ralph_sr
```

3. Desired information: Who is Ralph Sr. the grandfather of?

```
PROLOG command: grandfather (ralph_sr, X)
PROLOG response: X=wendy
                 X=amy
```

Obviously males are not the only parents of children. To be a bit more realistic we would have to specify the mothers too. We could add the following facts very easily.

1. Una Mae is the mother of Ralph.
2. Dottie is the mother of Wendy and Amy.
3. Frank and Dorothy are the father and mother of Dottie.

```
parent (ralph_sr, ralph)
parent (ralph, wendy)
parent (ralph, amy)
parent (una_mae, ralph)
parent (dottie, wendy)
parent (frank, dottie)
parent (dorothy, dottie)
grandfather (Gf,Gc) if parent (Gf, X) and parent (X, Gc)
```

Now with this additional data we can determine more relationships. For example, who are Wendy's grandfathers?

```
PROLOG command: grandfather (X,wendy)
PROLOG response: X=ralph_sr
                 X=una_mae
                 X=frank
                 X=dorothy
```

Oops! What happened? Well, grandfathers are obviously males and grandmothers are obviously females (a little piece of data that we have forgotten to tell the knowledge base.) This could be added very easily.

```
parent (ralph_sr, ralph)
parent (ralph, wendy)
parent (ralph, amy)
parent (una_mae, ralph)
parent (dottie, wendy)
parent (frank, dottie)
parent (dorothy, dottie)
male (ralph_sr)
male (ralph)
male (frank)
female (wendy)
female (amy)
female (una_mae)
female (dottie)
female (dorothy)
```

Now we will have to change our definition of a grandfather and add one for grandmother. Our new definition of a grandfather is a male who has a child who has a child. A grandmother is a female who has a child who has a child. A grandparent is either a grandfather or a grandmother. The new rules are

```
grandfather (Gf,Gc) if parent (Gf, X) and parent (X, Gc)
                    and male (Gf)
grandmother (Gm,Gc) if parent (Gm, X) and parent (X, Gc)
                    and female (Gm)
grandparent (Gp,Gc) if grandfather (Gp,Gc) or grandmother (Gp,Gc)
```

Note that there are several ways that we could have defined grandparent. We chose this one to illustrate the "or" condition.

The two biggest advantages of specifying rules in knowledge bases are

1. We can save space on secondary storage devices. If we know that a relationship is always true (example: a grandfather is a male who has a child who has a child); then why store this fact if we have the data to derive it.

2. We can infer things based on previously known facts and other derived relationships (example: a grandparent is either a grandfather or a grandmother).

The study of knowledge bases promises to be a fascinating one, but it is beyond the scope of this text.

PARTS OF A DBMS

No matter what the structure of the DBMS, they all are composed of two basic parts: the data definition part and the data manipulation part.

Data Definition

Data definition refers to how the structure of the database is communicated to the DBMS. The overall structure of the database is sometimes called the schema. The

Figure 1.9   A Schema Definition for a Network-Structured DBMS

```
SCHEMA NAME IS STUDENT-FACULTY-COURSE.

REALM NAME IS FILE1. CONTAINS 20 PAGES.
REALM NAME IS FILE2. CONTAINS 20 PAGES.

RECORD NAME IS STUDENT
    LOCATION MODE IS CALC USING STU-ID DUPLICATES ARE NOT
      ALLOWED; WITHIN REALM FILE1.
    STU-ID; PICTURE XXXX.
    STUDENT-NAME; PICTURE X(20).
    ADDRESS; PICTURE X(20).
    BIRTHDATE; PICTURE X(8).
    GENDER; PICTURE X(6); CHECK IS VALUE "MALE", "FEMALE".
RECORD NAME IS COURSE
    LOCATION MODE IS VIA STU-COURSE SET; WITHIN REALM FILE2.
    COURSE-ID; PICTURE X(6).
    COURSE-TITLE; PICTURE X(20).
    SECTION; PICTURE 99; CHECK IS RANGE 1 THRU 20.
RECORD NAME IS FACULTY
    LOCATION MODE IS CALC USING FAC-ID DUPLICATES ARE NOT
      ALLOWED; WITHIN REALM FILE2.
    FAC-ID; PICTURE XXX.
    FACULTY-NAME; PICTURE X(20).
    DEPARTMENT; PICTURE X(10).
    GENDER; PICTURE X(6); CHECK IS VALUE "MALE", "FEMALE".
    SALARY; PICTURE 99999.99.

SET NAME IS STU-COURSE OWNER IS STUDENT; ORDER IS SORTED.
    MEMBER IS COURSE; SORT KEY IS COURSE-ID ASCENDING.
SET NAME IS FAC-COURSE OWNER IS FACULTY; ORDER IS SORTED.
    MEMBER IS COURSE; SORT KEY IS COURSE-ID ASCENDING.
```

schema describes all the records, all the data items, all the files, all the sets (for CODASYL type DBMS), used in the database. This is usually specified through some type of special language called the data definition language (DDL). Each DBMS has its own DDL.

Not every user, either the end user or database specialist user, of the database needs access to every record or every data item in a record. There is a mechanism that is utilized to restrict access to records and/or data items in a record. This mechanism is called the subschema.

The schema is the global logical view of the complete database, and the subschema represents the user or program's view of the database. While it is true that a subschema could contain all the records and all the data items per record defined in the schema, this usually does not occur. The user has access to the database only through subschemas. This concept will be discussed at greater length later in the text.

To illustrate a DDL, we will use the CODASYL standard DDL and a generic version of an RDBMS DDL. We will not attempt to illustrate all the options in the CODASYL DDL as we simply want the reader to get the "flavor" of a DDL.

The CODASYL DDL is separated into four interrelated sections: the schema section, the realm section, the record section, and the set section. The schema section gives a name to the database, the realm section defines what files will be used to store the actual data, the record section defines all of the records and data items used in the database, and the set section defines all the sets used in the database. A sample schema is shown in Figure 1.9.

A sample subschema is shown in Figure 1.10.

Once the schema is created, usually by a text editor, it is compiled and an object schema is created. Next a subschema is created, again usually by a text editor. The subschema is also compiled. It must then be linked into the user's program in some manner. This is usually done through the system mapper or linkage editor.

Relational schemas are a bit different from conventional DBMS schemas in that neither the schemas have to be compiled nor do sets or data inversions have to be specified. (Relational database management systems rarely use the terms schema and subschema. We only use them here for consistency.) The only thing that is specified is the basic structure of the table. For illustrative purposes (Figure 1.11)

Figure 1.10 A subschema for a Network-Structured DBMS

```
SUBSCHEMA NAME IS MYSUBSCHEMA FROM STUDENT-FACULTY-COURSE.

REALMS ARE ALL.

RECORDS ARE STUDENT; INCLUDE STU-ID, STUDENT-NAME.
            COURSE; INCLUDE ALL.

SETS ARE STU-COURSE.
```

Figure 1.11   Schema for a Relational DBMS

```
CREATE TABLE STUDENT (STU-ID          CHAR (4),
                      STUDENT-NAME     CHAR (20),
                      ADDRESS          CHAR (20),
                      BIRTHDATE        DATE,
                      GENDER           CHAR (6));

CREATE TABLE COURSE  (COURSE-ID        CHAR (6),
                      COURSE-TITLE     CHAR (20),
                      SECTION          NUMBER (2));

CREATE TABLE FACULTY (FAC-ID           CHAR (3),
                      FACULTY-NAME     CHAR (20),
                      DEPARTMENT       CHAR (20),
                      GENDER           CHAR (6),
                      SALARY           NUMBER (8,2));
```

we will use the Structured Query Language (SQL), used in the ORACLE DBMS, method of defining tables.

Relational subschemas are created using views that will be described in Chapter 12, Creating and Utilizing Views.

Once these tables are created, data can be loaded directly or the table definitions can be mapped/linked into COBOL, FORTRAN, and PASCAL language programs, and data can be loaded into the tables by these programs.

All the descriptions of the data, both the global and the users' views, are stored in the database management system's data dictionary. Data dictionaries are discussed in Chapter 7.

Data Manipulation

Data manipulation refers to methods used to retrieve, add, modify, and delete data in a database. Each method is used throughout the operation of a database management system.

METHODS OF MANIPULATING DATA

There are four basic methods of data manipulation in databases: programming language interface, query languages, report writers, and system utilities. **Programming language interfaces** are generally used to modify database values and to produce reports that require sophisticated computations, such as complex statistical computations. **Query languages** are used to inquire into the database. Query languages are very good for performing *ad hoc* querying needed in today's fast-paced world of information retrieval. **Report writers** are designed to produce very long reports normally directed to the line printer. **System utilities** are used by the system manager (later on in the chapter we will see that this person is called the database administrator) in doing his or her job.

Programming Language Interface

Programming language interface (PLI), sometimes called the host language interface, refers to accessing the database through some type of programming language: COBOL, PL/1, Pascal, FORTRAN.

The CODASYL method of data manipulation in COBOL revolves around embedding some special verbs in the COBOL language to manipulate data. Some of these verbs are:

FIND	Retrieves a record and copies it into system buffers.
GET	Copies data from system buffers into program buffers.
STORE	Adds a new record occurrence into the database.
DELETE	Removes a record occurrence from the database.
CONNECT	Links a record occurrence into a set occurrence.
DISCONNECT	Delinks a record occurrence from a set occurrence.
MODIFY	Changes the value of specified data values.

Other languages simply make these verbs procedure calls.

The relational approach, using ORACLE examples, is to make calls to various ORACLE routines. ORACLE generally uses a preprocessor to convert embedded ORACLE commands to the necessary COBOL routines. (The exception to this is Harris ORACLE, which does not have a host language preprocessor.) Examples of COBOL routines to manipulate data are:

CPILON	Logs the COBOL program onto the ORACLE database.
CPIFCH	Retrieves a record occurrence from a table.
CPIOSQ	Executes a command passed to ORACLE as a text string.
CPIROL	Rollsback any changes made to the database.

Further discussion of Programming Language interfaces is beyond the scope of this text.

Query Languages

Query languages are stand-alone languages that allow rapid access, mostly in an on-line environment, to the database. Some of the languages are considered fourth generation languages (4GL). These languages do not have to be compiled/translated or linked before they are used. They are designed primarily for retrieval of data, although data maintenance use is usually allowed.

Query languages fall into one of two categories. The first category is called **command-oriented query languages**. This category encompasses all query languages in which the commands are specified in English-like text. The second category is called **screen-oriented query languages** or graphics-oriented query languages. In this category, the user enters commands through a fill-in-the-blank mechanism.

      Command-oriented query languages.   The following are examples of the VAX-11 DATATRIEVE query language, which is considered a command-oriented query language. It is not particularly important that you understand completely each and every example shown. At this point we only want you to get the "flavor" of what query languages are.

1. Display all data values for female students.

```
PRINT STUDENT WITH GENDER = "FEMALE"
```

2. Display the name and address of students born between October 9, 1945 and January 1, 1953.

```
PRINT NAME, ADDRESS OF STUDENT -
    WITH BIRTHDATE BETWEEN "9-OCT-45" AND "1-JAN-53"
```

3. Print the names, departments, and salaries of the faculty members in descending order of salary.

```
PRINT FACULTY-NAME, DEPARTMENT, SALARY OF FACULTY -
    SORTED BY SALARY DESCENDING
```

4. Print the names of the male faculty members earning between $20,000 and $40,000. Sort the result in ascending order of salary.

```
PRINT FACULTY-NAME OF FACULTY
    WITH GENDER = "MALE" AND -
    SALARY BETWEEN 20000 AND 40000
    SORTED BY SALARY ASCENDING
```

5. Insert a new faculty members record occurrence into the database.

```
STORE FACULTY
Enter FAC-ID: F01
Enter FACULTY-NAME: BEN NELSON
Enter DEPARTMENT: MANAGEMENT
Enter GENDER: MALE
Enter SALARY: 30000
```

6. Give every faculty member in the Computer Science Department a 50% raise.

```
MODIFY ALL FACULTY WITH DEPARTMENT = "COMP SCI" -
USING SALARY = SALARY * 1.5
```

7. Delete all members of the faculty who are assigned to the Computer Science Department.

```
ERASE ALL FACULTY WITH DEPARTMENT = "COMP SCI"
```

The following are the same examples written in ORACLE's query language **Structured Query Language (SQL)** another command-oriented query language.

1. Display all data values for female students.

```
SELECT * FROM STUDENT WHERE GENDER = 'FEMALE';
```

2. Display the name and address of students born between October 9, 1945 and January 1, 1953.

```
SELECT NAME, ADDRESS FROM STUDENT WHERE BIRTHDAY BETWEEN
'9-OCT-45' AND '1-JAN-53';
```

3. Print the names, departments, and salaries of the faculty members in descending order of salary.

```
SELECT FACULTY_NAME, DEPARTMENT, SALARY
FROM FACULTY ORDER BY SALARY DESC;
```

4. Print the names of the male faculty members earning between $20,000 and $40,000. Sort the result in ascending order of salary.

```
SELECT FACULTY-NAME FROM FACULTY
WHERE GENDER = 'MALE' AND
SALARY BETWEEN 20000 AND 40000
ORDER BY SALARY;
```

5. Insert a new faculty member's record occurrence into the database.

```
INSERT INTO FACULTY VALUES
('F01', 'BEN NELSON',
'MANAGEMENT','MALE',30000);
```

6. Give every faculty member in the Computer Science Department a 50% raise.

```
UPDATE FACULTY
SET SALARY = SALARY * 1.5 WHERE DEPARTMENT
= 'COMP SCI';
```

7. Delete all members of the faculty who are assigned to the Computer Science Department.

```
DELETE FACULTY WHERE DEPARTMENT = 'COMP SCI';
```

The SQL language will be covered later in the text beginning in Chapter 5, Introduction to ORACLE.

Screen oriented query languages.   One of the best screen-oriented query language is **Query-by-Example (QBE)**, an IBM product. In QBE a schematic of a table is drawn on the users VDU screen. The user can use several operators to retrieve (P.), update (U.), delete (D.), or insert (I.) to utilize the database. We will use our same seven examples that we have explained already to illustrate QBE's power.

1. Display all data values for female students.

Student	Stu-id	Student-Name	Address	Birthdate	Gender
	P.	P.	P.	P.	P.FEMALE

The P. (pronounced p dot) is the print operator. Any column in which the P. resides will display values on the VDU screen. The value FEMALE in the Gender box indicates a condition to be tested (gender = FEMALE). Therefore the command states ''Print the values of Stu-id, Student-Name, Address, Birthdate, and Gender for every record that contains the value FEMALE for gender. Note that the VDU's cursor must be moved around the screen so that the user can fill in the proper blanks to formulate the query. Once the boxes are filled in to the user's satisfaction, the ENTER key on the terminal is pressed, and the query results appear on the screen.

2. Display the name and address of students born between October 9, 1945 and January 1, 1953.

Student	Stu-id	Student-Name	Address	Birthdate	Gender
		P.	P.	DATE	

Conditions
DATE > 'Oct 9, 1945' & < 'Jan 1, 1953'

This example takes advantage of QBE's example element (DATE) and the Condition box. The example element DATE is QBE's method of linking the values stored in the box Birthdate to the Condition box. This query states ''Display the values of Student-Name and Address where the value of Birthdate is between October 9, 1945 and January 1, 1953.

3. Print the names, departments, and salaries of the faculty members in descending order of salary.

Faculty	Fac-id	Faculty-Name	Department	Gender	Salary
		P.DO.	P.		P.

Note that the DO. affixed to the P. command in the Faculty-Name box indicates that values to be displayed will be sorted in descending order on faculty name before printing.

4. Print the names of the male faculty members earning between $20,000 and $40,000. Sort the result in ascending order of salary.

Faculty	Fac-id	Faculty-Name	Department	Gender	Salary
		P.			AO.X

Conditions
X > 20000 & < 40000

5. Insert a new faculty member's record occurrence into the database.

Faculty	Fac-id	Faculty-Name	Department	Gender	Salary
I.	F01	Ben Nelson	Management	Male	30000

Note that the I. (for Insert) is placed under the table name in the schematic of the table.

6. Give every faculty member in the Computer Science Department a 50% raise.

Faculty	Fac-id	Faculty-Name	Department	Gender	Salary
U.			Comp Sci Comp Sci		SAL SAL*1.5

Again we have used the example element to indicate a variable value. The first line indicates that we want to extract a list of salaries for all persons assigned to the Computer Science Department. The second line indicates that the old values referred to by the example element $\underline{S}AL$ are to be updated by taking the current value of salary stored in each record and multiplying it by 1.5. This is indicated by placing the update operator (U.) in the second line of the command.

7. Delete all members of the faculty who are assigned to the Computer Science Department.

Faculty	Fac-id	Faculty-Name	Department	Gender	Salary
D.			Comp Sci		

The D. operator indicates that records are to be deleted from the table.

Report Writers

Report writers are stand-alone programs that give the user the ability to generate reports with such features as control breaks, summary totals, averages, maximums, minimums, and counts. This is somewhat like the Report Writer feature embedded into COBOL. Report writers are primarily designed for use in a batch environment. This is not to imply that they cannot be used in an online environment.

The following is a report writer example written in VAX-11 DATATRIEVE:

```
REPORT FACULTY SORTED BY DEPARTMENT, SALARY DESCENDING
SET COLUMNS_PAGE = 132
SET REPORT_NAME = "FACULTY SALARY REPORT" "BY DEPARTMENT"
AT BOTTOM OF DEPARTMENT PRINT SKIP 2,
 PRINT TOTAL SALARY USING $$$,$$$.99
PRINT DEPARTMENT, FACULTY-NAME, SALARY
END_REPORT
```

The following is the same report utilizing SQL:

```
SET LINESIZE 132
TITLE 'FACULTY SALARY REPORT BY DEPARTMENT'
BREAK ON DEPARTMENT SKIP 2
COMPUTE SUM OF SALARY ON DEPARTMENT
SELECT DEPARTMENT, FACULTY_NAME,
SALARY FROM FACULTY ORDER BY SALARY DESC;
```

The ORACLE Report Writer feature is described in Chapter 14, The Internal Report Writer.

System Utilities

System utilities are processors/procedures that allow the system manager to do such things as back up databases, load data records onto the database from nondatabase files, and restore databases from system or database crashes. These utilities are fairly standard for most database packages although some may have more features than others.

ORACLE utilities are described in Chapter 8.

DATABASE ADMINISTRATION

In every institution that has a DBMS there is a need for a database administrator. This can be one person or an entire department. The database administrator (DBA) is the caretaker of the database. His job is to allocate passwords/privileges to users, ensure that the integrity level of the data is at the highest level that it can possibly be, implement new versions/features of the database, assist in the design and implementation of databases, assist database programmers with problems, instruct users on new features, and act as a liaison between the institution and the database vendor.

SUMMARY

In this chapter we introduced some of the concepts utilized in database management systems. Concepts covered include some basic definitions necessary for us to get started in learning about DBMSs, the basic operations of a DBMS, the different structures of DBMSs, and methods of accessing data in a database. The role of the database administrator was also discussed. A sample database to assist in describing the various aspects of database management was also introduced.

Now that we have completed this chapter, you should be familiar with the following database concepts. If you are not sure what these terms mean, go back and review the various sections of the chapter that explain them.

A. Database
B. Database management system (DBMS)
C. Type/occurrence
D. Master file/transaction file
E. Data integrity
F. Data/information
G. Goals of a DBMS
H. How data is processed
   1. Retrieval
   2. Modification
      a. Adding record occurrences
      b. Deleting record occurrences
      c. Modifying data
         (1) Assigned modification
         (2) Computed modification

I. How DBMS are structured internally
   1. Hierarchical
   2. Network or CODASYL
   3. Inverted List
   4. Relational
J. Knowledge bases
K. Schema/subschema
L. Data definition language
M. Methods of manipulating data
   1. Programming Languages
   2. Query Languages
   3. Report Writers
   4. System Utilities
N. Database administration

Now that the foundation has been laid, let us move on to explore the area of relational DBMS in the next chapter.

EXERCISES

1. Explain the difference between a database and a database management system.
2. Explain the difference between a database and a knowledge base.
3. Select an application area where you feel databases could be used.
   a. What records could be used in the system?
   b. What are some of the data fields that you would place into these records?
   c. What integrity checks could be made?
   d. What sets can you visualize in the system?
   e. List some record, data item and set types and some occurrences of those types.
   f. Give some examples of the various types of data modifications that would occur in your system. What factors would cause record occurrences to be added to your system? What factors would cause record occurrences to be deleted from your system? What factors would cause assigned updates to take place in your system? What factors would cause computed updates to occur?
4. Discuss the role of a database administrator in an organization? What should his or her qualifications be? Should the DBA be one person or a group of people (a separate department)?
5. Explain the difference between a database key and a random access key. Why is direct access faster than random access?

2

The
Relational Approach

PURPOSE: The primary focus of this chapter is to introduce you to the terminology used in relational database management systems. Properties of the relational model and the rationale for design of the model are also explored.

Now that we understand what a database management system is and basically how it works, let us narrow our scope and concentrate on relational database management systems (RDBMS). Remember that we are still using the term database management systems to refer to general purpose database management systems.

Let us begin this chapter by describing some concepts that you must understand to be able to utilize the relational model of data. The reader should be aware that most of the concepts covered in this chapter are theoretical and are not necessarily implemented on any relational system in existence today. However, if you understand these concepts, it will be much easier for you to understand the implementation of the relational theory that we will describe later in the text.

HISTORY OF RELATIONAL DATABASES

The reader should remember back to Chapter 1 that the relational approach was developed by Dr. E. F. Codd of IBM in the late 1960s [1]. The technique of representing data in the form of two-dimensional tables was significantly different from the conventional models of data (the CODASYL model and the hierarchical model). It is a much simpler approach to understand and utilize than conventional models. For these two basic reasons the relational model should be the data model of the future.

Critics of the relational model point to the slow speed of execution as the prime detractor of the model. They claim that even though relational databases are easy to use by novices, the speed at which they retrieve data makes their use undesirable in the commercial marketplace. The problem of speed of execution will be addressed later in this text.

RELATIONAL TERMINOLOGY

Before we can explore the relational model, we must become familiar with some of the terminology used in describing it. We will start with some of the more elementary relational terminology and induce other concepts as needed.

Relations and Tables

The basic structure for the relational model is the relation. A **relation** is a two-dimensional structure that contains data. The name ''relation'' is taken from the mathematical theory of sets: it has nothing to do with the fact that the data stored in the relations is related (although it usually is). Relations are an abstract concept that are implemented through tables since tables are the closest data structure tool to represent relations that we have. In most cases it is acceptable to use the words ''relation'' and ''table'' interchangeably as tables are implementations of relations.

Tuples, Attributes, and Cardinality

Each row of the relation is called a **tuple** (rhymes with couple) and each column is called an **attribute** or field. The number of attributes or columns in a table is called the **degree of the relation**. A relation with only one column is called a **unary relation**. A relation with two columns in it is called a **binary relation**. A relation with three columns in it is called a **ternary relation**. A relation with four columns in it is called, you guessed it, **a relation of degree four**. Actually any relation can be referred to as a relation of degree *n* or an *n-ary* relation. *N*, naturally, refers to the number of columns in the relation.

The number of tuple occurrences in the relation is referred to as the *cardinality* of the relation.

Figure 2.1 illustrates the relational terminology that we have explored so far. The relation STUDENT is represented in a ternary table because it has three attributes: STU-ID, STUDENT-NAME, and ADDRESS. The cardinality of the table is 10, for it has 10 tuple occurrences stored in it.

Figure 2.1   Relational Terminology

RELATION OR **TABLE NAME: STUDENT**

```
STU-ID    STUDENT-NAME      ADDRESS              ← Attribute or
 S001     WENDY JONES       125 MAPLE AVE          field names
 S002     SAM WALES         3006 NAVAJO CL
 S003     CATHY SMITH       1600 PENN AVE        ← A tuple
 S004     DOTTIE STACY      10 DOWNING ST
 S005     JAY LANGER        GOLF COURSE RD
 S006     AMY LOPEZ         123 SUN RAY RD
 S007     SAM WATSON        225 TEST DRIVE
 S008     TAMMY REDD        113 MANCHESTER
 S009     TOMMY WADKINS     APPLE TREE DR
 S010     BEN TREVINO       BOWLING ALLEY
```

Domains

A domain is a set of acceptable values for a field or attribute. Domains are named and can be specified via a list of acceptable values, through rules, or by an algorithm.

An example of a domain specified by a list is the standard set of state abbreviation codes used in the U.S. mail system. This set could be called the STATE-CODES domain. This could be implemented by constructing a table that contains a list of all the acceptable abbreviations.

A domain specified by a set of rules could be a student's grade point average. The rule specifying grade point average could be

```
GPA is a real value computed to three decimal positions
defined on the range 0.000 to 4.000
```

An example of a domain specified by an algorithm could be that the selling price of an item must be the cost of the item plus at least 50% markup.

Attributes are defined over domains. For example, the STATE-OF-RESIDENCE field in the student's master file (table) could be defined over the STATE-CODES domain. Two or more attributes can be defined over the same domain. The student's overall grade point average and the grade point average within his or her major field are both defined over the GPA domain. By using the concept of domains in relational databases, we have built an additional integrity check into the database. Domains define the legal values for attributes utilized in the database.

Relational Database Table Notation

There is a very simple method of communicating to another person what the structure of a particular table looks like. To define a table, we specify the table name followed by the attributes of that table in parentheses. The notation for the three tables that we have been using for our examples in Chapter 1 would be:

```
STUDENT (STU-ID, STUDENT-NAME, ADDRESS, BIRTHDATE, GENDER)
COURSE  (COURSE-ID, COURSE-TITLE, SECTION-NO, STU-ID, FAC-ID)
FACULTY (FAC-ID, FACULTY-NAME, DEPARTMENT, GENDER, SALARY)
```

Keys

Keys in relational database serve two basic purposes: identification of tuples and creating relationships between tables. Keys can be made up of a single attribute, cleverly called single key attribute, or multiple attributes, also cleverly called multikey attributes, or composite or concatenated keys.

Candidate and primary keys.   **Candidate keys** are any attribute or combination of attributes (composite key) that uniquely identify each tuple (row) occurrence or future tuple occurrence in a table. One of the candidate keys is called the primary key. Let us look at one of our example tables to illustrate candidate and primary keys.

TABLE NAME: STUDENT

STU-ID	STUDENT-NAME	ADDRESS	BIRTHDATE	GENDER
S001	WENDY JONES	125 MAPLE AVE	10/25/65	FEMALE
S002	SAM WALES	3006 NAVAJO CL	1/10/60	MALE
S003	CATHY SMITH	1600 PENN AVE	2/22/22	FEMALE
S004	DOTTIE STACY	10 DOWNING ST	3/31/67	FEMALE
S005	JAY LANGER	GOLF COURSE RD	4/19/65	MALE
S006	AMY LOPEZ	123 SUN RAY RD	5/10/64	FEMALE
S007	SAM WATSON	225 TEST DRIVE	6/09/63	MALE
S008	TAMMY REDD	113 MANCHESTER	7/01/60	FEMALE
S009	TOMMY WADKINS	APPLE TREE DR	8/24/67	MALE
S010	BEN TREVINO	BOWLING ALLEY	9/30/66	MALE

A cursory look at the tuples in this table indicates that there are many candidate keys: STU-ID, STUDENT-NAME, ADDRESS, and BIRTHDATE. Note that each tuple occurrence has a unique value for these four attributes. About the only attribute that we could not use to identify uniquely each tuple is GENDER, for there is more than one occurrence of Male and Female. However, upon closer scrutiny, we should realize that even though every tuple in the table has a unique value for STUDENT-NAME, common sense tells us that sooner or later, we will get two people with the same name. The same is true with ADDRESS and BIRTHDATE. In actuality, we only have one acceptable attribute for the primary key and that is STU-ID (assuming that no two students will have the same STU-ID number). Even though we have eliminated the attributes STUDENT-NAME, ADDRESS, and BIRTHDATE from consideration for primary keys rather easily, this might not be so easy to do with "real-world" databases. If after eliminating some obvious attributes from consideration we still have more than one choice for primary key, the database designer(s) will simply have to select one of the candidate keys that seems the most reasonable to be the primary key.

A second example is needed to illustrate composite primary keys. Let us consider the following table.

TABLE NAME: COURSE

COURSE-ID	COURSE-TITLE	SECTION	STU-ID	FAC-ID
CSC100	INTRODUCTION TO COMPUTING	1	S001	J01
CSC100	INTRODUCTION TO COMPUTING	2	S002	S01
CSC200	PASCAL PROGRAMMING	1	S001	D01
CSC200	PASCAL PROGRAMMING	2	S003	S01
ACC200	PRINCIPLES OF ACCOUNTING I	1	S001	J02
ACC201	PRINCIPLES OF ACCOUNTING II	1	S004	J02
HIS200	HISTORY OF PIROGUES	1	S005	N01

In viewing the tuple occurrences in this table, we see that no one attribute uniquely identifies each tuple, so we will have to use a composite key of some type. We might consider using FAC-ID + STU-ID. However, if the same faculty member teaches the same student in two separate classes, we have a problem. Under the assumption that a student could not take the same class under the same faculty member more than once (i.e., the student takes the course in two separate sections during the same semester or, more realistically, over two different semesters), we will use the composite key of FAC-ID + STU-ID + COURSE-ID as the primary key of the table.

Primary keys are an integral part of the relational model of data, for they uniquely identify each tuple occurrence in a table. For this reason, a paramount guideline for constructing primary keys is that the primary key or any attribute participating in a composite primary key of a relation cannot have a null value. If the primary key of a relation is a unique identifier of the tuples in the table, how could a unique identifier have a value of null? This is a guideline effecting the integrity of the database. This guideline is referred to as entity integrity and it will be discussed more completely in Chapter 3.

Primary keys are usually underlined when specifying the tables in notational form. The primary keys of each of our three example tables are:

```
STUDENT (STU-ID, STUDENT-NAME, ADDRESS, BIRTHDATE, GENDER)
COURSE  (COURSE-ID, COURSE-TITLE, SECTION-NO, STU-ID, FAC-ID)
FACULTY (FAC-ID, FACULTY-NAME, DEPARTMENT, GENDER, SALARY)
```

Foreign keys. Foreign keys are used to "link" associated tables together. A foreign key is an attribute or a combination of attributes that is used as linking pins between tables. An attribute that is a foreign key in one table must be a primary key in another table. For example, if we consider the STUDENT and COURSE tables and we wanted to solve the query "List each student and the titles of the courses that they are currently taking,'' we could not solve that query directly from one table.

```
STUDENT ( STU-ID , STUDENT-NAME , ADDRESS , BIRTHDATE , GENDER )
COURSE ( COURSE-ID , COURSE-TITLE , SECTION-NO , STU-ID , FAC-ID )
```

We would have to take the student's name from the STUDENT table and the course titles from the COURSE table. We would have to perform some type of linking operation between the STUDENT table and the COURSE table over the common attribute STU-ID. (This operation is called a *join* in relational algebra, and it is described in the following chapter.) STU-ID is the primary key of the STUDENT table, and it is a foreign key in the COURSE table.

Since foreign keys represent links to primary keys, it makes sense that if a foreign key value exists in a table, value must exist as a primary key in some other table. The guideline is referred to as *referential integrity*. To illustrate the concept of referential integrity, let's use our STUDENT and COURSE tables.

TABLE NAME: STUDENT

STU-ID	STUDENT-NAME	ADDRESS	BIRTHDATE	GENDER
S001	WENDY JONES	125 MAPLE AVE	10/25/65	FEMALE
S002	SAM WALES	3006 NAVAJO CL	1/10/60	MALE
S003	CATHY SMITH	1600 PENN AVE	2/22/22	FEMALE
S004	DOTTIE STACY	10 DOWNING ST	3/31/67	FEMALE
S005	JAY LANGER	GOLF COURSE RD	4/19/65	MALE
S006	AMY LOPEZ	123 SUN RAY RD	5/10/64	FEMALE
S007	SAM WATSON	225 TEST DRIVE	6/09/63	MALE
S008	TAMMY REDD	113 MANCHESTER	7/01/60	FEMALE
S009	TOMMY WADKINS	APPLE TREE DR	8/24/67	MALE
S010	BEN TREVINO	BOWLING ALLEY	9/30/66	MALE

TABLE NAME: COURSE

COURSE-ID	COURSE-TITLE	SECTION	STU-ID	FAC-ID
CSC100	INTRODUCTION TO COMPUTING	1	S001	J01
CSC100	INTRODUCTION TO COMPUTING	2	S002	S01
CSC200	PASCAL PROGRAMMING	1	S001	D01
CSC200	PASCAL PROGRAMMING	2	S003	S01
ACC200	PRINCIPLES OF ACCOUNTING I	1	S001	J02
ACC201	PRINCIPLES OF ACCOUNTING II	1	S004	J02
HIS200	HISTORY OF PIROGUES	1	S005	N01

In the COURSE table, the attribute STU-ID is a foreign key to the STUDENT table. If you peruse the values of STU-ID in the COURSE table, you will notice that all the occurrences of this attribute (S001, S002, S003, S004, and S005) exist in the STU-ID attribute of the STUDENT table. If this condition exists, referential integrity exists. Referential Integrity would not exist if a tuple in the COURSE table with the value of S999 for STU-ID occurred. Remember, Referential Integrity means that every occurrence of a foreign key must refer to an existing occurrence of a primary key.

Foreign keys are not designated in the relational notation.

Redundant keys.   The last type of key that we will discuss is the redundant key. Redundant keys can only occur in composite keys. A redundant key is an attribute that participates in a primary key that is not needed. For example, if we had selected STU-ID + STUDENT-NAME as the primary key of the STUDENT table, STUDENT-NAME would be considered redundant, for we only need STU-ID to identify uniquely each tuple in the STUDENT table. Since redundant keys serve no useful purpose, they should not be utilized. We will see later in the text that redundant keys have the potential to cause serious problems in databases.

TYPES OF TABLES UTILIZED IN RELATIONAL DATABASES

There are three types of tables used in relational databases. The tables types are base tables, derived tables, and views.

Base Tables

Base tables are tables that are created via some type of data definition language command (such as ORACLE's CREATE TABLE command), and their data is stored permanently in secondary storage files. The majority of tables in a relational database are base tables.

Derived Tables

Derived tables are tables derived through some type relational data manipulation language command(s). The data in this type table is actual data, and hence redundant data, but it has been produced by some command(s) rather than being originally stored in the table. Derived tables are temporary tables, meaning that when you disconnect from the database, the derived tables and their associated data are lost. Derived tables can be saved, but when they are, they become base tables. Derived tables are designed to be used as temporary tables so the user will have less data (either fewer rows and/or fewer columns) to manage while working with the DBMS. Derived tables are usually created for some specific purpose (such as a report), and once that purpose is satisfied, the tables are released.

The following is an example of a derived table.

```
GUYS <- SELECT STUDENTS WHERE GENDER = 'MALE'
```

The command, which will be described in greater detail in the following chapter, creates a derived table called ''GUYS'' which consists of all the tuples from the STUDENT table where the value of the attribute GENDER is male.

Derived tables take on the same attribute characteristics (data types, sizes, etc.) as the base tables from which they are derived. Since they are temporary tables, derived tables usually do not have primary keys. Not all relational database management systems support the concept of derived tables. ORACLE does not support the concept of derived tables.

Views

Views are sometimes called virtual tables. **Virtual** in our context refers to something that appears to exist but in reality does not, such as virtual storage. This means that views appear to the user to be actual tables; however, the tuples are generated each time the view is utilized. Views consist of data derived from some type of relational data manipulation language command(s). The command(s) used to create the view is (are) called the view algorithm. The view algorithm is executed each time the view is utilized. This operation is transparent to the user. The view algorithm is stored permanently on the system's secondary storage in the system's data dictionary or catalog. Views can be derived from other views and/or from base tables but not from derived tables.

There are two basic differences between views and derived tables. The first difference is that a view is a dynamic table and a derived table is a static table. This means that when a change is made to one of the underlying tables composing the view, the view data is automatically updated. The reason for this is that the view algorithm is always reexecuted each time the view is utilized. The derived tables values remain unchanged for the command(s) producing the derived table is (are) not reexecuted each time the derived table is utilized. The second difference concerns the life of the view and the derived table. Once the user disconnects from the RDBMS, the derived table is lost. Since the view algorithm is stored in the RDBMS's system catalog, the view can be utilized during the user's next session on the system without having to redefine it.

There are two basic reasons for using views. First, views are used to compute values. For example, suppose our STUDENT table had the attributes QUALITY-POINTS-EARNED and HOURS-COMPLETED added to the table. Further suppose that we wanted to store the student's grade point average in the table. The storing of this field would be redundant, for it could be computed. We would use a view to compute a virtual attribute called GRADE-POINT-AVERAGE that would be computed by dividing the value of QUALITY-POINTS-EARNED by the value stored in HOURS-COMPLETED. This attribute appears as part of the view called STUDENT-VIEW, but its data values would not be stored on secondary storage. Only the command(s) used to generate the view is (are) stored on secondary storage. Naturally, any time the value of QUALITY-POINTS-EARNED and/or HOURS-COMPLETED is changed, the value of GRADE-POINT-AVERAGE is *automatically* updated.

Second, views are a means of restricting access to both rows and columns in a table. We could set up a view to allow faculty members in a department to "view" only the tuples of the students registered in their department. For example, faculty members in the Accounting Department would have access only to the records (tuples) pertaining to accounting majors. The view might also restrict the user to certain attributes in a table (i.e., STUDENT-NAME, ADDRESS, and HOURS-COMPLETED). Views are discussed in greater detail in Chapter 12, Creating and Using Views.

Views, as the name implies, are designed to be used only to view data and are not to be used for update. However, some implementations of the relational model allow the updating of views.

PROPERTIES OF THE RELATIONAL MODEL

Dr. Codd has outlined a set of properties for relational databases.[1] These properties must be strictly adhered to for the full power of the model to be realized. The properties of the relational model are

1. All data must be represented in tabular form.
2. All data must be atomic.
3. No duplicate tuples are allowed.
4. Tuples may be rearranged in almost any manner the user desires without changing the semantics of the tuples.

All Data Must Be Represented in Tabular Form

The user must perceive the data in tabular form, regardless of how it is physically represented. Physically, the data can be represented in any manner the implementer desires (actual tables, linked lists, etc.) as long as the user is shielded from this implementation. The user must have the ability to manipulate data in this tabular format without the need for recursive or looping structures. This does not mean that we cannot access tuples in a relational database in a language such as COBOL or Pascal and not use looping or recursive structures. It means that when we access the database through some type relational language such as relational algebra or relational calculus, we will not have to worry about looping or recursion to access tuples.

Another important characteristic of the relational model is that there are no user-visible pointers. Pointers may be used to represent such things as views, but these are transparent to the user.

All Data Must Be Atomic

Each cell in the relational database matrix can only contain one data value. Consider the following relation:

```
PROFESSOR ( PROF-ID, PROF-NAME, COURSES-TAUGHT)
```

If we look at the last attribute, COURSES-TAUGHT, we can see that if a professor teaches more than one course, we would have to place more than one value in the field COURSES-TAUGHT. Let us look at a sample tuple for Professor Mike Jones (PROF-ID = J001). It seems that the good professor has been assigned to teach CSC 100, Introduction to Pascal Programming, CSC 200, Data Structures, CSC 300, Operating Systems, and CSC 400, Artificial Stupidity. If we look at the professor's tuple occurrence, it might look as follows:

		CSC 400 - Artificial Stupidity
		CSC 300 - Operating Systems
		CSC 200 - Data Structures
J001	Mike Jones	CSC 100 - Intro to Pascal
PROF-ID	PROF-NAME	COURSES-TAUGHT

If you will notice, there are four values stored in the COURSES- TAUGHT attribute in Professor Jones' tuple occurrence. This is not allowed. If it were allowed, think about how this could be implemented. It could be implemented with some type pointer chain, but there are no visible pointers allowed in relational databases. A second method of implementation could be to allow variable-sized tuples.

```
PROFESSOR ( PROF-ID, PROF-NAME, COURSES-TAUGHT-1,
                                COURSES-TAUGHT-2,
                                .  .  .  .  ,
                                COURSES-TAUGHT-N)
```

Think about how you would limit the number of variable attributes that could be placed in a tuple. Think about some faculty members teaching one course and some teaching five courses. The tuple could have an indicator (another attribute) built into the tuple indicating how many actual occurrences of COURSES-TAUGHT would currently be stored in the tuple. Suppose there is some other field in the record that could have multiple values (such as names of students advised). Then we would have to have another indicator showing how many occurrences the professor had for this attribute. How would we allocate storage for this implementation? What would be the maximum number of courses taught by a professor? The maximum number of students advised? It would be very confusing for the nontechnical user to comprehend this. Therefore, to keep the representation simple, we will only be able to store one value in an attribute per tuple.

Does this mean that Professor Jones can only teach one course? Of course it doesn't. It means that we will only have to represent this condition some other way. That way is simply to build another table to store the courses taught. This would be done as follows.

```
PROFESSOR ( PROF-ID , PROF-NAME )
COURSES-TAUGHT ( PROF-ID , COURSE-NAME )
```

TABLE NAME: PROFESSOR   **TABLE NAME: COURSES-TAUGHT**

PROF-ID	PROF-NAME	PROF-ID	COURSE-NAME
J001	Mike Jones	J001	CSC 100 - Intro to Pascal
		J001	CSC 200 - Data Structures
		J001	CSC 300 - Operating Systems
		J001	CSC 400 - Artificial Stupidity

Do you see that by using this technique there is virtually no limit to the number of courses that Professor Jones can teach? Did you also realize the attribute PROF-ID in the COURSES-TAUGHT table is a foreign key? Actually, the technique of storing the course title and the course number in one field is also rather poor, but we will attack that problem at a later point in this text.

In summary, there can be only one value stored in an attribute of a tuple occurrence. By the way, this value can be "null". If you noticed that in the tuple occurrence with the four courses stacked into the one attribute, they formed a "pile of values." Therefore, another method of describing this property is to say that the tables must be represented with flat files. Any table that meets this condition is said to be in the First Normal Form. There will be more said about normal forms in Chapter 15, Designing Relational Databases.

No Duplicate Tuples Are Allowed

The third characteristic of relational databases is that duplicate tuples are not allowed in base tables. On the surface this seems like a trivial characteristic, for we have stated that each table must have a primary key, and the primary key by definition must be a unique value. Duplicate tuples become a particular problem in derived tables. There has been some discussion on whether derived tables have no designated primary key and, hence, could have duplicate tuples. Duplicate tuples should be eliminated from derived tables. Some implementations of relational databases automatically check for and delete duplicate tuples, some implementations require the user to execute some type DELETE DUPLICATE TUPLES command, and some other implementations do not care whether there are duplicate tuples in tables or not.

Rearrangement of Attributes and Tuples

The rearrangement of rows and columns should have no effect on the semantics of the data in a relational database table. This means that it doesn't make any difference where tuples are located in a table for location does not determine meaning. To illustrate this concept consider the following table.

```
PROFESSOR ( PROF-ID , PROFESSOR-NAME , AGE , GENDER )
```

TABLE NAME: PROFESSOR

PROF-ID	PROFESSOR-NAME	AGE	GENDER
P001	Jack Palmer	45	Male
P002	Amy Dancer	35	Female
P003	Arnold Hogan	40	Male
P004	Nancy Bradley	33	Female
P005	Frank Jones	29	Male

Does it change any information in the table if we were to rearrange the tuples in the table? Consider the following rearrangement of the PROFESSOR table.

TABLE NAME: PROFESSOR

PROF-ID	PROF-NAME	AGE	GENDER
P003	Arnold Hogan	40	Male
P001	Jack Palmer	45	Male
P005	Frank Jones	29	Male
P002	Amy Dancer	35	Female
P004	Nancy Bradley	33	Female

Of course it does not! We can now see that the order of the tuples does not change the semantics of the data.

If we rearrange the order of the columns, would it change the semantics of the data? Let's try it and see.

TABLE NAME: PROFESSOR

PROF-NAME	GENDER	AGE	PROF-ID
Jack Palmer	Male	45	P001
Amy Dancer	Female	35	P002
Arnold Hogan	Male	40	P003
Nancy Bradley	Female	33	P004
Frank Jones	Male	29	P005

The rearrangement of the columns does not appear to have any effect on what the tuples mean. Therefore, the columns can be rearranged without changing the meaning of the tuples.

In summary, we can rearrange the row and/or the columns and not change the meaning of our data, as long as we do not change both values at the same time.

BASIS FOR THE RELATIONAL MODEL

When Dr. Codd conceived the relational model, he had reasons for developing it.[2] His rationale was based on problems that he perceived with the construction of currently existing DBMSs. Dr. Codd stated that currently existing database management systems had failed in their effort in ''boosting productivity.'' His reasons for making this statement were threefold.

Why Currently Existing DBMSs Have Failed as Productivity Boosters

Database management systems were designed to assist the user in managing her data. It was assumed by users that since their data would be better managed, their productivity would naturally be increased. In considering currently existing DBMSs, Dr. Codd found three problems with this assumption.

First, with nonrelational systems, application developers were faced with learning irrelevant concepts such as CODASYL sets, next pointers, prior pointers, and owner pointers. Dr. Codd felt that users of DBMSs should not have to bother themselves with these complex concepts. The DBMS should keep track of such things and shield the user from having to know them.

Second, nonrelational DBMSs processed records one at a time. The user had to be aware of such conditions as end-of-file, end-of-set, and so on. Dr. Codd wanted users/programmers to be able to address groups of records at a time, which he referred to as ''set processing.'' The DBMS would take care of such trivial details as testing for end-of-file. These tests would be completely transparent to the user. Since the basis for RDBMS is the mathematical theory of sets, he chose the word ''set'' to refer to a group of records (in reality a subset of records) that have some type identity (e.g., a set of all male students). This definition of a set is used much in the manner of sets in Venn diagrams (Figure 2.2).

Please be aware that we now have two definitions of a set. The first is the so-called CODASYL set which refers to an owner-member relationship between record types. We will now refer to this relationship as a CODASYL set. The second is the relational definition of a set that comes from the mathematical theory of sets. Unless otherwise noted, in the remainder of this text when we refer to a set, we are referring to the relational set.

Third, database vendors originally treated ad hoc querying as an afterthought. Most vendors did not even furnish customers with any type of query facility. This

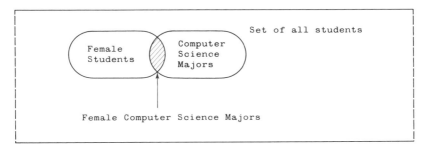

Figure 2.2   Venn Diagrams

has been changed in today's competitive world of database vendors, but in the late 1960s and early 1970s query languages were virtually unheard of. Query facilities are one of the most important selling points of modern DBMSs.

Solutions to the Problems

Given these three problem areas, Dr. Codd wanted to develop a method of processing data that solved these perceived problems. His solution was, of course, the relational model of data. He wanted to develop a model that provided the following:

1. **True data independence.** The new model was to provide the user with a "sharp, clear boundary" between the logical and physical aspects of database design and manipulation. The user would no longer have to worry about such things as traversing linked lists or considering which access path through the network structure was best to retrieve data. The user would simply state what data was needed, not how to get it.

2. **Communicability.** Since the underlying structure (the table) of the database is so simple, various users of the system (systems designers, programmers, end users, management) could communicate with each other concerning the database without operating through some database vernacular translator.

3. **Set processing.** The user should have the ability to work with large chunks of data as opposed to accessing one record at a time, *à la* conventional programming languages. The user should not be concerned with iterative looping structures common to most conventional languages.

In designing a solution to the problems by implementing these objectives, it was further decided to change the basic method of addressing data in databases. Data has always been addressed by position. To illustrate this concept, consider a simple two-dimensional array in any language. To access any data value in the array, we must know all of the following

1. The array name
2. The specific row where the data item is located
3. The specific column where the data item is located

The row-column intersection connotes a physical location.

In the relational model any data item can be addressed by value, not by physical position, no matter where it is located in the database. This method of addressing is called **associative addressing**. With the utilization of associative addressing, any data item can be addressed by means of three values. The three values are

1. The table name
2. The primary key value
3. The attribute name

This means that the user does not have to be concerned with where the data is stored. The system takes care of storing and retrieving the values for us. The system also determines the access path(s) to and from the data for the user. By combining this method of addressing data with the relational languages described in the following chapter and the table structure, the relational model was born.

Now that we understand the underlying structure of the relational model, we should now explore how data is manipulated in the relational model. That is the topic of our next chapter.

SUMMARY

The focus of this chapter was to introduce the reader to some of the relational terminology. The material covered in this chapter was initially defined by Dr. E. F. Codd in the late 1960s and early 1970s. The material was generally theoretical, but is essential to the understanding of the various implementations of the relational model of data.

We introduced the concepts of relations, tables, attributes, domains, and N-ary relations. Various types of keys, candidate, primary, foreign, composite, and redundant, associated with the relational model were also discussed. The three types of tables, base, derived, and views, were also presented. The chapter concluded with a discussion of Dr. Codd's rationale for designing the relational model.

Now that you have completed this chapter, you should be familiar with the following concepts:

A. Relation

B. Table

C. Attribute or field

D. Domain

E. Degree of a relation

F. Cardinality of a relation

G. Notation used to represent a table

H. Candidate keys

 I. Primary keys

J. Foreign keys

K. Entity integrity

L. Referential integrity

M. Composite keys

N. Redundant keys

O. Base tables

P. Derived tables

Q. Views

R. Properties of the relational model

S. Why existing DBMS have failed as productivity boosters

T. Associative addressing

EXERCISES

1. Explain the difference between a relation and a table.

2. Explain the difference between a primary key and a foreign key. Why do derived tables not have primary keys? Can they have foreign keys?

3. Explain what is meant by set processing. What is the difference between a CODASYL set and a relational set?

4. Explain why views cannot be generated from derived tables.

5. Why entity and referential integrity? Is it a worthwhile goal to strive for?

6. Consider the database that you "constructed" in Exercise 2 of Chapter 1. Using that database, contemplate the following questions:
How would you convert it to a relational database?
What tables would you have?
What attributes would you have in each table?
What domains would you have?
What would be primary key of each table?
What foreign keys are there in each table?
Which of your tables would be base tables?
Can you see a use for views? If so, which ones?

REFERENCES

1. Codd, E. F. "A Relational Model of Data for Large Shared Data Bases," *Communications of the ACM*, **13,** no. 6, 1970, 377–387.

2. Codd, E. F. "Relational Database: A Practical Foundation for Productivity," *Communications of the ACM*, **25,** no. 2, 1982, 109–117.

3

Data Manipulation via Relational Algebra

PURPOSE: The purpose of this chapter is to acquaint the user with the relational algebra data manipulation facilities of the relational model. Although the relational algebra facilities are basically theoretical, they are extremely helpful in understanding the various implemented relational data manipulation languages. The chapter concludes with a set of guidelines to determine if a database management system can be considered relational.

Data manipulation refers to methods of retrieving and changing data in the database. Dr. Codd has designed two levels of data manipulation languages: relational algebra, which is covered in this chapter, and relational calculus, which is covered in the following chapter. These languages are considered stand-alone query languages, even though provisions could be made to embed the commands within conventional programming languages. The languages are sometimes referred to as data sublanguages for they may not contain all the extras of regular languages such as function calls to compute various mathematical properties such as the sine, cosine, square root, and so on. These languages do not contain any provisions for extensive formatting of data.

Even though these languages have not been completely implemented on any industrial-strength database management system, they are very important, for the

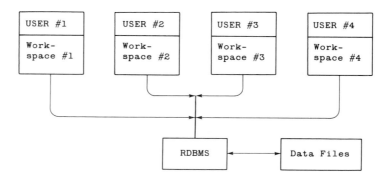

Figure 3.1   User Workspaces

concepts that they illustrate are critical to understanding data manipulation in implemented RDBMS.

CONCEPT OF A WORKSPACE

A workspace is a buffer area into which data is brought after it has been retrieved. It also acts as a staging area for data that is to be written out to data files stored on secondary storage devices. Workspaces are dynamic and can hold as much data as needed. Realistically, the workspace might be a virtual workspace with the parts that cannot fit into memory being swapped out of memory and retrieved as needed. This operation is transparent to the user. Each user of the system is automatically provided with a temporary workspace when she connects to the RDBMS. When the user disconnects from the RDBMS the workspace and its current contents are lost. (The user usually has the option of saving the contents of the workspace for recall at a later point in time.)

Conceptually you can picture a workspace in Figure 3.1.

SYNTAX OF DATA MANIPULATION LANGUAGE COMMANDS

Since both relational algebra and relational calculus are theoretical languages, there are no actual syntax rules for either. C. J. Date, in his book, *An Introduction to Database Systems*, does define a rigorous syntax for relational algebra [1]. Since these languages are being used only to illustrate data manipulation in RDBMS, you may use any reasonable syntax that you wish to represent the commands. We will use the convention that is used in the APL (**A P**rogramming **L**anguage), and that is if the results of a command are not assigned into something (e.g., a resultant table, see paragraphs that follow) via the assignment operator (←), they are displayed on the user's terminal. However, in an effort to remain consistent, we will attempt to use the same syntax for each of the algebra and calculus commands throughout this text. In addition, we will assume that the language syntax is free-field.

RELATIONAL ALGEBRA

Relational algebra is a sublanguage that was primarily designed for data retrieval, and that is where its power lies. This is not to say that data cannot be modified using relational algebra, it is just that the commands are more flexible for retrieving data. Relational algebra commands combine set theory commands with some commands that Dr. Codd designed specifically for the relational model.

One of the important concepts concerning relational algebra relates to how data is referenced. In a programming language we could use the statement

```
        A = B + C
   or   A := B + C;
   or   ADD B TO C GIVING A.
```

and we would know that A, B, and C were scalar variables. In relational languages, the variables refer to entire tables. This means that variables usually refer to "chunks" of tuples. This should become obvious to you as we step through our examples.

The output from a relational algebra command is always in the form of a table. This table is called the **resultant table**. This property is called **closure**. This is an important concept for it allows us to embed one relational algebra command inside of another.

SPECIAL RELATIONAL ALGEBRA COMMANDS

We begin our discussion of relational algebra with the special operators (select, project, join, and divide) designed for relational database management systems. We will then explore the traditional set operators (union, intersection, difference, and product) that have been adapted for the relational model. Since the syntax of relational algebra is rather arbitrary, we will present two syntaxes for each command. The first will be rather wordy, and the second more concise.

SELECT

The SELECT command takes a horizontal subset of records from a table. The SELECT command is sometimes referred to as RESTRICT so as not to confuse it with the SQL command SELECT, which is considerably more powerful than the relational algebra command SELECT. Since we have not yet introduced the SQL

SELECT command, we will refer to this command as the SELECT command. The first form of the syntax of the SELECT command is

```
SELECT table-name [WHERE θ]
```

The command notation guidelines that we will use to describe the relational algebra commands are as follows:

1. The brackets ([]) indicate that this part of the command is optional.
2. The uppercase words are required.
3. The lowercase words are user-supplied objects such as table names or attribute names.

An alternate and more concise syntax of the SELECT command is:

```
table-name [ [θ] ]  {Note that the inner brackets
                       are part of the syntax}
```

The symbol "table-name" obviously represents the table to be used in the selection process. The symbol θ, referred to as theta, represents any condition or set of conditions used as a filter for the tuples in the table. If θ is not present, the entire table is selected.

Let us use our now-famous example tables to illustrate some sample SELECT commands.

TABLE NAME: STUDENT

STU-ID	STUDENT-NAME	ADDRESS	BIRTHDATE	GENDER
S001	WENDY JONES	125 MAPLE AVE	10/25/65	FEMALE
S002	SAM WALES	3006 NAVAJO CL	1/10/60	MALE
S003	CATHY SMITH	1600 PENN AVE	2/22/22	FEMALE
S004	DOTTIE STACY	10 DOWNING ST	3/31/67	FEMALE
S005	JAY LANGER	GOLF COURSE RD	4/19/65	MALE
S006	AMY LOPEZ	123 SUN RAY RD	5/10/64	FEMALE
S007	SAM WATSON	225 TEST DRIVE	6/09/63	MALE
S008	TAMMY REDD	113 MANCHESTER	7/01/60	FEMALE
S009	TOMMY WADKINS	APPLE TREE DR	8/24/67	MALE
S010	BEN TREVINO	BOWLING ALLEY	9/30/66	MALE

1. Display the entire STUDENT table.

```
SELECT STUDENT
```

The alternate syntax would be as follows.

STUDENT

STU-ID	STUDENT-NAME	ADDRESS	BIRTHDATE	GENDER
S001	WENDY JONES	125 MAPLE AVE	10/25/65	FEMALE
S002	SAM WALES	3006 NAVAJO CL	1/10/60	MALE
S003	CATHY SMITH	1600 PENN AVE	2/22/22	FEMALE
S004	DOTTIE STACY	10 DOWNING ST	3/31/67	FEMALE
S005	JAY LANGER	GOLF COURSE RD	4/19/65	MALE
S006	AMY LOPEZ	123 SUN RAY RD	5/10/64	FEMALE
S007	SAM WATSON	225 TEST DRIVE	6/09/63	MALE
S008	TAMMY REDD	113 MANCHESTER	7/01/60	FEMALE
S009	TOMMY WADKINS	APPLE TREE DR	8/24/67	MALE
S010	BEN TREVINO	BOWLING ALLEY	9/30/66	MALE

2. Copy the entire STUDENT table into a derived table called DUPLICATE-STUDENTS.

```
DUPLICATE-STUDENTS <- SELECT STUDENT
```

or

```
DUPLICATE-STUDENTS <- STUDENT
```

3. Using a Theta SELECT, list all data on the MALE students.

```
SELECT STUDENTS WHERE GENDER = 'MALE'
```

or

```
STUDENT [GENDER = 'MALE']
```

STU-ID	STUDENT-NAME	ADDRESS	BIRTHDATE	GENDER
S002	SAM WALES	3006 NAVAJO CL	1/10/60	MALE
S005	JAY LANGER	GOLF COURSE RD	4/19/65	MALE
S007	SAM WATSON	225 TEST DRIVE	6/09/63	MALE
S009	TOMMY WADKINS	APPLE TREE DR	8/24/67	MALE
S010	BEN TREVINO	BOWLING ALLEY	9/30/66	MALE

4. List all data on the FEMALE students born before January 1, 1963.

```
SELECT STUDENT WHERE GENDER = 'FEMALE' AND
       BIRTHDATE < '1/01/63'
```

or

```
STUDENT [GENDER = 'FEMALE' & BIRTHDATE < '1/01/63']
```

```
STU-ID  STUDENT-NAME      ADDRESS         BIRTHDATE  GENDER
S003    CATHY SMITH       1600 PENN AVE   2/22/22    FEMALE
S008    TAMMY REDD        113 MANCHESTER  7/01/60    FEMALE
```

5. Create a derived table called MATURE-LADIES containing all the data on the female students born before January 1, 1963.

```
MATURE-LADIES <- SELECT STUDENT WHERE GENDER = 'FEMALE' AND
                 BIRTHDATE < '1/01/63'
```

or

```
    MATURE-LADIES <- STUDENT [GENDER = 'FEMALE' &
                     BIRTHDATE < '1/01/63']
```

PROJECT

If the SELECT command generates a horizontal subset of a table then the PROJECT command generates a vertical subset of a table. The syntax for the PROJECT command is:

```
    PROJECT attr1, attr2, . . ., attrN FROM table-name
```

or

```
    PROJECT table-name OVER attr1, attr2, . . . , attrN
```

An alternate syntax that could be used is:

```
        table-name [attr1, attr2, . . ., attrN]
```

The symbols attr1, attr2, . . ., attrN obviously represent the various attributes from the table "table-name." The reader will notice that there is no theta condition specified on the PROJECT operator. If there were a Theta PROJECT, it would function like a combination of the SELECT and PROJECT commands combined into one command.

Examples of the PROJECT command follow.

TABLE NAME: COURSE

```
COURSE-ID  COURSE-TITLE              SECTION  STU-ID  FAC-ID
CSC100     INTRODUCTION TO COMPUTING       1  S001    J01
CSC100     INTRODUCTION TO COMPUTING       2  S002    S01
CSC200     PASCAL PROGRAMMING              1  S001    D01
CSC200     PASCAL PROGRAMMING              2  S003    S01
ACC200     PRINCIPLES OF ACCOUNTING I      1  S001    J02
ACC201     PRINCIPLES OF ACCOUNTING II     1  S004    J02
HIS200     HISTORY OF PIROGUES             1  S005    N01
```

1. List out the names of the courses being taught.

```
PROJECT COURSE-TITLE FROM COURSE
```

or

```
COURSE [COURSE-TITLE]

COURSE-TITLE
INTRODUCTION TO COMPUTING
PASCAL PROGRAMMING
PRINCIPLES OF ACCOUNTING I
PRINCIPLES OF ACCOUNTING II
HISTORY OF PIROGUES
```

Notice that the duplicate tuples have been deleted from the resultant table.

2. Place a list of titles of the courses being taught into a derived table called CURRENT-COURSES.

```
CURRENT-COURSES <- PROJECT COURSE-TITLE FROM COURSE
```

or

```
CURRENT-COURSES <- COURSE [COURSE-TITLE]
```

3. List the STU-IDs and the COURSE-IDs of the courses that the students are taking.

```
PROJECT STU-ID, COURSE-ID FROM COURSE
```

or

```
COURSE [STU-ID, COURSE-ID]

STU-ID       COURSE-ID
S001         CSC100
S002         CSC100
S001         CSC200
S003         CSC200
S001         ACC200
S004         ACC201
S005         HIS200
```

4. We can use the PROJECT command to permute the order of the attributes.

```
PROJECT STU-ID, FAC-ID, COURSE-ID, SECTION,
        COURSE-TITLE FROM COURSE
```

or

```
COURSE [STU-ID, FAC-ID, COURSE-ID, SECTION, COURSE-TITLE]
```

STU-ID	FAC-ID	COURSE-ID	SECTION	COURSE-TITLE
S001	J01	CSC100	1	INTRODUCTION TO COMPUTING
S002	S01	CSC100	2	INTRODUCTION TO COMPUTING
S001	D01	CSC200	1	PASCAL PROGRAMMING
S003	S01	CSC200	2	PASCAL PROGRAMMING
S001	J02	ACC200	1	PRINCIPLES OF ACCOUNTING I
S004	J02	ACC201	1	PRINCIPLES OF ACCOUNTING II
S005	N01	HIS200	1	HISTORY OF PIROGUES

JOIN

The function of the JOIN command is to link tables together. To use a JOIN command, the two (or more) tables that are to be joined must have a common domain. The attributes that the domain ranges over can have different names, but they must be defined over the same domain. (Remember, attributes are defined over domains.) Actually, the tables do not "have" to contain a common attribute, but if they do not, the command makes very little sense to execute. (There is another command called the Cartesian product that does in fact join all the tuples of the first table to each of the tuples of the second table. This command is described later in this chapter.)

There are many different joins as shown next.

1. Simple or inner JOIN
2. Natural JOIN
3. Equi-JOIN
4. Theta JOIN
5. Outer JOIN

Simple JOIN.   In a Simple JOIN command, sometimes called an Inner JOIN, the system looks at each tuple in isolation and matches values over the common domain. The syntax of the JOIN command is

```
JOIN table-name1, table-name2 OVER common-attribute
```

The alternate syntax of the Simple JOIN command is as follows.

```
table-name1 [common-attribute] table-name2
```

The symbols table-name1 and table-name2 are the two tables that are to be joined together. The symbol common-attribute represents an attribute that is to be used in the join process. For now, we will assume that the JOIN attribute in both tables has the same attribute name.

The JOIN command selects the first tuple in table-name1 and attempts to match (compare for equality) the value in the JOIN attribute in each tuple to the value of the JOIN attribute in table-name2. If a match is found, a tuple consisting of all the attribute values in table-name1 concatenated with all the attribute values in table-name2 is generated. A new tuple is created for each match found. The match continues by comparing the JOIN attribute value in the second tuple of table-name1 with the JOIN attribute value in each tuple in table-name2. The process continues until all the tuples in table-name1 have been exhausted.

Let us use some subsets of the STUDENT and COURSE tables to illustrate the JOIN command. We will assume that the follow PROJECTs have been executed.

```
ST-TAB <- PROJECT STU-ID, STUDENT-NAME FROM STUDENT
CO-TAB <- PROJECT COURSE-ID, STU-ID, COURSE-TITLE FROM
          COURSE
```

SELECT ST-TAB

STU-ID	STUDENT-NAME
S001	WENDY JONES
S002	SAM WALES
S003	CATHY SMITH
S004	DOTTIE STACY
S005	JAY LANGER
S006	AMY LOPEZ
S007	SAM WATSON
S008	TAMMY REDD
S009	TOMMY WADKINS
S010	BEN TREVINO

Note: The common attribute is STU-ID

SELECT CO-TAB

COURSE-ID	STU-ID	COURSE-TITLE
CSC100	S001	INTRODUCTION TO COMPUTING
CSC100	S002	INTRODUCTION TO COMPUTING
CSC200	S001	PASCAL PROGRAMMING
CSC200	S003	PASCAL PROGRAMMING
ACC200	S001	PRINCIPLES OF ACCOUNTING I
ACC201	S004	PRINCIPLES OF ACCOUNTING II
HIS200	S005	HISTORY OF PIROGUES

1. List all the students taking courses and the titles of the courses that they are taking.

```
JOIN ST-TAB, CO-TAB OVER STU-ID
```

or

```
ST-TAB [STU-ID] CO-TAB
```

STU-ID	STUDENT-NAME	COURSE-ID	STU-ID	COURSE-TITLE
S001	WENDY JONES	CSC100	S001	INTRODUCTION TO COMPUTING
S001	WENDY JONES	CSC200	S001	PASCAL PROGRAMMING
S001	WENDY JONES	ACC200	S001	PRINCIPLES OF ACCOUNTING I
S002	SAM WALES	CSC100	S002	INTRODUCTION TO COMPUTING
S003	CATHY SMITH	CSC200	S003	PASCAL PROGRAMMING
S004	DOTTIE STACY	ACC201	S004	PRINCIPLES OF ACCOUNTING II
S005	JAY LANGER	HIS200	S005	HISTORY OF PIROGUES

Notice that since the student "WENDY JONES" is registered for three courses, three tuples are generated by the JOIN command. However, the students Amy Lopez, Sam Watson, Tammy Wadkins, and Ben Trevino do not take any courses (there are no tuples in the COURSE table with their STU-IDs) and hence no tuples are produced for the resultant table.

We can visualize the execution of the JOIN command as the execution of nested loops. The following set of pseudocode is an example of the JOIN command.

```
Read the first tuple from the ST-TAB table
While not end-of-table in the ST-TAB table
  Begin
    Read the first tuple in the CO-TAB table
    While not end-of-table in the CO-TAB table
      Begin
        If ST-TAB.STU-ID = CO-TAB.STU-ID
          then display the following attributes from the
                current ST-TAB table tuple:
                STU-ID, STUDENT-NAME and
              display the following attributes from the
                current CO-TAB table tuple:
                COURSE-ID, STU-ID, COURSE-TITLE
        Read the next tuple from the CO-TAB table
      End
    Read the next tuple from the ST-TAB table
  End
```

2. Store the list generated by the preceeding example one above in a derived table called STU-COURSES.

```
STU-COURSES <- JOIN ST-TAB, CO-TAB OVER STU-ID
```

or

```
STU-COURSES <- ST-TAB *STU-ID+ CO-TAB
```

Natural JOIN.   You will notice from Example 1 of the Simple JOIN that there is a duplicate attribute (STU-ID) in the resultant table. The reason for this is that the attribute STU-ID occurs in both tables. Since this is in fact a duplicate, it can be omitted and no information is lost. This JOIN with the duplicate attribute omitted is called a Natural JOIN. In the remainder of this text, when we perform a Simple JOIN operation, we will assume it to be a Natural JOIN. The resultant table in Example 1 with a Natural JOIN would look like

```
STU-COURSES <- JOIN ST-TAB, CO-TAB OVER STU-ID
```

Note that there is no change to the first format syntax of the command.

A version of the concise syntax is shown here. In this syntax the asterisk (*) indicates the Natural JOIN.

```
STU-COURSES <- ST-TAB [ST-TAB.STU-ID * CO-TAB.STU-ID] CO-TAB
```

Notice that since the attribute STU-ID appears in both tables, it must be qualified. The most common qualification format is to place the name of the table before the attribute and separate the two with a period.

TABLE NAME: STU-COURSES

STU-ID	STUDENT-NAME	COURSE-ID	COURSE-TITLE
S001	WENDY JONES	CSC100	INTRODUCTION TO COMPUTING
S001	WENDY JONES	CSC200	PASCAL PROGRAMMING
S001	WENDY JONES	ACC200	PRINCIPLES OF ACCOUNTING I
S002	SAM WALES	CSC100	INTRODUCTION TO COMPUTING
S003	CATHY SMITH	CSC200	PASCAL PROGRAMMING
S004	DOTTIE STACY	ACC201	PRINCIPLES OF ACCOUNTING II
S005	JAY LANGER	HIS200	HISTORY OF PIROGUES

Notice that the second occurrence of STU-ID is the one we have chosen to omit. That is just a convention that we have adopted. We could have just as easily omitted the first occurrence.

Equi-JOIN.   In all the example JOINs that we have viewed, the match condition has always been equality. Another term for this type join is the Equi-JOIN. As we have stated, whenever the match condition is not explicitly stated, we will assume an Equi-JOIN.

Theta JOIN.   In some situations we do not want to use an Equi-JOIN. We want to specify some type condition(s) other than equality. If the symbol θ again represents any condition or combination of conditions, we could specify a Theta JOIN as follow:

```
JOIN table-name1, table-name2 WHERE θ

or table-name1 [θ] table-name2
```

Here are some examples of Theta JOINs. Again we will use the ST-TAB and the CO-TAB tables for examples.

1. List the courses and students who do not match over STU-ID.

```
JOIN ST-TAB, CO-TAB WHERE ST-TAB.STU-ID ≠ CO-TAB.STU-ID
```

or

```
ST-TAB [ST-TAB ≠ CO-TAB.STU-ID] CO-TAB
```

STU-ID	STUDENT-NAME	COURSE-ID	STU-ID	COURSE-TITLE
S001	WENDY JONES	CSC100	S002	INTRO TO COMPUTING
S001	WENDY JONES	CSC200	S003	PASCAL PROGRAMMING
S001	WENDY JONES	ACC201	S004	PRINCIPLES OF ACCOUNTING II
S001	WENDY JONES	HIS200	S005	HISTORY OF PIROGUES
S002	SAM WALES	CSC100	S001	INTRO TO COMPUTING
S002	SAM WALES	CSC200	S001	PASCAL PROGRAMMING
S002	SAM WALES	CSC200	S003	PASCAL PROGRAMMING
S002	SAM WALES	ACC200	S001	PRINCIPLES OF ACCOUNTING I
S002	SAM WALES	ACC201	S004	PRINCIPLES OF ACCOUNTING II
S002	SAM WALES	HIS200	S005	HISTORY OF PIROGUES
S003	CATHY SMITH	CSC100	S001	INTRO TO COMPUTING
S003	CATHY SMITH	CSC100	S002	INTRO TO COMPUTING
S003	CATHY SMITH	CSC200	S001	PASCAL PROGRAMMING
S003	CATHY SMITH	ACC200	S001	PRINCIPLES OF ACCOUNTING I
S003	CATHY SMITH	ACC201	S004	PRINCIPLES OF ACCOUNTING II
S003	CATHY SMITH	HIS200	S005	HISTORY OF PIROGUES
S004	DOTTIE STACY	CSC100	S001	INTRO TO COMPUTING
S004	DOTTIE STACY	CSC100	S002	INTRO TO COMPUTING
S004	DOTTIE STACY	CSC200	S001	PASCAL PROGRAMMING
S004	DOTTIE STACY	CSC200	S003	PASCAL PROGRAMMING
S004	DOTTIE STACY	ACC200	S001	PRINCIPLES OF ACCOUNTING I
S004	DOTTIE STACY	HIS200	S005	HISTORY OF PIROGUES
S005	JAY LANGER	CSC100	S001	INTRO TO COMPUTING
S005	JAY LANGER	CSC100	S002	INTRO TO COMPUTING
S005	JAY LANGER	CSC200	S001	PASCAL PROGRAMMING
S005	JAY LANGER	CSC200	S003	PASCAL PROGRAMMING
S005	JAY LANGER	ACC200	S001	PRINCIPLES OF ACCOUNTING I
S005	JAY LANGER	ACC201	S004	PRINCIPLES OF ACCOUNTING II
S006	AMY LOPEZ	CSC100	S001	INTRODUCTION TO COMPUTING
S006	AMY LOPEZ	CSC100	S002	INTRODUCTION TO COMPUTING
S006	AMY LOPEZ	CSC200	S001	PASCAL PROGRAMMING
S006	AMY LOPEZ	CSC200	S003	PASCAL PROGRAMMING
S006	AMY LOPEZ	ACC200	S001	PRINCIPLES OF ACCOUNTING I
S006	AMY LOPEZ	ACC201	S004	PRINCIPLES OF ACCOUNTING II
S006	AMY LOPEZ	HIS200	S005	HISTORY OF PIROGUES
S007	SAM WATSON	CSC100	S001	INTRODUCTION TO COMPUTING
S007	SAM WATSON	CSC100	S002	INTRODUCTION TO COMPUTING

STU-ID	STUDENT-NAME	COURSE-ID	STU-ID	COURSE-TITLE
S007	SAM WATSON	CSC200	S001	PASCAL PROGRAMMING
S007	SAM WATSON	CSC200	S003	PASCAL PROGRAMMING
S007	SAM WATSON	ACC200	S001	PRINCIPLES OF ACCOUNTING I
S007	SAM WATSON	ACC201	S004	PRINCIPLES OF ACCOUNTING II
S007	SAM WATSON	HIS200	S005	HISTORY OF PIROGUES
S008	TAMMY REDD	CSC100	S001	INTRODUCTION TO COMPUTING
S008	TAMMY REDD	CSC100	S002	INTRODUCTION TO COMPUTING
S008	TAMMY REDD	CSC200	S001	PASCAL PROGRAMMING
S008	TAMMY REDD	CSC200	S003	PASCAL PROGRAMMING
S008	TAMMY REDD	ACC200	S001	PRINCIPLES OF ACCOUNTING I
S008	TAMMY REDD	ACC201	S004	PRINCIPLES OF ACCOUNTING II
S008	TAMMY REDD	HIS200	S005	HISTORY OF PIROGUES
S009	TOMMY WADKINS	CSC100	S001	INTRODUCTION TO COMPUTING
S009	TOMMY WADKINS	CSC100	S002	INTRODUCTION TO COMPUTING
S009	TOMMY WADKINS	CSC200	S001	PASCAL PROGRAMMING
S009	TOMMY WADKINS	CSC200	S003	PASCAL PROGRAMMING
S009	TOMMY WADKINS	ACC200	S001	PRINCIPLES OF ACCOUNTING I
S009	TOMMY WADKINS	ACC201	S004	PRINCIPLES OF ACCOUNTING II
S009	TOMMY WADKINS	HIS200	S005	HISTORY OF PIROGUES
S010	BEN TREVINO	CSC100	S001	INTRODUCTION TO COMPUTING
S010	BEN TREVINO	CSC100	S002	INTRODUCTION TO COMPUTING
S010	BEN TREVINO	CSC200	S001	PASCAL PROGRAMMING
S010	BEN TREVINO	CSC200	S003	PASCAL PROGRAMMING
S010	BEN TREVINO	ACC200	S001	PRINCIPLES OF ACCOUNTING I
S010	BEN TREVINO	ACC201	S004	PRINCIPLES OF ACCOUNTING II
S010	BEN TREVINO	HIS200	S005	HISTORY OF PIROGUES

If you work through the resultant table you will see that a tuple is generated anywhere the theta condition (ST-TAB.STU-ID $\neq$ CO-TAB.STU-ID) is satisfied. You should be aware that some of these theta conditions can produce very large resultant tables. Also notice that there are two columns with STU-ID, but the values in each tuple for the two attributes are different. We can infer from this that there is no such thing as a Natural Theta JOIN for the common attributes will never have the same values unless theta is equality.

Note that we again had to qualify the attribute STU-ID, for it appears in both tables.

The Theta JOIN is also used when we wish to perform an Equi-JOIN and the attribute names are different (both attributes are still defined over a common domain). To illustrate this, let's go back to our first Simple JOIN, list all of the students taking courses and the courses that they are taking. Let's further assume that the JOIN attributes have different names.

```
ST-TAB (STUDENT#, STUDENT-NAME)
CO-TAB (COURSE-ID, STU-ID )
```

We cannot use a Simple JOIN to link these two tables together, for there is no common attribute name. We must use the following Theta JOIN to link them together.

```
JOIN ST-TAB, CO-TAB WHERE STU-ID = STUDENT#
```

or

```
ST-TAB [STU-ID = STUDENT#] CO-TAB
```

Notice that the two attribute names do not have to be qualified; they are unique. The results of the JOIN are shown here.

STUDENT#	STUDENT-NAME	COURSE-ID	STU-ID	COURSE-TITLE
S001	WENDY JONES	CSC100	S001	INTRODUCTION TO COMPUTING
S001	WENDY JONES	CSC200	S001	PASCAL PROGRAMMING
S001	WENDY JONES	ACC200	S001	PRINCIPLES OF ACCOUNTING I
S002	SAM WALES	CSC100	S002	INTRODUCTION TO COMPUTING
S003	CATHY SMITH	CSC200	S003	PASCAL PROGRAMMING
S004	DOTTIE STACY	ACC201	S004	PRINCIPLES OF ACCOUNTING II
S005	JAY LANGER	HIS200	S005	HISTORY OF PIROGUES

Outer JOIN.   The Outer JOIN is similar to the Simple JOIN (sometimes called the Inner JOIN) except that tuples that do not meet the equality condition also generate a tuple containing null values for their attributes. The Outer JOIN must also have a common domain to join the two tables over. The format of the Outer JOIN is similar to that of the Simple JOIN except that we prefix the command with the word "OUTER." In the concise syntax, a plus sign (+) placed after the join condition indicates an Outer JOIN.

```
OUTER JOIN table-name1, table-name2 OVER common-attribute
```

or

```
table-name1 [table-name1.attr1 = table-name2.attr1+] table-name2
```

To illustrate the Outer JOIN, let us consider the following two tables.

TABLE NAME: STU

STU-ID	STUDENT-NAME
S001	WENDY JONES
S002	SAM WALES
S003	CATHY SMITH

TABLE NAME: COUR

COURSE-ID	STU-ID	COURSE-TITLE
CSC100	S001	INTRODUCTION TO COMPUTING
CSC100	S002	INTRODUCTION TO COMPUTING
CSC200	S001	PASCAL PROGRAMMING
CSC300	S004	DATA STRUCTURES

If we performed a simple Equi-JOIN on the two tables we would get the following output.

```
                    JOIN STU, COUR OVER STU-ID
```

or

```
                    STU [STU-ID] COUR
```

STU-ID	STUDENT-NAME	COURSE-ID	COURSE-TITLE
S001	WENDY JONES	CSC100	INTRODUCTION TO COMPUTING
S001	WENDY JONES	CSC200	PASCAL PROGRAMMING
S002	SAM WALES	CSC100	INTRODUCTION TO COMPUTING

Notice that no tuple was generated for student S003. The reason for this is that the STU.STU-ID of S003 is not listed in the COUR table and therefore no match occurs. There was also no tuple generated for COUR.STU-ID of S004, for there is no STU-ID of S004 in the STU table. Note that this last case violates the referential integrity rule we discussed in the previous chapter.

Using the same two tables but now performing an Outer JOIN produces different results.

```
            OUTER JOIN STU, COUR OVER STU-ID
            or  STU [STU.STU-ID = COUR.STU-ID+] COUR
```

STU-ID	STUDENT-NAME	COURSE-ID	STU-ID	COURSE-TITLE
S001	WENDY JONES	CSC100	S001	INTRODUCTION TO COMPUTING
S001	WENDY JONES	CSC200	S001	PASCAL PROGRAMMING
S002	SAM WALES	CSC100	S002	INTRODUCTION TO COMPUTING
S003	CATHY SMITH	\<NULL>	\<NULL>	\<NULL>
\<NULL>	\<NULL>	CSC300	S004	DATA STRUCTURES

The Outer JOIN produces two more tuples than the inner JOIN did. It produces a tuple for STU.STU-ID of S003 even though there is no corresponding S003 in the COUR table. Notice that the values of COURSE-ID, the second STU-ID, and COURSE-TITLE are all set to null. The last tuple is generated from COUR.STU-ID equal to S004. Notice the null values in these tuples (denoted \<NULL>).

DIVIDE

Division is another extremely powerful operator that implements a "vertical and." Remembering back to the Theta SELECT command, we could specify as many conditions as we wished to filter out the tuples in which we had no interest. However, all those conditions referred to the tuple that was being considered. In some instances we might want a test that would be run between tuples. The DIVIDE command provides such power.

The format of the DIVIDE command is

```
DIVIDE table-name1 BY table-name2 OVER common-attribute
```

The alternate syntax for the DIVIDE command is

```
table-name1 [table-name1.attr1 ÷ table-name2.attr2] table-name2
```

For the DIVIDE command to work correctly, table-name1 must be a binary table, and table-name2 must be a unary table. There must be a common domain in the two tables. The result will be a unary table defined over the noncommon attribute in table-name1.

To illustrate the DIVIDE command, let us create a binary table by projecting out the attributes STU-ID and COURSE-ID from the COURSE table and placing the results into a derived table called COURSE-TAKING.

```
COURSE-TAKING <- PROJECT STU-ID, COURSE-ID FROM COURSES
SELECT COURSE-TAKING
```

STU-ID	COURSE-ID
S001	CSC100
S002	CSC100
S001	CSC200
S003	CSC200
S001	ACC200
S004	ACC201
S005	HIS200

1. What are the STU-IDs of the students taking CSC100? To solve this query we will have to build a unary table: let's call it WHAT-COURSE with a single attribute called COURSE-ID and place CSC100 as the only tuple in the table. (Don't worry about how the table is created and how data gets into it at this point, just assume that the table is magically created and loaded.) The table should look as follows:

```
SELECT WHAT-COURSE
```

COURSE-ID
CSC100

Now we are ready to solve the query.

```
DIVIDE COURSES-TAKING BY WHAT-COURSE OVER COURSE-ID
```

or

```
COURSE-TAKING [COURSE-TAKING.COURSE-ID ÷
               WHAT-COURSE.COURSE-ID] WHAT-COURSE
```

```
STU-ID
S001
S002
```

Wow, this is really high-brow stuff! Did you realize that you could have solved the query with a simple SELECT and a PROJECT command?

```
TEMP <- SELECT COURSES-TAKING WHERE COURSE-ID = "CSC100"
PROJECT STU-ID FROM TEMP
```

The following example is a bit more realistic.

2. What are the STU-IDs of the students taking **both** CSC100 and CSC200? This will be a little more difficult to solve with a SELECT command. We could try the following SELECT command:

```
SELECT COURSES-TAKING WHERE COURSE-ID = "CSC100" AND
                            COURSE-ID = "CSC200"
```

This command will execute, but a null resultant table (a table with no tuples in it) will be generated. Do you see why? Remember that the SELECT command looks at one tuple at a time. How could the same tuple have two different values stored in the attribute COURSE-ID? What we need is a command that looks for a tuple with the value of "CSC100" in it, notes the corresponding STU-ID, then searches for a tuple with "CSC200" in COURSE-ID, then matches the value stored in STU-ID of the two tuples. If a match is found, the common value in STU-ID is placed in the resultant table. Do you see where this process ANDs tuples in a vertical manner? This is exactly what the DIVIDE command does.

To solve this query we simply have to add a new tuple containing "CSS200" to the WHAT-COURSE table and perform the DIVIDE command. Again, do not worry about how the new tuple gets added into the table at this point.

```
SELECT WHAT-COURSE

COURSE-ID
CSC100
CSC200
```

```
DIVIDE COURSES-TAKING BY WHAT-COURSE OVER COURSE-ID
```

or

```
COURSE-TAKING [COURSE-TAKING.COURSE-ID ÷
               WHAT-COURSE.COURSE-ID] WHAT-COURSE
```

```
STU-ID
S001
```

The DIVIDE command is very valuable. However, it is not implemented directly on most relational DBMSs.

SOME INTEGRATED EXAMPLES

Now that we have been exposed to these special relational algebra operators, let us explore their retrieval power by combining them to solve some queries. We will again use our three example tables.

```
STUDENT ( STU-ID, STUDENT-NAME, ADDRESS, BIRTHDATE, GENDER)
COURSE ( COURSE-ID, COURSE-TITLE, SECTION-NO, STU-ID, FAC-ID)
FACULTY ( FAC-ID, FACULTY-NAME, DEPARTMENT, GENDER, SALARY)
```

1. What are the names of the students who are taking CSC100? The following are the three relational algebra commands needed to solve this query.

```
TEMP1 <- SELECT COURSE WHERE COURSE-ID = "CSC100"
TEMP2 <- JOIN TEMP1, STUDENT OVER STU-ID
PROJECT STUDENT-NAME FROM TEMP2
```

The SELECT command extracts only those tuples where the COURSE-ID is equal to "CSC100." After the execution of this command, the derived table, TEMP1, contains the following tuples.

TABLE NAME: TEMP1

COURSE-ID	COURSE-TITLE	SECTION	STU-ID	FAC-ID
CSC100	INTRODUCTION TO COMPUTING	1	S001	J01
CSC100	INTRODUCTION TO COMPUTING	2	S002	S01

Notice that all we really need from the table TEMP1 are the STU-IDs of the students taking "CSC100": S001 and S002. The next thing that we have to do is to find what STUDENT-NAMEs are associated with S001 and S002. To do this, we must JOIN the TEMP1 table with the STUDENT table. After the execution of the JOIN command the table TEMP2 contains the following data.

TABLE NAME: TEMP2

COURSE-ID	COURSE-TITLE	SECTION	STU-ID	FAC-ID	STUDENT-NAME	ADDRESS	BIRTHDATE	GENDER
CSC100	INTRODUCTION TO COMPUTING	1	S001	J01	WENDY JONES	125 MAPLE AVE	10/25/65	FEMALE
CSC100	INTRODUCTION TO COMPUTING	2	S002	S01	SAM WALES	3006 NAVAJO CL	1/10/60	MALE

Now that we have the data that we need (the attribute STUDENT-NAME) we can simply PROJECT it out. The PROJECT operator would yield the following output:

```
PROJECT STUDENT-NAME FROM TEMP2

         STUDENT-NAME
         WENDY JONES
         SAM WALES
```

If you will refer back to the tables STUDENT and COURSE, you will find that the two students listed are the only ones currently taking the course CSC100.

For those of you who would like to use only one relational algebra command to solve this query the following embedded command is offered.

```
PROJECT STUDENT-NAME FROM (JOIN (SELECT COURSE WITH  COURSE
= "CSC100"), STUDENT OVER STU-ID)
```

You will notice that the only difference (other than the original query solution being composed of three relational algebra commands and this one being composed of only one) between our original solution to the problem and this condensed version is that in the condensed version, the system has to name the derived tables, whereas in the original version we gave them the names TEMP1 and TEMP2. Remember that the only reason that we can embed relational algebra commands inside one another is because of the property of closure, the output of every relational algebra command is a table.

You have also probably noticed that there are other methods of solving this query. Perhaps this command is less efficient, but here is another example solution to the query.

```
TEMP1 <- SELECT COURSE WHERE COURSE-ID = "CSC100"
TEMP2 <- PROJECT STU-ID FROM TEMP1
TEMP3 <- PROJECT STU-ID, STUDENT-NAME FROM STUDENT
TEMP4 <- JOIN TEMP2, TEMP3 OVER STU-ID
PROJECT STUDENT-NAME FROM TEMP5
```

2. List the names of all the female students being taught by female professors. (Does this sound like a familiar query?) The following set of relational algebra commands will satisfy this query.

```
STUDENT (STU-ID, STUDENT-NAME, ADDRESS, BIRTHDATE, GENDER)
COURSE (COURSE-ID, COURSE-TITLE, SECTION-NO, STU-ID, FAC-ID)
FACULTY (FAC-ID, FACULTY-NAME, DEPARTMENT, GENDER, SALARY)

    TEMP1 <- SELECT FACULTY WHERE GENDER = "FEMALE"
    TEMP2 <- PROJECT FAC-ID FROM TEMP1
    TEMP3 <- JOIN TEMP2, COURSE OVER FAC-ID
    TEMP4 <- JOIN TEMP3, STUDENT OVER STU-ID
    TEMP5 <- SELECT TEMP4 WHERE GENDER = "FEMALE"
    PROJECT STUDENT-NAME FROM TEMP5
```

Let's look at the various commands to determine how the final answer was produced. The first SELECT command extracts the female faculty members. The output from this command would be as follows.

```
TEMP1 <- SELECT FACULTY WHERE GENDER = "FEMALE"
```

TABLE NAME: TEMP1

FAC-ID	FACULTY-NAME	DEPARTMENT	GENDER	SALARY
S01	WENDY SWIMMER	COMP SCI	FEMALE	45,000
D01	AMY DANCER	COMP SCI	FEMALE	34,500

Actually, all we would need from this table is the FAC-IDs of the female faculty, so let's just project that column out of TEMP1 so that our JOIN won't create such a large table.

```
TEMP2 <- PROJECT FAC-ID FROM TEMP1
```

TABLE NAME: TEMP2

FAC-ID
S01
D01

Now we have to find out what courses FAC-IDs S01 and D01 teach. This can be done with a JOIN.

```
TEMP3 <- JOIN TEMP2, COURSE OVER FAC-ID
```

TABLE NAME: TEMP3

COURSE-ID	COURSE-TITLE	SECTION	STU-ID	FAC-ID
CSC100	INTRODUCTION TO COMPUTING	2	S002	S01
CSC200	PASCAL PROGRAMMING	1	S001	D01
CSC200	PASCAL PROGRAMMING	2	S003	S01

We will now use another JOIN to find which students take CSC100 and CSC200. The students are S002, S001, and S003.

```
TEMP4 <- JOIN TEMP3, STUDENT OVER STU-ID
```

TABLE NAME: TEMP4

COURSE-ID	COURSE-TITLE	SECTION	STU-ID	FAC-ID	STUDENT-NAME	ADDRESS	BIRTHDATE	GENDER
CSC100	INTRODUCTION TO COMPUTING	2	S002	S01	SAM WALES	3006 NAVAJO CL	1/10/60	MALE
CSC200	PASCAL PROGRAMMING	1	S001	D01	WENDY JONES	125 MAPLE AVE	10/25/65	FEMALE
CSC200	PASCAL PROGRAMMING	2	S003	S01	CATHY SMITH	1600 PENN AVE	2/22/22	FEMALE

Next we need to extricate the female tuples from TEMP4 with a SELECT command.

```
TEMP5 <- SELECT TEMP4 WHERE GENDER = "FEMALE"
```

TABLE NAME: TEMP5

COURSE-ID	COURSE-TITLE	SECTION	STU-ID	FAC-ID	STUDENT-NAME	ADDRESS	BIRTHDATE	GENDER
CSC200	PASCAL PROGRAMMING	1	S001	D01	WENDY JONES	3006 NAVAJO CL	10/25/65	FEMALE
CSC200	PASCAL PROGRAMMING	2	S003	S01	CATHY SMITH	125 MAPLE AVE	2/22/22	FEMALE

All that remains for us to do is to pull the students' names out of the TEMP5 table with a PROJECT command.

```
PROJECT STUDENT-NAME FROM TEMP5
```

STUDENT-NAME
WENDY JONES
CATHY SMITH

3. What are the names of the students taking the courses ''Introduction to Computing'' and ''Pascal Programming'' and ''Principles of Accounting I.''

```
STUDENT (STU-ID, STUDENT-NAME, ADDRESS, BIRTHDATE, GENDER)
COURSE (COURSE-ID, COURSE-TITLE, SECTION-NO, STU-ID, FAC-ID)
```

The relational algebra commands to retrieve this desired data are as follows.

```
TEMP1 <- SELECT COURSE WHERE COURSE-TITLE IN
         ["INTRODUCTION TO COMPUTING", "PASCAL PROGRAMMING",
          "PRINCIPLES OF ACCOUNTING I"]
TEMP2 <- PROJECT COURSE-ID FROM TEMP1
TEMP3 <- PROJECT COURSE-ID, STU-ID FROM TEMP1
TEMP4 <- DIVIDE TEMP3 BY TEMP2 OVER COURSE-ID
TEMP5 <- JOIN TEMP4, STUDENT OVER STU-ID
PROJECT STUDENT-NAME FROM TEMP5
```

The table TEMP1 contains the tuples for the courses Introduction to Computing, Pascal Programming, and Principles of Accounting. The ''IN'' operator is just a short way to do multiple OR conditions.

```
TEMP1 <- SELECT COURSE WHERE COURSE-TITLE IN
         ["INTRODUCTION TO COMPUTING", "PASCAL PROGRAMMING",
          "PRINCIPLES OF ACCOUNTING I"]
```

TABLE NAME: TEMP1

COURSE-ID	COURSE-TITLE	SECTION	STU-ID	FAC-ID
CSC100	INTRODUCTION TO COMPUTING	1	S001	J01
CSC100	INTRODUCTION TO COMPUTING	2	S002	S01
CSC200	PASCAL PROGRAMMING	1	S001	D01
CSC200	PASCAL PROGRAMMING	2	S003	S01
ACC200	PRINCIPLES OF ACCOUNTING I	1	S001	J02

We must now prepare for our DIVIDE command by producing a binary and a unary table. The first table that we want to produce is one containing the course numbers for the three courses. We are assuming that the three courses are listed in TEMP1 table. This would mean that there were students that are taking these three courses. If they were not, we would have to build a table containing the three COURSE-IDs.

TEMP2 <- PROJECT COURSE-ID FROM TEMP1

TABLE NAME: TEMP2

COURSE-ID
CSC100
CSC200
ACC200

The binary table contains the COURSE-IDs and the STU-IDs that take those courses.

TEMP3 <- PROJECT COURSE-ID, STU-ID FROM TEMP1

TABLE NAME: TEMP3

COURSE-ID	STU-ID
CSC100	S001
CSC100	S002
CSC200	S001
CSC200	S003
ACC200	S001

By dividing the table TEMP3 by TEMP2, we are able to extract the STU-IDs of the students taking CSC100, CSC200, and ACC200.

TEMP4 <- DIVIDE TEMP3 BY TEMP2 OVER COURSE-ID

TABLE NAME: TEMP4

STU-ID
S001

The student number does us no good without the student name to go with it. We need to use the JOIN command to find out who STU-ID S001 is.

```
TEMP5 <- JOIN TEMP4, STUDENT OVER STU-ID
```

STU-ID	STUDENT-NAME	ADDRESS	BIRTHDATE	GENDER
S001	WENDY JONES	125 MAPLE AVE	10/25/65	FEMALE

We can now PROJECT out the name of the student.

```
PROJECT STUDENT-NAME FROM TEMP5
```

STUDENT-NAME
WENDY JONES

These three examples should illustrate the very powerful retrieval capabilities of the four special relational algebra operators: SELECT, PROJECT, JOIN, and DIVIDE.

TRADITIONAL SET OPERATORS

There are four traditional set operations that can be applied to relational databases: UNION, INTERSECTION, DIFFERENCE, and a form of the Cartesian product (TIMES). All four operations utilize two tables.

For the first three operations to work correctly, the two tables involved must be **union compatible,** that is, the structures of the two tables must be identical, the degree of the two tables must be the same, and the order of the columns must also be exactly the same.

To illustrate the UNION, INTERSECTION, and DIFFERENCE commands, we will use the following two tables.

```
GREEKS-WHO-ARE-ATHLETES (STU-ID, STUDENT-NAME, ORGANIZATION)
GREEKS-WHO-ARE-SCHOLARS (STU-ID, STUDENT-NAME, ORGANIZATION)
```

Table occurrences are as follows:

TABLE NAME: GREEKS-WHO-ARE-ATHLETES

STU-ID	STUDENT-NAME	ORGANIZATION
S050	KIM RICHARDS	SIGMA EPISLON CHI DELTA
S051	FRANK WILSON	TAPPA KEGGA BEER
S052	DENNIS JONES	DELTA DEBITS
S053	BEN NELSON	GAMMA DELTA IOTA

TABLE NAME: GREEKS-WHO-ARE-SCHOLARS

STU-ID	STUDENT-NAME	ORGANIZATION
S050	KIM RICHARDS	SIGMA EPISLON CHI DELTA
S053	BEN NELSON	GAMMA DELTA IOTA
S054	PATTI SIMS	T.G.I.F.
S055	PHIL JONES	BIGG PHATTSSEAUX'S

Note that the two tables are union compatible. Also note that there is redundant data in the two tables.

Again as with the previous relational algebra operations, we will illustrate two different types of syntax. The first will be a more wordy; the second will be a more concise.

Union

The union of two tables combines the tuples from the two tables. The syntax for the union operations is as follows.

```
table-name1 UNION table-name2
```

The alternate form is

```
table-name1 ∪ table-name2
```

For example, if we wanted to combine the athletes and the scholars together, producing a table of Greeks who are either Athletes or Scholars or both, we could execute the following command.

```
GREEKS-WHO-ARE-ATHLETES UNION GREEKS-WHO-ARE-SCHOLARS
```

or

```
GREEKS-WHO-ARE-ATHLETES ∪ GREEKS-WHO-ARE-SCHOLARS
```

STU-ID	STUDENT-NAME	ORGANIZATION
S050	KIM RICHARDS	SIGMA EPISLON CHI DELTA
S051	FRANK WILSON	TAPPA KEGGA BEER
S052	DENNIS JONES	DELTA DEBITS
S053	BEN NELSON	GAMMA DELTA IOTA
S054	PATTI SIMS	T.G.I.F.
S055	PHIL JONES	BIGG PHATTSSEAUX'S

Again notice that the duplicate tuples are automatically removed from the resultant table.

Intersection

The intersection of two tables yields the tuples common to both tables. Both syntaxes of the INTERSECT command are shown:

```
table-name1 INTERSECT table-name2
```

or

```
table-name1 ∩ table-name2
```

Using our two example tables, if we wanted to find the students who are both athletes and scholars we could use the INTERSECT command.

```
GREEKS-WHO-ARE-ATHLETES INTERSECT GREEKS-WHO-ARE-SCHOLARS
```

or

```
GREEKS-WHO-ARE-ATHLETES ∩ GREEKS-WHO-ARE-SCHOLARS
```

STU-ID	STUDENT-NAME	ORGANIZATION
S050	KIM RICHARDS	SIGMA EPISLON CHI DELTA
S053	BEN NELSON	GAMMA DELTA IOTA

Difference

The difference between tables table-name1 and table-name2 is the tuples that belong to table-name1 but not to table-name2. This means that the common tuples between the two tables are deleted from table-name1. The two syntaxes of the difference command are

```
table-name1 MINUS table-name2
```

or

```
table-name1 - table-name2
```

Be aware that table-name1 MINUS table-name2 does not yield the same result as table-name2 MINUS table-name1. If we wanted to find the Greeks who are athletes but not scholars, we could execute the following command.

```
GREEKS-WHO-ARE-ATHLETES MINUS GREEKS-WHO-ARE-SCHOLARS
```

or

```
GREEKS-WHO-ARE-ATHLETES - GREEKS-WHO-ARE-SCHOLARS

STU-ID   STUDENT-NAME        ORGANIZATION
 S051    FRANK WILSON        TAPPA KEGGA BEER
 S052    DENNIS JONES        DELTA DEBITS
```

If we wanted the Greeks who are scholars but not athletes we would have to exchange the arguments to our difference command.

```
GREEKS-WHO-ARE-SCHOLARS MINUS GREEKS-WHO-ARE-ATHLETES
```

or

```
GREEKS-WHO-ARE-SCHOLARS - GREEKS-WHO-ARE-ATHLETES
```

```
STU-ID   STUDENT-NAME        ORGANIZATION
 S054    PATTI SIMS          T.G.I.F.
 S055    PHIL JONES          BIGG PHATTSSEAUX'S
```

Cartesian Product

The Cartesian product of two tables **joins** each tuple of table-name1 with each tuple of table-name2. There need not be a common attribute between the two tables as in the JOIN command. The format of the Cartesian product is

```
table-name1 TIMES table-name2
```

or

```
table-name1 * table-name2
```

To illustrate the Cartesian product (TIMES) we will create two more tables.

```
LIST-OF-POSSIBLE-MAJORS ( MAJOR-NAME )
```

TABLE NAME: LIST-OF-POSSIBLE-MAJORS

```
MAJOR-NAME
COMPUTER SCIENCE
MANAGEMENT INFORMATION SYSTEMS
ACCOUNTING
UNDERWATER BASKET WEAVING              {We have an expanded curriculum.}
```

If we wanted the permutation of every Greek who is a scholar with every possible major name, we could use the following Cartesian product. We will assume that we only want the student name from the GREEKS-WHO-ARE-SCHOLARS table. Do not get the impression that we can only get the Cartesian product from unary tables; we only did this to shorten our output.

```
GREEKS <- PROJECT STUDENT-NAME FROM GREEKS-WHO-ARE-SCHOLARS
GREEKS TIMES LIST-OF-POSSIBLE-MAJORS
```

or

```
GREEKS * LIST-OF-POSSIBLE-MAJORS
```

STUDENT-NAME	MAJOR-NAME
KIM RICHARDS	COMPUTER SCIENCE
KIM RICHARDS	MANAGEMENT INFORMATION SYSTEMS
KIM RICHARDS	ACCOUNTING
KIM RICHARDS	UNDERWATER BASKET WEAVING
FRANK WILSON	COMPUTER SCIENCE
FRANK WILSON	MANAGEMENT INFORMATION SYSTEMS
FRANK WILSON	ACCOUNTING
FRANK WILSON	UNDERWATER BASKET WEAVING
DENNIS JONES	COMPUTER SCIENCE
DENNIS JONES	MANAGEMENT INFORMATION SYSTEMS
DENNIS JONES	ACCOUNTING
DENNIS JONES	UNDERWATER BASKET WEAVING
BEN NELSON	COMPUTER SCIENCE
BEN NELSON	MANAGEMENT INFORMATION SYSTEMS
BEN NELSON	ACCOUNTING
BEN NELSON	UNDERWATER BASKET WEAVING

When there is a common attribute to link over, the Cartesian product becomes a superset of the JOIN command.

ANOTHER INTEGRATED EXAMPLE

Suppose that we wanted a list of students who are students at the university but are not currently enrolled in any classes. We could use one of our new commands to solve this query very readily.

```
STUDENT ( STU-ID, STUDENT-NAME, ADDRESS, BIRTHDATE, GENDER)
COURSE ( COURSE-ID, COURSE-TITLE, SECTION-NO, STU-ID, FAC-ID)
```

Our query is solved as follows.

```
TEMP1 <- PROJECT STU-ID, STUDENT-NAME FROM STUDENT
TEMP2 <- PROJECT STU-ID FROM COURSE
TEMP3 <- JOIN TEMP1, TEMP2 OVER STU-ID
TEMP4 <- PROJECT STUDENT-NAME FROM TEMP3
TEMP5 <- PROJECT STUDENT-NAME FROM STUDENT
TEMP5 MINUS TEMP4
```

The first two PROJECT commands are simply used to reduce the tables down to a more manageable size.

```
TEMP1 <- PROJECT STU-ID, STUDENT-NAME FROM STUDENT
```

TABLE NAME: TEMP1

STU-ID	STUDENT-NAME
S001	WENDY JONES
S002	SAM WALES
S003	CATHY SMITH
S004	DOTTIE STACY
S005	JAY LANGER
S006	AMY LOPEZ
S007	SAM WATSON
S008	TAMMY REDD
S009	TOMMY WADKINS
S010	BEN TREVINO

The second PROJECT is also used to extract the STU-IDs of the students currently taking classes. Again remember that the duplicate tuples (the STU-IDs of the students taking multiple classes) will be deleted.

```
TEMP2 <- PROJECT STU-ID FROM COURSE
```

TABLE NAME: TEMP2

STU-ID
S001
S002
S003
S004
S005

Next we want to find out who STU-IDs S001, S002, S003, S004 and S005 are. This is accomplished with a JOIN.

```
TEMP3 <- JOIN TEMP1, TEMP2 OVER STU-ID
```

TABLE NAME: TEMP3

STU-ID	STUDENT-NAME
S001	WENDY JONES
S002	SAM WALES
S003	CATHY SMITH
S004	DOTTIE STACY
S005	JAY LANGER

We now want a list of names of all students taking classes.

```
TEMP4 <- PROJECT STUDENT-NAME FROM TEMP3
```

TABLE NAME: TEMP3

STUDENT-NAME
WENDY JONES
SAM WALES
CATHY SMITH
DOTTIE STACY
JAY LANGER

In addition, we want the table TEMP5 to contain a list of all the students that we have on file.

```
TEMP5 <- PROJECT STUDENT-NAME FROM STUDENT
```

TABLE NAME: TEMP5

STUDENT-NAME
WENDY JONES
SAM WALES
CATHY SMITH
DOTTIE STACY
JAY LANGER
AMY LOPEZ
SAM WATSON
TAMMY REDD
TOMMY WADKINS
BEN TREVINO

Now that we have a list of all students and a list of the students taking classes, if we subtract the table containing the students taking classes from the table containing all students, what do we have left? The students that are not taking any classes.

```
TEMP5 MINUS TEMP4
```

```
STUDENT-NAME
AMY LOPEZ
SAM WATSON
TAMMY REDD
TOMMY WADKINS
BEN TREVINO
```

As you can see from these examples, relational algebra is a very powerful data manipulation tool. To illustrate how powerful it is, think about how much COBOL/Pascal/PL-1 code it would take to retrieve the tuples for our examples.

DATA MAINTENANCE VIA RELATIONAL ALGEBRA

Data maintenance (insertions and deletions) can be accomplished by using the traditional set operators of UNION and MINUS. Dr. Codd did not design an operator for modification of attribute values.

Insertion of New Tuples

The UNION command is used to add new tuples to a table. Suppose that we had a new student to be added to the GREEKS-WHO-ARE-SCHOLARS TABLE. The STU-ID is S056, the students name is JOE JOHNSON, and he belongs to the organization GAMMA DELTA IOTA. We could add the student into the table as follows.

```
GREEKS-WHO-ARE-SCHOLARS <- GREEKS-WHO-ARE-SCHOLARS UNION
{"S056", "JOE JOHNSON", "GAMMA DELTA IOTA"}
```

Notice that the values of the attributes are entered in positional order. This is just a convention that we have adopted for this text.

We could enter a tuple into a table even if we did not have all the data for each attribute in the tuple. This could be accomplished by entering the value NULL for unknown values. Be aware that the value of the primary key of a tuple cannot be null, remember entity integrity. Suppose that another new Greek athlete needed to be entered into our table, but we were not sure to what ORGANIZATION to which he belongs. We could add the new tuple occurrence as follows.

```
GREEKS-WHO-ARE-ATHLETES <- GREEKS-WHO-ARE-ATHLETES UNION
{"S057", "JACK PALMER", NULL}
```

Deletion of Tuples

The difference operator is used to delete tuples from a table. Suppose that we wanted to delete PHIL JONES from the GREEKS-WHO-ARE-ATHLETES (he got too corpulent and can't be on the mud wrestling team any more). This could be accomplished as follows.

```
GREEKS-WHO-ARE-ATHLETES <- GREEKS-WHO-ARE-ATHLETES MINUS
{"S055", "PHIL JONES", "BIGG PHATTSSEAUX'S"}
```

We could also delete tuples with wild card symbols. We will use the asterisk (*) as a wild card, meaning that any value can be in that attribute. Let's delete PHIL JONES again, but this time with wild cards. (We will assume that Phil was never deleted in the previous data maintenance command.)

```
GREEKS-WHO-ARE-ATHLETES <- GREEKS-WHO-ARE-ATHLETES MINUS
{*, "PHIL JONES", *}
```

The wild card concept gives us a method of deleting multiple tuples. We now want to delete all the Greek athletes who are members of TAPPA KEGGA BEER.

```
GREEKS-WHO-ARE-ATHLETES <- GREEKS-WHO-ARE-ATHLETES MINUS
{*, *, "TAPPA KEGGA BEER"}
```

We could even delete all the tuples in a table.

```
GREEKS-WHO-ARE-ATHLETES <- GREEKS-WHO-ARE-ATHLETES MINUS
{*, *, *}
```

Modification of Tuples

Modifications to attribute values could be implemented through some new relational operator such as CHANGE. Let's update DENNIS JONES' organization to ALPHA BETA DELTA.

```
CHANGE ORGANIZATION TO "ALPHA BETA DELTA" WHERE
STUDENT-NAME = "DENNIS JONES"
```

CONDITIONS NECESSARY FOR A DBMS TO BE CONSIDERED RELATIONAL

Since relational database management systems are the newest DBMS, and appear to be the better vehicle to manage data, most new DBMS packages have dubbed themselves ''relational.'' This has been done to assist in marketing their product.

However, to be called a RDBMS connotes that the package has certain properties and powers. It would be inappropriate for a DBMS to call itself relational if it did not have these properties and powers. In an effort to rectify this, a subcommittee of the American National Standards Institute (ANSI) called the Relational Task Group (RTG) surveyed 14 different RDBMS to develop a set of minimum conditions for a RDBMS to be called "fully relational"[2].

The first condition is that the user perceive that the data is represented in the form of a table. The second condition is that there be no user visible links between tables. Any pointer mechanism must be totally transparent to the DBMS users. The third condition is that the system support the relational algebra operators of SELECT, PROJECT, and either Equi-JOIN or Natural JOIN. The syntax of these operators can be whatever the implementer finds convenient, but she cannot resort to the use of recursion or iteration to implement the operators. The operators cannot be restricted by access path that might have been predefined.

Any system that meets these three requirements is considered **minimally relational.** A system that meets the first two requirements, but not the third, should be referred to as a tabular DBMS and not a relational DBMS.

For a DBMS to be considered fully relational, it must meet two additional criteria. The first is that the DBMS implement **all** the relational algebra operators without the use of looping or recursion and without restrictions due to predefined access paths. The second is that the DBMS support both entity and referential integrity. These integrity rules were introduced in the previous chapter. Remember that entity integrity means that no attribute composing the primary key of a relation is allowed to be null. Referential integrity means that every occurrence of a foreign key must refer to an existing primary key occurrence in another table.

SUMMARY

This chapter was dedicated to studying the theoretical data manipulation sublanguage relational algebra. The eight basic relational operators of SELECT, PROJECT, JOIN, DIVIDE, UNION, INTERSECT, MINUS, and TIMES were introduced. Examples of the operators were discussed. The chapter terminated with a discussion of the conditions necessary for a DBMS to be considered relational.

Upon completion of this chapter you should now be familiar with these concepts:

- **A.** Relational algebra
- **B.** Theta
- **C.** SELECT
- **D.** PROJECT
- **E.** INNER JOIN
- **F.** Natural JOIN

G. Equi-JOIN

H. Theta JOIN

I. Outer JOIN

J. DIVIDE

K. UNION

L. MINUS

M. INTERSECT

N. TIMES

O. Conditions necessary for a DBMS to be considered minimally relational

P. Tabular DBMS

Q. Conditions necessary for a DBMS to be considered fully relational

R. Entity integrity

S. Referential integrity

T. Closure

EXERCISES

1. What is the difference between an Inner JOIN and an Outer JOIN?

2. What is the difference between an Equi-JOIN and a Theta JOIN?

3. Why should entity and referential integrity be an integral part of a DBMS?

4. Why should there be a criterion for a DBMS to be considered relational?

5. What are the advantages of using relational algebra to retrieve data. Compare it to a conventional language such as COBOL.

6. What is closure and why is it important in relational algebra?

7. Given the example tables noted below, form the relational algebra expressions to solve the following queries.

```
STUDENT ( STU-ID, STUDENT-NAME, ADDRESS, BIRTHDATE, GENDER)
COURSE ( COURSE-ID, COURSE-TITLE, SECTION-NO, STU-ID, FAC-ID)
FACULTY ( FAC-ID, FACULTY-NAME, DEPARTMENT, GENDER, SALARY)
```

(a) What are the names and addresses of the male students born between January 1, 1960 and December 31, 1965?

(b) List the names of each faculty member and the titles of the courses that they teach.

(c) List the names of the Professors who teach both ACC201 and ACC202.

(d) Is there anyone born before December 25, 1967 taking the course The History of Pirogues?

(e) Are there any male and female students with the same birthdays?

(f) What students are taught by faculty members making over $42,500?

(g) The course The History of Pirogues has been changed to The History of Canoes. Make the change.

(h) The course Pascal Programming has been deleted from our curriculum. Delete these records. Think about what effect this has on the students registered in the class. How would you handle this in a real-world database? Remember referential integrity. (We will discuss this problem later in the text when we cover design of databases.)

REFERENCES

1. Date, C. J., *Introduction to Database Management Systems*, Vol 1, (4th ed.), Addison-Wesley, Reading, MA, 1986.
2. Schmidt, Joachim W. and Michael L. Brodie (eds) *Relational Database Systems*, Springer-Verlag, Berlin and Heidleberg, 1983.

4

Data Manipulation via Relational Calculus

PURPOSE: This chapter is dedicated to illustrating the use of relational calculus in manipulating data in the relational model. Various quantifiers are discussed along with the two basic types of relational calculus. An implementation of the calculus, DSL Alpha, is reviewed. The chapter concludes with a discussion of query optimization.

Relational algebra gave us a very powerful, albeit theoretical, sublanguage to manipulate data in data models. The primary use has been in the relational model. Relational algebra is certainly less procedural than is performing data manipulation via a conventional language; however, Dr. Codd has defined an even higher-level data manipulation sublanguage called relational calculus. There is even less procedurality in the relational calculus. A query that might take several relational algebra commands to solve will only take one relational calculus expression.

RELATIONAL CALCULUS

The calculus that Dr. Codd adapted to the relational model has it origins in set theory and logic. Specifically, **relational calculus** was developed from the branch of logic called predicate calculus. The relational calculus that we will be describing is generally referred to as **first-order predicate calculus**. The "first-order" refers to the fact that when the conditional part of the calculus expression (called the predicate) is evaluated, it must be evaluated as either true or false. For this reason when we refer to relational calculus, we are actually referring to the so-called first order predicate calculus. By the way, relational calculus has no relation to differential or integral calculus that is taught in mathematics curriculums.

As you will see as our discussion continues, relational calculus is actually more a notation than an actual language, although Dr. Codd has also designed an implementation of the calculus in a language that he called DSL Alpha (for Data SubLanguage Alpha). DSL Alpha will be discussed later in this chapter.

CALCULUS TERMINOLOGY AND NOTATION

Before we delve into any calculus expressions, there is a set of terminology, native to the calculus, that must be understood to utilize it.

Targets and Predicates

A calculus expression has two basic parts: the target and the qualifier or predicate. The **target of the expression** is what is wanted from the expression. What is wanted is usually an attribute, a list of attributes, a relation, or some combination thereof. This can be thought of as the output of a calculus expression. The **predicate** is the condition(s) to which the values in the target are subject. Just as with relational algebra, relational calculus is a theoretical sublanguage and therefore has no specific syntax, although again, C. J. Date has designed one in his text [1]. In the syntax we use in this text, the target will be placed in braces ([]) and will be separated from the predicate by a colon (:):

```
{target} : [predicate]
```

Notice that the predicate is optional in the expression. We will use the same convention for assigning the results of a calculus expression into a derived table as we did with the tables derived in relational algebra. This is also shown.

```
Derived-Table <- {target} : predicate
```

Dr. Codd used the word "workspace" to refer to a derived table in relational calculus.

Tuple Variables

When we used a relational algebra command, the syntax of the command gave us a reference point as to what tuples we were referring to in the command. For example, in the relational algebra command

```
SELECT STUDENT WHERE GENDER = "FEMALE"
```

we know that the attribute GENDER refers to the gender within the STUDENT table as opposed to the gender within the FACULTY table. The syntax of the command intimated that gender was from the STUDENT table. This is not always clear with relational calculus expressions.

Since we have no reference point for attribute names in the calculus notation (they could come from any relation), we will fully qualify all attribute names by using what is commonly called a tuple or range variable. The tuple variable is usually the name of the relation and is separated from the attribute name by a period. The purpose of the tuple variable is to qualify or restrict the values of the tuple attributes to those of a particular relation. For example, to differentiate between the attribute FAC-ID, which appears in both the COURSE and FACULTY tables, we would use COURSE.FAC-ID and FACULTY.FAC-ID.

Remember that a tuple variable ranges over a relation.

SOME EXAMPLES OF RELATIONAL CALCULUS

Some simple examples should introduce you to the retrieval power of relational calculus. The examples will naturally utilize our tables which we have come to know and love.

```
STUDENT (STU-ID, STUDENT-NAME, ADDRESS, BIRTHDATE, GENDER)
COURSE (COURSE-ID, COURSE-TITLE, SECTION-NO, STU-ID, FAC-ID)
FACULTY (FAC-ID, FACULTY-NAME, DEPARTMENT, GENDER, SALARY)
```

1. List all of the information on all of the students.

```
{STUDENT}
```

Notice that the calculus expression contains no predicate and the target is the complete relation STUDENT. The reason that we have no predicate is that we do not want to filter out any tuples. This is equivalent to the relational algebra command

```
SELECT STUDENT
```

2. List all the information on the female students.

```
{STUDENT} : STUDENT.GENDER = "FEMALE"
```

This query contains a predicate. It filters out only the tuples where the value of gender is female. The colon can be read as "where." This expression can be read as "Get the tuples from the STUDENT table where value of gender is equal to female." This is equivalent to the relational algebra command

```
SELECT STUDENT WHERE GENDER = "FEMALE"
```

3. List the names and salaries of the male faculty members in the Computer Science Department.

```
{FACULTY.NAME ,FACULTY.SALARY} : FACULTY.DEPT = "COMP SCI" &
                                 FACULTY.GENDER = "MALE"
```

This query contains a compound predicate. We will use the ampersand symbol (&) to represent the AND condition. The vertical bar (|) will be used to represent the OR condition, and the tilde (¯) will be used for the NOT condition. Note that this query contains a compound target. This expression is equivalent to the following two relational algebra commands:

```
TEMP1 <- SELECT FACULTY WHERE DEPT = "COMP SCI" AND
                              GENDER = "MALE"
PROJECT TEMP1 OVER NAME , SALARY
```

As we can see from this example, this query would be solved with two relational algebra commands. It would be up to the system and not the user to determine how the target would be produced. We can see from this example that the calculus is less procedural than even relational algebra.

4. Create a derived table called CS-GUYS that contains male faculty members or faculty members in the Computer Science Department.

```
CS-GUYS <- {FACULTY.NAME} :
           FACULTY.DEPT = "COMP SCI" |
           FACULTY.GENDER = "MALE"
```

QUANTIFIERS

A quantifier is something that tells us how many things satisfy the predicate. There are many different types of quantifiers found in logic: some, all, many, a few, almost all. There are only two that we will utilize in relational calculus: all and some.

The Universal Quantifier

The first quantifier is called the **universal quantifier**, usually stated as "all" or "for all". We will use the symbol ∀ to represent the universal quantifier. For any tuples to be retrieved, using the universal quantifier, all the tuples must evaluate the predicate of the calculus expression to true. For example, list the names and addresses of the students only if all are female. Using the universal quantifier, we could develop the following calculus expression to represent the query:

```
{STUDENT.STUDENT-NAME, STUDENT.STUDENT-ADDRESS} :
      ∀STUDENT(STUDENT.GENDER = "FEMALE")
```

This query is read "Get the names and addresses from the STUDENT table only if all tuples have gender equal to female." The result of this query would be either the entire STUDENT table, if there were only females in the table, or a null resultant table if any tuple's value of gender was not equal to female.

Notice the universal quantifier forms a vertical AND on the tuples. Retrieve all the tuples only if the value of gender in the first tuple is female, and the value of gender in the second tuple is female, and the value of gender in the third tuple is female, and so on.

The Existential Quantifier

The second type of quantifier is called the **existential quantifier** and is usually stated "some," "for some," or "there exists." We will use the symbol ∃ to represent the existential quantifier. The existential quantifier implies that we will retrieve the "some" tuples that satisfy the expression predicate. For example, list the names and addresses of the female students. Using the existential quantifier, we could develop the following calculus expression to represent this query.

```
{STUDENT.STUDENT-NAME, STUDENT.STUDENT-ADDRESS} :
      ∃STUDENT(STUDENT.GENDER = "FEMALE")
```

This query is read "Get the names and addresses from the STUDENT table for those tuples with gender equal to female." The result would be the tuples where the gender is equal to female or a null table if all of the tuples contained a value for gender other than female.

Notice that this same operation could be stated without the existential quantifier.

```
{STUDENT.STUDENT-NAME, STUDENT.STUDENT-ADDRESS} :
      STUDENT.GENDER = "FEMALE"
```

We have only used this expression to introduce you to the existential quantifier, there is more to it than this. We will explore the existential quantifier later on in this chapter.

WELL-FORMED FORMULAS

Well-formed formulas (WFFs) are the only acceptable type of formulas (conditions) for relational calculus expressions. We could state that a relational calculus expression must be a WFF or one of its acceptable permutations.

There are seven different permutations of WFF acceptable to relational calculus predicates.

1. Simple comparison. This is called a WFF. An example of a a simple comparison is

   ```
   STUDENT.GENDER = "FEMALE"
   ```

2. Negation of a simple comparison. This is denoted NOT WFF. An example would be

   ```
   NOT (STUDENT.GENDER = "FEMALE")
   ```

3. Using AND to connect two (or more) simple comparisons. This is denoted WFF1 AND WFF2. An example would be

   ```
   STUDENT.GENDER = "FEMALE" AND STUDENT.BIRTHDATE < "1/1/65"
   ```

4. Using OR to connect two (or more) simple comparisons. This is denoted WFF1 OR WFF2. An example would be

   ```
   STUDENT.GENDER = "FEMALE" OR STUDENT.BIRTHDATE < "1/1/65".
   ```

5. The use of the existential quantifier. This is denoted ∃tuple-variable(WFF). An example would be

   ```
   ∃STUDENT(STUDENT.GENDER = "FEMALE").
   ```

6. The use of the universal quantifier. This is denoted ∀tuple-variable(WFF). An example would be

   ```
   ∀STUDENT(STUDENT.GENDER = "FEMALE").
   ```

7. The use of the implication condition. This is denoted If WFF1 THEN WFF2. An example would be

   ```
   IF FACULTY.DEPARTMENT = "COMPUTER SCIENCE"
   THEN FACULTY.GENDER = "FEMALE" .
   ```

It implies that a condition is always true. This example implies that all Computer Science faculty members are female.

FREE AND BOUND VARIABLES

Free and bound variables refer to the scope of the tuple variable. This relates to the tuples that the variable has ''influence'' over.

Free-tuple variables are free to range over any tuple in the relation. Bound variables are "bound" to quantifiers. To determine to which quantifier the variable is bound, just look for the first WFF to the right of the quantifier. It is similar to a negation sign in a conventional language expression. A good analogy exists between local and global variables in a conventional programming language and free and bound variables. Free variables are analogous to global variables. Any subprogram can utilize their value. Bound variables are analogous to local variables, for their use is restricted to the subprogram currently in use.

Let's look at some of our previous examples to illustrate free and bound variables.

1. `{STUDENT} : STUDENT.GENDER = "FEMALE"`

In looking at this expression, you will notice that there are actually two tuple variables, one in the target and one in the predicate (they are both called STUDENT). However, since there are no quantifiers in this expression, they are both free variables.

2. `{FACULTY.NAME,FACULTY.SALARY} :`
                                    `FACULTY.DEPT = "COMP SCI" &`
                                    `FACULTY.GENDER = "MALE"`

Again in this expression we have four tuple variables, all called FACULTY, two in the target and two in the predicate. Each of the two variables in the predicate refers to a "tuple pointer" pointing to the same tuple in the FACULTY table. The same is true for the two tuple variables in the predicate. Again we have no quantifiers so they are all free variables.

3. `{STUDENT.STUDENT-NAME, STUDENT.STUDENT-ADDRESS} :`
         `∃STUDENT(STUDENT.GENDER = "FEMALE")`

This expression has a quantifier associated with the tuple variable STUDENT in the predicate. This variable is bound to that existential quantifier. Only free variables can occur in a target, but a predicate may contain free and/or bound variables.

JOIN QUERIES

If you will notice, none of our relational calculus example queries up to this point have required a join. The use of joins is certainly not restricted to relational algebra. The use of joins in relational calculus will require the use of quantifiers. Let us look at some queries that require the use of joins.

```
STUDENT (STU-ID, STUDENT-NAME, ADDRESS, BIRTHDATE, GENDER)
COURSE (COURSE-ID, COURSE-TITLE, SECTION-NO, STU-ID, FAC-ID)
FACULTY (FAC-ID, FACULTY-NAME, DEPARTMENT, GENDER, SALARY)
```

1. What are the names and birthdays of the students who are taking CSC100?

```
{STUDENT.STUDENT-NAME, STUDENT.BIRTHDAY} :
    ∃COURSE(COURSE.STU.ID = STUDENT.STU-ID &
        COURSE.COURSE-ID = "CSC100")
```

This query is interpreted as follows:

a. Take the STUDENT-NAME and BIRTHDAY of the first tuple in the STUDENT table.

b. Does that student's STU-ID match any STU-IDs in the COURSE table. If so, does that course's COURSE-ID equal "CSC100"? If yes, place that STUDENT.STUDENT-NAME and STUDENT.BIRTHDAY into the resultant table and continue processing. If no, continue processing.

Notice that the bound tuple variable COURSE was restricted by the existential quantifier. This means that only the tuples that matched over STU-ID and satisfied the restriction that COURSE-ID was equal to CSC100 were placed in the resultant table. The free variable STUDENT in the target is used to output the tuples that satisfy the predicate.

2. List the names of the female students who are taught by female faculty members. (This one keeps popping up.) If you will remember back to the previous chapter this query had to be solved by two joins. We will first attempt to solve this query with two relational calculus expressions and then reduce it to one expression.

```
TEMP1 <- {COURSE.STU-ID} :
    ∃FACULTY(COURSE.FAC-ID = FACULTY.FAC-ID &
    FACULTY.GENDER = "FEMALE")

{STUDENT.STUDENT-NAME} :   ∃TEMP1(TEMP.STU-ID = STUDENT.STU-ID
    & STUDENT.GENDER = "FEMALE")
```

The first calculus expression produced a list of STU-IDs that took courses under female faculty members, and the second expression took that list and used it to find out which of the STU-IDs belonged to female students.

Let's try it in one expression:

```
{STUDENT.STUDENT-NAME} :
∃COURSE(COURSE.STU-ID = STUDENT.STU-ID &
    STUDENT.GENDER = "FEMALE") &
∃FACULTY(COURSE.FAC-ID = FACULTY.FAC-ID &
    FACULTY.GENDER = "FEMALE")
```

Notice that we have embedded one existential quantifier inside the other. Upon scrutinizing this query, you might be able to come up with several other variations that would satisfy the query. Since the calculus notation is inherently theoretical, all other permutations of correct predicates would be correct. There is one form of predicates with multiple quantifiers that seems to be preferred, probably only because it is defined. This is called the prenex normal form. It simply means that all the quantifiers are taken out of the expressions and are placed to the left of the expression in order. This is analogous to placing a mathematical expression with parentheses in Polish notation and removing all the parentheses. The prenex normal form has only one set of parentheses enclosing the conditions. If we wished to place our predicate in the prenex normal form, it would look like this:

```
∃COURSE∃FACULTY(COURSE.STU-ID=STUDENT.STU-ID &
          STUDENT.GENDER = "FEMALE" &
          COURSE.FAC-ID = FACULTY.FAC-ID &
     FACULTY.GENDER = "FEMALE")
```

3. Are there any faculty members who teach all the classes? This query calls for the use of the universal quantifier.

```
{FACULTY.FAC-NAME} : ∀COURSE(COURSE.FAC-ID = FACULTY.FAC-ID)
```

We will discontinue our examples of relational calculus at this point for it is not our objective to make you an expert in relational calculus. It is, however, our goal to make you aware of the extreme power of the language so that you will be able to perceive the queries when they are implemented in ORACLE's SQL language. If you are interested in more information on relational calculus, we suggest that you acquire Date's text [1].

TYPES OF RELATIONAL CALCULUS

There are two methods of implementing relational calculus. The first is the type that Dr. Codd has suggested where the variables range over tuples. This is called **tuple-oriented relational calculus**. In the second type, variables range over domains. This is naturally called **domain-oriented relational calculus.** Since most of the RDBMS software that has been implemented today follows the tuple-oriented relational calculus (the major exception being Query-By-Example introduced in Chapter 1), we will not delve into the domain-oriented relational calculus. If you are interested in domain-oriented relational calculus, refer to a paper by Lacroix and Pirotte [2].

RELATIONALLY COMPLETE

One of the more important aspects that has come out of relational calculus is the term "relationally complete." For a language to be relationally complete, it must have at least the power of relational calculus. Obviously, relational completeness is a measure of the power of a relational language or package. It has been proven that relational algebra is relationally complete. For the proof, refer to Ullman's text [3].

Database implementers should strive for relational completeness, for if their software is missing some type retrieval function, the results could be disastrous. Remember what happened to the president of the university in Chapter 1, even though the data he wanted was stored in the university's database, he could not get it out in the manner he needed it. After all, what are databases for if not to produce timely and accurate information for users?

DATA SUBLANGUAGE ALPHA

DSL Alpha is an implementation of the relational calculus designed by E. F. Codd [4]. Although DSL Alpha was never fully implemented, the language QUEL (QUEry Language) that is used on the INGRES system is a representative implementation.

We will look at some of the basic DSL Alpha commands in order to give you the flavor of the "language." The retrieval command of Alpha is the GET command. The loosely defined syntax of the GET command is

```
GET INTO workspace target {: predicate}
```

Remember that Dr. Codd referred to a derived table as a workspace. Once data was placed into a workspace, it presumably could then be manipulated by a conventional language, displayed on a terminal screen, modified, and so on.

Let's assume that we wanted the names of the students in our STUDENT table. We would use the following DSL Alpha command:

```
GET INTO STU STUDENT.STUDENT-NAME
```

WORKSPACE (TABLE) NAME: STU

STUDENT-NAME
WENDY JONES
SAM WALES
CATHY SMITH
DOTTIE STACY
JAY LANGER
AMY LOPEZ
SAM WATSON
TAMMY REDD
TOMMY WADKINS
BEN TREVINO

If there would have been any duplicate tuples in the resultant workspace, they would have been automatically deleted.

There is one thing that we have purposely omitted from the example. DSL Alpha is a tuple-oriented relational calculus. Therefore, we must define a tuple variable for every relation that we want to use in our database. This is done through the RANGE command. The syntax of the RANGE command is as follows:

```
RANGE table-name tuple-variable-name
```

We could declare a tuple variable called STU-TV to range over the entire STUDENT table like this:

```
RANGE STUDENT STU-TV
```

Once the tuple variable has been declared, it remains in effect until the user changes or deletes it. We could use the tuple variable in the foregoing query as follows.

```
GET INTO STU STU-TV.STUDENT-NAME
```

One immediate benefit of tuple variables is that you could temporarily shorten table names via tuple variables. Tuple variables need only be used with quantifiers (existential or universal).

Let's look at a few more examples.

1. Get the names and salaries of the faculty members who earn over $40,000.

```
GET INTO RICH FACULTY.FACULTY-NAME, FACULTY.SALARY :
          FACULTY.SALARY > 40000
```

WORKSPACE NAME: RICH

FACULTY-NAME	SALARY
WENDY SWIMMER	45000

We did not have to use a RANGE command to create a tuple variable for this is a simple non-quantified retrieval.

2. Get the names and salaries of the faculty members who earn more than $30,000 and are members of the Computer Science Department. Retrieve the results in descending order by salary.

```
GET INTO BYTERS FACULTY.FACULTY-NAME, FACULTY.SALARY :
          FACULTY.SALARY > 30000 &
          FACULTY.DEPARTMENT = "COMP SCI"
          DOWN FACULTY.SALARY
```

WORKSPACE NAME: BYTERS

FACULTY-NAME	SALARY
AMY DANCER	34500
RAYMOND J. JOHNSON	40000
WENDY SWIMMER	45000

Notice that the order of the retrieved tuples is changed due to the DOWN, clause which obviously causes the sorting of the resultant workspace by FACULTY. SALARY. If there is a DOWN, there must be an UP. Again, since this was a nonquantified retrieval, we did not need to create a tuple variable.

3. Get the names of the students currently enrolled in CSC100. This query cannot be solved using only one table.

```
STUDENT (STU-ID, STUDENT-NAME, ADDRESS, BIRTHDATE, GENDER)
COURSE (COURSE-ID, COURSE-TITLE, SECTION, STU-ID, FAC-ID)
```

Therefore, we must declare the existence of a tuple variable.

```
        RANGE COURSE COU-TV
        GET INTO TAKING STUDENT.STUDENT-NAME :
            ∃COU-TV(STUDENT.STU-ID=COU-TV.STU-ID &
                COU-TV.COURSE = "CSC100")
```

WORKSPACE NAME: TAKING

STUDENT-NAME
WENDY JONES
SAM WALES

DSL Alpha was the first attempt to design a language to implement the relational calculus. Dr. Codd did design commands for inserting, deleting, and modifying tuples in relations, along with a set of standard statistical functions (average, count, sum, maximum, and minimum); however, we will not delve that deeply into the language. If you are interested in DSL Alpha, we suggest that you acquire the original article describing the language in detail [4]. Even though it was never directly implemented, it did make a significant contribution to the field of relational databases.

QUERY OPTIMIZATION

At this point you should be aware that the relational calculus predicates could be solved in more than one way. If there is a choice of steps to solve the query, it is hoped that the system will choose the ''best'' possible method of implementing the query. Selecting the best possible solution to solving a query is called optimization. Actually, the system might not recognize all possible solutions to the query solution or, it might take too long to evaluate all possible solutions, so the system might just try to improve on the current query solution.

There are two very important factors to consider when attempting to optimize a query: time and space. Time refers to the time that it takes to carry out the operations to solve the query. Space refers to how much space is needed to construct the intermediate tables to solve the query. To illustrate these factors, let us consider one of our example queries. We want the names of the students taking CSC100. As we have previously illustrated, the calculus expression that we have used to solve this query is:

```
RANGE COURSE COU-TV
GET INTO TAKING STUDENT.STUDENT-NAME :
     ∃COU-TV(STUDENT.STU-ID=COU-TV.STU-ID &
          COU-TV.COURSE = "CSC100")
```

In dissecting this query we realize that this query can be broken down into the following steps (these steps would be recognized and executed by the RDBMS).

1. Pull the tuples out of the table COURSE that pertain to CSC100. The only thing that we really need here is the STU-IDs of the students who take CSC100.
2. Find out which tuples in the STUDENT table match the tuples just retrieved in step 1. This gets us the tuples in the STUDENT table that match the list of STU-IDs retrieved in step 1.
3. Pull the names of the students whose STU-IDs match.

For illustration purposes, let us assume that the RDBMS converts the calculus expression into its equivalent relational algebra commands and then executes these commands. The relational algebra commands to accomplish this are

```
TEMP1 <- SELECT COURSE WHERE COURSE-ID = "CSC100"
TEMP2 <- JOIN TEMP1 AND STUDENT OVER STU-ID
PROJECT STUDENT-NAME FROM TEMP2
```

Another solution permutation of this query is

1. Connect all the tuples in the STUDENT table to the matching tuples in the COURSE table. This gives us a list of all the students and the courses that they are currently taking.
2. Pull out the tuples that pertain to the course CSC100.
3. Pull out the names of the students that meet the criteria in step 2.

The relational algebra commands to accomplish this are

```
TEMP1 <- JOIN STUDENT AND COURSE OVER STU-ID
TEMP2 <- SELECT TEMP1 WHERE COURSE-ID = "CSC100"
PROJECT STUDENT-NAME OVER TEMP2
```

Now that we have an alternate solution that produces exactly the same answer, which implementation does the system choose? To help us make a selection, let us look at the two tables involved in the solution.

TABLE NAME: STUDENT

STU-ID	STUDENT-NAME	ADDRESS	BIRTHDATE	GENDER
S001	WENDY JONES	125 MAPLE AVE	10/25/65	FEMALE
S002	SAM WALES	3006 NAVAJO CL	1/10/60	MALE
S003	CATHY SMITH	1600 PENN AVE	2/22/22	FEMALE
S004	DOTTIE STACY	10 DOWNING ST	3/31/67	FEMALE
S005	JAY LANGER	GOLF COURSE RD	4/19/65	MALE
S006	AMY LOPEZ	123 SUN RAY RD	5/10/64	FEMALE
S007	SAM WATSON	225 TEST DRIVE	6/09/63	MALE
S008	TAMMY REDD	113 MANCHESTER	7/01/60	FEMALE
S009	TOMMY WADKINS	APPLE TREE DR	8/24/67	MALE
S010	BEN TREVINO	BOWLING ALLEY	9/30/66	MALE

TABLE NAME: COURSE

COURSE-ID	COURSE-TITLE	SECTION	STU-ID	FAC-ID
CSC100	INTRODUCTION TO COMPUTING	1	S001	J01
CSC100	INTRODUCTION TO COMPUTING	2	S002	S01
CSC200	PASCAL PROGRAMMING	1	S001	D01
CSC200	PASCAL PROGRAMMING	2	S003	S01
ACC200	PRINCIPLES OF ACCOUNTING I	1	S001	J02
ACC201	PRINCIPLES OF ACCOUNTING II	1	S004	J02
HIS200	HISTORY OF PIROGUES	1	S005	N01

If we consider the first solution,

```
TEMP1 <- SELECT COURSE WHERE COURSE = "CSC100"
TEMP2 <- JOIN TEMP1 AND STUDENT OVER STU-ID
PROJECT STUDENT-NAME FROM TEMP2
```

The first operation to be executed is to remove the unneeded tuples in the COURSE table by selecting only the tuples that pertain to CSC100.

TABLE NAME: TEMP1

COURSE-ID	COURSE-TITLE	SECTION	STU-ID	FAC-ID
CSC100	INTRODUCTION TO COMPUTING	1	S001	J01
CSC100	INTRODUCTION TO COMPUTING	2	S002	S01

This reduces the size of the COURSE table, now called TEMP1, to two tuples instead of the seven in the original table. (We know that this is not a significant reduction in tuples, but we are just using these tables as examples. Industrial-strength databases might contain millions of tuples.)

Now all the system has to do is to match on STU-ID equaling S001 or S002. After the execution of the JOIN command, our table looks like this:

TABLE NAME: TEMP2

COURSE-ID	COURSE-TITLE	SECTION	STU-ID	FAC-ID	STUDENT-NAME	ADDRESS	BIRTHDATE	GENDER
CSC100	INTRODUCTION TO COMPUTING	1	S001	J01	WENDY JONES	125 MAPLE AVE	10/25/65	FEMALE
CSC100	INTRODUCTION TO COMPUTING	2	S002	S01	SAM WALES	3006 NAVAJO CL	1/10/60	MALE

As you can see, there are several attributes that are not needed to satisfy this query: from the COURSE table, COURSE-ID, COURSE-NAME, SECTION, and FAC-ID; and from the STUDENT table, ADDRESS, BIRTHDATE, and GENDER. (Remember that the field STU-ID is shown only once, for we are assuming a Natural JOIN.) These attributes could have been projected out to save space. This would have to be done by the system optimizer routine.

After the JOIN is executed, the attribute STUDENT-NAME is PROJECTed out to produce the final result.

In executing the second alternative,

```
TEMP1 <- JOIN STUDENT AND COURSE OVER STU-ID
TEMP2 <- SELECT TEMP1 WHERE COURSE = "CSC100"
PROJECT STUDENT-NAME FROM TEMP2
```

more space is initially utilized, for irrelevant tuples are generated, the ones not pertaining to CSC100.

The first command links the students that are taking classes with the classes that they are taking.

```
TEMP1 <- JOIN STUDENT AND COURSE OVER STU-ID
```

TABLE NAME: TEMP1

STU-ID	STUDENT-NAME	ADDRESS	BIRTHDATE	GENDER	COURSE-ID	COURSE-TITLE	SECTION	FAC-ID
S001	WENDY JONES	125 MAPLE AVE	10/25/65	FEMALE	CSC100	INTRODUCTION TO COMPUTING	1	J01
S001	WENDY JONES	125 MAPLE AVE	10/25/65	FEMALE	CSC200	PASCAL PROGRAMMING	1	D01
S001	WENDY JONES	125 MAPLE AVE	10/25/65	FEMALE	ACC200	PRINCIPLES OF ACCOUNTING I	1	J02
S002	SAM WALES	3006 NAVAJO CL	1/10/60	MALE	CSC100	INTRODUCTION TO COMPUTING	1	J01
S003	CATHY SMITH	1600 PENN AVE	2/22/22	FEMALE	CSC200	PASCAL PROGRAMMING	1	D01
S004	DOTTIE STACY	10 DOWNING ST	3/32/67	FEMALE	ACC201	PRINCIPLES OF ACCOUNTING II	1	J02
S005	JAY LANGER	TOTTINGHAM RD	4/19/65	MALE	HIS200	HISTORY OF PIROGUES	1	N01

This alternative generated five unnecessary tuples that must be deleted from the TEMP1 table via the SELECT command. There are also unnecessary attributes that are generated by this join. Perhaps two opening PROJECTs would have eliminated much of the data in the temporary tables and save some space and time. In our example tables, you will notice that not every student takes classes. This saves us additional time and space by not having to generate corresponding tuples to go with these tuples.

Therefore, we can state that with the data that we have, the first alternative saves some space and with it some time over the second alternative. The problem is that we had to execute both query solutions to determine that the first alternative was probably the best.

In general, the JOIN-type queries are the ones that the system has to try its best to optimize, for they are the most time consuming to execute and generate the most space for resultant tables. This means that JOINs should be placed as late as possible in the execute queue. However, it must be the job of the RDBMS to optimize queries, and this should be transparent to the user.

SUMMARY

This chapter was dedicated to introducing the reader to the concepts of relational calculus. Tuple-oriented relational calculus was stressed. Two quantifiers, existential and universal, were utilized to link tables together. An implementation of relational calculus called DSL Alpha was also discussed. The chapter terminated with a brief discussion of query optimization.

At this point you should be familiar with the following relational calculus terms:

A. Relational calculus expression

B. Target

C. Predicate/qualifier

D. Workspace

E. Tuple variable

F. Quantifier

G. Universal quantifier

H. Existential quantifier

I. Well-formed formulas

J. Free and bound variables

K. Tuple-oriented relational calculus

L. Domain-oriented relational calculus

M. Relational completeness

N. DSL Alpha

O. Query optimization

EXERCISES

1. Explain the difference between a free and a bound variable.

2. What is meant by a WFF?

3. Explain what is meant by relational completeness.

4. Discuss why query optimization is important. Why can't the user become involved?

5. Discuss the differences between relational algebra and relational calculus. Do you feel there is a need for completely implementing either or both? Which do you feel is easier for people with a technical background to learn? a nontechnical background?

6. Given the following relations, give the relational calculus expressions to solve the following queries.

```
STUDENT ( STU-ID, STUDENT-NAME, ADDRESS, BIRTHDATE, GENDER)
COURSE ( COURSE-ID, COURSE-TITLE, SECTION-NO, STU-ID, FAC-ID)
FACULTY ( FAC-ID, FACULTY-NAME, DEPARTMENT, GENDER, SALARY)
```

a. List all the male faculty members whose salary is less than $35,000.
b. List the female faculty members and the courses that they teach.
c. List the faculty members who teach the course Introduction to Computing.

REFERENCES

1. Date, C. J. *Introduction to Database Management Systems*, Vol 1, 4th ed., Addison-Wesley, Reading, MA, 1986.

2. Lacroix, M. and A. Pirotte "Domain-Oriented Relational Languages," *Proceedings of the Third International Conference on Very Large Data Bases*, October 1977.

3. Ullman, Jeffery *Principles of Database Systems*, 2nd ed., Computer Science Press, Rockville, MD, 1982.

4. Codd, E. F. "A Data Base Sublanguage Founded on Relational Calculus," *Proceedings of the 1977 ACM SIGFIDET Workshop on Data Description, Access, and Control*, November 1977.

5. Klenk, Virginia *Understanding Symbolic Logic* Prentice Hall, Englewood Cliffs, NJ, 1983.

5

Introduction to ORACLE

PURPOSE: Chapter 5 is designed to introduce you to the ORACLE RDBMS. The various components that make up the system are outlined and their function(s) are elaborated. Syntax of the ORACLE commands is presented. The different ORACLE utilities are also described.

ORACLE is an implemented relational database management system. ORACLE is produced, maintained, and marketed by the ORACLE Corporation in Belmont, California.

This chapter introduces you to the basic concepts of the ORACLE database management system. The component parts of the DBMS are introduced along with the basic syntax of the commands. ORACLE's two on-line command types are also explored. In our examples, ORACLE commands that the user inputs are always shown in a tint panel.

One important note on terminology before we begin. The ORACLE manuals use the terms rows and columns to refer to tuples and attributes. For this reason we will use the terms row/tuple and column/attribute interchangeably.

OVERVIEW OF ORACLE

ORACLE is a relational DBMS developed by the ORACLE Corporation (formerly Relational Software, Inc.). The original company was formed in 1977 and the first version of ORACLE was installed in 1979. It was originally installed on a DEC PDP-11 computer system but is available on many mainframes, minicomputers, and microcomputers today. As of January 1, 1988, there are over 500 installations running ORACLE.

The package was developed utilizing the "C" language. This was done to ensure maximum portability.

Systems On Which ORACLE Is Available

Even though the product was developed on a DEC PDP-11 computer system, it is available on the systems shown in Tables 5.1 and 5.2. This list of systems will certainly change over time, but it is presented as an illustration of the diversity of systems on which the package is available. As of May 15, 1987, the initial license fee (the second license fee is available at a discount) for the basic ORACLE system is between $1300, for microcomputer systems, and $144,000, for large mainframes. (These prices are obviously subject to change and are only included to give the reader a relative feel for the price of the software that we will be discussing through out this text.) The system is usually available to colleges and universities at a very substantial discount, provided that they only use it for a teaching tool.

One unique version of ORACLE is the one available for Harris computers. The Harris Corporation has acquired a licensing agreement from the ORACLE corporation for the package. Harris users interface directly with the Harris Corporation for the package. It is the same system that is available to users of other computer systems except that it has been tuned for Harris computer systems.

Vendor support services include maintenance agreements and ORACLE training courses. ORACLE's Premium Support Services are (as of May 1987) structured at four levels, shown in Table 5.3. Again these services are presented to give the reader a relative feel for the services provided by database vendors.

The ORACLE Corporation has developed courses entitled "Introduction to ORACLE" and "ORACLE Database Design" which are included with the price of each license.

System Components

The ORACLE DBMS consists of the ORACLE kernel, SQL (Structured Query Language) and UFI (User Friendly Interface) interfaces, system utilities, and Host Language Interface and several system utilities.

The basic component of the system is the ORACLE kernel. The kernel requires approximately 350K bytes of main memory. In systems that have smaller amounts of main memory, parts of the kernel are swapped in and out of memory as needed.

TABLE 5.1   MINICOMPUTER AND MAINFRAME SYSTEMS FOR WHICH ORACLE IS AVAILABLE

CPU	MODEL	Operating System
IBM	370/138–148	VM/CMS, MVS
IBM	370/158	VM/CMS, MVS
IBM	370/168	VM/CMS, MVS
IBM	4321–4331	VM/CMS, MVS
IBM	4341–4361	VM/CMS, MVS
IBM	4381–30xx	VM/CMS, MVS
IBM	9370	VM/CMS, MVS
Amdahl	V-6	VM/CMS, MVS, UTS
Amdahl	V-7, V-8	VM/CMS, MVS, UTS
NAS	System 6600	VM/CMS, MVS
NAS	System 8000	VM/CMS, MVS
NAS	System 9000	VM/CMS, MVS
DEC	PDP 11/44	RSX/11M Plus
DEC	PDP 11/70	RSX/11M Plus
DEC	VAX 11/730	VMS, UNIX V, UNIX 4.2
DEC	VAX 11/750	VMS, UNIX V, UNIX 4.2
DEC	VAX 11/780	VMS, UNIX V, UNIX 4.2
DEC	VAX 11/782	VMS, UNIX V, UNIX 4.2
DEC	VAX 11/785	VMS, UNIX V, UNIX 4.2
DEC	8978, 8974	VMS, UNIX V, UNIX 4.2
DEC	8800, 8700	VMS, UNIX V, UNIX 4.2
DEC	8650, 8550	VMS, UNIX V, UNIX 4.2
DEC	8600, 8500	VMS, UNIX V, UNIX 4.2
DEC	8530, 8300	VMS, UNIX V, UNIX 4.2
DEC	8350	VMS, UNIX V, UNIX 4.2
Data General	MV4000	AOS/VS
Data General	MV8000	AOS/VS
Data General	MV10000	AOS/VS
AT&T	3B20 S	UNIX V
AT&T	3B20 D	UNIX V
AT&T	3B20 A	UNIX V
Hewlett-Packard	HP 9000 Series 500	HP/UX
Apollo	Domain 460, 660, 300, 320	Aegis
Harris	H-60, H500, H700, H800, H1000, H1200	VOS

Source: Oracle Corporation, Belmont, CA.

SQL (pronounced ''sequel'') is the primary interface to ORACLE. It is generally considered an on-line query language. SQL is designed to be used primarily by on-line users; however, this does not preclude its use in batch processing. (See the Host Language Interface discussion that follows.) A sample SQL command is

```
SELECT STUDENT-NAME, ADDRESS
FROM STUDENT
WHERE GENDER = 'FEMALE';
```

TABLE 5.2   MICROCOMPUTER SYSTEMS AND WORKSTATIONS FOR WHICH ORACLE
IS AVAILABLE

CPU	MODEL	Operating System
IBM	PC/XT	PC DOS
IBM	COMPATIBLES	MS DOS
AT&T	3B2	UNIX V
TI	PROFESSIONAL	MS DOS
DEC	RAINBOW	MS DOS
DEC	MICRO II	RSX/11M PLUS
DEC	MICROVAX	MICRO VMS
FORTUNE	32:16	For: Pro(UNIX)
CT	MINIFRAME	CTIX
CT	MEGAFRAME	CTIX +
HP	9000 SERIES 200	HP/UX
Apollo WS		AEGIS

Source: Oracle Corporation, Belmont, CA.

The ORACLE kernel executes all SQL commands. We will examine more SQL
commands later in this chapter.

   UFI (pronounced ''you fee'') is the processor that allows on-line access to
SQL. Its commands allow for the formatting of queries, generating of reports, and
the accessing of the on-line HELP facility. A sample UFI command to format the
output of the SALARY attribute is:

```
COLUMN SALARY FORMAT $99,999
```

UFI is further described in this chapter.

TABLE 5.3   ORACLE PREMIUM SUPPORT SERVICES

Level	Annual Price	Description of Services
1	$ 10,000	Local customer service representatives guaranteed on-call service. Twenty-four hour toll-free support hot line at corporate headquarters. Access to on-line support system for problem reporting and tracking, mail facility, user bulletin board, and access to new and updated products on a trial basis. Five day's on-site technical assistance.
2	$ 20,000	Same as level 1 except that level 2 customers are given 15 days of on-site technical assistance plus 10 training units.
3	$ 50,000	Same as level 2 except the level 3 customers are given 35 days of on site technical assistance and 25 training units plus an annual executive briefing, a complete system audit, and a 10% discount on consulting services.
4	$200,000	Same as level 3 except that level 4 customers are given 250 days of on-site technical assistance and 50 training units.

Source: Oracle Corporation, Belmont, CA.

The various ORACLE utilities allow for the design of interactive applications (SQL*Forms), generation of reports (RPT, the report facility), bulk loading of data into ORACLE tables from external files (ODL, the ORACLE data loader), and the backing up of tables and data (the IMPORT/EXPORT facility). New utilities are constantly being added in an effort to improve the package. A sample EXPORT command is:

```
EXPORT BACKUPFILE  MY_ACCOUNT/MY_PASSWORD
```

These utilities are discussed through out the remainder of this text.

SQL commands can also be executed from within certain host programming languages such as FORTRAN, COBOL, and C. SQL is accessed through an interface mechanism called HLI (host language interface). A sample COBOL HLI command is:

```
CALL "CPILON" USING USERID, USERL, PASSWORD, PSWL, AUDIT, STAT,
```

A complete discussion of the host language interface is beyond the scope of this text.

System Overview

A diagram of the ORACLE DBMS is shown in Figure 5.1. Notice that all processors are linked directly into the ORACLE kernel. This allows the executing of SQL

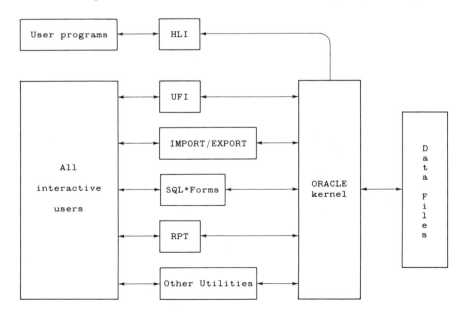

Figure 5.1   An Overview of Oracle

commands from these processors. More about this feature will be discussed later in the text.

USER FRIENDLY INTERFACE

UFI (User Friendly Interface) is an interactive processor that allows the user to communicate with ORACLE. Within UFI the user can do such things as

1. Modify the last SQL command.
2. Change the default format for any attribute, including the attribute heading.
3. Create simple reports with such things as control breaks, page headings, and control sums.
4. Log on and Log off ORACLE.
5. Direct output to a file for printing at a later time.
6. Write the last SQL command to an external file (external to ORACLE) so that it can be executed at a later time.
7. Access an on-line HELP system.

When the user connects to ORACLE via some type of terminal, he is connected to the UFI processor. At this point he can execute either UFI or SQL commands or disconnect from the system. The UFI prompt is

```
UFI>
```

which can be changed. To change the UFI prompt, you must use the SET UFIPROMPT "string" command. Once executed the UFI prompt is changed to whatever you enclose in the quotes. If you execute the UFI command SET TIME ON, the current time is displayed before each UFI prompt. Examples of changing UFI prompts are:

```
UFI> SET UFIPROMPT "My ORACLE Prompt:"
My ORACLE Prompt: SET TIME ON
11:12:32 My ORACLE Prompt: SET UFIPROMPT "UFI>"
1:12:59 UFI> SET TIME OFF
UFI>
```

Note that we have adopted the convention of displaying the user's input in a tint panel and ORACLE's output in regular type. These two commands are called SETs. There are many SET commands in UFI. Other UFI commands will be introduced throughout the text as needed. To see the current settings of all the UFI SET commands, type the UFI command SHOW ALL. If you only want to display the current setting of one SET command, type SET command-name. To illustrate, let's see the current value of UFIPROMPT and then all the current SETtings.

```
UFI > SHOW UFIPROMPT
Ufiprompt "UFI >"

UFI > SHOW ALL
Feedback on for 6 or more  records
Heading ON
Linesize 80
Numwidth 10
Spool ON
User is "BOOK"
Space 1
Worksize 8000
Lines will be wrapped
Pagesize 19
Showmode OFF
Pause is OFF
Ttitle OFF an is the 1st characters of the next select  statement
Btitle OFF an is the 1st characters of the next select  statement
Define "&" (Hex 26)
Ufiprompt "UFI>"
Underline "_" (Hex 2D)
Null ""
Verify ON
Scan ON
Termout ON
Echo ON
Headsep "|" (Hex 7C)
Maxdata 5000
Time OFF
Cmdsep OFF
Sqlterminator ";" (Hex 3B)
Ufiprefix "#" (Hex 23)
Release 40202
Autocommit OFF
Newpage 1
Long 80
Errorflag OFF
Trimout ON
```

STRUCTURED QUERY LANGUAGE

SQL is an outgrowth of a relational prototype system developed by IBM to determine if the relational model of data could be implemented. The prototype system was called System R, and the interface language developed for the system was called Structured English Query Language or SEQUEL. (Although some feel that it was actually a "sequel" to SQUARE, Specifying Queries in A Relational Environment [6], which IBM tried to implement on conventional CRTs and failed. IBM Research later redesigned the language and renamed it SEQUEL.) The language was later improved and called SEQUEL II, and the name was eventually shortened to SQL.

There are very few SQL commands, which makes the "language" very easy to learn. SQL is called a Fourth Generation Language (4GL) due to its immense power, conciseness, and low level of procedurality. The SQL language is considered by many authorities as an implementation of the relational calculus. A list of SQL commands and a brief description of each follows:

1. **SELECT** Used to retrieve data from a database.
2. **UPDATE** Used to modify attribute occurrences.
3. **INSERT** Used to add new tuples to tables.
4. **DELETE** Used to delete tuples from tables.
5. **CREATE** Used to create tables, views, and so on.
6. **ALTER** Used to modify the structure of tables, storage spaces, and so on.
7. **DROP** Used to delete tables, views, and so on.
8. **GRANT** Used to create a user-name and to give other system users privileges on your tables.
9. **REVOKE** Used to delete a user-name or recall the table privileges granted to other users.

The format of SQL commands is completely free-field, except that you cannot break a command in the middle of a word. Commands can be entered in either upper or lowercase. The following are some examples of acceptable SQL commands.

```
UFI> SELECT STUDENT-NAME FROM STUDENT WHERE GENDER = 'FEMALE';

UFI> SELECT STUDENT-NAME
  2  FROM STUDENT
  3   WHERE GENDER = 'FEMALE';

UFI> SELECT             student-name
  2            FROM
  3 student
  4                                                        WHERE
  5 gender
  6                        =
  7 'FEMALE'
  8 ;
```

As you can probably deduce by now each of the three commands shown produces a resultant table of the names of the female students. The resultant table would be displayed directly below the command.

```
UFI> SELECT STUDENT-NAME FROM STUDENT WHERE GENDER = 'FEMALE';
```

```
STUDENT-NAME
WENDY JONES
CATHY SMITH
DOTTIE STACY
AMY LOPEZ
TAMMY REDD
```

The semicolon after the statement tells ORACLE to execute the command. If you do not like the semicolon, you may use the UFI command SET SQLTERM "string" to change the SQL terminator symbol. For example, if you wanted to change the SQL terminator to a dollar sign ($), the UFI command would be

```
UFI> SET SQLTERM "$"

UFI> SELECT STUDENT-NAME FROM STUDENT WHERE GENDER = 'FEMALE'$

STUDENT-NAME
WENDY JONES
CATHY SMITH
DOTTIE STACY
AMY LOPEZ
TAMMY REDD
```

The following SQL command is illegal and would produce an error.

```
UFI> SELECT STU
   2 DENT-NAME FROM STUDENT WHERE GENDER = 'FEMALE';

SELECT STU
       *
Error at Line 1: 704      Invalid Column Name
```

Note the illegal break on the attribute STUDENT-NAME. Since the end-of-line is a terminator, ORACLE looks for the column (attribute) name STU and does not find it; hence an error is generated. You also cannot break a SQL command word (SELECT, FROM, WHERE, etc.) between lines. If a command contains an error, the error message is displayed directly below the command in error. A summary of all ORACLE error messages can be found in the ORACLE Language Reference Manual.

SQL is a language that is not restricted to ORACLE. It is available on several other RDBMS systems. IBM's relational DBMS, called DB2, and Relational Technology's INGRES have SQL interfaces. Some microcomputer DBMSs have adopted SQL (usually a subset of full SQL) as their interface language.

SQL is constantly being updated and redesigned by the various computer and software vendors. New commands are being implemented with each new release of SQL. (Remember that there is a difference between language design and language implementation.) Once all the designed commands are implemented into SQL, it can be considered "relationally complete." The first step in making SQL the de facto industry language occurred when the ANSI (American National Standards Institute) accepted it as a standard language for relational databases.

THE SQL COMMAND BUFFER

When SQL commands are entered, they are housed in a storage area called the **SQL Command Buffer**. Once the command is housed in the buffer it remains there until the next SQL command is entered. (There might be 5000 UFI commands entered between SQL commands, but as long as no new SQL commands are entered the command buffer remains unchanged.) There can be only one SQL command residing in the SQL command buffer.

As you have observed from the previous examples of SQL commands, the command can extend for several lines. If a command extends past one line, line numbers, beginning with line 2, are displayed to the left of each line. These numbers are used for reference only.

Once a SQL command resides in the buffer, it can be executed, modified, or stored to an external file. These operations are done with various UFI commands.

For example purposes, let us assume that the following SQL command resides in the SQL command buffer.

```
UFI> SELECT STUDENT-NAME
   2 FROM STUDENT
   3 WHERE GENDER = 'FEMALE'
   4 [RET]
```

Notice that the command did not end with a semicolon (;). This means that the command will not execute; it is only stored in the buffer. The [RET] refers to pressing the RETURN Key on your terminal. This tells ORACLE that this is the end of the command. Remember that the semicolon executes the command just entered, and the return key when enter from position 1 of a new input line terminates the entry into the buffer and does not execute the command.

Executing SQL Commands from the SQL Command Buffer

There are two ways to execute the SQL command currently stored in the buffer. The first method causes the command to be displayed, the command to be executed, and the output to be displayed. This method is done with the UFI command RUN.

```
UFI> RUN
   1 SELECT STUDENT-NAME
   2 FROM STUDENT
   3 WHERE GENDER = 'FEMALE'
```

```
STUDENT-NAME___
WENDY JONES
CATHY SMITH
DOTTIE STACY
AMY LOPEZ
TAMMY REDD
```

Note that when the command is displayed a semicolon is not needed to execute the command—the RUN command does it for you.

The second method of executing stored SQL commands is with the slash (/). The slash executes the command without first displaying it.

```
UFI>/
```

```
STUDENT-NAME___
WENDY JONES
CATHY SMITH
DOTTIE STACY
AMY LOPEZ
TAMMY REDD
```

Listing the Command in the SQL Buffer

It may sometimes become necessary to list the command currently housed in the buffer. This can be done with the LIST command.

```
UFI> LIST
    1   SELECT STUDENT-NAME
    2   FROM STUDENT
    3*  WHERE GENDER = 'FEMALE'
```

The asterisk (*) postfixed to line 3 indicates that this is the current line number. This becomes important when we want to edit a SQL command.

We may list just one line in the command buffer if we wish. To do this we place the number of the line that we want listed after the word LIST, a blank is optional. The line that we list becomes the current line.

```
UFI> LIST 2
    2*  FROM STUDENT
```

The LIST command does not allow the listing of ranges of lines.

Modifying SQL Commands

The are four types of modifications that can be done to a command currently residing in the SQL command buffer. The four types of modifications are

1. Inserting a new line in the command buffer.

2. Deleting a line from the buffer.

3. Changing a string of characters to a different string of characters.

4. Appending a string of characters onto the end of a line. All four modifications require you to make the line that you will modify the current line via the LIST command.

Inserting a New Line into the Buffer.   To insert a new line in between lines currently in the buffer, you must use the INPUT command. (You do not use the INSERT command because that is a SQL command utilized to insert new tuples in a table.) The INPUT inserts the new line <u>after</u> the current line. To illustrate this, let's insert some new lines after line 1.

```
UFI> LIST1
  1* SELECT STUDENT-NAME

UFI> INPUT
  2i  ,ADDRESS
  3i  ,STU-ID
  4i  [RET]

UFI> LIST
  1  SELECT STUDENT-NAME
  2  ,ADDRESS
  3  ,STU-ID
  4  FROM STUDENT
  5* WHERE GENDER = 'FEMALE'
```

Notice that UFI renumbers the lines in the buffer. The RET terminates the insertion of lines. The lowercase "i" indicates that you are in INPUT mode. If you want to add a line to the end of the buffer, simply make the last line current and begin inserting normally.

```
UFI> LIST
  1  SELECT STUDENT-NAME
  2  ,ADDRESS
  3  ,STU-ID
  4  FROM STUDENT
  5* WHERE GENDER = 'FEMALE'

UFI> INPUT
  6  AND BIRTHDATE = '01-JUL-60'
  7  [RET]
```

```
UFI>  LIST
   1   SELECT STUDENT-NAME
   2   ,ADDRESS
   3   ,STU-ID
   4   FROM STUDENT
   5   WHERE GENDER = 'FEMALE'
   6*  AND BIRTHDATE = '01-JUL-60'
```

Be aware that when we are adding lines to the bottom of the buffer, the lowercase "i" does not display, for we are not really inserting, we are actually appending to the end of the buffer.

There is no easy method of inserting a new line before line 1 in the buffer. To do it, you must insert your new line after the first line in the buffer, retype the first line, and then delete the current first line. The reason that you cannot insert a line before line 1 is that the first word that the ORACLE command line interpreter expects is a SQL command name (SELECT, INSERT, DELETE, etc.). Remember that in SQL's syntax, nothing can be placed before the command name in the SQL Command Buffer. If the command name is misspelled, you will not even get a line 2 designator.

Obviously once the SQL command in the buffer has been edited, it can then be executed, further edited, listed, or saved to an external file.

Deleting a Line from the Buffer.   To delete a line from the buffer, simply make the line that you wish to delete current, then type DEL for delete. You may only delete one line at a time, for there can be only one current line.

Be aware that you cannot enter the entire word DELETE for that is the SQL command for deleting tuples from tables.

Let's illustrate a delete with the line that we just added in the previous example.

```
UFI>  LIST
   1   SELECT STUDENT-NAME
   2   ,ADDRESS
   3   ,STU-ID
   4   FROM STUDENT
   5   WHERE GENDER = 'FEMALE'
   6*  AND BIRTHDATE = '01-JUL-60'

UFI>  DEL

UFI>  LIST
   1   SELECT STUDENT-NAME
   2   ,ADDRESS
   3   ,STU-ID
   4   FROM STUDENT
   5*  WHERE GENDER = 'FEMALE'
```

```
UFI> LIST3
   3   ,STU-ID

UFI> DEL

UFI> LIST
   1   SELECT STUDENT-NAME
   2   ,ADDRESS
   3   FROM STUDENT
   4*  WHERE GENDER = 'FEMALE'

UFI> LIST 2
   2   ,ADDRESS

UFI> DEL

UFI> LIST
   1   SELECT STUDENT-NAME
   2   FROM STUDENT
   3*  WHERE GENDER = 'FEMALE'
```

Appending to the End of a Line in the Buffer.   Sometimes it is very convenient simply to append a string of characters to the end of a line. To append to the end of a line we can use the cleverly named command APPEND. Let's assume that we wanted to add the string ",STU-ID, ADDRESS" to the end of the SELECT command. If we look at the buffer, we will see these lines.

```
UFI> LIST
   1   SELECT STUDENT-NAME
   2   FROM STUDENT
   3*  WHERE GENDER = 'FEMALE'
```

We see that we want to add the string to the end of line 1, so we must make it current.

```
UFI> LIST 1
   1*  SELECT STUDENT-NAME

UFI> APPEND ,STU-ID, ADDRESS

UFI> LIST
   1   SELECT STUDENT-NAME, STU-ID, ADDRESS
   2   FROM STUDENT
   3*  WHERE GENDER = 'FEMALE'
```

Notice that there is one blank space after the word APPEND. Any text specified after this one blank is appended to the end of the current line.

Changing Strings of Characters in the Buffer.   Changing strings of characters requires the use of the CHANGE command. The format of the CHANGE command is as follows:

```
CHANGE/string to search for/replacement string/
```

Let's assume that we want the command in the buffer to select the names, student IDs, and addresses of the male students instead of the females. We could use the CHANGE command to change the string FEMALE to the string MALE.

```
UFI> LIST
  1  SELECT STUDENT-NAME, STU-ID, ADDRESS
  2  FROM STUDENT
  3* WHERE GENDER = 'FEMALE'

UFI> CHANGE/FEMALE/MALE/

UFI> LIST
  1  SELECT STUDENT-NAME, STU-ID, ADDRESS
  2  FROM STUDENT
  3* WHERE GENDER = 'MALE'
```

Note that the strings do not have to match in length. The CHANGE command changes the first occurrence of the string in its left-to-right search, so it is your responsibility to make sure that your string is unique.

All of the UFI commands that we have discussed in this section can be abbreviated by using the first letter of the command (except for delete). The abbreviations that can be used are:

COMMAND	ABBREVIATION
RUN	R or /
LIST	L
INPUT	I
DELETE	DEL
APPEND	A
CHANGE	C

The SQL Command Buffer and External Files

Once you get a command the way you want it in the command buffer, you may wish to write the contents of the buffer out to a file so that you will not have to retype the command each time you wish to execute it. This is SQL's novel method of implementing procedures.

Saving the Contents of the Buffer.   To save the contents of the SQL command buffer by writing it out to a file, you must use the SAVE command. The syntax of the SAVE command is

```
SAVE filename
```

The name of the file (''filename'') that the buffer is to be saved into depends upon the naming conventions used on the system that ORACLE is running on. We will use the generic name ''filename'' to represent the file for purposes of this text. This command writes the contents of the SQL command buffer out to the designated file in text format (whichever one is native to your system). This file can be edited via the computer system's standard text editor if you wish to do so.

The SAVE command destroys the current contents of the file and replaces it with the contents of the command buffer. If you wish to append the contents of the command buffer to the end of the file, you must attach the APPEND clause to the SAVE command.

```
SAVE filename APPEND
```

Retrieving the Contents of a File into the Buffer.   The command to retrieve the contents of a file into the SQL command buffer is GET. The format of the GET command is as follows:

```
GET filename
```

This command copies the contents of the file into the command buffer. If there is more than one SQL and UFI command in the file only the last SQL command is retained in the buffer. The GET command only copies, it does not execute the commands. If you wish to execute the command currently residing in the buffer, you must type either RUN or a slash (/).

Executing the Commands Stored in a File.   The START command copies the contents of a file into the SQL command buffer and executes the command. If there is more than one command in the file, the START command will copy each command and execute each one in succession. The format of the START command is as follows:

```
START filename
```

The START command is a very efficient method of creating ''run streams'' or series of SQL commands that are executed quite frequently. START commands are very useful for executing groups of UFI formatting commands that are needed to make output easier to read. The drawback to executing UFI commands is that they can not be inserted into the file via the SAVE command; they must be created via your computer system's text editor. The reason for this is that UFI commands are not stored in the SQL command buffer and hence cannot be written directly to an external file. We will cover this concept in greater detail in the following chapter.

If you execute a START command, all commands in the file (both UFI and SQL) are displayed before they are executed. If you just want the output from the command displayed, insert the UFI command SET ECHO OFF before you execute the START command (or embed the command in the START file). When you want the commands displayed again, type the command SET ECHO ON.

The ORACLE package has some example START files that give examples of various SQL and UFI commands. These files are summarized in the Aside at the end of Chapter 8 of this text. We will refer to these commands at different points in this text. At that point you should execute these START files and observe their output.

ORACLE COMMENTS

ORACLE comments are called **remarks.** Remarks are entered via the REM command. Once ORACLE detects the string REM in the first six or three characters in the command line, it disregards the remainder of the command line. Examples of remarks are:

```
UFI> REMARK _ THIS IS A COMMENT _
UFI> REM        This is also acceptable.
```

Remarks are particularly useful when creating a START file with multiple commands. If a remark is in a START file and SET ECHO OFF has been executed, the remarks are not displayed.

We will use remarks in the remainder of the text to annotate different commands.

DIRECTING ORACLE OUTPUT TO A FILE

Any output produced by ORACLE can be spooled to an external file by executing the SPOOL filename command. This command will take all output that is displayed on your terminal screen and copy it out to a file. Once you have opened a spool file, you can direct your computer system to print the file or close the file. To close a spool file, you must type the UFI command SPOOL OFF. To close the file and direct the output to the system printer, type the command SPOOL OUT. An example of a spool file is:

```
UFI> REMARK . . . . . Open a spool file called MY-FILE.
UFI> SPOOL MY-FILE
UFI> REMARK . . . . . Execute a SQL command.
UFI> SELECT STUDENT-NAME FROM STUDENT WHERE GENDER =
  2 'FEMALE';

STUDENT-NAME_____
WENDY JONES
CATHY SMITH
DOTTIE STACY
AMY LOPEZ
TAMMY REDD

UFI> REMARK . . . . . Close the spool file and direct the
UFI> REMARK . . . . . output to the system printer.
UFI> SPOOL OUT
```

The forgoing sequence of commands opens a file called "MY-FILE" (we selected MY-FILE as a generic file name) and places the SQL command along with its output, including the remarks, into the file. Once the output from the command is placed in the file, the command SPOOL OUT closes the file and directs the file to the system printer. If we had entered the command SPOOL OFF, the file would have been closed but not directed to the printer. If you want it printed, you must exit ORACLE and direct the file to the printer through some operating system-level command. In either case (SPOOL OUT or SPOOL OFF) the file exists as a text file that can be edited via any text editor. If you do not close the file before you disconnect from ORACLE (via the EXIT command), it closes the file for you, but does not direct it to the system printer.

The output that is directed to the file is also displayed on your terminal. If you only want the output directed to the file and not to your screen, you must use the UFI command SET TERMOUT OFF. This suppresses all terminal output, including the UFI prompt. To bring the output back to your screen, type SET TERMOUT ON.

ENTERING AND LEAVING ORACLE

To use ORACLE in terminal mode, you must connect to the UFI processor. Once you have connected to ORACLE, you may enter SQL and/or UFI commands, change ORACLE accounts (called user-names) or exit the system.

ORACLE Identifiers

Anytime that you must furnish a "name" to ORACLE, that "name" is called an identifier. Identifiers are such things as table names, view names, attribute names, user-names, and so forth. The rules for valid identifiers are very simple.

1. They must contain between 1 and 30 characters.
2. They must start with an alphabetic character.
3. They can contain any combination of numbers, letters, or the special characters dollar sign ($), pound sign (#), at sign (@), and underscore (__).
4. They must be unique for that class of objects. For example, you could not have two tables with the identifier ABCD, but you could have a table and an attribute with the name ABCD.
5. They cannot be an ORACLE reserved word. A complete list of ORACLE reserved words can be found in Appendix D. Be aware that this list changes with each new version of ORACLE that is released.

Examples of valid and invalid identifiers are

```
Valid                    Invalid
MY_TABLE                 123_TABLE       {Begins with a number}
MY_#$$@#TABLE            #_OF_STUDENTS {Begins with a non-letter}
YOO_HOO_SAILOR           THIS_IDENTIFIER_HAS_TOO_MANY_CHARACTERS
what$A$GEEK              STUDENT-NAME    {Illegal character}
```

User-names

Entry into ORACLE is made through a user-name. A user-name is a named collection of all the tables and views that a user wants to keep together. For security purposes, each user-name has an associated password. Once you create anything within your user-name, no other user's can access it unless you grant them the privilege (discussed in Chapter 13) or they know your user-name and password.

Do not confuse an ORACLE user-name with your system log-on name. Your system log-on name (sometimes called a system account) gets you into your computer system, and your ORACLE user-name gets you into ORACLE. You may enter any ORACLE user-name from any system account.

Your user-name and password is assigned to you by your ORACLE database administrator (DBA) and are therefore considered identifiers.

When created, ORACLE user-names are granted certain privileges. There are three levels of privileges that can be granted.

1. CONNECT, lowest-level privilege. Creates a user-name and allows the user only the privilege of accessing tables and views from other accounts. This assumes that the other user-names have explicitly granted this user-name the privilege of accessing the tables and/or views.
2. RESOURCE, allows the user to create his own tables and views. This user-name must also have CONNECT privilege.
3. DBA, highest level privilege. This grants the user-name unlimited power. This allows the user to create and remove all other user-names and to access

any table or view in any user-name. This is the only type user that can change the password of another user-name. DBA privilege implies both CONNECT and RESOURCE privilege.

The GRANT Command.   User-names are created through the GRANT command. The syntax of the GRANT command is as follows:

```
GRANT CONNECT TO user-name1 [,user-name2, . . .] IDENTIFIED BY
      password1 [,password2, . . .]

GRANT RESOURCE TO user-name1 [,user-name2, . . .]

GRANT DBA TO user-name1 [,user-name2 ,. . .] IDENTIFIED BY
      password1 [,password2 ,. . .]
```

Notice that the RESOURCE privilege does not allow for a password. The reason for this is that the user-name must have CONNECT privilege before it can be granted RESOURCE privilege.

Examples of GRANT commands are

```
UFI> GRANT CONNECT TO MY_USER_NAME IDENTIFIED BY MY_PASSWORD;

Grant succeeded.

UFI> GRANT RESOURCE TO MY_USER_NAME;

Grant succeeded.

UFI> GRANT CONNECT TO WENDY_BISLAND, AMY_BISLAND,
   2 JANET_PONDER IDENTIFIED BY DAUGHTER_#1, DAUGHTER_#2,
   3 MY_STUDENT_GRADER;

Grant succeeded.

UFI> GRANT DBA TO DOTTIE_BISLAND, KAREN_SOKATCH
   2 IDENTIFIED BY MY_WIFE, MY_SUPER_REVIEWER;

Grant succeeded.
```

The GRANT command can only be executed from user-names with DBA privilege.

The REVOKE Command.   User-names can be eliminated by using the REVOKE command. The format of the REVOKE command is:

```
REVOKE privilege FROM user-name1 [,user-name2 ,. . .]
```

Examples of the REVOKE command follow:

```
UFI> REVOKE CONNECT FROM MY_USER_NAME;

Revoke succeeded.

UFI> REVOKE RESOURCE FROM MY_USER_NAME;

Revoke succeeded.

UFI> REVOKE CONNECT FROM AMY_BISLAND, WENDY_BISLAND;

Revoke succeeded.
```

Notice that the user-name's password did not have to be specified when revoking privileges. This is because the REVOKE command can only be executed from a user-name with DBA privilege.

Note that the GRANT and the REVOKE commands are SQL commands. A semicolon must be placed after the command for it to execute.

Connecting to ORACLE

To enter the ORACLE DBMS in terminal mode, you must type the command UFI from the operating system-level prompt. If this is done correctly, you should get a message that looks something like this. (We will assume that you have logged onto your computer system and are at the operating system prompt level, which we will further assume is an dollar sign ($).)

```
$UFI

ORACLE Utilities, Copyright (c) 1979, 1980, 1981, 1982, RSI

UFI version 3.5 - on Mon Dec 23 13:26:47 1985

Connecting to: ORACLE

Processing database: ORACLE V4.2.2 - Production (25-Oct-1985)

Enter user-name: MY_USER_NAME

Enter password: MY_PASSWORD

UFI>
```

Notice that the system asks for your ORACLE user-name and password. (Actually you do not get the password notice until you enter the user-name.) Once you have successfully entered your user-id and password correctly, you are ready to begin to enter UFI and/or SQL commands as evidenced by the UFI> prompt.

If you wish to enter both your user-name and password at the same time simply separate the two by a slash (/).

```
Enter User-name: MY_USER_NAME/MY_PASSWORD

UFI>
```

Disconnecting from ORACLE

Whenever you wish to exit the ORACLE DBMS, you need only type the command EXIT.

```
UFI> EXIT

Logged off from ORACLE.

$        < Assumed to be your operating system prompt.
```

At this point you are back to the operating system level of your system and should receive your operating system prompt.

Connecting to Another User-name

Once you have entered ORACLE under one user-name, you may transfer to another user-name as long as you know the user-name and password of the other account. To enter another user-name, you must use the UFI command CONNECT. The format of the CONNECT command is

```
CONNECT user-name/password
```

An example of the CONNECT command is:

```
UFI> CONNECT ANOTHER_USER_NAME/ANOTHER_PASSWORD

Connected.

                        UFI>
```

Notice that if there is a user-name ANOTHER_USER_NAME with the password ANOTHER_PASSWORD, you will get the message "Connected." If there is not, you will get an error message that looks like this:

```
UFI> CONNECT ANOTHER_USER_NAME/ANOTHER_PASSWORD
```

```
ERROR: 1017  Invalid username/password - Logon denied.

Warning: You are no longer connected to  ORACLE!
```

The CONNECT command saves time in that you do not have to exit ORACLE and then reconnect to change user-names.

You may be connected to only one user-name at a time. The connection to one user-name implies the disconnection from the current user-name.

SQL*FORMS

The SQL*Forms is a processor designed for the nondatabase professional who needs to use a database to perform her job. It is a screen–oriented facility that can be used with a wide variety of CRT terminals. It can be used to enter data, retrieve data, and modify data in an ORACLE database. It also provides capability of data and operation validation needed for various types of integrity checks.

A detailed discussion of SQL*Forms is beyond the scope of this text.

THE IMPORT/EXPORT FACILITY

At some point in the database's life it becomes necessary to off load the data table descriptions, view descriptions, and actual data to external files. This might be done for backup purposes or to change versions of ORACLE or to transport the database to another computer system. This task is made very easy by the IMPORT/EXPORT facility. The EXPORT processor copies all of the table definitions, view definitions, and tuples into an external file. The IMPORT processor copies the table definitions, view definitions, and tuples from an external file back into a user-name.

The IMPORT/EXPORT facility is discussed at greater length in Chapter 8.

THE HOST LANGUAGE INTERFACE

Utilizing the host language interface the user can write programs in either FORTRAN, COBOL, or C and execute embedded SQL commands directly from these programs. This is a particularly attractive feature for maintenance of the database. This feature makes the conventional programming languages much more powerful vehicles for accessing ORACLE databases.

A detailed discussion of the host language interface to ORACLE is beyond the scope of this text.

THE ORACLE BULK DATA LOADER

It sometimes becomes very tedious to load volumes of data records into a database. This becomes particularly inefficient when the data records (soon to be tuples) are already in an external file. This data file might have been produced by some conventional language program, statistical package, or data gathering mechanism.

The ORACLE bulk data loader (ODL) is designed to ease the burden of loading volumes of data currently stored in an external file(s) into ORACLE tables. ODL is described further in Chapter 8.

THE ORACLE REPORT WRITER

Simple reports (with control breaks, page headings, control sums) can be produced via certain UFI commands, but more sophisticated reports (word processor-type reports with data extracted from ORACLE tables) are generally produced via the ORACLE report writer facility (RPT). The report writer can be used to produce the following types of reports.

1. Preprinted invoices
2. Mailing labels
3. Columnar reports with multiple levels of subtotals
4. Nested reports
5. Side-by-side reports with data from different SQL queries

The report writer facility can be utilized to produce letters, memoranda, and other types of correspondence. The simple ORACLE Report Writer is discussed in Chapter 14, but a discussion of the external report writer is beyond the scope of this text.

THE ORACLE HELP FACILITY

ORACLE has a built-in HELP facility that gives syntax descriptions, examples, and a text description of all SQL and UFI commands. (The ORACLE DBA might not have loaded the HELP facility on your system due to the large amount of memory that it uses.) To access the HELP facility, you may type the word HELP, and the system will respond with a screen containing all the UFI and SQL commands that it has help on. If you know which command that you want help on, simply type HELP command-name. Two examples of the HELP processor follow.

```
UFI> HELP
```

HELP

Syntax	
HELP [SQL reserved words | User Friendly Interface commands]	

SQL				
Query	Joins	Outer Join	Subquery	Repeating
SELECT	FROM	WHERE	GROUP BY	HAVING
ORDER BY	DELETE	INSERT	ALTER TABLE	UPDATE
CREATE TABLE	CREATE INDEX	CREATE VIEW	CREATE SYNONYM	GRANT
DROP TABLE	DROP INDEX	DROP VIEW	DROP SYNONYM	REVOKE
ALTER CLUSTER	CONNECT BE	LIKE	ALTER PARTITION	
CREATE CLUSTER	CREATE SPACE	DEFINITION	CREATE PARTITION	

UFI				
ECHO	NEWPAGE	PAGESIZE	LINESIZE	WRAP
START	PAUSE	SPACE	NUMWIDTH	FEEDBACK
BREAK ON	COMPUTE SUM OF COLUMN		FORMAT	Editing

Examples	
HELP SELECT	
HELP CREATE INDEX	
HELP PAGESIZE	

UFI> HELP SPOOL

SPOOL

Syntax 1	
SPOOL filename	

Syntax 2	
SPOOL OFF	

Syntax 3	
SPOOL OUT	

Examples	
SPOOL DIARY	
SPOOL HARDCOPY	
SPOOL OFF	
This command is used to open an operating system file to which all output generated by UFI will be written, or to cause a previously opened file to be closed and optionally scheduled for printing.	

SPOOL filename will open the specified file for spooling. If a file for spooling is already opened, it will be closed. If a file name extension is not specified, the default will be that one used by the operating system for the line printer output.

SPOOL OFF will close the file currently opened for spooling. SPOOL OUT will close the file currently opened for printing and schedule that file for printing. This option assumes that the operating system supports spooling and that it has been generated to do so. Note that once the file has been printed, the file may, depending on the operating system, be deleted.

THE ORACLE DATABASE ADMINISTRATOR

The ORACLE database administrator is a person or a group of persons who have the powers of creating new user-names, passwords, and other ORACLE-related administrative tasks. The ORACLE DBA works in a user-name that has DBA privilege. This means that they have powers not granted to regular accounts, so that they can accomplish their duties. There are some other powers that the ORACLE DBA has that will be discussed at the proper time.

SUMMARY

This chapter was dedicated to introducing you to ORACLE. We discussed how the ORACLE system was structured, the two types of on-line commands (UFI and SQL), and the SQL command buffer. Management of the buffer was also described. We further explored how to connect to ORACLE via user-names and passwords. The chapter concluded with a brief discussion of the various ORACLE utilities.

After completing this chapter the following terms/commands should be familiar to you.

A. ORACLE kernel	**K.** SET SQLTERM
B. UFI	**L.** SHOW UFIPROMPT or TIME or
C. SQL	SQLTERM
D. SHOW	**M.** RUN
E. SHOW ALL	**N.** /
F. SQL command buffer	**O.** LIST
G. ORACLE utilities	**P.** INPUT
H. SET UFIPROMPT	**Q.** DEL
I. SET TIME	**R.** APPEND
J. SET ALL	**S.** CHANGE

T. SAVE
U. GET
V. START
W. SET TERMOUT
X. REMARK
Y. SPOOL
Z. ORACLE identifiers
AA. ORACLE user-name and password
BB. EXIT
CC. CONNECT

DD. GRANT
EE. REVOKE
FF. User-name privileges (CONNECT, RESOURCE, DBA)
GG. SQL*Forms
HH. IMPORT/EXPORT facility
II. The host language interface
JJ. The ORACLE bulk data loader
KK. The ORACLE report writer
LL. The HELP facility

EXERCISES

1. Explain the function of the SQL command buffer.
2. Explain why SQL commands end in a semicolon and UFI commands do not. (You won't find this question explicitly answered in the chapter, you will have to think about it.)
3. What is the difference between the UFI command CONNECT and the CONNECT privilege given to user-names.
4. Secure a user-name and password from you friendly ORACLE DBA. Try to connect to ORACLE. Try out some of the UFI commands that we have discussed in the chapter. Try the following.
   a. Change your UFI prompt.
   b. Make the time appear after your UFI prompt.
   c. Try out the HELP facility.
   d. SHOW all the current settings of the SET commands.
   e. SHOW the current value of SQLTERM.
   f. Type in the following SQL command

   ```
   SELECT STUDENT-NAME, ADDRESS
   FROM STUDENT
   WHERE GENDER = 'FEMALE'    <- Do not end it with a ;
   ```
   Now that it is in the SQL command buffer, try to edit it. Make sure that you use the LIST, INPUT, DEL, APPEND, and CHANGE commands. Next try to RUN the command. Why didn't it execute? Why won't any SQL command execute?

   g. Type the following SQL command.

   ```
   GRANT DBA TO your_name IDENTIFIED BY your_password;
   ```
   Did the command execute? Why not?
   h. Type the following command.

   ```
   CONNECT HARLEY_SMIDLAPP/HORSE_FACE
   ```
   Did it work? Why not?
   i. Exit the system after you have finished exploring the system all that you want.

REFERENCES

1. *Harris ORACLE Reference Manual*, Harris Corporation, Ft. Lauderdale, FL, Release 4.1.4, May 1985.

2. *Harris ORACLE User's Guide*, Harris Corporation, Ft. Lauderdale, FL, February 1984.

3. *Harris ORACLE Database Administrator's Guide*, Harris Corporation, Ft. Lauderdale, FL, Release 4.2.2, September 1985.

4. *Harris ORACLE Utilities Manual*, Harris Corporation, Ft. Lauderdale, FL, Release 3.1.4, October 1984.

5. *SQL*Forms Designer's Reference - Version 2.0* ORACLE Corporation, Belmont, CA, 1986.

6. "Specifying Queries as Relational Expressions: The SQUARE Data Sublanguage," R. F. Boyce, D. D. Chamberlain, W. F. King, and M. M. Hammer, *Communications of the ACM*, 18, no. 11, 1975, 621–628.

7. "Implementaion of a Structured English Query Language," M. M. Astrahan and D. D. Chamberlain, *Communications of the ACM*, 18, no. 10, 1975, 580–587.

8. "SEQUEL2: a Unified Approach to Data Definition, Mainipula- tion, and Control," D. D. Chamberlain, et al, *IBM Journal of Research and Development*, 20, no. 6, 1976, 560–575.

6

Simple Retrieval and Formatting

PURPOSE: The purpose of this chapter is to introduce the SQL SELECT command. The method of implementing a predicate utilizing a WHERE clause is also explored. Sorting of the resultant table is described along with the various data formatting techniques.

The mechanism for retrieving data from ORACLE databases is the SELECT command. The SELECT command is much more powerful than is the relational algebra SELECT command. For this reason some of the more recent relational database authors have begun using the name RESTRICT to refer to the relational algebra SELECT operator. The SQL SELECT command actually combines the Relational Algebra operators SELECT, PROJECT, JOIN, and CATRESIAN PRODUCT.

This chapter illustrates the implementation of the relational algebra SELECT and PROJECT commands via the SQL SELECT command. Chapter 9 discusses the JOIN and CARTESIAN PRODUCT commands.

Since one SELECT command has the capability of retrieving virtually any type data stored in an ORACLE database, it is considered by many as an implementation of the relational calculus introduced in Chapter 4.

THE SYNTAX OF THE SELECT/FROM COMMAND

In this chapter we will describe a very simple version of the SELECT command. In the chapters that follow, especially Chapter 9 - JOIN Queries, we will expand the command. The syntax diagram of the SELECT shown next contains only the parts that we will discuss in this chapter. In presenting the syntax of the SELECT command and all remaining commands, we will use the following representations:

1. Capital letters represent mandatory words.
2. Anything in brackets ([]) represent optional parts of the command.
3. Lowercase letters represent values that you must furnish to the command.

If you wish to see the complete syntax diagram, see Appendix B.

```
SELECT [DISTINCT] <select-expression(s)>
FROM   table-name1 [,table-name2, , , ,]
[WHERE θ]
[ORDER BY attribute1 [DESC] [, attribute2 [DESC] , , , ,]]
```

The SELECT expression can be any combination of the following:

1. The asterisk (*) which indicates all attributes of the table. The attributes are displayed in the order that they were listed when the table definition was created. An alternative to the asterisk is table-name*. The use of this option will be explained later in the text.
2. Attribute names(s): Any combination of attributes found in the table. The attributes are displayed in the order that they are listed. Attribute names are separated by commas.
3. Arithmetic expressions: The standard arithmetic operators +, -, *, and / can be used to compute values.
4. SYSDATE: The system date displayed in a DD-MON-YY format.
5. ROWNUM: This is a virtual column that is generated as each tuple is being displayed. It is the sequential integers from one to n, where n represents the last tuple displayed.

There are more items that can be part of the select list, but we will defer until Chapter 9 before discussing them.

The ''table-name'' is the table or view that we want ORACLE to search to retrieve the desired data. Notice that the words SELECT and FROM are mandatory parts of the command. For this reason the command is sometimes referred to as the SELECT/FROM command.

The optional theta expression (WHERE θ), utilized with the WHERE clause, represents any set of conditions needed to filter out the unwanted tuples. The WHERE clause is described in greater detail later in this chapter.

The ORDER BY clause indicates that the resultant table will be sorted. This will be described later in this chapter.

When a SELECT command is executed, the results are stored in a temporary workspace. The default value for the workspace size is 8000 bytes. This value is usually adequate for most queries. However, some queries, usually involving some type of JOIN, might require additional workspace area. The workspace area can be altered with the UFI command SET WORKSIZE N. For example, if we wanted to increase the workspace size to 15,000 bytes, we could execute the following command:

```
UFI> SET WORKSIZE 15000
```

The workspace size should be left alone unless a query produces the following error message: "Context Area Too Small." At this point, you should change the size of the work space. The maximum value of WORKSIZE depends upon the type computer system on which ORACLE is running.

EXAMPLES OF THE SELECT COMMAND

The examples of the SELECT command will utilize our three tables.

```
STUDENT (STU-ID, STUDENT-NAME, ADDRESS, BIRTHDATE, GENDER)
COURSE (COURSE-ID, COURSE-TITLE, SECTION, STU-ID, FAC-ID)
FACULTY (FAC-ID, FACULTY-NAME, DEPARTMENT, GENDER, SALARY)
```

1. List all the tuples in the FACULTY table.

```
UFI> SELECT * FROM FACULTY;

FAC-ID FACULTY-NAME_____ DEPARTMENT GENDER SALARY
  J01   RAYMOND J. JOHNSON COMP SCI   MALE    40000
  S01   WENDY SWIMMER      COMP SCI   FEMALE  45000
  D01   AMY DANCER         COMP SCI   FEMALE  34500
  J02   BOB JONES          ACCOUNTING MALE    35000
  N01   JACK NELSON        HISTORY    MALE    28000
```

After examining the above output, you should be aware of several salient points.

A. The output is displayed directly below the SELECT command.

B. Each attribute column has a heading that is automatically displayed. This attribute column heading is the name given the attribute when the table was created. The CREATE TABLE command is discussed in the following chapter.

C. Each attribute has one blank space between column headings. This can be changed with the UFI command SET SPACE N, where N is the number of spaces to be "displayed" between attribute columns. It can be any integer number between 0 and 10.

D. The underlined line below each attribute column name indicates how many display column spaces are allocated to display the attribute. These values are determined from the attribute size as defined in the CREATE TABLE command. The exception to this is numeric data that is always displayed in 10 column-wide fields. This can be changed with the UFI command SET NUMWIDTH N. This command affects the display of all numeric data. The command is in effect until it is changed or the user disconnects from the system. If you do not like the underscore character, you may change it via the UFI command SET UNDERLINE <character>.

E. The values in the attribute SALARY are not preceded by a dollar sign nor do they have embedded commas. This can be changed with the UFI formatting command COLUMN, which is discussed later in this chapter.

F. Alphabetic data and attribute headings are left justified and numeric data and headings are right justified.

G. The tuples are listed in the order in which they were inserted into the table. (You can't tell this from the output shown on the screen, but take our word for it.)

H. This example does not show it, but if our tables were to have more than 19 lines of output, ORACLE would automatically scroll the top lines of output off the screen. By doing this, you might miss some important data. By using the UFI command SET PAUSE ON, the system will freeze the screen after each set of 19 lines are displayed. One screen of output will remain on the screen until the terminal's ENTER/RETURN key is pressed. This continues until all the tuples have been displayed. SET PAUSE OFF turns this command off.

Remember that the asterisk displays all the attributes of the table in the order that they were defined in the CREATE TABLE command, which is the SQL command used to create a table definition—see Chapter 7, Creating Tables.

2. Change the size of the print width of the SALARY field and execute the query again.

```
UFI> SET NUMWIDTH 6
UFI> SELECT * FROM FACULTY;

FAC-ID FACULTY-NAME       DEPARTMENT GENDER SALARY
  J01  RAYMOND J. JOHNSON COMP SCI   MALE    40000
  S01  WENDY SWIMMER      COMP SCI   FEMALE  45000
  D01  AMY DANCER         COMP SCI   FEMALE  34500
  J01  BOB JONES          ACCOUNTING MALE    35000
  N01  JACK NELSON        HISTORY    MALE    28000
```

Unless explicitly changed by the SET NUMWIDTH command, we will assume that NUMWIDTH has been set to six for the remaining example queries in this section.

3. Change the spacing between columns to three and repeat the query.

```
UFI> SET SPACE 3
UFI> /

FAC-ID     FACULTY-NAME_____     DEPARTMENT     GENDER     SALARY
J01        RAYMOND J. JOHNSON       COMP SCI       MALE       40000
S01        WENDY SWIMMER            COMP SCI       FEMALE     45000
D01        AMY DANCER               COMP SCI       FEMALE     34500
J01        BOB JONES                ACCOUNTING     MALE       35000
N01        JACK NELSON              HISTORY        MALE       28000
```

4. Change the spacing between attribute columns back to one and display an asterisk in place of the underline character under the attribute headings.

```
UFI> SET SPACE 1
UFI> SET UNDERLINE *
UFI> /

FAC-ID FACULTY-NAME_____ DEPARTMENT GENDER SALARY
J01    RAYMOND J. JOHNSON COMP SCI   MALE   40000
S01    WENDY SWIMMER      COMP SCI   FEMALE 45000
D01    AMY DANCER         COMP SCI   FEMALE 34500
J01    BOB JONES          ACCOUNTING MALE   35000
N01    JACK NELSON        HISTORY    MALE   28000
```

5. Using the table-name.* item in the SELECT expression, list the STUDENT table.

```
UFI> SET UNDERLINE _
UFI> SELECT STUDENT.* FROM STUDENT;

STU-ID STUDENT-NAME_ ADDRESS_____ BIRTHDATE GENDER
S001   WENDY JONES   125 MAPLE AVE  25-OCT-65 FEMALE
S002   SAM WALES     3006 NAVAJO CL 10-JAN-60 MALE
S003   CATHY SMITH   1600 PENN AVE  22-FEB-22 FEMALE
S004   DOTTIE STACY  10 DOWNING ST  31-MAR-67 FEMALE
S005   JAY LANGER    GOLF COURSE RD 19-APR-65 MALE
S006   AMY LOPEZ     123 SUN RAY RD 10-MAY-64 FEMALE
S007   SAM WATSON    225 TEST DRIVE 09-JUN-63 MALE
S008   TAMMY REDD    113 MANCHESTER 01-JUL-60 FEMALE
S009   TOMMY WADKINS APPLE TREE DR  24-AUG-67 MALE
S010   BEN TREVINO   BOWLING ALLEY  30-SEP-66 MALE

10 records selected.
```

Notice that the attribute BIRTHDATE is displayed in a somewhat different format from what we have presented in the previous examples. The width of a date field is established at nine columns and the default date format is DD-MON-YY. This can be changed as we shall see in Chapter 10.

Further notice the message ''10 records selected'' below the resultant table output. This message is displayed whenever seven or more tuples (records) are placed in the resultant table. This message can be changed via the UFI command SET FEEDBACK NN, where NN represents the number of records that must be selected before the message is displayed. For example, if we wanted the message displayed when 12 or more tuples are retrieved, we would use the following feedback command.

```
UFI> SET FEEDBACK 12
```

The select expression STUDENT.* has the same effect as .*

6. List only the names and birthdates of the students. This command combines the relational algebra PROJECT with the relational algebra SELECT command.

```
UFI> SET FEEDBACK 12
UFI> SELECT STUDENT-NAME, BIRTHDATE FROM STUDENT;

STUDENT-NAME_____   BIRTHDATE
WENDY JONES          25-OCT-65
SAM WALES            10-JAN-60
CATHY SMITH          22-FEB-22
DOTTIE STACY         31-MAR-67
JAY LANGER           19-APR-65
AMY LOPEZ            10-MAY-64
SAM WATSON           09-JUN-63
TAMMY REDD           01-JUL-60
TOMMY WADKINS        24-AUG-67
BEN TREVINO          30-SEP-66
```

7. List the names and birthdays of the students. Number the tuples retrieved.

```
UFI> SELECT ROWNUM, STUDENT-NAME, BIRTHDATE FROM STUDENT;

ROWNUM STUDENT-NAME_____   BIRTHDATE
     1 WENDY JONES          25-OCT-65
     2 SAM WALES            10-JAN-60
     3 CATHY SMITH          22-FEB-22
     4 DOTTIE STACY         31-MAR-67
     5 JAY LANGER           19-APR-65
     6 AMY LOPEZ            10-MAY-64
     7 SAM WATSON           09-JUN-63
     8 TAMMY REDD           01-JUL-60
     9 TOMMY WADKINS        24-AUG-67
    10 BEN TREVINO          30-SEP-66
```

Remember that ROWNUM is a numeric virtual column and its value does not exist until the tuple is displayed.

8. What would the salary structure look like if we doubled each faculty member's salary?

```
UFI> SET NUMWIDTH 10
UFI> SELECT FACULTY-NAME, SALARY, SALARY*2 FROM FACULTY;

FACULTY-NAME_____ __SALARY SALARY*2
RAYMOND J. JOHNSON       40000    80000
WENDY SWIMMER            45000    90000
AMY DANCER               34500    69000
BOB JONES                35000    70000
JACK NELSON              28000    56000
```

Note that the computed column is given the heading of the algorithm that is used to compute the column. If the column is not wide enough to fit the heading, the heading is truncated. This query also illustrates that columns can be computed. This feature is further discussed in Chapter 11.

9. List the names of the courses being taught.

```
UFI> SELECT COURSE-TITLE FROM COURSE;

COURSE-TITLE_____
INTRODUCTION TO COMPUTING
INTRODUCTION TO COMPUTING
PASCAL PROGRAMMING
PASCAL PROGRAMMING
PRINCIPLES OF ACCOUNTING I
PRINCIPLES OF ACCOUNTING II
HISTORY OF PIROGUES
```

Notice that the courses Introduction to Computing and Pascal Programming are listed twice. This illustrates the fact that ORACLE does not automatically eliminate duplicate tuples. To eliminate duplicate tuples, we must utilize the DISTINCT clause of the SELECT command.

```
UFI> SELECT DISTINCT COURSE-TITLE FROM COURSE;

COURSE-TITLE_____
INTRODUCTION TO COMPUTING
PASCAL PROGRAMMING
PRINCIPLES OF ACCOUNTING I
PRINCIPLES OF ACCOUNTING II
HISTORY OF PIROGUES
```

THE WHERE CLAUSE

The WHERE clause with its associated theta condition is used to restrict the tuples that enter the resultant table. The SELECT command when used in conjunction with the WHERE clause is the ORACLE implementation of the relational algebra THETA SELECT command. The basic syntax of the WHERE clause is

```
WHERE θ1 [[AND | OR θ2] , , ,]
```

The syntax of theta consists of the following.

```
<value1> operator <value2>

or [NOT]n IN (value1, value2, , , ,)

or [NOT] BETWEEN value1 AND value2

or [NOT] LIKE string
```

For now we will restrict the values of <value1> and <value2> to any of the following:

1. An attribute
2. A numeric constant
3. A string constant
4. A data constant
5. An arithmetic expression
6. A value generated by ORACLE (example: ROWNUM)

The value of string in the LIKE clause is naturally any character string.
The acceptable values for the operators that we will cover in this chapter are:

=	Equal to.
!=	Not equal to.
>	Greater than.
<	Less than.
>=	Greater than or equal to.
<=	Less than or equal to
[NOT] IN	Multiple OR conditions.
[NOT] LIKE	String matching.
[NOT] BETWEEN	Range matching.

In addition to these operators, the standard Boolean operators of AND, OR, and NOT are available. None of these three operators have any precedence. If precedence is needed, parentheses must be utilized.

EXAMPLES OF SIMPLE THETAS

Since SQL is almost readable English, the WHERE clauses need very little explanation. We will only furnish explanations where we feel that they are needed with the following examples.

1. List all the attributes of all of the female students.

```
UFI> SELECT * FROM STUDENT WHERE GENDER = 'FEMALE';

STU-ID STUDENT-NAME___  ADDRESS_____  BIRTHDATE GENDER
S001   WENDY JONES      125 MAPLE AVE   25-OCT-65 FEMALE
S003   CATHY SMITH      1600 PENN AVE   22-FEB-22 FEMALE
S004   DOTTIE STACY     10 DOWNING ST   31-MAR-67 FEMALE
S006   AMY LOPEZ        123 SUN RAY RD  10-MAY-64 FEMALE
S008   TAMMY REDD       113 MANCHESTER  01-JUL-60 FEMALE
```

Note that the string constant FEMALE was enclosed in single quotes ('). It could have optionally been enclosed in double quotes ('').

2. List all the data on faculty members who earn more than $35,000.

```
UFI> SET NUMWIDTH 6
UFI> SELECT * FROM FACULTY WHERE SALARY > 35000;

FAC-ID FACULTY-NAME_____  DEPARTMENT GENDER SALARY
J01    RAYMOND J. JOHNSON  COMP SCI   MALE    40000
S01    WENDY SWIMMER       COMP SCI   FEMALE  45000
```

3. List the names of the faculty members who earn more than $35,000.

```
UFI> SELECT FACULTY-NAME FROM FACULTY WHERE SALARY > 35000;

FACULTY-NAME_____
RAYMOND J. JOHNSON
WENDY SWIMMER
```

4. List all the data on faculty members who earn more than $35,000 and are females.

```
UFI> SELECT * FROM FACULTY WHERE SALARY > 35000
   2 AND GENDER = 'FEMALE';
```

```
FAC-ID FACULTY-NAME___ DEPARTMENT GENDER SALARY
S01    WENDY SWIMMER   COMP SCI   FEMALE 45000
```

5. List all the attributes of the faculty members who are not in the Computer Science department.

```
UFI> SELECT * FROM FACULTY WHERE DEPARTMENT != 'COMP SCI';

FAC-ID FACULTY-NAME___ DEPARTMENT GENDER SALARY
J01    BOB JONES       ACCOUNTING MALE   35000
N01    JACK NELSON     HISTORY    MALE   28000
```

6. List the names and salaries of the first three faculty members found in the FACULTY table.

```
UFI> SELECT FACULTY-NAME, SALARY
  2  FROM FACULTY
  3  WHERE ROWNUM <= 3;

FACULTY-NAME_____ SALARY
RAYMOND J. JOHNSON 40000
WENDY SWIMMER      45000
AMY DANCER         34500
```

7. List all the attributes of the first three female students.

```
UFI> SELECT *
  2  FROM STUDENT
  3  WHERE GENDER = 'FEMALE' AND ROWNUM <= 3;

STU-ID STUDENT-NAME_____ ADDRESS_____ BIRTHDATE GENDER
S001   WENDY JONES       125 MAPLE AVE    25-OCT-65 FEMALE
S003   CATHY SMITH       1600 PENN AVE    22-FEB-22 FEMALE
S004   DOTTIE STACY      10 DOWNING ST    31-MAR-67 FEMALE
```

TESTING MULTIPLE OR CONDITIONS

Sometimes it becomes necessary to test multiple conditions with the Boolean operator OR. For example, we might want a list of faculty members who are either in the Accounting or the History departments. This could be accomplished with the following SELECT command.

```
UFI> SELECT * FROM FACULTY
  2  WHERE DEPARTMENT = 'ACCOUNTING'
  3     OR DEPARTMENT = 'HISTORY';
```

```
FAC-ID FACULTY-NAME_ DEPARTMENT GENDER SALARY
J01    BOB JONES     ACCOUNTING MALE   35000
N01    JACK NELSON   HISTORY    MALE   28000
```

Specifying multiple OR conditions becomes tedious when there are many conditions to test. An alternative to specifying multiple OR conditions explicitly is to use the IN or NOT IN operator. The format of the IN operator is:

```
attribute [NOT] in (attribute-list)
```

This query could have been specified much more easily as follows.

```
UFI> SELECT * FROM FACULTY
   2 WHERE DEPARTMENT IN ('ACCOUNTING', 'HISTORY');
```

By inserting the word NOT before IN, we could have retrieved all the tuples where the department was not equal to Accounting or History.

```
UFI> SELECT * FROM FACULTY
   2 WHERE DEPARTMENT NOT IN ('ACCOUNTING', 'HISTORY');
```

```
FAC-ID FACULTY-NAME_____ DEPARTMENT GENDER SALARY
J01    RAYMOND J. JOHNSON COMP SCI   MALE   40000
S01    WENDY SWIMMER      COMP SCI   FEMALE 45000
D01    AMY DANCER         COMP SCI   FEMALE 34500
```

RANGE RETRIEVAL

Suppose we would like to retrieve the tuples for all the faculty members who earn between $30,000 and $40,000. Normally this query could be solved as follows.

```
UFI> SELECT * FROM FACULTY
   2 WHERE SALARY => 30000 AND SALARY <= 40000;
```

```
FAC-ID FACULTY-NAME_____ DEPARTMENT GENDER SALARY
J01    RAYMOND J. JOHNSON COMP SCI   MALE   40000
D01    AMY DANCER         COMP SCI   FEMALE 34500
J02    BOB JONES          ACCOUNTING MALE   35000
```

Again SQL provides an easy method of specifying a range of values with the BETWEEN operator. The syntax of the BETWEEN operator is:

```
[NOT] BETWEEN lower-value AND higher-value
```

Our range query could have been solved very readily as follows.

```
UFI> SELECT * FROM FACULTY
  2  WHERE SALARY BETWEEN 30000 AND 40000;
```

FAC-ID	FACULTY-NAME	DEPARTMENT	GENDER	SALARY
J01	RAYMOND J. JOHNSON	COMP SCI	MALE	40000
D01	AMY DANCER	COMP SCI	FEMALE	34500
J02	BOB JONES	ACCOUNTING	MALE	35000

If we had wanted all the faculty members who do not earn between $30,000 and $40,000, that is, less than $30,000 or greater than $40,000, we could have used the NOT BETWEEN operator.

```
UFI> SELECT * FROM FACULTY
  2  WHERE SALARY NOT BETWEEN 30000 AND 40000;
```

FAC-ID	FACULTY-NAME	DEPARTMENT	GENDER	SALARY
S01	WENDY SWIMMER	COMP SCI	FEMALE	45000
N01	JACK NELSON	HISTORY	MALE	28000

STRING SEARCHES

For attributes with the data type of character, it becomes necessary to perform string searches. String searches fall into two categories: full-string searches and substring searches.

Full-String Searches

Full-string searches constitute searching the entire attribute field. For example, if an attribute called STUDENT-NAME were defined as a character field 20 positions long, and we wanted to search it for the string "AL WILSON", we could use the expression

```
WHERE STUDENT-NAME = 'AL WILSON'
```

Even though there are only 9 characters in the string, ORACLE understands that what we really mean is that we are testing for is the first 9 characters of the string, it assumes that the remaining 11 characters are blank.

When performing string searches, we are not restricted to utilizing only the equals operator. Here are some examples of string searches utilizing other operators.

```
STUDENT-NAME > 'M' True for all tuples with STUDENT-NAME greater
               than 'M----------------' and less than or equal
               to 'ZZZZZZZZZZZZZZZZZZZZ'. The dash symbol (-)
               represents a blank character.

STUDENT-NAME = 'CONNIE JONES' True for all tuples where the value of
               STUDENT-NAME is not equal to 'CONNIE JONES'.

STUDENT-NAME BETWEEN 'A' AND 'B' True for all tuples where
               STUDENT-NAME begins with the letter 'A'.

STUDENT-NAME NOT BETWEEN 'A' AND 'B' True for all tuples where
               STUDENT-NAME does not begin with the letter 'A'.

STUDENT-NAME IN ('BEN NELSON', 'JANE ADDAMS', 'JANET WILSON',
               'SUSAN JOHNSON', 'JOAN SMITH') - True for all tuples
               where STUDENT-NAME is equal to any of the five
               names listed. Notice that the strings do not have
               to be the same length.
```

One final note concerning full-string searches: string searches are always case sensitive. This means that not only must the string match character for character, but it also must match character for character in the same case. For example, the following expression would generate a FALSE.

```
'Janet Martin' = 'JANET MARTIN'
```

There is a method of changing cases of character strings via the UPPER and LOWER functions. These functions are discussed in Chapter 11.

Substring Searches

Substrings, as the name implies, are subparts of strings. For example, we might want to find all the students whose first name is 'MIKE'. We could do this with some ingenuity by using the BETWEEN operator in the WHERE clause.

```
WHERE STUDENT-NAME BETWEEN 'MIKEAAAAAAAAAAAAAAAA'
                   AND 'MIKEZZZZZZZZZZZZZZZZ'
```

The LIKE operator with the percent wild card.   The preceeding predicate would only search for the substring MIKE' in the first four positions. Suppose we wanted to search for the substring 'MIKE' anywhere in the string. Fortunately ORACLE has provided us with a substring search operator. This operator is called LIKE. To illustrate the LIKE operator, let's use it to solve our substring problem.

```
WHERE STUDENT-NAME LIKE 'MIKE%'
```

Notice that we did not use an equals operator (=); we used the LIKE operator in place of it. The LIKE operator can only be used when searching character strings. Further notice the percent sign (%) in the string. The percent sign is called a wild card, and it means that it does not matter what the remainder of the string contains once we have found the characters 'MIKE' in the first four characters. This still does not solve our problem of finding the substring 'MIKE' within the string STUDENT-NAME. To accomplish this, we would simply add a percent sign in front of the substring 'MIKE' as follows.

```
WHERE STUDENT-NAME LIKE '%MIKE%'
```

Suppose that we now want STUDENT-NAMEs that do not contain the string 'MIKE'. We could accomplish this very easily by inserting the word NOT in front of LIKE.

```
WHERE STUDENT-NAME NOT LIKE '%MIKE%'
```

We are not restricted to just one substring within our LIKE command. Suppose that we wanted to retrieve all the tuples where the STUDENT-NAME is 'MIKE JONES'. If we specify our predicate as

```
WHERE STUDENT-NAME = 'MIKE JONES'
```

or

```
WHERE STUDENT-NAME LIKE '%MIKE JONES%'
```

we would not retrieve such names as 'MIKE A. JONES' or 'MIKE B. JONES' or 'MIKE FRED JONES'. To accomplish this, we must specify two different substrings within the LIKE command as follows.

```
WHERE STUDENT-NAME LIKE '%MIKE%JONES%'
```

Note that we have three wild cards in the string. This substring translates into the following:

```
Find  the  STUDENT-NAMEs  that contain the  substring  'MIKE'
followed by the substring 'JONES'. It doesn't make any
difference how many characters are in between the two
substrings.
```

The LIKE operator with the underline wild card.   The LIKE operator has another wild card that allows the user to search for characters in a particular position in a string. This wild card is the underline character (—). To illustrate, suppose that we wanted to develop a predicate that retrieved tuples where the third letter of the student's name was a ''k.'' We could utilize the underline wild card to specify this:

```
WHERE STUDENT-NAME LIKE '__K_____'
```

We could have specified this predicate a bit more easily by utilizing a combination of the two wild cards:

```
WHERE STUDENT-NAME LIKE '__K%'
```

The underlined wild card acts as a place holder in that it allows any character to be in that position, but it allows the user to specify that a substring be in a particular position of the string to be searched.

SORTING OUTPUT

Normally, the tuples in the resultant table are presented in the order that they were inserted in the table. The resultant tuple forms a ''stack'' data structure in that the first tuple entered in the table searched is the first one displayed, assuming that it meets the search criteria.

If we want the order of the tuples selected for the resultant table rearranged, we can use the ORDER BY clause. This clause does not permanently rearrange the tuples in the data files, it only temporarily rearranges them in the resultant table.

The format of the ORDER BY clause is

```
ORDER BY attribute-name1 | expression1 [DESC]
     [,attribute-name2 | expression2 [DESC]] [,. . .]
```

The ORDER BY clause is always used in conjunction with the SELECT command. The default order of the sort is ASCENDING (the smallest value is listed first). Any null values are always listed first regardless of the direction of the sort.

Let's look again at some of the SELECT commands that we illustrated at the beginning of the chapter and affix the ORDER BY clause to them.

1. Display all the data on faculty in ascending order by salary.

```
UFI> SET NUMWIDTH 6
UFI> SELECT * FROM FACULTY ORDER BY SALARY;

FAC-ID FACULTY-NAME_____ DEPARTMENT GENDER SALARY
  N01    JACK NELSON            HISTORY    MALE    28000
  D01    AMY DANCER             COMP SCI   FEMALE  34500
  J02    BOB JONES              ACCOUNTING MALE    35000
  J01    RAYMOND J. JOHNSON     COMP SCI   MALE    40000
  S01    WENDY SWIMMER          COMP SCI   FEMALE  45000
```

2. Display all the data on faculty in descending order by salary.

```
UFI> SELECT * FROM FACULTY ORDER BY SALARY DESC;

FAC-ID  FACULTY-NAME            DEPARTMENT GENDER  SALARY
S01     WENDY SWIMMER           COMP SCI   FEMALE  45000
J01     RAYMOND J. JOHNSON      COMP SCI   MALE    40000
J02     BOB JONES               ACCOUNTING MALE    35000
D01     AMY DANCER              COMP SCI   FEMALE  34500
N01     JACK NELSON             HISTORY    MALE    28000
```

3. List the faculty members who earn between $30,000 and $40,000. List the females before the males.

```
UFI> SELECT * FROM FACULTY
  2  WHERE SALARY BETWEEN 30000 AND 40000
  3  ORDER BY GENDER;

FAC-ID  FACULTY-NAME         DEPARTMENT GENDER  SALARY
D01     AMY DANCER           COMP SCI   FEMALE  34500
J02     BOB JONES            ACCOUNTING MALE    35000
J01     RAYMOND J. JOHNSON   COMP SCI   MALE    40000
```

We are not restricted to sorting on one sort key (attribute). If we specify more than one sort key, the first one specified becomes that major sort key (the first field sorted on), the second one specified becomes the second sort key, and so on. Each sort key may specify the word DESC to sort only that set of values in descending order. In the following example we want to list all the data on the faculty members sorted by gender and salary.

```
UFI> SELECT * FROM FACULTY ORDER BY GENDER, SALARY;

FAC-ID  FACULTY-NAME            DEPARTMENT GENDER  SALARY
S01     WENDY SWIMMER           COMP SCI   FEMALE  45000
D01     AMY DANCER              COMP SCI   FEMALE  34500
J01     RAYMOND J. JOHNSON      COMP SCI   MALE    40000
J02     BOB JONES               ACCOUNTING MALE    35000
N01     JACK NELSON             HISTORY    MALE    28000
```

Notice that SQL sorts the females before the males (ascending order). Then if there is a tie between the value of gender in two or more tuples (two or more tuples have the same value of gender), SQL breaks the tie with the value of salary.

If we wanted the same query except that we wanted the males listed before the females, but the salaries still in ascending order, we would have to make one minor change in the query. We would insert the word DESC after GENDER to denote descending order.

```
UFI> SELECT * FROM FACULTY ORDER BY GENDER DESC, SALARY;

FAC-ID FACULTY-NAME_____ DEPARTMENT GENDER SALARY
N01    JACK NELSON        HISTORY    MALE   28000
J02    BOB JONES          ACCOUNTING MALE   35000
J01    RAYMOND J. JOHNSON COMP SCI   MALE   40000
D01    AMY DANCER         COMP SCI   FEMALE 34500
S01    WENDY SWIMMER      COMP SCI   FEMALE 45000
```

Any data type, except LONG, can be sorted. (We will discuss the specific data types available in ORACLE SQL in Chapter 7, Creating Tables.) Here is an example of sorting DATE data.

```
UFI> SELECT STUDENT-NAME, BIRTHDATE FROM STUDENT
   2 ORDER BY BIRTHDATE;

STUDENT-NAME_____ BIRTHDATE
CATHY SMITH        22-FEB-22
SAM WALES          10-JAN-60
TAMMY REDD         01-JUL-60
SAM WATSON         09-JUN-63
AMY LOPEZ          10-MAY-64
JAY LANGER         19-APR-65
WENDY JONES        25-OCT-65
BEN TREVINO        30-SEP-66
DOTTIE STACY       31-MAR-67
TOMMY WADKINS      24-AUG-67

10 records selected
```

This query lists the students in chronological order by birthdate. The sort key can even be a computed expression.

```
UFI> SET NUMWIDTH 10
UFI> SELECT FACULTY-NAME, SALARY, SALARY*2 FROM FACULTY
   2 ORDER BY SALARY*2;

FACULTY-NAME_____ ____SALARY __SALARY*2
BOB JONES              28000     56000
AMY DANCER             34500     69000
JACK NELSON            35000     70000
RAYMOND J. JOHNSON     40000     80000
WENDY SWIMMER          45000     90000
```

If the virtual attribute ROWNUM is used, ROWNUM is generated from the original order of the tuples. Remember, ROWNUM is a virtual attribute and is generated when the resultant table is created. Therefore, it is generated before the resultant table is sorted. If we display the ROWNUM from a sorted table, the virtual attribute ROWNUM is displayed in its original order.

```
UFI> SELECT ROWNUM, FACULTY-NAME, SALARY, SALARY*2
   2 FROM FACULTY
   3 ORDER BY SALARY*2;

ROWNUM FACULTY-NAME            SALARY  SALARY*2
     5 JACK NELSON              28000     56000
     3 AMY DANCER               34500     69000
     4 BOB JONES                35000     70000
     1 RAYMOND J. JOHNSON       40000     80000
     2 WENDY SWIMMER            45000     90000
```

Note that ROWNUM gives us the original position (row number) in the unsorted resultant table. This means that we cannot use the ROWNUM attribute to retrieve the top n or bottom n sorted tuples (example: What are the names of the faculty members who earn the top/bottom three salaries?) from the table. This type query is handled utilizing subqueries, which are described in Chapter 10.

FORMATTING OUTPUT

Once you have become proficient with the SELECT command, you may not be completely satisfied with the manner in which ORACLE displays the data. At this point in the text, the only formatting commands that we have discussed are the SET NUMWIDTH N, which sets the default width for display of all numeric data, and SET SPACE N which sets the number of columns between attributes in the resultant table. The display format of the data can be modified to produce your output in a more pleasing manner. With ORACLE's formatting capabilities, you can do such things as

1. Change the attribute headings.
2. Change the format of the displayed data.
3. Specify a value to be displayed for null values.
4. Change the width of an output line.

Removing All Attribute Headings

If you want to display the values selected without headings, you must use the UFI command SET HEADING OFF.

```
UFI> SET HEADING OFF
UFI> SELECT FACULTY-NAME
  2  FROM FACULTY;
```

```
RAYMOND J. JOHNSON
WENDY SWIMMER
AMY DANCER
BOB JONES
JACK NELSON
```

This is particularly useful when you want to create a file via the SPOOL command that can be used as an external data file for a program written in a conventional language.

To turn the attribute headings back on, execute the SET HEADING ON command.

Changing the Attribute Headings

There are two methods of changing attribute headings. The first is directly within the SELECT, command and the second is through the COLUMN command. We will discuss the first method here and the second method in the following section.

We can temporarily change the attribute heading of any attribute by leaving one blank space after the attribute name in the SELECT list and then specifying the new attribute heading. For example, if we wanted to change the attribute heading for FACULTY-NAME to "NAME-OF-FACULTY," we could do it as follows.

```
UFI> SELECT FACULTY-NAME NAME-OF-FACULTY
  2  FROM FACULTY;
```

```
NAME-OF-FACULTY___
RAYMOND J. JOHNSON
WENDY SWIMMER
AMY DANCER
BOB JONES
BEN NELSON
```

If we wanted to rid the heading of the underline symbols so that the heading were NAME OF FACULTY, we would enclose the new attribute heading in double ('') quotes.

```
UFI> SELECT FACULTY-NAME "NAME OF FACULTY"
  2  FROM FACULTY;
```

```
NAME OF FACULTY___
RAYMOND J. JOHNSON
WENDY SWIMMER
AMY DANCER
BOB JONES
BEN NELSON
```

The reason that quotes must surround a new heading with embedded blanks is that a blank is a delimiter (signaling the end of new attribute header). If the quotes did not surround the string of characters, ORACLE would take NAME as the new attribute heading and expect a comma between NAME and OF. When it does not find one, it generates an error as follows:

```
UFI> SELECT FACULTY-NAME NAME OF FACULTY
   2 FROM FACULTY;

SELECT FACULTY-NAME NAME OF FACULTY
                                  *
ERROR at line 1:   923    missing FROM keyword
```

If we wished to get a "stacked" attribute heading, we could place vertical bars (|) where we wanted the end of a line to be.

```
UFI> SELECT FACULTY-NAME "NAME|OF|FACULTY"
   2 FROM FACULTY;

NAME
OF
FACULTY_____
RAYMOND J. JOHNSON
WENDY SWIMMER
AMY DANCER
BOB JONES
BEN NELSON
```

This method of altering attribute titles is particularly useful when we compute the value of attributes.

```
UFI> SET NUMWIDTH 10
UFI> SELECT FACULTY-NAME, SALARY, SALARY*2 "DOUBLE|SALARY"
   2  FROM FACULTY;

                                        DOUBLE
FACULTY-NAME_____  ____SALARY  ____SALARY
RAYMOND J. JOHNSON        40000       80000
WENDY SWIMMER            45000       90000
AMY DANCER              34500       69000
BOB JONES              35000       70000
JACK NELSON            28000       56000
```

One important point to remember concerning altering attribute headings is that if the new heading is longer than the number of columns allocated to display the attribute, the field width is expanded to accomodate the new head.

```
UFI> SET NUMWIDTH 10
UFI> SELECT FACULTY-NAME, SALARY, SALARY*2 "DOUBLE|SALARY"
   2 FROM FACULTY;

                                         DOUBLE
FACULTY-NAME_____ ____SALARY ____SALARY
RAYMOND J. JOHNSON        40000        80000
WENDY SWIMMER            45000        90000
AMY DANCER              34500        69000
BOB JONES               35000        70000
JACK NELSON             28000        56000
```

If we use the SELECT command to change attribute headings, the change is only in effect for that one execution of the SELECT command. If we want formatting commands to carry over to subsequent SELECTs, we must consider using the COLUMN command.

The COLUMN Command

The UFI command COLUMN can be used for many different formatting functions. It can be used to specify new attribute headings, change the display format of attribute values, and specify values to display if an attribute has a null value.

The COLUMN command(s) remain in effect until the user changes the values or until the user disconnects from the system. This means that the next time that you connect to ORACLE, you must reset your COLUMN settings. It is very useful to use your system's text editor to construct a "start file" that contains all the COLUMN commands that are needed to format the attributes in your database. Once this is done, it becomes very easy simply to start your format file instead of typing in several COLUMN commands every time that you connect to ORACLE.

The format of the UFI command COLUMN is as follows.

```
COL[UMN] [ ? | <attribute> [<option> . . .] ]
```

The values of <attribute> can be an attribute name, an attribute heading, an expression, or a constant.

The values of <option> can be any of the following:

1. ?
2. ALI[AS] <string>
3. CLE[AR]
4. DEF[AULT]
5. FOLD_B[EFORE] [0 1]
6. FOR[MAT] <mask>
7. HEA[DING] <string>
8. HEADS[EP] <character>

9. JUS[TIFY] [L[EFT]   R[IGHT]   C[ENTER]]

10. LIKE <attribute>

11. NEWL[INE]

12. NOPRI[NT]

13. PRI[NT]

14. NUL[L] <string>

15. OFF

16. ON

17. TEMP[ORARY]

18. TRU[NCATED]

19. WRA[PPED]

Notice that most of these options can be shortened. However, in the interest of readability, we will always use the long version of the option name. If you want to see what the abbreviated version of each command is, enter COLUMN ?. Not all of these options will be discussed in this chapter. Those that are not are discussed later on, throughout the text.

Specifying attribute headings   The COLUMN command is a much more powerful method of specifying attribute headings than specifying a heading as a part of the SELECT command. Examples of the COLUMN command to set new headings are:

```
UFI> COLUMN FACULTY-NAME HEADING NAME-OF-FACULTY
UFI> SELECT FACULTY-NAME
   2  FROM FACULTY;

NAME-OF-FACULTY_____
RAYMOND J. JOHNSON
WENDY SWIMMER
AMY DANCER
BOB JONES
JACK NELSON

UFI> REMARK . . ... Remove the underlines
UFI> COLUMN FACULTY-NAME HEADING 'NAME OF FACULTY'
UFI> /

NAME OF FACULTY_____
RAYMOND J. JOHNSON
WENDY SWIMMER
AMY DANCER
BOB JONES
JACK NELSON
```

```
UFI> REMARK . . ... Stack the attribute heading
UFI> COLUMN FACULTY-NAME HEADING 'NAME|OF|FACULTY'
UFI> /

NAME
OF
FACULTY_____
RAYMOND J. JOHNSON
WENDY SWIMMER
AMY DANCER
BOB JONES
JACK NELSON
```

Unlike altering the heading via the SELECT command the COLUMN command allows either single quotes (') or double quotes ('') to define headings containing spaces. Notice that in the last example, the vertical bar (|) was used as the heading separator. If you wish to change this, you may use the UFI command SET HEADSEP <character> to change the heading separator character.

```
UFI> SET HEADSEP $
UFI> COLUMN FACULTY-NAME HEADING 'NAME$OF$FACULTY'
UFI> /

NAME
OF
FACULTY_____
RAYMOND J. JOHNSON
WENDY SWIMMER
AMY DANCER
BOB JONES
JACK NELSON
```

Headings for character attributes are always left justified and headings for numeric data are always right justified. If we wish to change this, we would use the JUSTIFIED option of the COLUMN command. The three acceptable values for the JUSTIFIED option are LEFT, RIGHT, and CENTER.

```
UFI> REMARK Let's set the heading separator back to |
UFI> SET HEADSEP
UFI> COLUMN FACULTY-NAME HEADING 'NAME|OF|FACULTY' JUSTIFY RIGHT
UFI> /

NAME
OF
FACULTY_____
RAYMOND J. JOHNSON
WENDY SWIMMER
AMY DANCER
BOB JONES
JACK NELSON
```

Notice that the data is not JUSTIFIED RIGHT, only the heading is moved. Let's now center the heading. Notice that we only have to specify the justification and not the entire heading again.

```
UFI> COLUMN FACULTY-NAME JUSTIFY CENTER
UFI> /

NAME
OF
FACULTY_____
RAYMOND J. JOHNSON
WENDY SWIMMER
AMY DANCER
BOB JONES
JACK NELSON
```

If after you look at the output from a particular attribute and decide that you do not like it and want to return to the default values, you may simply use the DEFAULT option of the COLUMN command.

```
UFI> COLUMN FACULTY-NAME DEFAULT
UFI> /

FACULTY-NAME_____
RAYMOND J. JOHNSON
WENDY SWIMMER
AMY DANCER
BOB JONES
JACK NELSON
```

A similar option to DEFAULT exists. This option is called CLEAR. CLEAR also resets the formatting and heading values to the default values. In addition, it removes the attribute from the set of attribute values for which the COLUMN command has been utilized. It removes all evidence that a COLUMN command was ever used for the attribute. The format for the CLEAR option is:

```
COLUMN attribute CLEAR
```

Formatting attribute values.   Now that we have discussed the various options for the attribute headers, let's explore formatting of the actual values of the attributes. To format attribute values we must use the FORMAT option of the COLUMN command. The format of this option is:

```
COLUMN [attribute name|attribute heading|expression] FORMAT <mask>
```

The value of the format mask can be any of the following values or combination of values.

9   The numeral represents a single digit much in the manner of COBOL formatting with the PICTURE clause.

0   A zero is printed in this position.

A   The capital letter A represents a single character of data.

B   Blanks are displayed if this numeric field contains a zero.

.   A decimal point is displayed in this position.

,   A comma is displayed in this position.

$ A floating dollar sign is displayed before the left-most nonzero digit of a numeric field.

V   The decimal point is suppressed when displaying non integer numbers.

MI   A minus sign is displayed to the right of negative numbers.

PR   Brackets (<>) are placed around negative numbers.

The various format masks are illustrated in Table 6.1.

The number specified after the "A" in the character format mask is called a repeat factor. Notice that a repeat factor can be used with the "A" format mask but not with the "9" mask.

By using the FORMAT option of the COLUMN command, we can now format the SALARY attribute of the FACULTY table.

TABLE 6.1   EXAMPLES OF FORMAT MASKS

Format Mask	Raw Data Value	Displayed Value	
9999	1234	1234	
9999	123	123	
9,999	1234	1,234	
9,999	123	123	
999.99	123.45	123.45	
999.99	123	123.00	
999V99	123.45	12345	
999.00	123.45	123.00	
B9,999.99	1234.56	1,234.56	
B9,999.99	0		
9999	12345	####	
9999	-123	-123	
9999	-1234	####	
9999MI	-1234	1234-	
9999PR	-1234	<1234>	
$9,999.99	1234.56	$1,234.56	
AAAAA	ABCDE	ABCDE	
A5	ABCDE	ABCDE	
A3	ABCDE	ABC	
		DE	*Excess is wrapped+
a3	ABCDE	ABC	
		DE	
A4	ABC	ABC-	[- = a blank]

```
UFI> COLUMN SALARY FORMAT $999,999.99
UFI> SELECT * FROM FACULTY;

FAC-ID  FACULTY-NAME_____  DEPARTMENT  GENDER  ____SALARY
J01     RAYMOND J. JOHNSON  COMP SCI    MALE      $40,000
S01     WENDY SWIMMER       COMP SCI    FEMALE    $45,000
D01     AMY DANCER          COMP SCI    FEMALE    $34,500
J02     BOB JONES           ACCOUNTING  MALE      $35,000
N01     JACK NELSON         HISTORY     MALE      $28,000
```

Formatting strings.   The "A" format mask is used to format character strings. Suppose that the string is too long to fit on your screen or your printer page. What happens to the excess characters? This is handled by the WRAP or TRUNC option used for formatting strings. WRAP tells ORACLE to display all the text that it can using the default format. If ORACLE can't fit the entire text string on one output line, the data is wrapped around to a second and third line until all the text is displayed. TRUNC tells ORACLE to truncate the text after the first line of output.

Let's use FACULTY-NAME to illustrate TRUNC and WRAP.

```
UFI> SELECT FACULTY-NAME FROM FACULTY;

FACULTY-NAME_____
RAYMOND J. JOHNSON
WENDY SWIMMER
AMY DANCER
BOB JONES
JACK NELSON
```

We can tell from the dashes displayed below the attribute heading that there were 16 spaces allocated for the attribute FACULTY-NAME when the table was created. Now let's reformat FACULTY-NAME to 10 characters.

```
UFI> COLUMN FACULTY-NAME FORMAT A10
UFI> /

FACULTY-NA

RAYMOND J.
JOHNSON

WENDY SWIM
MER

AMY DANCER
BOB JONES
JACK NELSO
N
```

Note that the names in the table that are 10 characters or less, are displayed on one output line.

```
UFI>  REMARK What happens if we use TRUNC?
UFI>  COLUMN FACULTY-NAME TRUNC
UFI>  /


FACULTY-NA
RAYMOND J.
WENDY SWIM
AMY DANCER
BOB JONES
JACK NELSO
```

Why did we not have to set the first example to WRAP? Because WRAP is the default setting. We would only have to use WRAP if we changed the default setting from WRAP to TRUNC and we wanted to change the setting back to its original value.

Formatting computed expressions.   Formatting computed expressions is no different from formatting any other numeric value. The only problem is that since the expression forms a virtual attribute and it does not have an attribute name, how do we refer to it? We have several options. Let's use our "double salary" example to illustrate these options.

```
UFI>  SELECT FACULTY-NAME, SALARY, SALARY * 2
   2  FROM FACULTY;


FACULTY-NAME_____ ____SALARY __SALARY*2
RAYMOND J. JOHNSON      40000     80000
WENDY SWIMMER          45000     90000
AMY DANCER             34500     69000
BOB JONES              35000     70000
JACK NELSON            28000     56000
```

The first method of referring to the expression is to use an attribute heading in the SELECT command. We could then use the attribute heading to refer to the expression.

```
UFI>  SELECT FACULTY-NAME, SALARY, SALARY * 2   DOUBLE
   2  FROM FACULTY;

FACULTY-NAME_____ ____SALARY ____DOUBLE
RAYMOND J. JOHNSON      40000     80000
WENDY SWIMMER          45000     90000
AMY DANCER             34500     69000
BOB JONES              35000     70000
JACK NELSON            28000     56000
```

```
UFI> COLUMN DOUBLE FORMAT $99,999 HEADING `DOUBLE|SALARY'

UFI> SELECT FACULTY-NAME, SALARY, SALARY * 2 DOUBLE
   2 FROM FACULTY;


                                         DOUBLE
FACULTY-NAME_____ ____SALARY ____SALARY
RAYMOND J. JOHNSON    40000    $80,000
WENDY SWIMMER         45000    $90,000
AMY DANCER           34500    $69,000
BOB JONES            35000    $70,000
JACK NELSON          28000    $56,000
```

Notice that we executed the COLUMN command before the SELECT command. In the COLUMN command we referred to the attribute name DOUBLE that did not exist at the time. Further, notice that we used DOUBLE only as a reference point, for we changed the attribute heading.

A second method of referring to an expression is simply to place the expression in the COLUMN command.

```
UFI> COLUMN SALARY*2 FORMAT $99,999 HEADING `DOUBLE|SALARY'
```

When we specify the expression directly, notice that blanks are not allowed in the expression. Again the reason is that blanks are delimiters.

The third method is to use the COLUMN command to declare an alias for the expression, then use the alias to format the expression.

```
UFI> COLUMN SALARY*2 ALIAS DOUBLE
UFI> COLUMN DOUBLE FORMAT $99,999 HEADING `DOUBLE|SALARY'
```

Formatting null values. Null values ordinarily display as all blanks. To illustrate this, let's assume that one of our faculty members, Amy Dancer, has just joined the staff at our university and her pay rate has not been officially approved yet. When we entered Miss Dancer's tuple we entered a value of Null for SALARY. (Insertion of tuples is covered in Chapter 8.) This value will be updated when her pay rate becomes officially approved. If we listed out all of our faculty, notice that Amy Dancer's salary appears as a blank.

```
UFI> SELECT * FROM FACULTY;

FAC-ID FACULTY-NAME_____ DEPARTMENT GENDER SALARY
J01    RAYMOND J. JOHNSON COMP SCI   MALE   40000
S01    WENDY SWIMMER      COMP SCI   FEMALE 45000
D01    AMY DANCER         COMP SCI   FEMALE
J02    BOB JONES          ACCOUNTING MALE   35000
N01    JACK NELSON        HISTORY    MALE   28000
```

This can be changed by using the UFI command SET NULL <string>. For example, if we wanted to display the string "N/A" for NULL we would do the following.

```
UFI> SET NULL N/A
UFI> /

FAC-ID FACULTY-NAME_____ DEPARTMENT GENDER SALARY
 J01    RAYMOND J. JOHNSON COMP SCI   MALE    40000
 S01    WENDY SWIMMER      COMP SCI   FEMALE  45000
 D01    AMY DANCER         COMP SCI   FEMALE    N/A
 J02    BOB JONES          ACCOUNTING MALE    35000
 N01    JACK NELSON        HISTORY    MALE    28000
```

Unfortunately, this value is displayed for all values of null that are displayed in any attribute in any table. We might want to personalize the value of null in the SALARY attribute.

```
UFI> COLUMN SALARY NULL 'Not Approved' FORMAT $999,999,999
UFI> SELECT * FROM FACULTY;

FAC-ID FACULTY-NAME_____ DEPARTMENT GENDER _____SALARY
 J01    RAYMOND J. JOHNSON COMP SCI   MALE       $40,000
 S01    WENDY SWIMMER      COMP SCI   FEMALE     $45,000
 D01    AMY DANCER         COMP SCI   FEMALE Not Approved
 J02    BOB JONES          ACCOUNTING MALE       $35,000
 N01    JACK NELSON        HISTORY    MALE       $28,000
```

Note that the field size for SALARY had to be increased to fit the null message. If the attribute field size had not been increased, the text message would have been wrapped or truncated depending upon which option was in effect at the time.

Miscellaneous formatting commands.   All COLUMN commands remain in effect until the user changes them or disconnects from the system. It is sometimes useful temporarily to use certain headings and format masks. This can be accomplished by adding the word TEMPORARY to the COLUMN command.

```
COLUMN SALARY FORMAT $99,999 TEMPORARY
```

The effect of the TEMPORARY option is to invoke the COLUMN command the next time that the attribute (SALARY, in this example) is used in a SELECT. After it is used once, the default formatting values are restored.

Another method of temporarily disabling COLUMN commands is through the use of the OFF option. If we want to disable the current settings of the COLUMN command temporarily, we can use the following command.

```
               COLUMN SALARY OFF
```

The effect of this command is to disable the current settings of the COLUMN command (both headings and formats) executed for the SALARY attribute. The default settings are now in effect, but the current settings are not lost, they are only disabled. When we want to turn them back on, we would use this command:

```
               COLUMN SALARY ON
```

Here is an example of the COLUMN ON/OFF command:

```
UFI> COLUMN SALARY FORMAT $99,999
UFI> SELECT FACULTY-NAME, SALARY, SALARY*2 "DOUBLE SALARY"
  2  FROM FACULTY;

FACULTY-NAME_____ ____SALARY DOUBLE_SAL
RAYMOND J. JOHNSON    $40,000      80000
WENDY SWIMMER         $45,000      90000
AMY DANCER            $34,500      69000
BOB JONES             $35,000      70000
JACK NELSON           $28,000      56000

UFI> COLUMN SALARY OFF
UFI> /

FACULTY-NAME_____ ____SALARY DOUBLE_SAL
RAYMOND J. JOHNSON     40000      80000
WENDY SWIMMER          45000      90000
AMY DANCER             34500      69000
BOB JONES              35000      70000
JACK NELSON            28000      56000
```

If you have several attributes that need to be formatted similarly, ORACLE has the LIKE option for the column command. The function of the LIKE option is to copy the COLUMN specifications for one attribute into another attribute.

```
      UFI> COLUMN SALARY FORMAT $99,999
      UFI> COLUMN SALARY*2 LIKE SALARY
```

Sometimes there is one (or more) column(s) that you do not wish displayed. A method of accomplishing this is to list all the attributes in the table except the one(s) that you do not wish displayed. ORACLE has a much easier method of eliminating one or more attributes from the display. To accomplish this, you may use the NOPRINT option on that column. Neither the headings nor the attribute values will be printed until you turn the NOPRINT option off.

```
UFI> SELECT * FROM STUDENT;

STU-ID STUDENT-NAME___  ADDRESS_____  BIRTHDATE GENDER
S001   WENDY JONES      125 MAPLE AVE   25-OCT-65 FEMALE
S002   SAM WALES        3006 NAVAJO CL  10-JAN-60 MALE
S003   CATHY SMITH      1600 PENN AVE   22-FEB-22 FEMALE
S004   DOTTIE STACY     10 DOWNING ST   31-MAR-67 FEMALE
S005   JAY LANGER       GOLF COURSE RD  19-APR-65 MALE
S006   AMY LOPEZ        123 SUN RAY RD  10-MAY-64 FEMALE
S007   SAM WATSON       225 TEST DRIVE  09-JUN-63 MALE
S008   TAMMY REDD       113 MANCHESTER  01-JUL-60 FEMALE
S009   TOMMY WADKINS    APPLE TREE DR   24-AUG-67 MALE
S010   BEN TREVINO      BOWLING ALLEY   30-SEP-66 MALE

10 records selected
UFI> REMARK . . ... Turn off the printing of ADDRESS
UFI> COLUMN ADDRESS NOPRINT
UFI> /

STU-ID STUDENT-NAME___  BIRTHDATE GENDER
S001   WENDY JONES      25-OCT-65 FEMALE
S002   SAM WALES        10-JAN-60 MALE
S003   CATHY SMITH      22-FEB-22 FEMALE
S004   DOTTIE STACY     31-MAR-67 FEMALE
S005   JAY LANGER       19-APR-65 MALE
S006   AMY LOPEZ        10-MAY-64 FEMALE
S007   SAM WATSON       09-JUN-63 MALE
S008   TAMMY REDD       01-JUL-60 FEMALE
S009   TOMMY WADKINS    24-AUG-67 MALE
S010   BEN TREVINO      30-SEP-66 MALE

10 records selected
UFI> REMARK . . ... Turn it back on
UFI> COLUMN ADDRESS PRINT
UFI>  /

STU-ID STUDENT-NAME___  ADDRESS_____  BIRTHDATE GENDER
S001   WENDY JONES      125 MAPLE AVE   25-OCT-65 FEMALE
S002   SAM WALES        3006 NAVAJO CL  10-JAN-60 MALE
S003   CATHY SMITH      1600 PENN AVE   22-FEB-22 FEMALE
S004   DOTTIE STACY     10 DOWNING ST   31-MAR-67 FEMALE
S005   JAY LANGER       GOLF COURSE RD  19-APR-65 MALE
S006   AMY LOPEZ        123 SUN RAY RD  10-MAY-64 FEMALE
S007   SAM WATSON       225 TEST DRIVE  09-JUN-63 MALE
S008   TAMMY REDD       113 MANCHESTER  01-JUL-60 FEMALE
S009   TOMMY WADKINS    APPLE TREE DR   24-AUG-67 MALE
S010   BEN TREVINO      BOWLING ALLEY   30-SEP-66 MALE

10 records selected
```

Finally, a table has been created that contains more than 80 output characters in a line and will not fit on your output screen. This table must be displayed in parts or written to your system's print facility. Normally print facilities have wider output lines than do terminal screens. If you SPOOL your output to the system print facility, you must change the size of an output line. This can be done with the UFI command SET LINESIZE NN. The NN represents the maximum number of characters allowed in an output line. This number is usually 132 for most printers. To change the size of the output line to 132 characters, use the following UFI command.

```
UFI> SET LINESIZE 132
```

DISPLAYING THE CURRENT SETTINGS OF THE COLUMN COMMAND

At times we might have made so many changes to headings and formats of attributes that we can't remember what the current settings are. ORACLE has a method of displaying the current settings of an attribute. To get the current settings, simply type

```
COLUMN <attribute name>
```

This will display the current values for the attribute heading and format. For example if we wanted the current settings for the attribute FACULTY-NAME, we would type the following.

```
UFI> COLUMN FACULTY-NAME
COLUMN    FACULTY-NAME ON
FORMAT    A10
TRUNCATE
```

We can even display the current settings of temporary column headings. Remember that DOUBLE was a temporary heading for SALARY*2.

```
UFI> COLUMN DOUBLE
COLUMN    DOUBLE ON
HEADING   'DOUBLE|SALARY' (SEP WAS '|')
FORMAT    $99,999
```

If we want the settings for all the columns that have been defined in this terminal session, we can type just the word COLUMN.

```
UFI> COLUMN
COLUMN    FACULTY-NAME ON
FORMAT    A10
TRUNCATE
```

```
COLUMN    DOUBLE ON
HEADING   'DOUBLE|SALARY' (SEP WAS '|')
FORMAT    $99,999
COLUMN    ADDRESS
NOPRINT
```

Attributes that have been "cleared" via the command are not displayed.

```
COLUMN <attribute-name> CLEAR
```

SUMMARY

In this chapter we learned that the basic retrieval command for ORACLE was the SELECT/FROM command. Predicates could be added to the command via the WHERE clause. The ORDER BY clause caused the output from the SELECT command to be sorted in either ascending or descending order. The second part of the chapter was dedicated to formatting the various attributes that could be displayed.

Upon completion of this chapter, you should be familiar with the following ORACLE commands and terms.

A. SELECT/FROM

B. WHERE

C. DISTINCT

D. SYSDATE

E. ROWNUM

F. SELECT *

G. SET NUMWIDTH

H. SET SPACE

I. Theta operators

J. OR, AND, and NOT

K. Testing multiple OR conditions

L. BETWEEN

M. Full-string searches

N. Substring searches

O. LIKE

P. Wild card string operands

Q. ORDER BY

R. DESC

S. Attribute headers

T. COLUMN

U. HEADING

V. SET HEADSEP

W. FORMAT

X. Format masks

Y. WRAP-TRUNC

Z. NULL

AA. SET NULL

BB. DEFAULT

CC. CLEAR

DD. ALIAS

EE. ON/OFF

FF. SET LINESIZE

EXERCISES

1. Explain the function of the DISTINCT clause of the SELECT command.
2. If we used the data currently stored in our STUDENT example table, could we get the names of the students to display in alphabetical order? Why not? What would we have to do to our data to be able to display the student names in alphabetical order?
3. Utilizing data from the following tables, formulate the necessary SELECT commands to retrieve the following data.

```
STUDENT ( STU-ID, STUDENT-NAME, ADDRESS, BIRTHDATE, GENDER)
COURSE ( COURSE-ID, COURSE-TITLE, SECTION-NO, STU-ID, FAC-ID)
FACULTY ( FAC-ID, FACULTY-NAME, DEPARTMENT, GENDER, SALARY)
```

a. Display the names of all female students.
b. Display two values of gender stored in the STUDENT table. Make sure that male is listed before female.
c. Remove the attribute headings from the attribute STUDENT-NAME, then write the names and addresses of all of the male students out to an external file called "guys."
d. List the names of the students who have a double "l" in their names.
e. List the student table out in reverse order. (Tuple 10 would be listed first, tuple 9 would be listed second, etc.)
f. Suppose our beloved faculty were getting a 50% raise for the next school year. List each faculty name, his or her current salary, the amount of his raise, and his or her new salary. Be sure to set up realistic headings for the new computed attributes and format them reasonably.
g. List the names of the faculty members who earn between $30,000 and $40,000, but not equal to exactly $35,000. display the results in descending order of SALARY.
h. List the student IDs of the students currently taking classes.
i. List the titles of the courses being taught in alphabetical order.

REFERENCES

1. *Harris ORACLE Reference Manual.* Harris Corporation, Ft. Lauderdale, FL, Release 4.1.4, May 1985.
2. *Harris ORACLE User's Guide.* Harris Corporation, Ft. Lauderdale, FL, February 1984.
3. *ORACLE Reference Manual.* ORACLE Corporation, Belmont, CA, Release 4.0. May 1985.
4. *ORACLE User's Guide.* ORACLE Corporation, Belmont, CA, Release 4.0, May 1985.

$$7$$

Creating Tables, Indexes, Storage Spaces, and Partitions

PURPOSE: The purpose of this chapter is to illustrate how ORACLE base tables are created and altered. Creation and usage of indexes is also discussed. The chapter concludes with a discussion of how data and indexes are organized and stored in external data files.

In the previous chapter we discussed how data is retrieved from ORACLE tables. This chapter will explain how those tables are created. The following chapter discusses how data is inserted into the tables. This chapter examines the creation and usage of indexes. Data and indexes are not organized in a helter-skelter fashion; rather they are stored in an organized manner. These storage techniques are explored in this chapter.

In the two previous chapters we have used a tint to indicate what the user entered on each SQL or UFI command. We will no longer do this for the remainder of the book.

CREATING ORACLE TABLES

ORACLE tables are created with the SQL command CREATE TABLE. The syntax of the CREATE TABLE command is:

```
CREATE TABLE table-name
 (attribute-name1 data-type [[NOT] NULL]
 [,attribute-name2 data-type [[NOT] NULL]] ,, , ,)
 [SPACE space-name]
```

The symbols table-name, attribute-name, and space-name are all identifiers and, hence, follow all of the identifier syntax rules for naming. The values for data-type can be any of the four ORACLE valid data types: CHAR, DATE, LONG, and NUMBER. These data types are discussed in the following section of this chapter. The NULL clause tells ORACLE that null values either are [NULL] or are not [NOT NULL] allowed for this attribute. Space-name designates where the data for this table is to be stored. This concept is discussed later in this chapter. The maximum number of attributes that an ORACLE data table can have is 254.

ORACLE DATA TYPES

There are four different data types allowed in ORACLE databases. Two of these data types, CHAR and LONG, identify the data values as being character strings. The data type DATE contains a specially formatted attribute that contains dates. The data type NUMBER allows attributes to contain any numeric data values.

By designating an attribute to be a particular data type, the user is restricting the kind of data that can be inserted into a particular attribute column. If you try to insert a new tuple into a table and the value that you attempt to place into an attribute column does not match in type, ORACLE generates an error. The same thing will happen if you attempt to change a value currently stored in the attribute value of a tuple and the data types do not match. This is a type of integrity check that ORACLE performs for you free of charge.

The CHAR Data Type

Attributes of data type CHAR contain character strings. The format of the CHAR data type is:

```
CHAR (maximum length of the character string)
```

The value in parentheses must be an integer number value between 1 and 240. This means that the shortest character string that we can have is 1 character long and the longest is 240 characters. If we specify a character type longer than 240 characters, ORACLE will automatically change the data type to LONG (see the paragraphs that follow). If we attempt to store a character string longer than the defined length, ORACLE generates an error and will not store the tuple.

Numeric values can be stored as character strings, and if the user attempts to perform any arithmetic operation with them, ORACLE temporarily converts the numeric strings to numbers and performs the computation. The disadvantage of storing numeric values as character strings is that the use of the COLUMN command to format the values is restricted.

The DATE Data Type

The data type DATE allows any valid date between January 1, 4712 b.c. to December 31, 4711 a.d. This means that if you plan to utilize the ORACLE database to help you plan your future activities, you will not be able to plan anything for New Year's Day 4712 a.d. or any date thereafter, sorry!

The format or the DATE data type is simply

```
DATE
```

There is no width specification with the DATE data type for the default display width is defined as nine characters. Dates are entered and displayed in the following format:

```
dd-MON-yy
```

The "dd" represents the day of the month specified as an integer between 1 and 31 depending on the month. "MON" is the first three letters of the month, and "yy" represents the last two digits of the year. The first two digits of the year are assumed to be "19." We will show you how to change these default values later in this text. ORACLE will automatically validate the value of dates either input or changed.

The value of date attributes are displayed in the foregoing format. If the value of an attribute of type DATE was October 9, 1945 (a famous birthday), the value would be displayed as:

```
09-OCT-45
```

Remember that this is only the default format and can be changed. Methods of changing the format of date data for input are discussed in Chapter 8, and methods or reformatting date data for output are discussed in Chapter 10. We will also see in these chapters that the DATE data type can also contain time values.

The LONG Data Type

LONG is another type of string data type. The purpose of the data type LONG is to allow for long character strings (hence the clever name). An attribute of type LONG can contain up to 65,536 characters. Remember that the maximum string length for an attribute of data type CHAR is 240. The format of the data type LONG is

LONG

Again notice that this data type does not have a length value associated with it. The reason is that when you specify the data type LONG, you get the maximum string length. Don't worry, the space taken up by the string is allocated efficiently as we will see later on in this chapter.

When displaying attributes with the data type LONG, UFI only returns the first 80 characters of the string. If you desire more than the first 80 characters, you must utilize the UFI command SET LONG N. The value N represents the maximum number of characters that you want retrieved for the attribute of data type LONG.

```
UFI> SET LONG 200
```

This command changes the default for the number of characters retrieved from 80 to 200.

Even though this data type is handy for storing long character strings, it does have several severe restrictions.

1. There can be only one attribute per table with the data type LONG.
2. An attribute of the data type LONG cannot appear anywhere in a WHERE clause. This includes the objects of functions or in expressions.
3. An index cannot be created on an attribute with the data type LONG. (Indexes are discussed later in this chapter.)
4. A table containing an attribute with the data type LONG cannot be part of a cluster. (See Chapter 9 for more information on clusters.)
5. Not all ORACLE utilities can handle tables with attributes of type LONG.
6. Attributes of data type LONG cannot be formatted via the UFI command COLUMN.

The NUMBER Data Type

Attributes of the data type NUMBER are designed to store both integer and real numbers. The format of the NUMBER data type is

```
NUMBER [(number width [,precision])]
```

If we do not make a width specification, then a number of any size can be assigned into the attribute. The maximum width that can be specified is machine dependent, but ORACLE can only accurately store numbers of up to a certain number of significant digits. This value is also machine dependent. Precision is lost if a number with greater than this number of digits is stored into the attribute.

The optional width specification limits the size of the number that can be inserted into an attribute with the NUMBER data type. For example, if we specified an attribute with the data type

NUMBER (5)

we would be restricting our values to integer numbers between the values -99999 and 99999. Notice that the sign is not considered a position. If we enter a real number into an attribute with the foregoing data type, the number would be rounded and then truncated.

Precision indicates how many decimal places we want to keep for real numbers. For example, if we wished to store numbers as large as 999.99, we would use the following specification:

NUMBER (5,2)

Again notice that the decimal point is not considered as a position. If a number is greater than two digits to the right of the decimal place, it is rounded to two decimal places before being stored.

Remember, the width and precision are used only to restrict the size of the number stored in the attribute, not to format it. Formatting is handled by the SET NUMWIDTH and the COLUMN commands.

NULL VALUES

The system constant NULL can be assigned into any attribute, no matter what the data type is.

Null is a special value that indicates that the value for that attribute in a particular tuple does not exist. Remember back to the previous chapter when we had a faculty member, Amy Dancer, who had been hired but her salary rate had not been approved. Suppose that we wanted to insert Miss Dancer's tuple in the FACULTY table to indicate that she was currently a member of the faculty. However, we could not realistically enter a value of zero for the attribute SALARY for Miss Dancer's salary is not zero, it just hasn't been assigned a value yet. Another reason for not entering a zero value for salary is that if we wanted to compute the average salary for the faculty, we would get an artificially low value for the average. Null values are not used in computing arithmetic values. If we tried to enter a value of blank (' ') into the SALARY attribute, an attribute defined as NUMBER, an error would result.

EXAMPLES OF CREATE TABLE COMMANDS

To illustrate the CREATE TABLE command, let's create tables for our example tables.

```
STUDENT (STU-ID, STUDENT-NAME, ADDRESS, BIRTHDATE, GENDER)
COURSE (COURSE-ID, COURSE-TITLE, SECTION-NO, STU-ID, FAC-ID)
FACULTY (FAC-ID, FACULTY-NAME, DEPARTMENT, GENDER, SALARY)

UFI> CREATE TABLE STUDENT (STU_ID CHAR (6) NOT NULL,
  2                        STUDENT_NAME CHAR (17),
  3                        ADDRESS CHAR (20),
  4                        BIRTHDATE DATE,
  5                        GENDER CHAR (6));

Table created.

UFI> CREATE TABLE COURSE (COURSE_ID CHAR (6) NOT NULL,
  2                       COURSE_TITLE CHAR (27),
  3                       SECTION_NO NUMBER (2),
  4                       STU_ID CHAR (6) NOT NULL,
  5                       FAC_ID CHAR (6) NOT NULL);

Table created.

UFI> CREATE TABLE FACULTY (FAC_ID CHAR (6) NOT NULL,
  2                        FACULTY_NAME CHAR (18),
  3                        DEPARTMENT CHAR (10),
  4                        GENDER CHAR (6),
  5                        SALARY NUMBER (5));

Table created.
```

When these three tables were created, notice that certain attributes in each table were affixed with the clause NOT NULL. If you will remember, these were the attributes that we selected as the primary keys of the tables. If you will further remember, one of the guidelines for primary keys was that they could not contain a null value. ORACLE has no direct means of specifying which attribute(s) participate in the primary key, so we must affix the NOT NULL clause to the attribute(s) to ensure that the primary keys do not become contaminated with null values.

Be aware that just because we specify that an attribute has the NOT NULL clause affixed to it, it is not automatically a primary key. The NOT NULL clause can be used as a form of integrity check on an attribute. For example, we could affix the NOT NULL clause to the attributes BIRTHDATE and GENDER of the STUDENT table to ensure that when a new tuple is added to the table, the values of BIRTHDATE and GENDER have values.

Once a table has been created, it is ready to receive data. Inserting data into tables is discussed in the following chapter.

DROPPING TABLES

Tables can be removed from the database via the SQL command DROP TABLE. Dropping a table implies that the associated tuples will also be deleted. The format of the DROP TABLE command is

```
DROP TABLE table-name
```

A table can only be dropped by its creator or a user with DBA privilege.

Dropping tables invalidates any views utilizing the dropped table. Dropping a table also automatically drops any indexes that pertain to the table. If we wanted to drop our STUDENT table, we would use the following command.

```
UFI> DROP TABLE STUDENT;

Table dropped.
```

ALTERING TABLES

Once a table has been created, it can be altered in two ways.

1. Another attribute(s) can be added to the end of the table's attribute list. The new attribute(s) are added to the ''right-hand'' side of the table.
2. The data type or size of an attribute(s) can be changed.

Attributes cannot be dropped from tables.

These two table alterations are accomplished via the SQL command ALTER TABLE. It is important to note that these alterations can be made even if the table currently contains data. Since there are two separate types of alterations that can be performed on a table, there are two separate command syntaxes.

The one table alteration that cannot be accomplished directly is deleting an attribute. To delete an attribute of a table, we must create another table with the desired attributes. We will then have to copy the desired attributes from the first table into our recently created table. This copying is accomplished through the SQL INSERT/SELECT command which is described in Chapter 8.

Adding Attributes to Tables

The syntax of the ALTER TABLE ADD command is:

```
ALTER TABLE table-name

{ ADD attribute-name data-type [[NOT] NULL] |
    ADD (attribute-name1 data-type [[NOT] NULL]
        [,attribute-name1 data-type [[NOT] NULL], . . .]) }
```

All attributes added will be appended to the right side of the table and will be assigned null values. To illustrate the ALTER TABLE ADD command, let's assume that we wanted to add the attribute ''years of service'' to the FACULTY table. We have decided to call this attribute YR-SVC and will restrict it to two-digit integers. This attribute will be added to the table as follows.

```
UFI> ALTER TABLE FACULTY ADD YR-SVC NUMBER (2);

Table altered.

UFI> SET NUMWIDTH 6
UFI> SELECT * FROM FACULTY;

FAC-ID FACULTY-NAME_____ DEPARTMENT GENDER SALARY YR-SVC
J01     RAYMOND J. JOHNSON     COMP SCI   MALE    40000
S01     WENDY SWIMMER          COMP SCI   FEMALE  45000
D01     AMY DANCER             COMP SCI   FEMALE  34500
J02     BOB JONES              ACCOUNTING MALE    35000
N01     JACK NELSON            HISTORY    MALE    28000
```

Notice that all the values in the YR_SVC attribute are not displayed because they were automatically set to NULL. The values will be updated through the UPDATE command, which is discussed in the following chapter.

Modifying Data Types and Sizes

The syntax of the ALTER TABLE MODIFY command is:

```
ALTER TABLE table-name

{ MODIFY attribute-name data-type [[NOT] NULL] |
  MODIFY (attribute-name1 data-type [+NOT] NULL]
    [,attribute-name1 data-type [[NOT] NULL], . . .]}
```

The data type of an attribute can be changed only if the attribute contains all null values. The width of attribute of data type CHAR or NUMBER can always be increased. Remember that the data types DATE and LONG have no width specification. **Attributes can only be decreased in size only if all the occurrences for that attribute are null**.

Let's assume that we are considering hiring a very prominent faculty member, Dr. Randy Jones, and in an effort to attract the illustrious person to our school, we will have to pay him big bucks. In fact, we will have to pay him in excess of $100,000. If you will remember back to the beginning of this chapter, we allocated only five positions for the attribute SALARY in the FACULTY table. We must alter this attribute size.

```
UFI> ALTER TABLE FACULTY MODIFY SALARY NUMBER (6);

Table altered.
```

Note that the attribute alteration can be made even though there is data in the table.

THE USE OF INDEXES IN ORACLE

Indexes are analogous to inverted list structures discussed in Chapter 1. Another method of conceptualizing an index is to think of an index at the back of a book. An index in a book is a list of keywords used in the book and the page numbers where the key words are used. A database index is a list of database keys (similar to the book pages in the analogy we just used) of tuples that have the same value for a designated attribute. For example, if we created an index for the value gender in the FACULTY table, the actual indexes might look something like the following.

DATA TABLE NAME: FACULTY

DBK	FAC-ID	FACULTY-NAME	DEPARTMENT	GENDER	SALARY
T01	J01	RAYMOND J. JOHNSON	COMP SCI	MALE	40000
T02	S01	WENDY SWIMMER	COMP SCI	FEMALE	45000
T03	D01	AMY DANCER	COMP SCI	FEMALE	34500
T04	J02	BOB JONES	ACCOUNTING	MALE	35000
T05	N01	JACK NELSON	HISTORY	MALE	28000

The attribute DBK stands for database key. (This attribute has been added for illustration purposes only and would not be an actual attribute of the table.) We have used the simplified values T01 through T05 for illustration purposes only. The actual value of DBK is something that ORACLE calls ROWID, which is discussed later in this chapter.

Let us now assume that we wanted to create an index on the attribute GENDER. Our index would look like this:

Attribute Value	DBK of Tuples with the Attribute Value
FEMALE	T02, T03
MALE	T01, T04, T05

These lists are kept in a B*-tree organized file. Notice that the attribute values are kept in lexicographic order. In actuality, the entire attribute value would not have to be kept. It would only have to keep enough of the attribute value to determine uniqueness of the string. Only the first letter of the string, either M or F, would be necessary to determine uniqueness in our example.

These indexes are automatically updated anytime a new tuple is added to the table, a tuple is deleted, or the value of GENDER is changed.

Creation of Indexes

Indexes are created with the CREATE INDEX command. The syntax of the CREATE INDEX command is:

```
CREATE [UNIQUE] INDEX index-name
    ON table-name (attribute-name1 [,attribute-name2, . . .])
    [ {SYSSORT | NOSYSSORT} ]
    [ PCTFREE value1 ]
    [ {COMPRESS | NOCOMPRESS} ]
    [ ROWS = value2 ]
```

The UNIQUE clause guarantees that all of the values of the attribute will be unique. The symbol "index-name" is the name of the index. Index-name is an identifier. The only reason that we must give an index a name is so that if we want to drop it, we will have a reference point.

Since ORACLE indexes are kept in B*-tree files, the values of the attribute values must be in sorted order when the index is created. ORACLE gives you the option of using the system sort routine to order the values of the index or not sorting the values before inserting them into the B*-tree. If you specify SYSSORT, ORACLE will use the system sort utility to sort the index values before it begins creation of the B*-tree. If you specify NOSYSSORT, it will not sort the index values before creating the B*-tree. This means that the B*-tree is created dynamically, and hence, more reorganizing of the indexes is needed. This should bring up an obvious question: When do you use each sort option? The ORACLE Corporation recommends using the system sort routine when there are more than 100 tuples in the table upon which you wish to create and index. SYSSORT is the default value.

The value of PCTFREE is the percentage of free space that is left for inclusion of new values on the index page. The default value is 20. This means that when the index is first created, each index page will be 80% full. New tuples that are inserted will cause the index(es) for the table to be updated. If possible, the new database keys will be placed on the same page as the database keys with similar characteristics. If an overflow occurs, the system will not fail, but its retrieval efficiency begins to degrade as the list of keys must overflow to a second page. If we set PCTFREE to a high percentage value it will be efficient if your database is very volatile (tuples are frequently added to and deleted from the table). If the database is fairly stable (tuples are infrequently added to and deleted from the table), the percentage should be set fairly low. Adjusting this percentage is one of the tasks for the database administrator.

As we alluded to, the entire value of the attribute does not have to be stored, only enough of the attribute to make it unique. This compression of attribute values saves space. If we use the NOCOMPRESS option, the entire value of the attribute is stored on the index pages. This option requires more space, but makes indexed retrieval faster, for ORACLE can read the values directly from the index pages without looking at any data pages. The default value is COMPRESS.

The value of ROWS specifies the maximum number of unique values of the index. By specifying a fairly accurate value for ROWS, the speed of the sorting algorithm will be enhanced.

The ORACLE Corporation recommends that this value be estimated for tables containing more than 5000 tuple occurrences.

Let's use our example tables to illustrate how to create indexes.

```
UFI> CREATE INDEX GENDER_TYPE ON FACULTY (GENDER);

Index created.

UFI> REMARK . . .. . . We will suffix each primary key with

UFI> REMARK . . .. . . the characters _PK

UFI> CREATE UNIQUE INDEX STUDENT_PK ON STUDENT(STU_ID)
  2    NOSYSSORT;

Index created.

UFI> CREATE UNIQUE INDEX COURSE_PK ON
  2    COURSE (STU_ID, FAC_ID, COURSE_ID) NOSYSSORT;

Index created.

UFI> CREATE UNIQUE INDEX FACULTY_PK ON
  2    FACULTY (FAC_ID) NOSYSSORT;

   Index created.

UFI> CREATE INDEX MONEY ON FACULTY(SALARY) NOSYSSORT
  2    PCTFREE 30 ROWS=6000;
```

Once an index is created, all system operations involving the index are transparent to the user. If the user attempts to retrieve tuples with some type WHERE clause, the system determines if the attributes in the WHERE clause are indexed or not. If they are, the system utilizes the index(es) to retrieve the tuples. If not, the system will have to utilize a plain old sequential search through the tuples.

Indexes can be created for any data type except LONG.

Dropping Indexes

Indexes are dropped with the DROP INDEX command. The format of the DROP INDEX command is:

```
DROP INDEX index-name
```

To illustrate the DROP INDEX command, let's drop one of the indexes that were created in the previous section.

```
UFI> DROP INDEX MONEY;

Index dropped.
```

Indexes can only be dropped by the user who created the index or a user with DBA authority.

Validating Indexes

When a computer system has any type of malfunction, some of the files may become contaminated. It is always nice to be able to check the validity of data. If the files containing table indexes became contaminated, it could cause major problems in the ORACLE. Contamination could be caused by hardware failures, software failures, malicious tampering, and so forth. Periodically you should check the correctness of your indexes. This can be done with the VALIDATE INDEX command. The syntax of this command is simply

```
VALIDATE INDEX index-name
```

If we wanted to validate the index called STUDENT-PK, we would do it as follows.

```
UFI> VALIDATE INDEX STUDENT_PK;

Index validated.
```

If you attempt to validate an index and any other message other than "Index validated" is displayed, your index has become contaminated. If this happens you should drop the index and re-create it.

Why Use Indexes?

To index or not to index, that is the question. This is a problem that can affect the overall database performance. In most industrial installations, this question must be answered by the database administrator.

Indexes certainly have their advantages and disadvantages. The use or nonuse of indexes breaks down to the database choices of speed or storage space.

Indexes definitely speed up the retrieval of tuples. If we want to search a table for tuples that have a particular value of an attribute (GENDER='FEMALE'), indexed retrieval is very fast and efficient. The reason for this is that once ORACLE has established what attribute is to be searched (GENDER) and what value is to searched for (FEMALE), it has a list of the exact locations of the tuples with that value. If the item is not indexed, ORACLE will have to search tuple by tuple for the value.

Indexes are also a method of implementing primary keys of tables. If we create a unique index over the attribute(s) that form the primary key of the table, we will ensure that the primary key will always be a unique identifier of each tuple in the table. The values of foreign keys should also be indexed, for indexes will make join queries (see Chapter 9) execute faster. Whether we should make the index unique or not is a design question. This question is addressed in Chapter 13.

If indexes are so wonderful, why shouldn't we index each attribute of each table to guarantee the fastest possible retrieval of data? Of course, the answer to this question is space problems. If we create an index, we must give up the space to store the values of that index. We must decide whether we want to give up that extra storage to guarantee the uniqueness of the primary key and to speed up the retrieval of data.

In general, indexes are usually inefficient in two distinct situations.

1. When we have an attribute that has very few distinct values. Our example index on gender would be relatively inefficient in an industrial database. If we have a table that contains 10,000 tuple occurrences, with a fairly equal distribution of males and females, the list of database keys would be approximately 50% of the size of the table. This would generate many index page overflows. The search time would become longer and longer, after each new tuple occurrence is added to the table.

2. When we have attributes that have many distinct values. An example of this is any primary key. The reason that this situation is inefficient is that we would have very few database keys (one if the index is built on a primary key) per database value. This would lead to very inefficient use of the index space.

How many indexes should a table have? That depends on the type of index, the values of the index, how much secondary storage we have, and how much will the index be used. As a general guideline, the ORACLE Corporation recommends no more than two or three indexes per table.

A final point on the creation of indexes: When should indexes be created? Should they be created right after the table structure has been created and there are no tuples in the table. Or should they be created after the tables have been initially loaded with data, before any data maintenance is done. There are two schools of thought to answering this question.

The database administrators recommend that the table be initially loaded with data and then the index is created. This method will create the index much faster for the sort algorithm will sort all the index values at once and then insert them into the B*-tree.

The database designers (see Chapter 15) prefer that the index be created before any data is loaded into the database. Their thinking is that the integrity of the primary and foreign keys will be maintained by not allowing the data tables to become contaminated with duplicate values. However, this method is extremely slow, for ORACLE must insert a new tuple, then stop and update all the indexes for the table, then store the next tuple, then update all the indexes.

THE DATA DICTIONARY

All information pertaining to all ORACLE tables is stored in the ORACLE data dictionary. Such information as the table name, the attributes of a table, their data types and sizes, and whether the attribute will accept null values or not are examples of information stored in the data dictionary. Note that we did not say that tuple data was stored in the data dictionary, only information *about* the table is stored in the data dictionary. This is generally referred to as metadata. All the information stored in the data dictionary is also stored in data tables. You may treat these tables as you would any other ORACLE table: that is, you may retrieve data from them via the SELECT/FROM command. You may not alter the data dictionary tables in any manner.

To find out what data dictionary tables exist and what information is stored in each table, type the SQL command

```
UFI> SELECT * FROM DTAB;

TNAME             REMARKS
REFERENCE DATE   ORACLE CATALOG AS OF 10-MAY-84, INSTALLED ON  23-DEC-85 12:19:25
CATALOG          PROFILE OF TABLES ACCESSIBLE TO USER, EXCLUDING DATA DICTIONARY
COL              SPECIFICATIONS OF COLUMNS IN TABLES CREATED BY THE USER
COLUMNS          SPECIFICATIONS OF COLUMNS IN TABLES (EXCLUDING DATA DICTIONARY)
DEPENDENCIES     BASE AND DEPENDENT TABLES AND VIEWS CREATED BY USER
DTAB             DESCRIPTION OF TABLES & VIEWS IN ORACLE DATA DICTIONARY
EXTENTS          DATA STRUCTURE OF EXTENTS WITHIN TABLES
INDEXES          INDEXES CREATED BY USER & INDEXES ON TABLES CREATED BY USER
PARTITIONS       FILE STRUCTURE OF FILES WITHIN PARTITIONS - FOR DBA USE ONLY
SESSIONS         RECORD OF LOGIN SESSIONS FOR USER
SPACES           SELECTION OF SPACE DEFINITIONS FOR CREATING TABLES & CLUSTERS
STORAGE          DATA AND INDEX STORAGE ALLOCATION FOR USER'S OWN TABLES
SYSCATALOG       PROFILE OF TABLES AND VIEWS ACCESSIBLE TO THE USER
SYSCOLAUTH       DIRECTORY OF COLUMN LEVEL UPDATE GRANTS BY OR TO THE USER
SYSCOLUMNS       SPECIFICATIONS OF COLUMNS IN ACCESSIBLE TABLES AND VIEWS
SYSEXTENTS       DATA STRUCTURE OF TABLES THROUGHOUT SYSTEM - FOR DBA USE ONLY
SYSINDEXES       LIST OF INDEXES, UNDERLYING COLUMNS, CREATOR, AND OPTIONS
SYSSTORAGE       SUMMARY OF ALL DATABASE STORAGE - FOR DBA USE ONLY
SYSTABALLOC      DATA AND INDEX SPACE ALLOCATIONS FOR ALL TABLES - FOR DBA'S
SYSTABAUTH       DIRECTORY OF ACCESS AUTHORIZATION GRANTED BY OR TO THE USER
SYSUSERAUTH      MASTER LIST OF ORACLE USERS - FOR DBA USE ONLY
SYSUSERLIST      LIST OF ORACLE USERS
SYSPROGS         LIST OF PROGRAMS PRECOMPILED BY USER
SYSVIEWS         QUOTATION OF SQL TEXT UPON WHICH SYSTEM VIEWS ARE BASED
TAB              LIST OF TABLES, VIEWS, CLUSTERS AND SYNONYMS CREATED BY THE USER
TABALLOC         DATA AND INDEX SPACE ALLOCATIONS FOR ALL USER'S TABLES
TABQUOTAS        TABLE ALLOCATION (SPACE) PARAMETERS FOR TABLES CREATED BY USER
VIEWS            QUOTATIONS OF THE SQL STATEMENTS UPON WHICH VIEWS ARE BASED
28 Records selected.
```

This list of tables is usually updated with each new release of ORACLE. For this reason, if you type this command, your output might not match what is displayed here.

In lieu of discussing each of these dictionary tables at this point, we will discuss the tables when appropriate throughout the text.

There are several dictionary tables that we can utilize at this point in the text. These tables are TAB, COL, INDEXES, SESSIONS, and SYSUSERLIST.

The Data Dictionary Table TAB

The table TAB contains the names of all of the tables, views, clusters (see Chapter 9), and synonyms (see Chapter 12) that have been created in the current user-name.

Assuming that you have created the three tables described earlier and you have created no other tables, the table TAB should look as follows.

```
UFI> SELECT * FROM TAB;

TNAME__ TABTYPE _CLUSTERID
STUDENT TABLE
COURSE  TABLE
FACULTY TABLE
```

The value of TABTYPE (table type) can be table, view, or cluster. (Views and clusters are discussed later in the text.)

The Data Dictionary Table COL

The dictionary table COL contains all of the columns of all of the tables that have been created in the current user-name. When accessing the table COL, you will most probably be interested in only one table. To restrict your access to only one table, use the WHERE clause in conjunction with the SELECT/FROM command.

```
UFI> COLUMN TNAME FORMAT A7
UFI> COLUMN COLNO FORMAT 99999
UFI> COLUMN CNAME FORMAT A12
UFI> COLUMN COLTYPE FORMAT A7
UFI> COLUMN WIDTH LIKE COLNO
UFI> COLUMN SCALE LIKE COLNO
UFI> COLUMN NULLS FORMAT A8
UFI> SELECT * FROM COL WHERE TNAME = 'STUDENT';

TNAME__ COLNO CNAME_____ COLTYPE WIDTH SCALE NULLS
STUDENT     1 STU-ID       CHAR        6       NOT NULL
STUDENT     2 STUDENT-NAME CHAR       17       NULL
STUDENT     3 ADDRESS      CHAR       20       NULL
STUDENT     4 BIRTHDATE    DATE       21       NULL
STUDENT     5 GENDER       CHAR        6       NULL
```

Notice that we had to do some formatting of the table columns before we displayed the contents of the table. If this were not done, the table display would wrap around to two lines and become difficult to read.

The Data Dictionary Table INDEXES

The function of the INDEXES table is to keep track of the indexes created by the user. It contains such information as the index name, who created the index, what table does the index pertain to, and whether it is a concatenated index.

```
UFI> SET WORKSIZE 10000
UFI> COLUMN INAME FORMAT A10
UFI> COLUMN ICREATOR FORMAT A8
UFI> COLUMN TNAME FORMAT A8
UFI> COLUMN CREATOR FORMAT A7
UFI> COLUMN COLNAMES FORMAT A8
UFI> COLUMN INDEXTYPE FORMAT A9
UFI> COLUMN COLNUMBERS FORMAT 999999999999
UFI> COLUMN IORD FORMAT A4
UFI> COLUMN COMP FORMAT A8
UFI> COLUMN CONCATID FORMAT 999999999
UFI> SELECT * FROM INDEXES;
```

INAME	ICREATOR	TNAME	CREATOR	COLNAMES	INDEXTYPE	COLNUMBERS	IORD	CONCATID
STUDENT-PK	BOOK	STUDENT	BOOK	STU-ID	UNIQUE	1	ASC	
COURSE-PK	BOOK	COURSE	BOOK	STU-ID	UNIQUE	1	ASC	1
COURSE-PK	BOOK	COURSE	BOOK	FAC-ID	UNIQUE	2	ASC	1
COURSE-PK	BOOK	COURSE	BOOK	COURSE-ID	UNIQUE	3	ASC	1
FACULTY-PK	BOOK	FACULTY	BOOK	FAC-ID	UNIQUE	1	ASC	

Be aware that this query requires an expanded workspace. We have set the WORKSIZE parameter to 10,000, but we only have three indexes. If your system has more indexes, the WORKSIZE parameter may have to be set to a larger number for the command to execute properly. If you attempt to execute the command and the error message ''Context Area Too Small'' appears, simply adjust your WORKSIZE parameter.

The Data Dictionary Table SESSIONS

Sometimes it is necessary to determine when you were connected to ORACLE and what you did when you were connected. ORACLE keeps track of every connection to ORACLE and what was done during that session. This table is available to each user. The table (actually it is a view) only allows you to see connections to the user-name that you are currently logged onto.

```
UFI> SELECT * FROM SESSIONS;
```

LOGIN	LOGOUT	LOGREAD	PHYSREAD	LOGWRITE	DEADLOCKS	ERROR
24-DEC-85	24-DEC-85	8	0	5	0	
26-DEC-85	26-DEC-86	10	0	0	0	

The Data Dictionary Table SYSUSERLIST

ORACLE keeps a list of all the valid user-names in the system in a data dictionary table. Parts of this table are made available to users via a view called SYSUSERLIST.

```
UFI> SELECT * FROM SYSUSERLIST;

____USERID USERNAME_____ TIMESTAMP C D R
       6                                   23-DEC-85
       0 SYS                               23-DEC-85 Y Y Y
       1 PUBLIC                            23-DEC-85
       2 SYSTEM                            23-DEC-85 Y Y Y
       3 RBB                               23-DEC-85 Y Y
       4 BOOK                              23-DEC-85 Y   Y
       5 JANET_PONDER                      23-DEC-85 Y   Y
```

As you can see from the table, each user has a USERID. The first USERID (6 in the table) is the USERID of the next account to be created. TIMESTAMP is the date and time (remember that the time part of a date field is not part of the default display format) that the user-name was created. The letters "C," "D," and "R" stand for connect authority, DBA authority, and resource authority. The letter "Y" means that the user- name has the authority and null means that it does not. The actual attribute headings are CONNECTAUTH, DBAAUTH, and RESOURCEAUTH.

The SYSUSERLIST is convenient if you wish to CONNECT to another account but you have forgotten the exact user-name. Note that the password for the user-names does not display in SYSUSERLIST.

THE DESCRIBE COMMAND

Sometimes the COL table can be inconvenient to access or remember. A faster method of listing the attributes of a table is with the UFI command DESCRIBE. The format of the DESCRIBE command is as follows.

```
DESCRIBE table-name
```

To illustrate the describe command, let's "describe" the FACULTY table.

```
UFI> DESCRIBE FACULTY

  # size csize type            name
  1    6     6 2  character    FAC-ID
  2   17    17 2  character    FACULTY-NAME
  3   10    10 2  character    DEPARTMENT
  4    6     6 2  character    GENDER
  5    5    40 1  numeric      SALARY
```

STORAGE OF DATA

ORACLE stores data for tuples in a very efficient manner. Each data value is stored in the minimum number of bytes possible. Data separators (unprintable characters) are placed between data values so as to reduce the amount of actual data storage needed to store tuples. When we execute a SQL command to retrieve data, ORACLE retrieves it from its "packed" format and presents it in formatted fashion.

For example, if we executed the following SQL command,

```
UFI> SELECT * FROM FACULTY;

FAC-ID FACULTY-NAME_____ DEPARTMENT_ GENDER SALARY
J01    RAYMOND J. JOHNSON      COMP SCI    MALE   40000
S01    WENDY SWIMMER           COMP SCI    FEMALE 45000
D01    AMY DANCER              COMP SCI    FEMALE 34500
J02    BOB JONES               ACCOUNTING  MALE   35000
N01    JACK NELSON             HISTORY     MALE   28000
```

the data is retrieved and formatted for us. These operations are transparent to the user. Even though the data appears to fall into nice neat columns, it might actually be stored as follows.

```
J01@RAYMOND J. JOHNSON@COMP SCI@MALE@40000@S02@WENDY SWIMMER
@COMP SCI@FEMALE@45000@D01@AMY DANCER@COMP SCI@FEMALE@34500@
J02@BOB JONES@ACCOUNTING@MALE@35000@N01@JACK NELSON@HISTORY@
MALE@28000
```

We have used the symbol @ to represent the data separator. This is not the actual symbol that is used to separate the data; we are just using it for illustrative purposes.

The obvious disadvantage of this scheme is that every time data is retrieved, it must be reformatted. However, the storage savings and flexibility will generally outweigh the disadvantages of the reformatting efforts.

ORACLE DATA STORAGE ORGANIZATION

Data storage for ORACLE tables is divided into partitions. Partitions are implemented through data files. These files must reside on a direct access storage device (DASD), usually magnetic disks. Tables consist of two separate parts: the data part and the index part. Both data and index parts are stored in partitions.

Data and indexes for tables are directed to partitions by means of storage spaces. Storage spaces are templates that describe the data and index storage space allocated for each table. Many tables can have data allocated via the same storage space template. Storage spaces describe to ORACLE how much space, measured in data pages, to allocate for the data and indexes for each table.

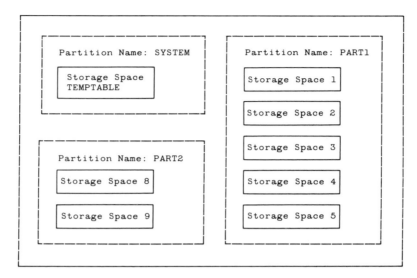

Figure 7.1

It is important to note that storage spaces do not allocate storage space, they are only a model for allocating storage space. The space is allocated when tuple occurrences are added to the table.

The relationship between partitions and storage spaces is shown in Figure 7.1. Partitions contain both data and index values. These values are stored in accordance with storage space definitions. The number of table and index values that can be stored within a partition depends on the size of the partition, the number of tuple occurrences in the table, the number of indexes, and the storage space parameters. As we will see later a storage space does not contain the actual data; it is only a template to store the data.

When ORACLE is initially loaded onto your system it contains one partition called SYSTEM and one storage space called TEMPTABLE. All the system (data dictionary) tables are located in the SYSTEM partition in accordance with the storage space TEMPTABLE. The SYSTEM partition is the default partition. This means that **if users do not explicitly direct their table data to another partition, it will automatically reside in the SYSTEM partition**. This is not a good practice, for the SYSTEM partition will soon be flooded with user data and indexes. Once the SYSTEM partition is full, nothing can be added to the database: no new user can be added, no new tables can be created, and no data can be added to any table. **User data and indexes should always be directed into user partitions**.

Creating Partitions

Only users with DBA authority can create partitions. We will briefly describe the process of creating partitions only for informational purposes.

The first thing that must be done to create a partition is to give the partition a name. This is done with the SQL command CREATE PARTITION. The format of this command is:

```
CREATE PARTITION partition-name
```

Partition-name is considered an identifier and therefore follows all the basic rules for naming identifiers. For example, if we wanted to create a partition called PART1, we would issue the following command.

```
UFI> CREATE PARTITION PART1;

Partition created.
```

The second thing that must be done to create a partition is to create a file name at the operating system level that will be used to hold the values in the partition. This file must contain contiguous storage. This usually evolves from the execution of an operating system command.

Finally, the file must be added to the partition via the ALTER PARTITION command. The syntax of the ALTER PARTITION command is:

```
ALTER PARTITION partition-name ADD FILE 'filename'
```

Let's assume that we have created a contiguous file called FILE1 at the operating system level and we wish to add it to our recently created partition called PART1. The following SQL command would alter our partition.

```
UFI> ALTER PARTITION PART1 ADD FILE 'FILE1';

Partition altered.
```

The size of a partition can be increased by generating another database file and adding it to the partition. The database cannot currently handle more than 16 database files per partition.

Creating Space Definitions

Space definitions are a model for how table data and indexes are stored. Each user-name should have their own space definition(s). The creation of space definitions is usually considered a database administrator's function in most ORACLE installations. However, this function can be performed by the user. Space definitions are created through the SQL command CREATE SPACE DEFINITION. The syntax of the CREATE SPACE DEFINITION command is:

```
CREATE SPACE DEFINITION space-definition-name
```

```
┌─────────┐ DATAPAGES ([ INITIAL allocation    ] ┌─────────┐
│         │            [ ,INCREMENT allocation]  │         │
│         │            [ ,MAXEXTENTS quota     ] │         │
└─────────┘            [ ,PCTFREE percentage   ]) └─────────┘

  ┌─────────┐ INDEXPAGES ([ INITIAL allocation    ] ┌─────────┐
  │         │             [ ,INCREMENT allocation]  │         │
  │         │             [ ,MAXEXTENTS quota     ]) │         │
  └─────────┘                                        └─────────┘
```

```
[PARTITION partition-name]
```

The symbol space-definition-name is an identifier. The options DATAPAGES and INDEXPAGES should be self-explanatory. ORACLE's method of allocating storage is an incremental one. Instead of initially allocating all the requested storage for a space definition, ORACLE only requests storage when it is needed.

INITIAL refers to the number of pages of storage that are initially allocated to store either data or indexes. This storage is allocated when the first tuple occurrence is inserted into the table. The default value for INITIAL is 5 pages. This means that when you insert the first tuple into a table using the storage space definition, 10 pages of storage (5 for data and 5 for indexes) are allocated to your table, assuming that you do not change the value of either or both of the INITIALs.

INCREMENT refers to the number of pages that will be allocated when you fill the number of INITIAL pages (either data or index) allocated. The default value for INCREMENT is 25. This means that when you overflow the initial 5 data pages, you will get an additional 25 pages to store any additional data or indexes that you might add to your tables.

MAXEXTENTS is the number of increments of INCREMENT pages that are allowed. The default value for MAXEXTENTS is 16. A common error in ORACLE installations is "MAXEXTENTS EXCEEDED." This means that you have run out of space in your space definition, and if you wish to add more tuple occurrences to your table, you must alter this value. This operation is discussed later in this chapter.

If the default values are not changed, there is a maximum of 405 data and 405 index pages that can be allocated for each table that utilizes the storage space definition.

Extent	Pages Allocated	Cumulative Total
INITIAL	5	5
1	25	30
2	25	55
3	25	80
4	25	105
/	/	/
15	25	380
16	25	405

PCTFREE is only relevant for data pages. It refers to the amount of free space allocated for expansion of data values (remember ORACLE packs data values as tightly as possible) or adding of additional attributes to currently existing tables. The default value for PCTFREE is 20. If you do not anticipate altering your tables very much, then you might want to consider setting the value of PCTFREE very small. If you set PCTFREE very small and then decide to alter your tables, ORACLE will run much slower for it must do extra searching for the additional attribute values.

The partition-name is obviously the name of the partition that we want to insert the storage space into. If the partition-name is omitted, the storage space uses the SYSTEM partition. All the operations that we have just described are completely transparent to the user.

To illustrate the creation of storage spaces, let us consider our sample database with the three tables: STUDENT, COURSE, and FACULTY. Since this is only an example and probably will not be changed very much, we will allocate very little space for the storage space in which we will store our tabular data and indexes.

```
UFI> CREATE SPACE DEFINITION SCHOOL
  2      DATAPAGES (INITIAL 5,
  3                 INCREMENTS 5,
  4                 MAXEXTENTS 5,
  5                 PCTFREE 10),
  6      INDEXPAGES (INITIAL 3,
  7                  INCREMENTS 3,
  8                  MAXEXTENTS 3)   PARTITION PART1;

Space created,
```

Dropping Storage Spaces

Storage space definitions can be dropped by the user-name that created them or by any user-name with DBA authority. To drop a space definition, we must use the DROP SPACE command. The syntax of the command is

```
DROP SPACE space-definition name
```

If we wanted to drop the space definition called SCHOOL, we would issue the following SQL command.

```
UFI> DROP SPACE SCHOOL;
```

```
Space dropped.
```

By dropping a storage space definition, what ORACLE actually means is closing a storage space for further use. Once a storage space has been dropped, no other table can be created using that space definition name. The tables that currently utilize the now-defunct space definition are unaffected. Remember that the table data and indexes actually reside in a partition, not in the space definition, so dropping a space definition does not effect previously created tables.

Altering Storage Spaces

Once a storage space has been created any of its parameters can be altered via the ALTER SPACE command. Changing the parameters of a space definition has no effect on the tables currently residing in the storage space. Only new tables are affected. The syntax for the ALTER SPACE command is:

```
ALTER SPACE space-definition-name

        DATAPAGES ([ INITIAL allocation    ]
                   [ ,INCREMENT allocation]
                   [ ,MAXEXTENTS quota     ]
                   [ ,PCTFREE percentage  ])

        INDEXPAGES ([ INITIAL allocation    ]
                    [ ,INCREMENT allocation]
                    [ ,MAXEXTENTS quota    ])

    [ PARTITION partition-name]
```

Only the parameter values that are specified are modified.

Suppose that we have realized that the INCREMENT value of DATAPAGES is too small and should be set to 10. This could be changed very easily with the following command.

```
UFI> ALTER SPACE SCHOOL DATAPAGES (INCREMENT 10);
```

```
Space altered.
```

Placing Table Data and Indexes into Storage Spaces

Placing table data into a partition is a simple matter of affixing the SPACE clause to end of the CREATE TABLE command. To illustrate, let's re-create our three tables as follows.

```
UFI> REMARK Let's drop the tables first
UFI> DROP TABLE STUDENT;

Table dropped.

UFI> DROP TABLE COURSE;

Table dropped.

UFI> DROP TABLE FACULTY;

Table dropped.

UFI> CREATE TABLE STUDENT (STU_ID CHAR (6) NOT NULL,
   2                       STUDENT_NAME CHAR (17),
   3                       ADDRESS CHAR (20),
   4                       BIRTHDATE DATE,
   5                       GENDER CHAR (6)) SPACE SCHOOL;

Table created.

UFI> CREATE TABLE COURSE (COURSE_ID CHAR (6) NOT NULL,
   2                      COURSE_TITLE CHAR (20),
   3                      SECTION_NO NUMBER (2),
   4                      STU_ID CHAR (6) NOT NULL,
   5                      FAC_ID CHAR (6) NOT NULL))
   6                      SPACE SCHOOL;

Table created.

UFI> CREATE TABLE FACULTY (FAC_ID CHAR (6) NOT NULL,
   2                       FACULTY_NAME CHAR (17),
   3                       DEPARTMENT CHAR (10),
   4                       GENDER CHAR (6),
   5                       SALARY NUMBER (5)) SPACE SCHOOL;

Table created.

UFI> CREATE UNIQUE INDEX STUDENT_PK ON STUDENT(STU_ID);
   2 NOSYSSORT

Index created.
```

```
UFI> CREATE UNIQUE INDEX COURSE_PK ON
  2   COURSE (STU_ID, FAC_ID, COURSE_ID) NOSYSSORT;

Index created.

UFI> CREATE UNIQUE INDEX FACULTY_PK ON
  2   FACULTY (FAC_ID) NOSYSSORT;

Index created.
```

Obviously by dropping the tables we will lose the data stored in them. We must re-create the tuples via the INSERT command illustrated in the following chapter.

Since the indexes are associated with tables, they are automatically placed in the same storage space with the data tables.

As you can see from the example, more than one table can utilize the same storage space definition. Remember that each table has its own storage space definition and the definition parameters are specified for each table that uses that definition.

Data Dictionary Tables Related to Storage Spaces

There are three data dictionary tables that are useful for determining how much storage that you are currently using.

The first of these tables is cleverly called STORAGE. It shows how much space your data and indexes are taking up.

```
UFI> SET NUMWIDTH 7
UFI> SELECT * FROM STORAGE;
```

NAME	TYPE	WHICH	STORAGE	EXTENTS
COURSE	TABLE	DATA	5	1
COURSE	TABLE	INDEX	3	1
FACULTY	TABLE	DATA	5	1
FACULTY	TABLE	INDEX	3	1
STUDENT	TABLE	DATA	5	1
STUDENT	TABLE	INDEX	3	1

```
6 Records selected.
```

The second table, SPACES, reminds you of what values you specified on your storage space(s) definition.

```
UFI> COLUMN SNAME FORMAT A8
UFI> COLUMN PNAME FORMAT A8
UFI> COLUMN PCT FORMAT 999
UFI> SELECT * FROM SPACES
```

SNAME	DATA1	DATA2	EXT-MAX	INDEX1	INDEX2	MAX-EXT	PCT	PNAME
TEMPTABLE	20	100	240	20	100	240	1	SYSTEM
SCHOOL	5	5	5	3	3	3	10	SCHOOL

The third table is EXTENTS, which indicates where the extents have been stored.

```
UFI> COLUMN NAME FORMAT A7
UFI> SELECT * FROM EXTENTS;

NAME___ TYPE___ WHICH    STORAGE    STARTING      ENDING____
STUDENT TABLE   DATA         5         46           50
STUDENT TABLE   INDEX        3         51           53
COURSE  TABLE   DATA         5         54           58
COURSE  TABLE   INDEX        3         59           61
FACULTY TABLE   DATA         5         62           66
FACULTY TABLE   INDEX        3         67           69
```

The STARTING and ENDING are the starting and end block addresses relative to the partition in which extents reside.

ROWID: THE ORACLE DATABASE KEY

Storage on most computer systems is organized by blocks or pages. A block is the smallest unit of storage used by the ORACLE database system. For example, on Harris Computer Systems, a block consists of eight sectors or 2688 bytes. Most tuples are smaller than 2688 bytes, so more than one tuple will fit in a block. There must be a method to access records from within a block.

In Chapter 1 of this text we introduced the concept of a database key. We noted that a database key was a "specific location of a record in a database." ORACLE calls its database keys ROWIDs. ROWID is a predefined value consisting of three subparts.

1. Relative block address, This represents the block number within the partition.

2. Relative record number, This is the record or tuple number within the block.

3. Partition number, This is the number of the partition where the tuple resides.

The value of ROWID is generated when a new tuple is stored into a table. The value of ROWID can be displayed as a virtual attribute. It is displayed as three sets of hexadecimal numbers with periods separating each subpart.

```
<Relative Block Address>.<Relative Record #>.<Partition#>
```

The following is an example of a SELECT command. Be aware that if you try to execute the same command, your values of ROWID will probably be different from the displayed values of ROWID. The reason for this is that your tuples are probably stored in different locations from ours.

```
UFI> SELECT ROWID, FACULTY.* FROM FACULTY;

ROWID_____ FAC-ID FACULTY-NAME_____ DEPARTMENT GENDER SALARY
00000270.0001.0002 J01    RAYMOND J. JOHNSON COMP SCI   MALE   40000
00000270.0002.0002 S01    WENDY SWIMMER      COMP SCI   FEMALE 45000
00000270.0003.0002 D01    AMY DANCER         COMP SCI   FEMALE 34500
00000270.0004.0002 J02    BOB JONES          ACCOUNTING MALE   35000
00000270.0005.0002 N01    JACK NELSON        HISTORY    MALE   28000
```

SUMMARY

This chapter described how ORACLE data tables are created and altered. We also discussed what indexes were and how they assisted ORACLE in retrieving data and preserving the uniqueness of primary keys. Methods of organizing data and index storages were also explored. After reading this chapter, you should be familiar with the following commands, concepts, and terms.

A. CREATE TABLE
B. ORACLE data types (CHAR, DATE, LONG, NUMBER)
C. SET LONG
D. NULL
E. DROP TABLE
F. ALTER TABLE ADD
G. ALTER TABLE MODIFY
H. CREATE INDEX
I. CREATE UNIQUE INDEX
J. SYSSORT/NOSYSSORT
K. PCTFREE
L. COMPRESS/NOCOMPRESS
M. ROWS=
N. DROP INDEX
O. The ORACLE data dictionary
P. DTAB
Q. TAB
R. COL

S. DESCRIBE
T. How ORACLE data is actually stored in tables
U. ROWID
V. The relationship between partitions and storage spaces
W. CREATE PARTITION
X. ALTER PARTITION
Y. CREATE SPACE DEFINITION
Z. INITIAL
AA. INCREMENT
BB. MAXEXTENTS
CC. PCTFREE
DD. DATAPAGES
EE. INDEXPAGES
FF. DROP SPACE
GG. ALTER SPACE
HH. Placing data and indexes into a storage space

EXERCISES

1. Explain the difference between a partition and a storage space.
2. Find out how big a page size is on your computer system.

3. What two things do we have to do to attributes designated as primary keys to ensure that the primary key guidelines are followed?

4. Explain what information the following data dictionary tables provide.

   a. TAB
   b. COL
   c. INDEXES
   d. SESSIONS
   e. SYSUSERLIST
   f. STORAGE
   g. SPACES
   h. EXTENTS

4. Perform the following operations ORACLE on your system. It would probably be helpful to you if you opened a SPOOL file to capture all the output from the commands so that you could study it at a later point.

   a. Find out the names of the partitions on your ORACLE system. This information should be available from either your teacher and/or your ORACLE database administrator.
   b. Create a storage space in the appropriate partition.
   c. Create the tables that we have outlined in this chapter. We will use them to illustrate the concepts covered in the remainder of this text.
   d. Display the contents of the system table DTAB.
   e. Display the contents of the system table TAB.
   f. Display the contents of COL for all your tables.
   g. Display the contents of COL for one of your tables.
   h. DESCRIBE some of your tables.
   i. Add the attribute YR—SVC to the FACULTY table.
   j. DESCRIBE the FACULTY table.
   k. Change the length of the attribute SALARY in the FACULTY table to six numeric positions.
   l. DESCRIBE the FACULTY table.
   m. Drop the FACULTY table.
   n. Display the contents of TAB.
   o. Create some indexes on your tables.
   p. Display the contents of the system table INDEXES.
   q. Drop one of the indexes that you just created.
   r. Display the contents of INDEXES.

REFERENCES

1. *Harris ORACLE Reference Manual.* Harris Corporation, Ft. Lauderdale, FL, Release 4.1.4, May 1985.

2. *Harris ORACLE User's Guide.* Harris Corporation, Ft. Lauderdale, FL, February 1984.

3. *Harris ORACLE Database Administrator's Guide.* Harris Corporation, Ft. Lauderdale, FL, Release 4.2.2, September 1985.

8

Data Maintenance

PURPOSE: The purpose of this chapter is to introduce you to the various types of data maintenance capabilities of ORACLE. The ORACLE data loader and IMPORT/EXPORT system utilities are illustrated. The commit and rollback features of ORACLE are also explored.

Data maintenance consists of three basic operations:

1. Adding new tuples to tables.
2. Deleting currently existing tuples from tables.
3. Modifying values of currently existing tuples.

In industrial databases, these three operations are usually performed by writing programs in conventional languages and linking those programs to ORACLE databases via the Host Language Interface (HLI). However, as an introduction to the ORACLE data maintenance commands, we will introduce the various maintenance commands directly in this chapter.

When data in a database is being altered, certain problems can occur. These problems usually revolve around concurrent access of tuples. For databases with concurrent users, data maintenance provides some interesting problems. For example, if two users attempt to update the same tuple simultaneously, which user's update takes place first? Suppose that we have a hardware failure during the execution of a series of updates. How do we know which tuples have been updated? How would we recover from a disk failure in which all the data on a disk was lost? The concurrency problem is addressed in Chapter 13, and the hardware/software failure problems are discussed in this chapter.

THE INSERT COMMAND

The purpose of the INSERT command is to add tuples to our tables. Each new tuple is added as the last tuple in our table. There is no way to place a tuple in any location but the last tuple in a table. Tuples can be appended one at a time directly into the table or SELECTed from other tables.

The INSERT command can be executed in any of the following three methods:

1. As a direct SQL command
2. Through the ORACLE bulk data loader system utility.
3. Through the Host Language Interface to some conventional (host) programming language.

There are two separate syntaxes for the INSERT command.

```
INSERT INTO table-name
    [ (attribute-name1, attribute-name2, . . .) ]
    VALUES (value1, value2, . . .)
```

or

```
INSERT INTO table-name
    [ (attribute-name1, attribute-name2, . . .) ]
    SELECT select-list
    FROM table-name
    [ WHERE θ ]
    [ GROUP BY attribute-name [ HAVING conditions ]]
```

The Simple INSERT Command

To illustrate the simple INSERT command, let's add another tuple in the student table. Let's assume that the new student's data is as follows:

Student ID:	S011
Student Name:	Dottie Wilson
Address:	1600 Penn Ave
Birthdate:	October 10, 1965
Gender:	Female

The following INSERT command will append the new tuple to the table STU-DENT.

```
UFI> INSERT INTO STUDENT VALUES ('S011', 'DOTTIE WILSON',
   2  '1600 PENN AVE', '10-OCT-65', 'FEMALE');

Record inserted.
```

Notice that we listed the values of the attributes in the order of attributes in the table definition. Remember the DESCRIBE table-name command if you forget the order of the attributes. ORACLE will match values to attributes on a position-by-position basis. As long as the data types and/or lengths do not conflict, the new tuple is added to the table. If any error occurs, an error message is displayed, and the tuple is not added to the table. Also notice that each value was specified within a set of quotes. All data of types CHAR, DATE, or LONG must be entered in quotes. All data of type NUMBER is entered without quotes. The student's birthdate must be converted to the dd-mon-yy format before it is input. Only one tuple at a time can be entered into a table via this simple format of the INSERT command. A value must be entered for each attribute in the table.

To illustrate the inserting of numeric data, let's add a new faculty member to the FACULTY table. Remember that the FACULTY table contains the numeric attribute SALARY. Let's insert the following tuple.

```
   Faculty ID: L01
 Faculty name: Leo Jones
   Department: Management
       Gender: Male
       Salary: $45,000

UFI> INSERT INTO FACULTY VALUES ('L01', 'LEO JONES',
   2  'MANAGEMENT', 'MALE', 45000);

Record inserted.
```

If we wish to enter the attribute values in a different order from that specified in the table definition, we must specify the order of the attributes. Let's enter another tuple with the attributes in a different order.

```
    Birthdate: November 22, 1963
 Student Name: Winston Neely
   Student ID: S012
       Gender: Male
      Address: #1 Bulldog Dr.

UFI> INSERT INTO STUDENT
   2  (BIRTHDATE, STUDENT_NAME, STU_ID, GENDER, ADDRESS)
```

```
3   VALUES ('22-NOV-63', 'WINSTON NEELY', 'S012', 'MALE',
4   '#1 BULLDOG ''SDR.');
```

```
Record inserted.
```

Notice that the attributes values are listed in the same order as the attributes in the list in line 2 of the SQL command buffer. Also, note that the value of ADDRESS contains a single quote. The method of inserting a single quote is the same as it is in most conventional programming languages, use two consecutive single quote marks (not a double quote).

If we wish to insert a null value for an attribute, there are two methods of accomplishing it. The first method consists of placing the ORACLE constant NULL in the attribute's place in the value list. For example, suppose that we wanted to insert the following tuple into the student table.

```
   Student ID: S013
 Student Name: Bonny Simpson
      Address: Unknown
    Birthdate: Unknown
       Gender: Female
```

```
UFI> INSERT INTO STUDENT VALUES ('S013', 'BONNY SIMPSON',
  2   NULL, NULL, 'FEMALE');
```

```
Record inserted.
```

Note that the word NULL is not enclosed in quotes. The reason for this is that NULL is a predefined constant.

The second method of inserting a null value for an attribute is to specify the attribute names in an attribute list and omit the name of the attribute(s) that are to be set to null values. Any items not specified in the attribute list are automatically set to null values. Let's use the same example that we used earlier to illustrate this method.

```
UFI> INSERT INTO STUDENT
  2   (STU-ID, STUDENT_NAME, GENDER)
  3   VALUES ('S013', 'BONNY SIMPSON', 'FEMALE');
```

```
Record inserted.
```

By executing this command, we would insert a duplicate tuple into our table. (We just inserted the same tuple in the previous example.) Note that ORACLE does not automatically check for duplicate tuples. However, if we had created a unique index on the attribute STU-ID, the system would have flagged the above execution of the INSERT command with the error message of "DUPLICATE INDEX VALUE ."

If we want to enter today's date into an attribute (of type DATE), we can use the predefined constant SYSDATE. SYSDATE is a constant and does not require quotes.

Copying Tuples from Other Tables

The second method of inserting tuples consists of copying data from other tables. This technique produces another base table as the actual data is permanently saved. This method produces duplicate data and, except in rare instances, should be avoided.

To utilize this technique, a new table must be created with the desired attributes before executing the INSERT command. To illustrate this technique, let's create a table that will contain only the tuples of the male faculty members. The first order of business is to create the new table that we will call MALE-FACULTY.

```
UFI> CREATE TABLE MALE-FACULTY (FAC-ID CHAR (6) NOT NULL,
   2                            FACULTY_NAME CHAR (18),
   3                            DEPARTMENT CHAR (6),
   4                            GENDER CHAR (6),
   5                            SALARY NUMBER (5))
   6                            SPACE SCHOOL;

Table created.

UFI> REMARK . . ... Now let's load the table

UFI> INSERT INTO MALE_FACULTY
   2 SELECT * FROM FACULTY WHERE GENDER = 'MALE';

   3  Records created.
```

The structure of the new table does not have to match the structure of the "old" table. For example, suppose that we wanted to construct another table that contained only female faculty members. Why should the new table contain the attribute GENDER when we know that all the tuples are female (actually tuples do not have a gender, the data that is represented in the tuples belong to females)? Let's further assume that we wish to add an additional attribute called HIGHEST DEGREE EARNED (which we will call HI_DEGREE) to our table. Again we must create the new table before we can insert any data into the table.

```
UFI> CREATE TABLE FEMALE-FACULTY (FAC_ID CHAR (6) NOT NULL,
   2                              FACULTY_NAME CHAR (18),
   3                              DEPARTMENT CHAR (6),
   4                              SALARY NUMBER (5)),
   5                              HI_DEGREE CHAR (3))
   6                              SPACE SCHOOL;

Table created.
```

```
UFI> REMARK . . ... Load the table with data

UFI> INSERT INTO FEMALE_FACULTY
   2   (FAC_ID, FACULTY_NAME, DEPARTMENT, SALARY)
   3   SELECT FAC_ID, FACULTY_NAME, DEPARTMENT, SALARY
   4   FROM FACULTY WHERE GENDER = 'FEMALE';

2 Records created.
```

Since we did not wish to copy all the attributes from the FACULTY table to the FEMALE-FACULTY table, we must specify in the SELECT command the attributes that we want copied. Notice that the attribute HI-DEGREE does not appear in the FACULTY table, so its value is set to null for each tuple copied. These null values can be changed with the UPDATE command discussed later in this chapter.

SQL Variables

Even though the INSERT command is relatively easy to use, if we wanted to enter several tuples at a time, it would become very tedious. SQL variables are a solution to this problem. A SQL variable is a variable that can be used in conjunction with an INSERT command. The format of a SQL variable is a string of characters preceded by an ampersand (&) or a double ampersand (&&). The ampersand character can be changed by the use of the UFI command SET DEFINE <char> command. The maximum string length of a SQL variable name is 15 characters. The following are examples of legal SQL variables:

```
&NAME, &AGE, &salary, &1, &22, &TEST1
```

These SQL variables are used as placeholders for constant values in the value list of the INSERT command. When the INSERT command is executed, the user is prompted with

```
Enter value for <SQL variable string>:
```

At this point the user inputs the value for the attribute represented by the string.

SQL variables are temporary entities as they are not stored in the data dictionary. This means when you exit ORACLE, the current values of the SQL variables are lost.

Executing INSERT commands with SQL variables.   Let's illustrate SQL variables by appending a new faculty member tuple to the FACULTY table. The following faculty member has decided to teach at our university.

```
     Faculty ID: L05
   Faculty Name: Jim Adams
     Department: Foreign Language
         Gender: Male
         Salary: $35,000

UFI> INSERT INTO FACULTY VALUES (&FAC_ID, &FACULTY_NAME,
   2  &DEPARTMENT, &GENDER, &SALARY);

Enter value for FAC_ID: 'L05'
Enter value for FACULTY_NAME: 'JIM ADAMS'
Enter value for DEPARTMENT: 'FORN LANG'
Enter value for GENDER: 'MALE'
Enter value for SALARY: 35000

UFI> INSERT INTO FACULTY VALUES ('L05', 'JIM ADAMS',
   2  'FORN LANG', 'MALE', 35000);

1 Record created.
```

Notice that after ORACLE finishes prompting the user for values, it echoes the INSERT statement with the values substituted for the variables. This is done automatically so that you can verify that the correct values have been placed in the attributes. If you do not wish the INSERT statement echoed, you can execute the UFI command SET VERIFY OFF. Naturally to turn the INSERT echo back on, we must execute the UFI command SET VERIFY ON command.

If you study the INSERT example, you will notice that the values for FAC-ID, FACULTY-NAME, DEPARTMENT, and GENDER have quotes placed around them. The reason is that these values belong to attributes of type CHAR. Values for types CHAR, LONG, and DATE must be enclosed in single quotes. The value for the attribute SALARY (35000) is not enclosed in quotes for it is of type NUMBER. This inconvenience can be taken care of very simply. If we know that the attribute value will require quotes, we can place the quotes around the SQL variable(s). When ORACLE detects quotes around SQL variables, it now only searches for a carriage return as the only value delimiter.

Let's change our example to reflect this new knowledge.

```
UFI> INSERT INTO FACULTY VALUES ('&FAC_ID', '&FACULTY_NAME',
   2  '&DEPARTMENT', '&GENDER', &SALARY);


Enter value for FAC_ID: L05
Enter value for FACULTY_NAME: JIM ADAMS
Enter value for DEPARTMENT: FORN LANG
Enter value for GENDER: MALE
Enter value for SALARY: 35000
```

```
UFI> INSERT INTO FACULTY VALUES ('L05', 'JIM ADAMS',
  2  'FORN LANG', 'MALE', 35000);

1 Record created.
```

In all the examples, we have used the attribute name as the string post-fixed to the ampersand. Remember that this string is what is displayed after the "Enter value for" string. It does not have to be the attribute name. It could be some shortened form of the attribute name or simply a number. This concept is illustrated below.

```
UFI> INSERT INTO FACULTY VALUES ('&FID', '&1', '&DEPT',
  2  '&SEX', &2);

Enter value for FID: L05
Enter value for 1: JIM ADAMS
Enter value for DEPT: FORN LANG
Enter value for SEX: MALE
Enter value for 2: 35000

UFI> INSERT INTO FACULTY VALUES ('L05', 'JIM ADAMS',
  2  'FORN LANG', 'MALE', 35000);

1 Record created.
```

At this point SQL variables may seem like more trouble than they are worth. However, if you will remember, ORACLE stores the last SQL command in the SQL buffer. One of the options that we have with a command stored in the SQL buffer is to execute it (either with RUN or /). If we wanted to enter several tuples into a table, we could simply set up an INSERT command with SQL variables and continue executing it as many times as we wish. If the command were to be used frequently, it could be stored in a START file and copied into the SQL buffer from an external file and executed. To illustrate this concept, let's use the INSERT command to append several tuples to the FACULTY table.

```
UFI> REMARK . . ... Turn INSERT Echo Off

UFI> SET VERIFY OFF

UFI> INSERT INTO FACULTY VALUES ('&FAC_ID', '&FACULTY_NAME',
  2  '&DEPT', '&SEX', &SALARY);

Enter value for FAC-ID: D05
Enter value for FACULTY_NAME: WENDY WILSON
Enter value for DEPT: INFO SYSTEMS
```

```
Enter value for SEX: FEMALE
Enter value for SALARY: 38000

1 Record created.

UFI> REMARK . . ... Let's execute the same command again

UFI> /

Enter value for FAC_ID: C02
Enter value for FACULTY_NAME: AMY GRIFFIN
Enter value for DEPT: MUSIC
Enter value for SEX: MALE
Enter value for SALARY: 39000

1 Record created.
```

Short-term variables. If the SQL variable is preceded by one ampersand, it is called a short-term variable. This means that the value is defined for only one execution of the INSERT command. A new value must be entered with each execution of the INSERT command. Each execution of the INSERT command will cause the prompt "Enter value for" to be displayed.

Long term variables. If the SQL variable is preceded by two ampersands, it is called a long-term variable. This means that once the variable is assigned a value, that value remains in effect until the user changes it, "undefines" it, or exits the system. To illustrate the long-term variable, let's assume that we wanted to insert several tuples into the FACULTY table. Let's further assume that all the faculty members that we were entering are members of the Computer Science Department and are all males.

```
UFI> REMARK . . ... Turn INSERT Echo Back On
UFI> SET VERIFY ON
UFI> INSERT INTO FACULTY VALUES ('&FAC_ID', '&FACULTY_NAME',
   2  '&&DEPARTMENT', '&&GENDER', &SALARY);

Enter value for FAC_ID: H02
Enter value for FACULTY_NAME: JACK WILSON
Enter value for DEPARTMENT: COMP SCI
Enter value for GENDER: MALE
Enter value for SALARY: 35000

Old:  2  '&&DEPARTMENT', '&&GENDER', &SALARY);
New:  2  'COMP SCI', 'MALE', 35000);

UFI> INSERT INTO FACULTY VALUES ('H02', 'JACK WILSON',
   2  'COMP SCI', 'MALE', 35000);

1 Record created.
```

```
UFI> /

Enter value for FAC_ID: W03
Enter value for FACULTY_NAME: TIM SMITH
Enter value for SALARY: 38000

Old:  2  '&&DEPARTMENT', '&&GENDER', &SALARY);
New:  2  'COMP SCI', 'MALE', 38000);

UFI> INSERT INTO FACULTY VALUES ('W03', 'TIM SMITH',
   2  'COMP SCI', 'MALE', 38000);

1 Record created.
```

Notice that once the values of &&DEPARTMENT and &&GENDER were established, ORACLE did not prompt for the values again.

There is a second method of establishing the existence of a long-term variable. This consists of using the UFI command DEF <variable-name>=<value> command. The double ampersand is not used to define long-term variables in the DEF command for only long-term variables can be used in the DEF command. Using this method, we could assign values to SQL variables as follows:

```
UFI> DEF DEPARTMENT='COMP SCI'

UFI> DEF GENDER=MALE

UFI> REMARK . . .. Execute the INSERT command again

UFI> INSERT INTO FACULTY VALUES ('&FAC_ID', '&FACULTY_NAME',
   2  '&&DEPARTMENT', '&&GENDER', &SALARY);

Enter value for FAC_ID: S04
Enter value for FACULTY_NAME: RALPH SMITH
Enter value for SALARY: 41000

Old:  2  '&&DEPARTMENT', '&&GENDER', &SALARY);
New:  2  'COMP SCI', 'MALE', 41000);

UFI> INSERT INTO FACULTY VALUES ('S04', 'RALPH SMITH',
   2  'COMP SCI', 'MALE', 41000);

1 Record created.
```

Note that even though the long-term variables defined in the DEF command are not preceded by a double ampersand, when they are used in the INSERT command, they are. When ORACLE encounters the long-term variables &&DEPARTMENT and &&GENDER in the INSERT command, it checks to see if they have been assigned a value. If they have, no prompt is generated and the current value is used. If they have not been assigned a value, a prompt is displayed and ORACLE waits for an assignment.

The value of the long term variable GENDER is not enclosed in quotes. If the value of a long-term variable does not contain a delimiter (blank, single quote, or the CMDSEP character), it does not have to be enclosed in quotes.

Long-term variables may also have numeric names. The following DEF command looks a little strange, especially to mathematicians, but it works.

```
UFI> DEF 1=2
```

This command sets the long-term variable &&1 to the numeric value two.

The value of a long-term variable can be changed by using the DEF command and simply assigning it a new value. A long-term variable can be "undefined" with the UFI command UNDEFINE <variable-name>. UNDEFINE can be shortened to UNDEF.

```
UFI> UNDEFINE DEPARTMENT

symbol DEPARTMENT was "COMP SCI"
```

Other uses of variables.   SQL variables do not have to be used exclusively in INSERT commands. They may be used in any SQL command. Below are some examples of the use of variables in SELECT commands.

```
SELECT * FROM STUDENT WHERE GENDER = '&&SEX';
SELECT &&1 FROM FACULTY WHERE SALARY > &&2;
SELECT &&1 FROM &&2 WHERE &&3 != &&4;
SELECT * FROM FACULTY WHERE DEPARTMENT = '&1';
```

The use of long-term variables with the START command.   The UFI command START can be used to copy commands (both UFI and/or SQL) commands from external files into the SQL command buffer and execute them. The command becomes much more powerful when we can specify parameters in the START command. The values of these parameters correspond to long-term variables specified as numbers (&&1, &&2, &&3, etc.). The format of the START command is the same as we specified it in Chapter 5, except that we can now expand the command with a parameter list.

```
START filename parameter-list
```

where parameter-list is a list of constants separated by blanks corresponding to &&1, &&2, &&3, and so on.

For example, suppose that the following INSERT command was stored in a start-file called PUTITIN.

```
INSERT INTO FACULTY VALUES (&&1, &&2, &&3, &&4, &&5);
```

We could execute this INSERT command with the following START command.

```
UFI> START PUTITIN  C04 "ANNE WHITE" MARKETING FEMALE 39999

UFI>  INSERT INTO FACULTY VALUES ('C04', 'ANNE WHITE', 'MARKETING', 'FEMALE', 39999)

1 Record created.
```

The START command with parameters is not limited to use only to the INSERT command. It can be used with any other SQL command. The start-file is usually created by using the computer system's text editor.

THE DELETE COMMAND

The purpose of the DELETE command is to remove tuples from ORACLE tables. The syntax of the DELETE command is:

```
DELETE [FROM] table-name [ WHERE θ ]
```

Any tuple for which the theta condition(s) is true is removed from the table. If the optional WHERE clause is omitted, all tuples are removed from the table. This command does not remove the table definition from the data dictionary. Remember that the DROP command must be used for this.

The following are examples of the DELETE command.

```
UFI> REMARK . . .. Let's assume that no new tuples were
UFI> REMARK . . .. added to the tables STUDENT and FACULTY
UFI> DELETE FROM STUDENT WHERE STUDENT_NAME = "SAM WALES";
1 record deleted.

UFI> DELETE FROM FACULTY WHERE GENDER = "FEMALE";

2 records deleted.

UFI> DELETE COURSE;

6 Records deleted.
```

THE UPDATE COMMAND

Modification of attribute values is done through the UPDATE command. The syntax of the UPDATE command is:

```
UPDATE table-name
SET attribute-name1 = {expression1 | NULL}
   [,attribute-name2 = {expression2 | NULL} . . .]
[WHERE θ ]
```

The UPDATE command will modify whatever attributes have been specified for whichever tuples the theta condition(s) is (are) evaluated to be true. Omission of the WHERE clause causes the attribute(s) of all tuples to be modified.

The expression can be a simple constant or any valid ORACLE expression.

The following are examples of the ORACLE UPDATE command.

```
UFI> REMARK . . .. Change RAYMOND J. JOHNSON's department to
UFI> REMARK . . .. INFORMATION PROCESSING
UFI> UPDATE FACULTY SET DEPARTMENT = 'INFO PROC'
   2  WHERE FACULTY_NAME = 'RAYMOND J. JOHNSON';

1 Record updated.

UFI> REMARK . . .. Give all faculty members a 20% raise!!!
UFI> UPDATE FACULTY SET SALARY = SALARY * 1.2;

5 Records updated.

UFI> REMARK . . .. Wendy Swimmer has just won the lottery
UFI> REMARK . . .. and decides that she no longer needs a
UFI> REMARK . . .. salary - set her salary to null
UFI> UPDATE FACULTY SET SALARY = NULL
   2  WHERE FACULTY_NAME = 'WENDY SWIMMER';

1 Record updated.
```

Notice that the UPDATE command allows both assigned updates (SET DEPARTMENT = 'INFO PROC') and computed updates (SET SALARY =SALARY * 1.2).

If we wanted to update more than one attribute in a tuple(s), we would simply separate the attributes with commas.

```
UFI> UPDATE FACULTY
   2  SET DEPARTMENT = 'INFO SYSTEMS ,
   3       SALARY = SALARY * 1.25
   4  WHERE FACULTY-NAME = 'JACK NELSON';

1 Record updated.
```

As of version 4.2.2 of ORACLE, a SELECT command cannot be used in the set clause.

COMMIT AND ROLLBACK

When any data maintenance is performed on an ORACLE table, the user has the option of allowing those data changes to be written directly out to the data files holding the actual data or holding all the changes in a buffer area and writing the changes out to the data files at a later time. This entire process is described later in this chapter.

The UFI command COMMIT is used to make any changes made to tables permanent by writing the changes out to data files. The UFI command ROLLBACK backs out all changes that have been made since the last COMMIT was executed.

If you want all your data maintenance changes to be committed as soon as they are executed, then you should use the UFI command SET AUTOCOMMIT IMM. This ensures that all changes to data are committed immediately after the command is executed. If AUTOCOMMIT is set to IMM, there is no possibility of performing a rollback as the changes are not stored in a buffer. If we set AUTOCOMMIT to OFF (SET AUTOCOMMIT OFF), any change made to a table will cause the table to be locked in exclusive mode. This means that no other user can modify any tuple in the table until you either commit or roll back the changes. Other users may retrieve tuples from the table, but they will not have access to any of the modified tuples. The default setting for AUTOCOMMIT is OFF.

It is important to note that if an error is made during data maintenance, all changes from the last commit point are lost.

The following is a sample ORACLE data maintenance session using COMMITs and ROLLBACK. We will assume that for this session that the value of AUTOCOMMIT is OFF.

```
UFI> REMARK . . .. Let's make a bunch of changes to our data
```

```
    Assume that we have made
      100 data maintenance
    changes to our tables.
```

```
UFI> COMMIT
```

```
Commit complete
```

```
    Assume that we have made
    100 more data maintenance
    changes to our tables.
```

```
UFI> REMARK . . .. We now realize that we have made an error in
UFI> REMARK . . .. the last batch of changes and we want the
UFI> REMARK . . .. tuples "unchanged"
UFI> ROLLBACK
```

```
Rollback complete
```

The COMMIT and ROLLBACK only affect data changes and not table restructure changes (ALTER TABLE ADD/MODIFY).

THE ORACLE BULK DATA LOADER UTILITY

A second method of inserting tuples into an ORACLE table is to use the ORACLE bulk data loader (ODL) utility. ODL is a utility and is executed via operating system-level commands. The function of ODL is to read records that have been previously stored in a sequential data file and append them to an ORACLE table.

Executing the ODL utility involves the use of three files.

1. The raw data file. This is the sequential file(s) that contain(s) the data that is to be loaded into an ORACLE table.
2. The error log file. This file is produced by ODL after the raw data file has been read. It contains statistics such as the number of records processed, the number of records that contained detectible errors, error messages, and so forth.
3. The ODL command file. This file consists of the ODL commands necessary to do such things as:
    a. Define the format of the data of the records in the raw data file.
    b. Give the operating system name of the raw data file.
    c. Tell ODL which table to load the data into.
    d. Tell ODL how many records to load and how many to skip over before loading begins.

Invoking the ORACLE bulk data loader

ODL must be invoked from the operating system level of your computer system. Since different systems have different operating system prompts, we will use the $ as a generic prompt character. The command to invoke ODL is:

```
$ODL cf lf uname [-S#] [-L#] [-C#] [-E#] [db=dbname] [-?]
```

where

cf is the name of the command file.

lf is the name of the log file.

uname is the user's ORACLE user-name/password.

-S# is the number of input records to skip before beginning to load data. The default value is zero.

-L# is the maximum number of records to load into the table after skipping S records. If L is zero, ODL loads records until end of file is achieved. The default value is zero.

-C# is the number of records to load until a commit occurs. If the value of C is zero, ODL commits at end of file. The default value for C is 100. The ORACLE Corporation advises not to set this value greater than 500 for the buffer area that stores the uncommitted tuples will overflow if the value of C is set very high.

-E# is the number of rejected (erroneous) records the ODL will allow before it stops processing. If this value is zero, ODL will continue processing until end-of-file is reached, regardless of how many errors are detected. The default value is 50. However, if ODL detects an error in the first record, ODL stops processing regardless of what value E was set to.

db=dbname is the name of a remote database to connect to. This parameter can only be used on systems configured for remote databases. Remote databases are databases that exist primarily on another computer system that is networked in with your computer system. Remote database features are beyond the scope of this text.

-? is the option that causes only information about the current version of ODL to be displayed. This includes such information as the version number, installation date, and so forth. This option will not execute the processor. It is mainly used to ensure that the correct version of the processor is installed. Any parameter not specified will receive the default value.

Constructing the ODL Command File

The function of the ODL command file is to communicate to ODL such information as the name and format of the raw data file, which attributes will be loaded with values, and so forth. The ODL command file is composed of three statements written in the ODL command language (naturally). These three statements are:

1. The DEFINE RECORD command which is used to define the format of the data in the raw data file.
2. The DEFINE SOURCE command which is used to define the input media for the raw data file.
3. The FOR EACH RECORD command which defines the mapping of data from the raw data file and the ORACLE table.

This file will most probably be created by you or your DBA through your system's text editor.

The DEFINE RECORD command.   The function of the DEFINE RECORD command is to specify the format of the records in the raw data file. The syntax of the command is:

```
DEFINE RECORD record-name AS field-description1
                         [, field-description2 [, . . . ]];
```

where

record-name is a user-defined name of the record. This name will only be used for reference purposes within ODL and hence does not have to match any ORACLE table name. However, for documentation purposes, it is a good idea to make this record-name match the table name into which we will place these record occurrences.

field-description contains the field-name, field-width, and field-location of each data field in the raw data file record. The syntax of the field description is as follows:

```
field-name (CHAR [ (field-width) ]
          [ , LOC [( ] | - )] number])
```

where

field-name is an internal reference for a data field. This name does not have to match the attribute-name into which it is being mapped.

CHAR [(field-width)] specifies the width (in number of characters) of the data field. The default field width is one. Note that the clause is preceded by the letters CHAR. CHAR must be used for attributes of any data type. ODL handles conversion to type DATE or NUMBER.

LOC [(+ | -)] number specifies the column where the data field begins on the input record. If a sign does not precede the number, an absolute location from the beginning of the input record is assumed. The first byte of the input record is numbered zero. A sign in front of the number indicates a relative position move. A negative sign indicates a move to the left and a positive sign indicates a move to the right. If this clause is omitted, ODL assumes that the data field begins directly after the previously defined field.

As an example of the DEFINE record command, let's consider a data record for the STUDENT table:

```
Byte                  1111111111222222222233333333334444444444555555555
Numbers →  01234567890123456789012345678901234567890123456789012345678
Data →     S025    MAGGIE JOHNSON    PSYCHO DR,        10-MAY-60 MALE
Values     ---                       ----------                  -----
           STU_ID ---------          ADDRESS           --------- GENDER
                  STUDENT_NAME                         BIRTHDATE
```

The DEFINE RECORD command used to define the above record is:

```
DEFINE RECORD STUDENT AS
     STU_ID (CHAR (6)),
     NAME (CHAR (17)),
     ADDRESS (CHAR (20)),
     BIRTHDATE (CHAR (9)),
     SEX (CHAR (6));
```

In this example the data fields were specified in the same order as they appear on the input record. There are also no filler columns between data values; therefore, the LOCation clause was not needed in this example. Also be aware that these formats are fixed, so all records in the input data file must have the same format.

You may also notice in the above example that Student name is listed as NAME and gender is listed as SEX. We could have listed the five data fields as A, B, C, D, and E if we so desired. This is, in our opinion, would be very poor documentation.

Suppose that our raw data file was not formatted so conveniently. Consider the following format.

```
Byte                  1111111111222222222233333333334444444444555555555566
Numbers ->0123456789012345678901234567890123456789012345678901
          -------------------------------
Data --> MALE    MAGGIE JOHNSON    PSYCHO  DR,             10-MAY-60  S025
Values   ---                       -----------                       ---
         GENDER   ---------        ADDRESS               ---------   STU-ID
                  STUDENT_NAME                           BIRTHDATE
```

In this data record the fields have been scrambled and spaces have been inserted between the fields GENDER and STUDENT-NAME (record position 6) and BIRTH-DATE and STU-ID (record position 53). There is also one space before GENDER in the beginning of the record (record position 0). The DEFINE RECORD command to define this record format is:

```
DEFINE RECORD STUDENT AS
    STU_ID (CHAR (6), LOC (55)),
    NAME (CHAR (17), LOC (8)),
    ADDRESS (CHAR (20)),
    BIRTHDATE (CHAR (9)),
    SEX (CHAR (6), LOC (-61));
```

Note that the fields ADDRESS and BIRTHDAY do not have LOCation clauses affixed to their definition for the value of ADDRESS is directly behind the data field NAME and BIRTHDATE is directly behind ADDRESS.

The DEFINE SOURCE command.   The purpose of the DEFINE SOURCE command is to define the input media for the raw data file. The syntax of the DEFINE SOURCE command is:

```
DEFINE SOURCE source-name source-parameters
    CONTAINING record-name;
```

where

source-name is a user-generated name that is not used for anything.

source-parameters specify the operating system name(s) of the raw data file(s). The format of the source parameters is

```
FROM file-name1 [, file-name2 ] , , ,
LENGTH number-of-bytes
```

where

file-name is the operating system name of the raw data file(s).

number-of-bytes is number of bytes in each record.

record-name is the name of the record as defined in the DEFINE RECORD command.

Let's assume that our data file is called STUDATA. If we further assume that STUDATA is formatted as we described in our first example in the DEFINE RECORD section, the DEFINE SOURCE command to relate the STUDATA file to the STUDENT record is

```
DEFINE SOURCE MYSOURCE
FROM STUDATA LENGTH 59 CONTAINING STUDENT;
```

Remember that the record positions are numbered beginning at zero, so if our maximum position number was 58, we actually have 59 bytes in the record.

The FOR EACH RECORD command.   The purpose of the FOR EACH RECORD command is to map the data defined in the raw data file to the attributes of an ORACLE table. The syntax for the FOR EACH RECORD command is

```
FOR EACH RECORD
   INSERT INTO table-name (attribute1 [,attribute2] , , , ,) :
                 <data-item1 [,data-item2] , , , ,>
   NEXT RECORD
```

where

table-name is the name of the ORACLE table where the data is to be loaded.

attribute is the name of the attribute of the ''table-name'' table that is to receive the data.

data-item is the name of the data item defined in the DEFINE RECORD command. Please note that the angle brackets (<>) are a mandatory part of the command.

The FOR EACH RECORD command maps the raw data file into the STUDENT table that we have created is:

```
FOR EACH RECORD INSERT INTO STUDENT
  (STU_ID, STUDENT_NAME, ADDRESS, BIRTHDAY, GENDER) :
  <STU_ID, NAME,          ADDRESS, BIRTHDAY, SEX>
NEXT RECORD
```

A complete example of the ODL command file.   The following command would be placed in the ODL command file via some text editor.

```
DEFINE RECORD STUDENT AS
    STU_ID (CHAR (6)),
    NAME (CHAR (17)),
    ADDRESS (CHAR (20)),
    BIRTHDATE (CHAR (9)),
    SEX (CHAR (6));

DEFINE SOURCE MYSOURCE
FROM STUDATA LENGTH 59 CONTAINING STUDENT;

FOR EACH RECORD INSERT INTO STUDENT
  (STU_ID, STUDENT_NAME, ADDRESS, BIRTHDAY, GENDER) :
  <STU_ID, NAME,          ADDRESS, BIRTHDAY, SEX>
NEXT RECORD
```

You may load only one table per ODL command file.

Executing ODL

Let's assume that we had created our ODL command file, and it is called ODLCF. We now wish to load the data records stored in STUDATA into our ORACLE table STUDENT. We will assume that the table STUDENT resides in the ORACLE user-name CLASS and it has the password ABC affixed to it. The following ODL execution will append the raw data records to the table STUDENT.
(Again we are assuming the dollar sign to be the operating system prompt.)

```
$ODL ODLCF ERRF CLASS/ABC -CO
```

Since we did not want to skip over any records or limit the number of tuples generated, the S and L parameters of the ODL command were omitted. Once this utility has terminated, the user is advised to display the contents of ERRF, the error log file to determine if any errors occurred in processing.

The error log file contains counts of the number of records read, the number of records successfully loaded into the ORACLE table, and a count of the number of errors detected.

There are three types of errors that can occur when executing ODL commands. These errors are

1. Control statement errors. These are usually syntax errors or detectable logical errors. There are usually three types of control statement errors. The formats of these errors are:

   a. Message ON LINE line-number COLUMN column-number where
      message is a text string of the error message. Examples of messages are "String too large," "Number too large," "Quoted literal not ended," "Illegal character", and the ever popular "Bad number".

      line-number is the line number in the ODL Control File where the error was detected.

      column-number is the column number of the "line number" line where the error was detected.

   b. SYNTAX ERROR LINE line-number ON INPUT symbol where
      symbol identifies the symbol that ODL detects as an error.

   c. symbol : message ON OR ABOUT LINE line-number where
      symbol can be a record field, source, record name, table, or symbol.
      message is a text string indicating the nature of the detected error. Examples of error messages are "Field is improperly aligned," "Source from clause is missing," "Record too large for source," "Table col/field count mismatch," and "Undefined record field."

2. ODL fatal errors - These are usually generated from resource (usually lack of a sufficient amount of memory to execute the processor) or internal problems to ODL. The format of these errors is

   ```
   ODL FATAL ERROR : message
   ```

   where message is usually one of the following:
   a. Out-of-parse stack space
   b. Out-of-heap space
   c. Out-of-table space

   The last two errors can probably be eliminated by executing ODL with more memory. If the message "Out-of-parse stack space" occurs, you should report this to your system database administrator.

3. ORACLE errors. These are internal ORACLE errors. The format of these errors is as follows.

   ```
   subroutine ERROR : message
   ```

   where
      subroutine is the name of the ORACLE subroutine that has failed.
      message is an ORACLE error message.

THE IMPORT AND EXPORT SYSTEM UTILITIES

It sometimes becomes necessary to copy the contents of ORACLE user-names out to external files. This could be done for several reasons.

1. To keep a backup copy of all the tables in a user-name.
2. To transport all the tables from a user-name to another unconnected (non networked) computer system.
3. To allow for the change of the width or type of an attribute.
4. To allow for the installation of a new version of ORACLE on your computer system. Although it is not always necessary to export databases when an upgrade is done, it is an option that the database administrator has. The installation notes that come with the new version will advise the database administrator whether to export or not.

ORACLE provides two system utilities to perform these tasks. EXPORT (EXP) allows the user to copy various items from a user-name out to an external file. IMPORT (IMP) allows the user to copy items from an external file into user-name tables. Both the utilities are executed at the operating system level as they are not UFI commands. Only the owner (creator) of a table can export items from a user-name. Any user with access to the external file can import items into a user-name.

Users have a choice of which items they may wish to export and import. Their choices are to:

1. Export all the tables and/or views (views are discussed in Chapter 11) from a user-name
2. Export only selected tables from a user-name
3. Export only the definition of tables, but not the actual data (tuples)
4. Import the tables and/or views stored in an external file
5. Import tables and/or views into a different ORACLE user-name

If a table or a view has been exported to an external file, you should not try to use a text editor or any other mechanism to edit or modify the items in that file. Once items have been exported to an external file, the only method of returning these items to an ORACLE user-name is via the import utility.

The EXPort Utility

The basic function of the EXPort utility is to copy items from a user-name into an external file. The format of the EXPort Utility is:

```
$EXP [user-name/password]
```

What is exported depends upon what privileges the exporter has. If the user has DBA privilege, the following items can be exported.

1. The user's current privilege(s)
2. Space definitions
3. Clusters
4. Grants on tables
5. Table definitions
6. Table row occurrences
7. Views
8. Synonyms (see Chapter 13)
9. Indexes

If the user does not have DBA privilege, he may only export the following items.

1. Table definitions
2. Table row occurrences
3. Grants on tables
4. Indexes
5. Clusters

Note that the non-DBA user does not get space definition commands placed in their export file.

The utility will prompt the user for the user-name and password if it is not specified on the EXPort execution command. If this is entered correctly, the user is asked to respond to a series of prompts to determine the following items.

1. The name of the external file that the material is to be exported to. If no name is specified, EXPDATA is assumed. The default file name on most systems is EXPDATA or EXPDAT.DMP. Check with your database administrator for your default export file name.

2. Do we want to export everything in the user-name, or do we want to specify the only certain tables be exported.

3. Do we want to export grants (privileges) on tables? This concept will be explained in Chapter 13.

4. Do we want to export only the table definitions and not the data (the rows) associated with the table.

Before we step through an example of the EXPort utility, we will introduce the IMPort utility, so that we can develop a more comprehensive example.

The IMPort Utility

If the EXPort utility is used to copy items from ORACLE user-names out to external files, then the IMPort utility copies items from external files into user-names. Obviously the only objects that can be imported are those that were exported. The format of the IMPort utility is:

```
$IMP [user-name/password]
```

If an object has been exported from a user-name with DBA privilege, it cannot be imported into a user-name without DBA privilege. If an object is imported into a different user-name/password from the user-name/password that exported it, the import facility displays the following message.

```
Warning: the data was exported by <USERNAME>, not by you
```

The import facility will ask the importer if he wants to suppress errors generated by any CREATE TABLE commands if the table already exists. It will also ask if the row occurrences are to be imported even though they were exported.

Examples of EXPort and IMPort Usage

Let's assume that our three favorite tables, STUDENT, COURSE, and FACULTY, all reside in the user-name MY-USER-NAME, which has CONNECT and RESOURCE privileges. We will further assume that the password MY-PASSWORD has been affixed to MY-ACCOUNT. If we wished simply to back up our user-name, we could export our table definitions and data out to a file called MYFILE. This could be accomplished as follows.

```
$EXP MY_USER_NAME/MY_PASSWORD

Export version 4.2.2 - on Sun Feb 09 14:59.55 1986

Connecting to: ORACLE
Processing database: ORACLE V4.2.2 (Rev. 00) 09-Feb-1986

Export file: EXPDATA>    <CR>

U(sers), or T(ables): U>    <CR>

Export Grants (Y/N): N>    <CR>

Export the rows (Y/N): Y>    <CR>

Exporting MY_USER_NAME
```

Note that, in this example, we took the default file name (EXPDATA) as the export file name, exported the entire user name by selecting the user's option, did not export any grants by selecting "N" in the export grants option, and exported all the row occurrences by selecting "Y" in response to the export rows prompt. The default value is selected by pressing the CARRIAGE RETURN key designated by <CR> in our example.

Let's now export only the table definition and data from the STUDENT table out to a file called MYFILE1.

```
$EXP MY_USER_NAME/MY_PASSWORD

Export version 4.2.2 - on Sun Feb 09 14:59.55 1986

Connecting to: ORACLE

Processing database: ORACLE V4.2.2 (Rev. 00) 09-Feb-1986

Export file: EXPDATA>    MYFILE1 <CR>

U(sers), or T(ables): U>    T <CR>

Export the rows (Y/N): Y>     <CR>

Table name: >    STUDENT

10 rows exported

Table name: >    <CR>
```

Let's now assume that we wanted to export only the table definitions of the FACULTY and the COURSE tables to a file called MYFILE2.

```
$EXP MY_USER_NAME/MY_PASSWORD

Export version 4.2.2 - on Sun Feb 09 14:59.55 1986

Connecting to: ORACLE

Processing database: ORACLE V4.2.2 (Rev. 00) 09-Feb-1986

Export file: EXPDATA>    MYFILE1

U(sers), or T(ables): U>    T <CR>

Export the rows (Y/N): Y>    N <CR>

Table name: >    FACULTY <CR>
```

```
0 rows exported

Table name: >      COURSE <CR>

0 rows exported

Table name: >      <CR>
```

If we wanted to (re)create the tables and load them with exported data, we would execute the following IMPort command.

```
$IMP MY_USER_NAME/MY_PASSWORD

Import Version 4.2.2 - Sun Feb 09 15:29:19 1986

Connecting to: ORACLE

Processing database: ORACLE V4.2.2 (Rev. 00) 09-Feb-1986

Import file: EXDATA>    <CR>

Ignore create errors due to object existence (Y/N): Y>    N <CR>

Import grants (Y/N): Y>    <CR>

Import the rows (Y/N): Y>    <CR>

Inserting into table "STUDENT": 10 rows
Inserting into table "COURSE": 7 rows
Inserting into table "FACULTY": 5 rows
```

JOURNALIZING

When any data maintenance is performed on any ORACLE table, a record is kept of the change(s). In the instance of a data modification, information is kept on what the tuple looked like before the change and after the change was made. These records are kept in two journal files. The ''before-the-change'' images are kept in a file called the Before-Image Journal File (BIJ). The ''after-the-change'' images are kept in a file called the After-Image Journal File (AIJ).

What Actually Happens When Data Maintenance Occurs

When the user executes an INSERT, UPDATE, or DELETE command, it causes changes to be made in the database tables. Those changes are recorded (actually the commands that cause the changes are recorded). This is done in a user transparent area of memory called the System Global Area (SGA). This area is shared by all ORACLE processes. The SGA is composed of two elements: the Cache Buffers and the Before-Image Buffers. Data that is read from or written to the data files containing the actual tuples is always stored temporarily in the cache buffers. Data that is read from or written to the Before-Image Journal File is always stored temporarily in the Before-Image Buffers.

When a SELECT, UPDATE, INSERT, or DELETE command is executed the data pages containing the desired tuples are copied from the data files into the Cache Buffers. If the buffers are full and a new data page must be copied into the Cache Buffers, the Least Recently Used (LRU) algorithm determines which page to copy back to the database files to make room for the new data page.

When data maintenance occurs (UPDATE, DELETE, or INSERT commands are executed), the following things happen to the data page containing the altered tuple(s). The page containing the tuple is copied from the data file into three places:

1. The Cache Buffers
2. The Before-Image Buffers
3. The Before-Image Journal File

The reason for copying the data into the Before-Image Journal File is that it guarantees an unmodified copy of the image in case a ROLLBACK is executed. Any modification takes place in the Cache Buffers. If some other user wants access to the data being modified, he gets the data from the before-image buffer. If the data that the second user needs has been pushed out of the Before Image Buffers, it must be recopied back into the Before-Image Buffers. When the original user COMMITs the changes, the altered data is copied from the Cache Buffers out to the data files. The data pages in the Before-Image Buffers and Before-Image Journal File are marked ''free,'' unless some other user is currently reading the original version of the data. In this case those pages remain in the Before-Image Buffers until all queries involving the original data are finished. If the database is running in a period of high data maintenance, the Least Recently Used algorithm might have already forced some data pages to be copied back to the data files.

The process just described is completely transparent to the user. But if the process is understood by the user, his overall knowledge and understanding of ORACLE will increase.

Why Should We Use After-Image Journalizing

Even though the before-image journalizing occurs automatically in ORACLE, after-image journalizing does not. After-image journalizing must be enabled. This is usually done by the database administrator. If after-image journalizing is enabled, the modified data is also written out to the After Image Journal File.

The basic reason for using after-image journalizing is to be able to recover from system or hardware failures. Let's assume that we have an industrial database

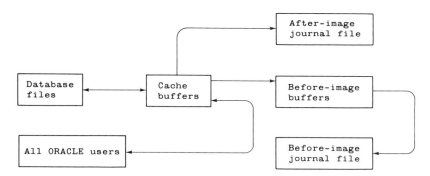

Figure 8.1   The Relationship Among ORACLE Users, Buffers, and Journal Files

that keeps track of our company's sales orders. Whenever a sale is made for one of our products, a new tuple is entered into our database. These orders are checked for correctness, and if an error is found, the necessary modification(s) to the tuple(s) is made. Suppose that we back up our database every Friday night via the EXPort utility. Our database is running absolutely perfectly until Thursday afternoon at 2:00 P.M. when we have a system failure. The disk where our data files are kept has an irrecoverable disk crash. This is where all our sales records are stored. What do we do to recover? The database administrator will have to run the IMPort utility to establish the database to where it was after the Friday night export. Once this is done, the DBA can now use the After Image Journal (AIJ) Utility to roll the database forward until just before the system crash on Thursday. If this capability were not available, then each transaction (sales order) would have to be reentered into the system. (That is only assuming we can acquire each sales order from the past week.) For this reason alone, after-image journalizing should be seriously considered for all industrial databases. On the other hand, after-image journalizing requires quite a bit of extra disk space. We get back to the perplexing problem of safety versus space. This is a problem that must be addressed by the database administrator.

The relationships among the ORACLE users, the buffers, and the journal files are shown in Figure 8.1.

SUMMARY

This chapter discussed how to enter tuples into ORACLE tables, delete tuples from tables, and modify tuples currently residing in tables. We also discussed how to bulk load data into tables from external files via the ORACLE bulk data loader utility (ODL). A method of backing up data tables and views via the EXPort and IMPort system utilities was explained. The chapter concluded with a discussion of before-image and after-image journalizing.

Upon completion of this chapter, you should now be familiar with the following terms, concepts, and commands.

A. INSERT	**O.** The ODL control file
B. INSERT/SELECT	**P.** DEFINE RECORD
C. Short term variables	**Q.** DEFINE SOURCE
D. Long term variables	**R.** FOR EACH RECORD
E. SET VERIFY ON/OFF	**S.** The ODL raw data file
F. SET DEFINE <char>	**T.** The ODL error log file
G. DEF	**U.** ODL errors
H. UNDEFINE	**V.** EXPort
I. START filename <parameters>	**W.** IMPort
J. DELETE	**X.** Journalizing
K. UPDATE	**Y.** The Before Image Journal File
L. COMMIT	**Z.** The Before Image Buffer
M. ROLLBACK	**AA.** The Cache Buffer
N. ODL	**BB.** The After Image Journal File

EXERCISES

1. Explain the difference between long-term and short term variables. When would each be used?

2. Explain how you could use the START command with parameters to insert tuples. Retrieve tuples.

3. Explain how the ODL command file is constructed. What constitutes the file?

4. Explain how journalizing works in ORACLE.

5. Assuming that you have created the three tables (Student, Faculty, and Course) as per Exercise 4c in Chapter 7, use the INSERT command to load the data for the tables. Before you attempt any of these commands, you should open a SPOOL file so that you can record your actions for later study.

    a. Use the simple INSERT to load the five tuples of the FACULTY table. When you are finished loading the table, be sure to COMMIT the changes.

    b. Use short-term variables to load the seven tuples of the COURSE table. When you are finished loading the table, be sure to COMMIT the changes.

    c. Use ODL to load the ten tuples of the student table. ODL will automatically commit the changes for you.

6. Set up some acceptable output formats (via COLUMN commands) for the attributes in the three tables. Display all the data in your tables. EXIT ORACLE and build an external file with all your formatting commands. Get back into your user-name and START your format file. Try to display the various tuples in each of the tables.

7. Perform the following data maintenance commands:
   a. Delete all male tuples from the STUDENT table.
   b. Change Raymond J. Johnson's Department to Accounting.
   c. Change all of the male student's majors to H_2O Polo.
   d. Give every faculty member a 40% raise.
   e. Add the following faculty member to the FACULTY table.

```
            Fac ID: T03
      Faculty Name: Steve Smithson
        Department: Phys Ed
            Gender: Male
            Salary: \36,000
```

   f. Add the following student to the STUDENT table.

```
            Stu ID: S075
      Student Name: Marvin Smith
           Address: Unknown
         Birthdate: Unknown
            Gender: Male
```

   g. Roll back all your changes.

```
┌─────────────────────────────────────────────────────────┐
│                        ASIDE                            │
└─────────────────────────────────────────────────────────┘
```

Even though we have given you a set of data that you can use to practice the various ORACLE commands, there is another source of example data. This database consisting of four tables is provided for you by the ORACLE Corporation. It usually comes with your system. This data is stored in a special account on each system. You should ask your instructor or database administrator whether this data exists on your system. If it does, you should copy it into your user-name so that you will have more practice data to work with.

To access this sample database, you must use the START command. The START command to create and load the four data tables is shown next. Again you should open a SPOOL file to record the action.

```
UFI> SPOOL MYFILE
UFI> START acct-nameSQLBLD
```

```
┌───────────────────────────┐
│   All the CREATE          │
│   and INSERT commands     │
│   are executed here       │
└───────────────────────────┘
```

```
UFI> REMARK . . .. Do what ever else you want to do here
UFI> SPOOL OUT
```

This command accesses a file called SQLBLD, which is stored in the account "acct-name." SQLBLD contains the necessary CREATE commands to build the bonus data tables. Those tables are as follows.

EMP. Contains 14 tuples representing employees of a firm.

DEPT. Contains 4 tuples representing the four departments of the firm.

SALGRADE, Contains 5 tuples representing the five salary grades within the firm.

BONUS, Contains zero tuples representing bonuses earned by the firm's employees. This table will be loaded with later commands.

The data for these tables are placed in the SYSTEM partition, so they should be removed whenever you have finished with them. These tables are used for most of the examples used in the ORACLE manuals.

There are additional START files that contain commands to illustrate the various SQL and UFI commands. The file name and a brief explanation of what it illustrates follows.

Filename	Description
SQLBLD	Creates and loads the tables EMP, DEPT, BONUS, and SALGRADE.
DATADEF	Creates and loads the table PROJ.
SELECT	Executes some simple SELECT commands.
WHERE	Illustrates various WHERE clauses.
ORDERBY	Illustrates various sort options.
GROUPBY	Illustrates the GROUP BY clause.
MANIP	Various forms of the INSERT, DELETE, and UPDATE are shown.
RECOVERY	Illustrates COMMIT and ROLLBACK.
NULL	Illustrates the use of null values.
ALTER	Illustrates how to change and add columns to tables.
DICTSTRU	Illustrates how to retrieve data from system tables.
CONTENT	Illustrates how to view information of tables.
EXPRESS	Illustrates the use of expressions in SELECT's.
DATE	Illustrates the use of the DATE data type.
JOIN	Illustrates the use of JOIN queries.
SUBQUERY	Illustrates the use of the subquery.
VIEWS	Creates and retrieves data from views.

This list of illustrative files could expand each time a new feature(s) is added to ORACLE.

REFERENCES

1. *Harris ORACLE Reference Manual*. Harris Corporation, Ft. Lauderdale, FL, Release 4.1.4, May 1985.

2. *Harris ORACLE User's Guide*. Harris Corporation, Ft. Lauderdale, FL, February 1984.

3. *Harris ORACLE Database Administrator's Guide*. Harris Corporation, Ft. Lauderdale, FL, Release 4.2.2, September 1985.

4. *Harris ORACLE Utilities Manual*. Harris Corporation, Ft. Lauderdale, FL, Release 3.1.4, October 1984.

9

JOIN Queries

PURPOSE: This chapter illustrates the implementation of the relational algebra JOIN operator. The Equi-JOIN, Theta JOIN, Outer JOIN, and the Cartesian product are explored along with an efficient method of designing storage when heavy join activity is expected in a database.

In all the queries that we have discussed up to this point in the text, we used only one table to solve the query. If that were all the retrieval power that ORACLE had, it would be just another file management system. Perhaps the most powerful feature of relational databases is the ability to implement the relational algebra operator JOIN.

The JOIN Query

The purpose of the JOIN query is to link two or more tables together across a common attribute(s). There is no special ORACLE command to implement the JOIN query. The FROM and WHERE clauses of the SELECT command are all that are needed. The FROM clause specifies the tables that are to be joined and the WHERE clause specifies the join condition(s).

THE EQUI-JOIN

To illustrate the JOIN query, let's try to solve the query "What courses are taught by members of the faculty?" As you can see by the following tables, we cannot solve this query with only one table.

```
COURSE (COURSE-ID, COURSE-TITLE, SECTION-NO, STU-ID, FAC-ID)
FACULTY (FAC-ID, FACULTY-NAME, DEPARTMENT, GENDER, SALARY)
```

TABLE NAME: COURSE

COURSE-ID	COURSE-TITLE	SECTION	STU-ID	FAC-ID
CSC100	INTRODUCTION TO COMPUTING	1	S001	J01
CSC100	INTRODUCTION TO COMPUTING	2	S002	S01
CSC200	PASCAL PROGRAMMING	1	S001	D01
CSC200	PASCAL PROGRAMMING	2	S003	S01
ACC200	PRINCIPLES OF ACCOUNTING I	1	S001	J02
ACC201	PRINCIPLES OF ACCOUNTING II	1	S004	J02
HIS200	HISTORY OF PIROGUES	1	S005	N01

TABLE NAME: FACULTY

FAC-ID	FACULTY-NAME	DEPARTMENT	GENDER	SALARY
J01	RAYMOND J. JOHNSON	COMP SCI	MALE	40000
S01	WENDY SWIMMER	COMP SCI	FEMALE	45000
D01	AMY DANCER	COMP SCI	FEMALE	34500
J02	BOB JONES	ACCOUNTING	MALE	35000
N01	JACK NELSON	HISTORY	MALE	28000

Structure of the Equi-JOIN

To refresh your memory, we will first solve this query with the following two relational algebra commands.

```
TEMP <- JOIN FACULTY, COURSE OVER FAC-ID
PROJECT FACULTY-NAME, COURSE-TITLE FROM TEMP
```

If you will peruse the two commands carefully, you will notice that there are three important aspects to the commands.

1. The FACULTY and COURSE tables are joined together.
2. The join is an Equi-JOIN with the common attribute being FAC-ID.
3. The attributes FACULTY-NAME and COURSE-TITLE are projected out of the resultant table.

We must incorporate these three aspects into the ORACLE SELECT command to solve this query:

```
UFI> SELECT FACULTY-NAME, COURSE-TITLE
  2  FROM FACULTY, COURSE
  3  WHERE FACULTY.FAC-ID = COURSE.FAC-ID;

FACULTY-NAME_____ COURSE-TITLE_____
RAYMOND J. JOHNSON  INTRODUCTION TO COMPUTING
WENDY SWIMMER       INTRODUCTION TO COMPUTING
WENDY SWIMMER       PASCAL PROGRAMMING
AMY DANCER          PASCAL PROGRAMMING
BOB JONES           PRINCIPLES OF ACCOUNTING I
BOB JONES           PRINCIPLES OF ACCOUNTING II
JACK NELSON         HISTORY OF PIROGUES
```

Notice that the two attributes that we desired displayed are simply listed in the select list of the SELECT command. The two tables that are to be joined are listed in the FROM clause (the order of listing is irrelevant). The Equi-JOIN condition (FACULTY.FAC-ID = COURSE.FAC-ID) is specified in the WHERE clause. Note that since FAC-ID appears in both tables, the attributes must be qualified. The qualification is accomplished by placing the table name followed by a period before the attribute name. Even though FACULTY-NAME and COURSE-TITLE come from two different tables, they do not have to be qualified for they are unique attributes in the two tables specified in the FROM clause.

The Equi-JOIN with Theta Conditions

Let's expand our example to include a listing of only the courses taught by Raymond J. Johnson again utilizing relational algebra to solve this query with the following commands.

```
TEMP <- JOIN FACULTY, COURSE OVER FAC-ID
TEMPA <- PROJECT TEMP OVER FACULTY-NAME, COURSE-TITLE
SELECT TEMPA WHERE FACULTY-NAME = 'RAYMOND J. JOHNSON'
```

(Remember that the relational algebra SELECT command is different from the ORACLE SELECT command.)

This can be accomplished very easily in SQL by appending a second part to the WHERE clause of the previous command.

```
UFI> SELECT FACULTY-NAME, COURSE-TITLE
  2  FROM FACULTY, COURSE
  3  WHERE FACULTY.FAC-ID = COURSE.FAC-ID
  4    AND FACULTY-NAME = 'RAYMOND J. JOHNSON';


FACULTY-NAME_____ COURSE-TITLE_____
RAYMOND J. JOHNSON  INTRODUCTION TO COMPUTING
```

Notice that this SQL SELECT command combines three relational algebra operators, SELECT, PROJECT, and JOIN, into one command.

OPTIMIZING JOIN QUERIES

Be aware that the predicate of the foregoing command could have been specified in the reverse order.

```
UFI> SELECT FACULTY_NAME, COURSE_TITLE
  2  FROM FACULTY, COURSE
  3  WHERE FACULTY_NAME = 'RAYMOND J. JOHNSON'
  4    AND FACULTY.FAC-ID = COURSE.FAC_ID;
```

Since there are two conditions specified in the predicate, the command could be executed two ways. The first method would consist of joining each tuple of the FACULTY table to each tuple of the COURSE table where the values of FAC-ID matched. Then eliminate all tuples where the value of the attribute FACULTY-NAME was not equal to "RAYMOND J. JOHNSON." This is shown by the following relational algebra sequence.

```
TEMP <- JOIN FACULTY, COURSE OVER FAC-ID
TEMPA <- PROJECT TEMP OVER FACULTY-NAME, COURSE-TITLE
SELECT TEMPA WHERE FACULTY-NAME = 'RAYMOND J. JOHNSON'
```

The second method consists of eliminating the non-'RAYMOND J. JOHNSON' tuples before the join is executed. This is shown in the following relational algebra sequence.

```
TEMP <- SELECT FACULTY WHERE FACULTY-NAME = 'RAYMOND J. JOHNSON'
TEMPA <- JOIN TEMPA AND COURSES OVER FAC-ID
PROJECT TEMPA OVER FACULTY-NAME, COURSE-TITLE
```

Note that the second series of commands is much more efficient, the reason being that only the necessary tuples are joined to the matching tuples from the FACULTY table.

This example is designed to illustrate that the order in which the WHERE conditions are executed *does* make a difference. As we stated in Chapter 4, the process of determining the most efficient method of executing a query is called optimization. This should be the responsibility of the software and not the user. You may specify the conditions in any order that you wish in an ORACLE command and ORACLE will optimize the execution of the predicate conditions as efficiently as it possibly can. This usually consists of postponing the execution of the join part of the predicate to the latest possible time.

THETA JOINS

Although most JOIN conditions that you will encounter will probably be Equi-JOINs, ORACLE will handle any relational operator including =, !=, >, <, >=, and <=, BETWEEN, and LIKE.

Suppose for some reason we want a list of courses that each faculty member did <u>not</u> teach. This query could be solved with the use of the not equals operator (!=).

```
UFI> SELECT FACULTY-NAME, COURSE-TITLE
   2  FROM FACULTY, COURSE
   3  WHERE FACULTY.FAC-ID != COURSE.FAC-ID;

FACULTY-NAME_____ COURSE-TITLE_____
WENDY SWIMMER       INTRODUCTION TO COMPUTING
AMY DANCERER        INTRODUCTION TO COMPUTING
BOB JONES           INTRODUCTION TO COMPUTING
JACK NELSON         INTRODUCTION TO COMPUTING
RAYMOND J. JOHNSON  INTRODUCTION TO COMPUTING
AMY DANCER          INTRODUCTION TO COMPUTING
BOB JONES           INTRODUCTION TO COMPUTING
JACK NELSON         INTRODUCTION TO COMPUTING
RAYMOND J. JOHNSON  PASCAL PROGRAMMING
WENDY SWIMMER       PASCAL PROGRAMMING
BOB JONES           PASCAL PROGRAMMING
JACK NELSON         PASCAL PROGRAMMING
RAYMOND J. JOHNSON  PASCAL PROGRAMMING
AMY DANCER          PASCAL PROGRAMMING
BOB JONES           PASCAL PROGRAMMING
JACK NELSON         PASCAL PROGRAMMING
RAYMOND J. JOHNSON  PRINCIPLES OF ACCOUNTING I
WENDY SWIMMER       PRINCIPLES OF ACCOUNTING I
AMY DANCER          PRINCIPLES OF ACCOUNTING I
JACK NELSON         PRINCIPLES OF ACCOUNTING I
RAYMOND J. JOHNSON  PRINCIPLES OF ACCOUNTING II
WENDY SWIMMER       PRINCIPLES OF ACCOUNTING II
AMY DANCER          PRINCIPLES OF ACCOUNTING II
JACK NELSON         PRINCIPLES OF ACCOUNTING II
RAYMOND J. JOHNSON  HISTORY OF PIROGUES
WENDY SWIMMER       HISTORY OF PIROGUES
AMY DANCER          HISTORY OF PIROGUES
BOB JONES           HISTORY OF PIROGUES

28 records selected.
```

If we wanted the courses that RAYMOND J. JOHNSON did not teach, we could structure our query as follows.

```
UFI< SELECT FACULTY-NAME, COURSE-TITLE
   2   FROM FACULTY, COURSE
   3   WHERE FACULTY.FAC-ID != COURSE.FAC-ID
   4     AND FACULTY-NAME = 'RAYMOND J, JOHNSON';

FACULTY-NAME_____     COURSE-TITLE_____ _____
RAYMOND J, JOHNSON INTRODUCTION TO COMPUTING
RAYMOND J, JOHNSON PASCAL PROGRAMMING
RAYMOND J, JOHNSON PASCAL PROGRAMMING
RAYMOND J, JOHNSON PRINCIPLES OF ACCOUNTING I
RAYMOND J, JOHNSON PRINCIPLES OF ACCOUNTING II
RAYMOND J, JOHNSON HISTORY OF PIROGUES

6 records selected,
```

Notice that the first tuple in the resultant table contains the COURSE-TITLE Introducion to Computing. Our tables indicate that Raymond J. Johnson does in fact teach this class. Why then does this tuple get generated? The fact is that another instructor, one Miss Amy Dancer, teaches this course too. It is Miss Dancer's COURSE-TITLE of Introduction to Computing that is joined to Mr. Johnson's tuple.

This example was designed only to illustrate the use of the Theta JOIN. If it bothers you that we did not get the correct answer, wait until we get to the section on the Outer JOIN.

AN EXTENDED EXAMPLE WITH JOINS

To illustrate the power of joins in ORACLE, let's consider the following example. Let's assume that we have created a table called GRADES that contains the test scores of our various students. The table GRADES was created as follows.

```
UFI> CREATE TABLE GRADES (STU-ID CHAR (6) NOT NULL,
   2                        STUDENT-NAME CHAR (14),
   3                        TEST1 NUMBER (3),
   4                        TEST2 NUMBER (3),
   5                        TEST3 NUMBER (3),
   6                        FINAL_EXAM NUMBER (3))
   7                        SPACE SCHOOL_SPACE;

Table created,
```

This table is designed to contain the test grades for our students. The table has been loaded with these INSERT commands.

```
UFI> INSERT INTO GRADES VALUES ('S001', 'WENDY JONES',
   2   98, 95, 93, 92);

1 Record created,
```

```
UFI> INSERT INTO GRADES VALUES ('S002', 'SAM WALES',
   2   88, 85, 83, 82);

1 Record created.

UFI> INSERT INTO GRADES VALUES ('S003', 'CATHY SMITH',
   2   78, 75, 73, 72);

1 Record created.

UFI> INSERT INTO GRADES VALUES ('S004', 'DOTTIE STACY',
   2   68, 65, 63, 62);

1 Record created.

UFI> INSERT INTO GRADES VALUES ('S005', 'JAY LANGER',
   2   14, 28, 63, 45);

1 Record created.
```

We can use the following command to display the current status of the student's grades.

```
UFI> SELECT * FROM GRADES;

STU_ID STUDENT_NAME__ _____TEST1 _____TEST2 _____TEST3 FINAL_EXAM
S001   WENDY JONES           98         95         93         92
S002   SAM WALES             88         85         83         82
S003   CATHY SMITH           78         75         73         72
S004   DOTTIE STACY          68         65         63         62
S005   JAY LANGER            14         28         63         45
```

Determining a Letter Grade via a Theta Join

This output is satisfactory if we just want to view the students' grades. However, it would be more beneficial if we could compute the students' average grade. Let's assume that we sum the first three tests and then weight the final exam twice. Our average algorithm would look like this:

$$\text{AVERAGE} = (\text{TEST1} + \text{TEST2} + \text{TEST3} + (2/\text{FINAL\_EXAM}) \mid 5$$

We could implement this by using the above formula in a SELECT command.

```
UFI> SELECT GRADES.*, (TEST1+TEST2+TEST3+(2*FINAL_EXAM))/5
   2   FROM GRADES;
```

```
STU-ID STUDENT-NAME__ _____TEST1 _____TEST2 _____TEST3 FINAL-EXAM
(TEST1+TEST2+TEST3+(2*FINAL_EX
S001   WENDY JONES            98        95        93        92
                             94
S002   SAM WALES              88        85        83        82
                             84
S003   CATHY SMITH            78        75        73        72
                             74
S004   DOTTIE STACY           68        65        63        62
                             64
S005   JAY LANGER             14        28        63        45
                             39
```

The attribute heading for the computed attribute is not as nice as we would like. Remember that the maximum length of a column heading is 30 characters. This can be adjusted with the following COLUMN commands.

```
UFI> COLUMN TEST1 FORMAT 99999
UFI> COLUMN TEST2 FORMAT 99999
UFI> COLUMN TEST3 FORMAT 99999
UFI> COLUMN (TEST1+TEST2+TEST3+(2*FINAL_EX HEADING AVE
UFI> COLUMN AVE FORMAT 999.99
UFI> /

STU-ID STUDENT-NAME__ TEST1 TEST2 TEST3 FINAL-EXAM ___AVE
S001   WENDY JONES       98    95    93         92  94.00
S002   SAM WALES         88    85    83         82  84.00
S003   CATHY SMITH       78    75    73         72  74.00
S004   DOTTIE STACY      68    65    63         62  64.00
S005   JAY LANGER        14    28    63         45  39.00
```

Notice the COLUMN command creating the heading ''AVE.'' The arithmetic expression used to refer to the virtual attribute is specified by only the first 30 characters of the expression. Again, the reason for this is that the maximum length of attribute labels is 30 characters, even though the arithmetic expression used to define the attribute is actually 36 columns wide, we could only use the first 30 characters.

What we would now like to do is assign the student a letter grade based on his average. The grading scale that we will use is as follows:

Average	Letter Grade
90 and above	A
89 to 80	B
79 to 70	C
69 to 60	D
59 and below	F

What we have established is a range of averages for our various letter grades. We have a high value (average) and a low value (average) for each letter grade. What we must do now is to transform our grading scale into an ORACLE table. The table will have three attributes: LOW-VALUE, HIGH-VALUE, and GRADE. The table is created as follows.

```
UFI> CREATE TABLE GRADE-SCALE (LOW-VALUE NUMBER (4,1),
   2                           HIGH-VALUE  NUMBER (4,1),
   3                           GRADE CHAR (1))
   4                           SPACE SCHOOL-SPACE;

Table created.

UFI> REMARK . . .. Now we must load our table with values.
UFI> INSERT INTO GRADE-SCALE VALUES (90.0, 100.0, 'A');

   1 Record created.

UFI> INSERT INTO GRADE-SCALE VALUES (80.0, 89.9, 'B');

   1 Record created.

UFI> INSERT INTO GRADE-SCALE VALUES (70.0, 79.9, 'C');

1 Record created.

UFI> INSERT INTO GRADE-SCALE VALUES (60.0, 69.9, 'D');

1 Record created.

UFI> INSERT INTO GRADE-SCALE VALUES (0.0, 59.9, 'F');

1 Record created.

UFI> COLUMN LOW-VALUE FORMAT 99999999.9
UFI> COLUMN HIGH_VALUE FORMAT 99999999.9
UFI> COLUMN GRADE FORMAT A5
UFI> SELECT * FROM GRADE-SCALE;

_LOW-VALUE HIGH-VALUE GRADE_
      90.0      100.0 A
      80.0       89.9 B
      70.0       79.9 C
      60.0       69.9 D
        .0       59.9 F
```

We can now use the join facility of SQL to assign each student a letter grade.

```
UFI> SELECT GRADES.*, (TEST1+TEST2+TEST3+(2*FINAL_EXAM))/5,
   2    GRADE
   3    FROM GRADES, GRADE-SCALE
   4    WHERE (TEST1+TEST2+TEST3+(2*FINAL-EXAM))/5 BETWEEN
   5    LOW-VALUE AND HIGH-VALUE;
```

STU-ID	STUDENT-NAME	TEST1	TEST2	TEST3	FINAL-EXAM	AVE	GRADE
S001	WENDY JONES	98	95	93	92	94.00	A
S002	SAM WALES	88	85	83	82	84.00	B
S003	CATHY SMITH	78	75	73	72	74.00	C
S004	DOTTIE STACY	68	65	63	62	64.00	D
S005	JAY LANGER	14	28	63	45	39.00	F

The Coup de Grace

And now for the coup de grace. Why should we store the name of the student in the GRADES table when we already have it stored in the STUDENT table? We will now re-create the GRADE table *without* the STUDENT-NAME attribute.

```
UFI> DROP TABLE GRADES;

 Table dropped.

UFI> CREATE TABLE GRADES (STU-ID CHAR (6) NOT NULL,
   2                      TEST1 NUMBER (3),
   3                      TEST2 NUMBER (3),
   4                      TEST3 NUMBER (3),
   5                      FINAL-EXAM NUMBER (3))
   6                      SPACE SCHOOL-SPACE;

Table created.

UFI> REMARK . . .. Now reload the table

ZUFI> INSERT INTO GRADES VALUES ('S001', 98, 95, 93, 92);

1 Record created.

UFI> INSERT INTO GRADES VALUES ('S002', 88, 85, 83, 82);

1 Record created.

UFI> INSERT INTO GRADES VALUES ('S003', 78, 75, 73, 72);

1 Record created.

UFI> INSERT INTO GRADES VALUES ('S004', 68, 65, 63, 62);

1 Record created.
```

```
UFI> INSERT INTO GRADES VALUES ('S005', 14, 28, 63, 45);

1 Record created,
```

Now we want to get the students' test scores from the GRADES table, their names from the STUDENT table, and their letter grades from the GRADE-SCALE table. This will involve the joining of three tables.

```
UFI> SELECT GRADES.STU-ID, STUDENT-NAME, TEST1, TEST2, TEST3,
   2        FINAL-EXAM, (TEST1+TEST2+TEST3+(2*FINAL-EXAM))/5, GRADE
   3   FROM GRADES, GRADE-SCALE, STUDENT
   4   WHERE (TEST1+TEST2+TEST3+(2*FINAL-EXAM))/5 BETWEEN
   5         LOW-VALUE AND HIGH-VALUE
   6     AND STUDENT.STU-ID = GRADES.STU-ID;
```

STU-ID	STUDENT-NAME	TEST1	TEST2	TEST3	FINAL-EXAM	AVE	GRADE
S001	WENDY JONES	98	95	93	92	94.00	A
S002	SAM WALES	88	85	83	82	84.00	B
S003	CATHY SMITH	78	75	73	72	74.00	C
S004	DOTTIE STACY	68	65	63	62	64.00	D
S005	JAY LANGER	14	28	63	45	39.00	F

We can extend this example even further and request only the tuples of the students who have scored above the grade of "C." Let us also assume that we want the tuples displayed in descending order by GRADE.

```
UFI> SELECT STUDENT_NAME, GRADES.*,
   2        (TEST1+TEST2+TEST3+(2*FINAL_EXAM))/5, GRADE
   3   FROM GRADES, GRADE-SCALE, STUDENT
   4   WHERE (TEST1+TEST2+TEST3+(2*FINAL_EXAM))/5 BETWEEN
   5         LOW_VALUE AND HIGH_VALUE
   6     AND STUDENT.STU_ID = GRADES.STU_ID;
   7     AND GRADE < 'C' ORDER BY GRADE;
```

STUDENT-NAME	STU-ID	TEST1	TEST2	TEST3	FINAL-EXAM	AVE	GRADE
WENDY JONES	S001	98	95	93	92	94.00	A
SAM WALES	S002	88	85	83	82	84.00	B

THE USE OF TABLE LABELS

Table labels are a shortcut method of specifying a table name. A table label is in effect only for the statement in which it is defined. To define a table label, simply leave one blank space after the table name in the FROM clause and specify the table label. For example if we wanted to rename the STUDENT table temporarily as S, we could use the following FROM clause.

```
FROM STUDENT S
```

Table labels are particularly useful when executing joins with complex WHERE clauses. Let's use the previous JOIN query to illustrate the use of table labels.

```
UFI> SELECT STUDENT_NAME, G.*,
  2        (TEST1+TEST2+TEST3+(2*FINAL_EXAM))/5, GRADE
  3  FROM GRADES G, GRADE-SCALE, STUDENT S
  4  WHERE (TEST1+TEST2+TEST3+(2*FINAL_EXAM))/5 BETWEEN
  5        LOW_VALUE AND HIGH_VALUE
  6    AND S.STU_ID = G.STU_ID;
  7    AND GRADE < 'C' ORDER BY GRADE;
```

Note the we used the table label "S" and "G" to rename the tables GRADES and STUDENT. We did not rename GRADE_SCALE, for it was not directly specified in the WHERE clause. Further note that if had need to we could have used the short form of the GRADE table (G.*) to indicate that we wanted to display the attributes from the GRADES table.

THE OUTER JOIN

We can use the Equi-JOIN to illustrate how we could retrieve the names of the students and the courses that they take.

```
UFI> SELECT STUDENT-NAME, COURSE-TITLE
  2  FROM STUDENT, COURSE
  3  WHERE STUDENT.STU-ID = COURSE.STU-ID;

STUDENT-NAME_____    COURSE-TITLE_____
WENDY JONES           INTRODUCTION TO COMPUTING
WENDY JONES           PASCAL PROGRAMMING
WENDY JONES           PRINCIPLES OF ACCOUNTING I
SAM WALES             INTRODUCTION TO COMPUTING
CATHY SMITH           PASCAL PROGRAMMING
DOTTIE STACY          PRINCIPLES OF ACCOUNTING II
JAY LANGER            HISTORY OF PIROGUES
```

But suppose that we wanted to determine which students did not take any courses. We can see from the following two tables that we cannot use an Equi-JOIN to solve this query.

```
STUDENT (STU-ID, STUDENT-NAME, ADDRESS, BIRTHDATE, GENDER)
COURSE (COURSE-ID, COURSE-TITLE, SECTION-NO, STU-ID, FAC-ID)
```

TABLE NAME: STUDENT

STU-ID	STUDENT-NAME	ADDRESS	BIRTHDATE	GENDER
S001	WENDY JONES	125 MAPLE AVE	25-OCT-65	FEMALE
S002	SAM WALES	3006 NAVAJO CL	10-JAN-60	MALE
S003	CATHY SMITH	1600 PENN AVE	22-FEB-22	FEMALE
S004	DOTTIE STACY	10 DOWNING ST	31-MAR-67	FEMALE
S005	JAY LANGER	GOLF COURSE RD	19-APR-65	MALE
S006	AMY LOPEZ	123 SUN RAY RD	10-MAY-64	FEMALE
S007	SAM WATSON	225 TEST DRIVE	09-JUN-63	MALE
S008	TAMMY REDD	113 MANCHESTER	01-JUL-60	FEMALE
S009	TOMMY WADKINS	APPLE TREE DR	24-AUG-67	MALE
S010	BEN TREVINO	BOWLING ALLEY	30-SEP-66	MALE

TABLE NAME: COURSE

COURSE-ID	COURSE-TITLE	SECTION	STU-ID	FAC-ID
CSC100	INTRODUCTION TO COMPUTING	1	S001	J01
CSC100	INTRODUCTION TO COMPUTING	2	S002	S01
CSC200	PASCAL PROGRAMMING	1	S001	D01
CSC200	PASCAL PROGRAMMING	2	S003	S01
ACC200	PRINCIPLES OF ACCOUNTING I	1	S001	J02
ACC201	PRINCIPLES OF ACCOUNTING II	1	S004	J02
HIS200	HISTORY OF PIROGUES	1	S005	N01

By perusing these tables we can see that students Amy Lopez, Sam Watson, Tammy Redd, Tommy Wadkins, and Ben Trevino do not take any courses for their STU-IDs do not appear in the STU-ID attribute of the COURSE table.

One method of solving this query is through the use of the Outer JOIN. The Equi-JOIN and/or Theta JOIN produces a tuple in the resultant table only if the join condition(s) is (are) met. The Outer JOIN produces a tuple in the resultant table whether the join condition is met or not. If the condition is not met, the Outer JOIN produces null values for the attributes of the ''second'' table when the join condition is not met. (The Outer JOIN is described in detail in Chapter 3.) For example, let's illustrate the Outer JOIN by joining the tuples for students Dottie Stacy and Tammy Redd to the tuples in the COURSE table.

```
UFI> SELECT STUDENT-NAME, COURSE-TITLE
  2   FROM STUDENT, COURSE
  3   WHERE STUDENT.STU-ID = COURSE.STU-ID (+)
  4     AND STUDENT-NAME IN ('DOTTIE STACY', 'TAMMY REDD');
```

STUDENT-NAME	COURSE-TITLE
DOTTIE STACY	PRINCIPLES OF ACCOUNTING II
TAMMY REDD	

Note that since Tammy Redd does not take any courses, the value of COURSE-TITLE in her tuple is null and hence displayed as a blank. The results of this join are different from an Equi-JOIN in that the tuple for Tammy Redd would not be generated in a simple join. The reason is that Tammy Redd does not have a corresponding tuple in the COURSE table.

Note that the plus sign (+) differentiates the Equi-JOIN from the Outer JOIN. The plus sign is placed after the attribute COURSE.STU-ID, for we want the tuples from the COURSE table joined to the STUDENT table. (Does this make the STUDENT table the joiner and COURSE table the joinee?) The null values will be generated for the COURSE attributes that do not have a corresponding value in the STUDENT table. This is the reason that the value of COURSE-TITLE is null for the Tammy Redd tuple. If we had placed the plus sign beside STUDENT.STU-ID, then if there was a course that had no student registered, it would have generated a null value for STUDENT-NAME. For example, suppose we had added the following tuple to the COURSE table.

```
COURSE-ID COURSE-TITLE_____ SECTION STU-ID FAC-ID
HIS333    HISTORY OF ROUND DANCING         1           D03
```

Note that in actuality this tuple could not be generated, for STU-ID is part of the primary key of the COURSE table, and we know that the value of the primary key of a table cannot be null. However, for purposes of this example, let's assume that we had somehow inserted this tuple in the COURSE table and executed an Outer JOIN with position of the plus sign changed, the results would be as follows.

```
UFI> SELECT STUDENT_NAME, COURSE_TITLE
  2  FROM STUDENT, COURSE
  3  WHERE STUDENT.STU_ID (+) = COURSE.STU_ID
  4    AND STUDENT_NAME = 'DOTTIE STACY'
  5    AND COURSE_TITLE IN ('PRINCIPLES OF ACCOUNTING II',
  6                         'HISTORY OF ROUND DANCING');

STUDENT-NAME_____    COURSE-TITLE_____
DOTTIE STACY          PRINCIPLES OF ACCOUNTING II
                      HISTORY OF ROUND DANCING
```

If we executed the Outer JOIN on the complete STUDENT table, we would get the following output.

```
UFI> SELECT STUDENT_NAME, COURSE_TITLE
  2  FROM STUDENT, COURSE
  3  WHERE STUDENT.STU_ID = COURSE.STU_ID (+);

STUDENT-NAME_____    COURSE-TITLE_____
WENDY JONES           INTRODUCTION TO COMPUTING
```

```
          WENDY JONES          PASCAL PROGRAMMING
          WENDY JONES          PRINCIPLES OF ACCOUNTING I
          SAM WALES            INTRODUCTION TO COMPUTING
          CATHY SMITH          PASCAL PROGRAMMING
          DOTTIE STACY         PRINCIPLES OF ACCOUNTING II
          JAY LANGER           HISTORY OF PIROGUES
          AMY LOPEZ
          SAM WATSON
          TAMMY REDD
          TOMMY WADKINS
          BEN TREVINO

          12 records selected.
```

This doesn't give us quite what we are looking for as it gives us the names of the students who are taking courses <u>and</u> the names of the students who are not taking courses. To satisfy our sample query fully, we will have to find some method of extracting only the tuples where the value of COURSE-TITLE is null. The complete SQL command is:

```
UFI> SELECT STUDENT_NAME, COURSE_TITLE
  2  FROM STUDENT, COURSE
  3  WHERE STUDENT.STU_ID = COURSE.STU_ID (+)
  4    AND COURSE_TITLE IS NULL;

STUDENT-NAME_____ COURSE-TITLE_____
AMY LOPEZ
SAM WATSON
TAMMY REDD
TOMMY WADKINS
BEN TREVINO
```

Note that we did not have to display the attribute COURSE-TITLE in the above query if we did not want to. We included it to show that its value was null in each of the retrieved tuples.

JOINING A TABLE TO ITSELF

In certain very rare instances we may need to be able to join a table to itself. This can be accomplished very easily in ORACLE. All we have to do is to use different table labels to give the same table two different names. For example, if we wanted to join the FACULTY table to itself, we could use the following FROM clause.

```
FROM FACULTY F1, FACULTY F2
```

To illustrate a use for joining a table to itself, consider the following table.

TABLE NAME: PERSONNEL

FAC-ID	FACULTY-NAME	BOSS-ID	TITLE-OR-RANK	SALARY
D02	GREG DAVIS		PRESIDENT	$80,000
M01	SCOTT MIZE	D02	DEAN	$60,000
S02	LARRY SIMPSON	D02	DEAN	$44,000
N02	NICK NORMAN	S02	DEPARTMENT CHAIR	$50,000
C01	JAN CARNER	M01	DEPARTMENT CHAIR	$42,000
H01	BYRON HOGAN	S02	DEPARTMENT CHAIR	$43,000
F01	LEE FALDO	S02	DEPARTMENT CHAIR	$45,000
J01	RAYMOND J. JOHNSON	F01	PROFESSOR	$40,000
S01	WENDY SWIMMER	F01	PROFESSOR	$45,000
D01	AMY DANCER	F01	ASSOC PROFESSOR	$34,500
J02	BOB JONES	C01	ASSOC PROFESSOR	$35,000
N01	JACK NELSON	N02	INSTRUCTOR	$28,000
N03	BEN NELSON	H01	ASSIST PROFESSOR	$30,000
S03	MARK STEWART	H01	ASSIST PROFESSOR	$30,500
C02	PAT CARNER	H01	PROFESSOR	$44,000

Who Makes More than Their Bosses?

The classic query to illustrate joining a table to itself is to find the names of the employees who earn more than their bosses. Before we discuss solving this query, let's examine the table to learn what data we have stored in it. A very important piece of information that we have in this table is that we can determine who works for whom. (This relationship forms a tree structure, which will be discussed fully in the next chapter.) Notice that we have two attributes in each tuple called FAC-ID and BOSS-ID. The attribute BOSS-ID contains the FAC-ID of the employee's boss. For example, notice that faculty member Raymond J. Johnson works under the supervision of Lee Faldo. We know this is true because Raymond J. Johnson's BOSS-ID is ''F01'' and that is the FAC-ID of Lee Faldo. Note that even though FAC-ID and BOSS-ID have different attribute names, they are defined over the same common domain: the list of faculty identifiers. (Domains are, of course, not directly specifiable in ORACLE.) Notice that the president of the university has no boss. (College presidents would probably disagree with this statement.) We know this because the value of the president's BOSS-ID is null.

To solve this query we will have to perform the two operations. The first thing that we must do is to find the employees whose BOSS-ID is equal to the FAC-ID of another tuple. We will do this by joining the PERSONNEL table to itself over the common domain, faculty identifier (BOSS-ID = FAC-ID). This will create a table of employees and their bosses. This is illustrated with the Equi-JOIN command

```
UFI> SELECT E.FACULTY-NAME, E.SALARY, B.FACULTY-NAME, B.SALARY
  2  FROM PERSONNEL E, PERSONNEL B
  3  WHERE E.BOSS-ID = B.FAC-ID;
```

For output of this command see table on page 242.

Note the comment that we have placed above the resultant table heading. (*This comment is not part of the table output, we have entered it in for expository purposes only.*) The comment illustrates that the first five attributes of the resultant table are referred to by the table label "E," for Employee, and the second five attributes are referred to by the table label "B," for Boss. Finally, note that in each tuple of the resultant table the value of the attribute BOSS-ID in the "E" part of the table is equal to the value of FAC-ID in the "B" part of the table.

Once we have found each employee's boss, the second thing that we must do is compare the boss's salary against the employee's salary. This can be done by adding the following condition to the command predicate.

```
E.SALARY > B.SALARY
```

Since we have the attribute SALARY in the resultant table twice, we must have some method of differentiating between the two attributes. The table labels "E" and "B" are used for this.

The following SQL command will solve the proposed query.

```
UFI> SELECT E.FACULTY-NAME, E.SALARY "FAC SAL",
  2  B.FACULTY-NAME "BOSS NAME", B.SALARY "BOSS SAL"
  3  FROM PERSONNEL E, PERSONNEL B
  4  WHERE E.BOSS-ID = B.FAC-ID
  5    AND E.SALARY > B.SALARY;

FACULTY-NAME____ FAC_SAL BOSS_NAME_____ BOSS_SAL
NICK NORMAN      $50,000 LARRY SIMPSON    $44,000
LEE FALDO        $45,000 LARRY SIMPSON    $44,000
PAT CARNER       $44,000 BYRON HOGAN      $43,000
```

Note that we have placed attribute headings above the two salary attributes and the boss attribute to improve the readability of the output.

The reason that we had to join the table to itself to solve this query is because we had to perform intertuple comparisons. We had to compare the value of SALARY in one tuple to the value of SALARY in related tuples of the PERSONNEL table. Once we joined the PERSONNEL table to itself, we placed the two values of SALARY (E.SALARY and B.SALARY) in the same row (even though it is a virtual row). It is now a simple task to compare the two values. The reason that we had to specify two different table labels is so we could differentiate the two FACULTY-NAMEs and the two SALARYs.

		———————— Referred to by Table Label "E" ————————				———————— Referred to by the Table Label "E" ————————			
FAC_ID	FACULTY_NAME	BOSS_ID	TITLE_OR_RANK	SALARY	FAC_ID	FACULTY_NAME	BOSS_ID	TITLE_OR_RANK	SALARY
M01	SCOTT MIZE	D02	DEAN	$60,000	D02	GREG DAVIS		PRESIDENT	$80,000
S02	LARRY SIMPSON	D02	DEAN	$44,000	D02	GREG DAVIS		PRESIDENT	$80,000
N02	NICK NORMAN	S02	DEPARTMENT CHAIR	$50,000	S02	LARRY SIMPSON	D02	DEAN	$44,000
C01	JAN CARNER	M01	DEPARTMENT CHAIR	$42,000	M01	SCOTT MIZE	D02	DEAN	$60,000
H01	BYRON HOGAN	S02	DEPARTMENT CHAIR	$43,000	S02	LARRY SIMPSON	D02	DEAN	$44,000
F01	LEE FALDO	S02	DEPARTMENT CHAIR	$45,000	S02	LARRY SIMPSON	D02	DEAN	$44,000
J01	RAYMOND J. JOHNSON	F01	PROFESSOR	$40,000	F01	LEE FALDO	S02	DEPARTMENT CHAIR	$45,000
S01	WENDY SWIMMER	F01	PROFESSOR	$45,000	F01	LEE FALDO	S02	DEPARTMENT CHAIR	$45,000
D01	AMY DANCER	F01	ASSOC PROFESSOR	$34,500	F01	LEE FALDO	S02	DEPARTMENT CHAIR	$45,000
J02	BOB JONES	C01	ASSOC PROFESSOR	$35,000	C01	JAN CARNER	M01	DEPARTMENT CHAIR	$42,000
N01	JACK NELSON	N02	INSTRUCTOR	$28,000	N02	NICK NORMAN	S02	DEPARTMENT CHAIR	$50,000
N03	BEN NELSON	H01	ASSIST PROFESSOR	$30,000	H01	BYRON HOGAN	S02	DEPARTMENT CHAIR	$43,000
S03	MARK STEWART	H01	ASSIST PROFESSOR	$30,500	H01	BYRON HOGAN	S02	DEPARTMENT CHAIR	$43,000
C02	PAT CARNER	H01	PROFESSOR	$44,000	H01	BYRON HOGAN	S02	DEPARTMENT CHAIR	$43,000

Who Earns More Money than Professor Johnson?

A second example of joining a table to itself could be to display the names of all the faculty members who earn more than Raymond J. Johnson. Since Raymond J. Johnson's salary is stored in the FACULTY table that we have been using, let's use it to solve this query.

```
FAC-ID FACULTY-NAME_____  DEPARTMENT  GENDER SALARY
J01    RAYMOND J. JOHNSON COMP SCI     MALE   40000
S01    WENDY SWIMMER      COMP SCI     FEMALE 45000
D01    AMY DANCER         COMP SCI     FEMALE 34500
J02    BOB JONES          ACCOUNTING   MALE   35000
N01    JACK NELSON        HISTORY      MALE   28000
```

We must join Raymond J. Johnson's tuple to each existing tuple in the FACULTY table so that we can compare Professor Johnson's salary to each of his colleague's salaries. The join is accomplished as follows.

```
UFI> SELECT A.FACULTY-NAME,A.SALARY,B.FACULTY-NAME,B.SALARY
   2   FROM FACULTY A, FACULTY B
   3   WHERE A.FACULTY-NAME = 'RAYMOND J. JOHNSON';
```

I----- Referred to by the Table Label "A" -----I					I----- Referred to by the Table Label "B" -----I				
FAC_ID	FACULTY_NAME	DEPARTMENT	GENDER	SALARY	FAC_ID	FACULTY_NAME	DEPARTMENT	GENDER	SALARY
J01	RAYMOND J. JOHNSON	COMP SCI	MALE	40000	J01	RAYMOND J. JOHNSON	COMP SCI	MALE	40000
J01	RAYMOND J. JOHNSON	COMP SCI	MALE	40000	S01	WENDY SWIMMER	COMP SCI	FEMALE	45000
J01	RAYMOND J. JOHNSON	COMP SCI	MALE	40000	D01	AMY DANCER	COMP SCI	FEMALE	34500
J01	RAYMOND J. JOHNSON	COMP SCI	MALE	40000	J02	BOB JONES	ACCOUNTING	MALE	35000
J01	RAYMOND J. JOHNSON	COMP SCI	MALE	40000	N01	JACK NELSON	HISTORY	MALE	28000

Again note that since we are using a duplicate set of attributes, we must use table labels to differentiate between the salary of Professor Johnson and his colleagues. The value of Professor Johnson's salary ($40,000) appears in each tuple, so we can compare it (A.SALARY) to the value of salary (B.SALARY) of each of his colleagues.

The complete SELECT command to solve the query is:

```
UFI> SELECT A.FACULTY-NAME JOHNSON, A.SALARY "JOHNSON SAL",
   2   B.FACULTY-NAME "OTHER FAC", B.SALARY "OTH SAL"
   3   FROM FACULTY A, FACULTY B
   4   WHERE A.FACULTY-NAME = 'RAYMOND J. JOHNSON'
   5     AND B.SALARY > A.SALARY;
```

```
JOHNSON_____  JOHNSON_SAL OTHER_FAC_____  OTH_SAL
RAYMOND J. JOHNSON        40000 WENDY SWIMMER      45000
```

Although this is one method of solving this query, a much more efficient method is illustrated in the next chapter, in the section dedicated to subqueries.

GENERATING CARTESIAN PRODUCTS THROUGH JOINS

If you will remember back to Chapter 3, a Cartesian product joins two tables together without regard to linking attributes. The Cartesian product joins each tuple of the first table to each tuple of the second table. This makes the Cartesian product a superset of the JOIN command.

The Cartesian product can be implemented in SQL by specifying two (or more) table names in the FROM clause and not specifying a JOIN condition in the WHERE clause. A word of caution about the Cartesian product: if there are n tuples in the first table and m tuples in the second table, then the resultant table will have n times m tuples. The Cartesian product is used to generate all possible combinations of tuples from two tables.

To illustrate the Cartesian product, suppose we wanted to match each faculty member with the students Wendy Jones and Sam Wales. (We could have matched every student with every faculty member, but that operation would have generated 50 tuples, and we thought that would take up too much print space in the book.)

```
UFI> SELECT FACULTY-NAME, STUDENT-NAME
  2  FROM FACULTY, STUDENT
  3  WHERE STUDENT-NAME IN ('WENDY JONES', 'SAM WALES');


FACULTY-NAME_____  STUDENT-NAME
RAYMOND J. JOHNSON  WENDY JONES
WENDY SWIMMER       WENDY JONES
AMY DANCER          WENDY JONES
BOB JONES           WENDY JONES
JACK NELSON         WENDY JONES
RAYMOND J. JOHNSON  SAM WALES
WENDY SWIMMER       SAM WALES
AMY DANCER          SAM WALES
BOB JONES           SAM WALES
JACK NELSON         SAM WALES

10 Records selected.
```

CLUSTERS

Even though the JOIN operation is the most powerful operation in relational databases, it is also the most time consuming. The primary reason for this is that ORACLE will have to read a tuple from the first table and then read all the tuples from the second table in an attempt to satisfy the JOIN condition(s). It will then read the second tuple in the first table and then read all the tuples in the second table. (See the example of how a JOIN resembles nested loops in Chapter 3.) For example, suppose that our JOIN condition were

```
STUDENT.STU-ID = COURSE.STU-ID
```

ORACLE would have to signal to the computer system to read the page of secondary storage where the first value of STUDENT.STU-ID was stored, the first tuple of the STUDENT table. Then the pages where all the values of COURSE.STU-ID were stored would have to be read to determine if a match existed. Next, the page with the second tuple of the STUDENT table would be read and all the pages containing the COURSE table tuples would have to be reread. This process continues until the supply of STUDENT tuples is exhausted. As you can see, this is a very time-consuming process, and if we can speed it up in any way, we should do it.

Normally the data for the two tables is stored on different pages (blocks) in the storage space(s). This forces the computer system to perform many physical reads. It would certainly speed up execution of JOIN queries if we could store the tuples with common values on the same physical page. This concept is called **clustering**. Clustering is only useful if Equi-JOINs are needed. Clusters causes the physical storage space in the database to be rearranged.

If the user perceives that in the day-to-day operations of a database certain tables will be joined frequently, it would probably behoove him to consider clustering. Clustering should improve the overall performance of a database if a significant number of Equi-JOINs are performed between tables. This does not mean what we cannot search the table(s) in other ways (simple WHERE clauses), but it is less efficient than if the table(s) were not clustered.

The ORACLE Corporation has determined that clustering should improve system performance by a factor between two and three times.

Creating a Cluster

Before clusters can be used they must be created. Clusters are created via the CREATE CLUSTER command. The command syntax is:

```
CREATE CLUSTER cluster-name (attribute1 data-type1
                            [, attribute2 data-type2 , , ,])
        [SPACE storage-space]
```

The attribute(s) that is specified is the attribute that will be used in the Equi-JOIN. For example, if we perceived that we would be joining our STUDENT table and our COURSE table over the common attribute STU-ID, we could create a cluster as follows.

```
UFI> CREATE CLUSTER STU-COURSE (FAC-ID CHAR(6))
   2   SPACE SCHOOL_SPACE;

Cluster created.
```

Note that the attribute name, data type, and size are exactly the same as the original data declarations in the CREATE TABLE command. Also be aware that since we are rearranging storage space we have the option of specifying a storage space name.

At this point ORACLE does not know which tables will be joined so as to take advantage of clustering. The ALTER CLUSTER command must be used to inform ORACLE the cluster in which to store the data tables. The format of the ALTER CLUSTER command is:

```
ALTER CLUSTER cluster-name ADD TABLE table-name
WHERE [cluster-name.]attribute1 = [table-name.]attribute2
[AND [cluster-name.]attribute3 = [table-name.]attribute4 . . .]
```

Let's add the STUDENT table to the cluster.

```
UFI> ALTER CLUSTER STU_COURSE ADD TABLE STUDENT
   2   WHERE STU_COURSE.STU-ID = STUDENT.STU-ID;

Cluster altered.
```

Now we will insert the values from the COURSE table.

```
UFI> ALTER CLUSTER STU-COURSE ADD TABLE COURSE
   2   WHERE STU_COURSE.STU-ID = STUDENT.STU-ID;

Cluster altered.
```

These ALTER CLUSTER commands cause tuples from the two tables with the same value of STU-ID to be stored on the same physical page in secondary storage; that is, it will cluster the tuples around common values of STU-ID. Remember that the use of clusters rearranges the physical storage space used to store tables that are included in the cluster. The table(s) still exist, but their tuples have been physically rearranged in secondary storage.

There are four important rules about clusters that must be remembered.

1. A table can only reside in one cluster at any one instant in time.
2. Tables with an attribute of the data type LONG cannot be clustered.
3. Clusters do not affect the syntax of any SQL command.
4. At least one of the attributes in the CREATE CLUSTER command must have the restriction of not allowing null values.

If we plan to join more than two tables then we may want to place the third, fourth, fifth, and so on tables in the cluster. A table may be removed from the cluster by executing the ALTER CLUSTER DROP command. The format of this command is:

```
        ALTER CLUSTER cluster-name DROP TABLE table-name
```

For example, if we wanted to drop the table COURSE from the STU-COURSE cluster, we would execute the following command.

```
    UFI> ALTER CLUSTER STU-COURSE DROP TABLE COURSE;

    Cluster altered.
```

This command also rearranges physical storage when executed.

Dropping Clusters

If at any time we wish to drop a cluster we can execute the DROP CLUSTER command. The syntax of the command is:

```
            DROP CLUSTER cluster-name
```

Be aware that a cluster cannot be dropped until all tables have been removed, via the ALTER CLUSTER cluster-name DROP TABLE table-name command, from the cluster.

```
 UFI> REMARK . . .. We will assume that the ALTER CLUSTER
 UFI> REMARK . . .. command above has been executed removing
 UFI> REMARK . . .. the table COURSE from the cluster.
 UFI> ALTER CLUSTER STU-COURSE DROP TABLE STUDENT;

 Cluster altered.

 UFI> DROP CLUSTER STU-COURSE;

 Cluster dropped.
```

The Effect of Clusters on Indexes

When a cluster is created, an index called a cluster index is automatically created on the attribute(s) specified in the CREATE CLUSTER command. This index is similar to the index created with the CREATE INDEX command. This index keeps the tuples in ascending order by cluster value. This could save system space because, if the attributes in each table were indexed via the CREATE INDEX command, two indexes would have to be maintained. The cluster maintains both indexes in one cluster index. Therefore it is not reasonable to maintain an index on an attribute that is part of a cluster.

If you have created a multicolumn index on a table and that table is added to a cluster, *it causes problems in the data dictionary*. The solution to this problem is to drop the multicolumn index, add the table to the cluster, then re-create the multi-column index.

SUMMARY

This chapter discussed the most powerful operator in relational databases: the JOIN operator. Various types of joins were illustrated such as the Equi-JOIN, Theta JOIN, and Outer JOIN. Optimization of JOIN operations was also explored. The Cartesian product, which is a superset of a join, was also illustrated. A method of storing tuples, called clustering, that can be used to store frequently joined tables efficiently was also illustrated.

After completion of this chapter, the reader should be familiar with the following commands, terms, and concepts.

A. JOIN query	**G.** Table labels
B. Equi-JOIN	**H.** Clusters
C. Theta JOIN	**I.** CREATE CLUSTER
D. Outer JOIN	**J.** ALTER CLUSTER ADD
E. Optimization of JOIN queries	**K.** ALTER CLUSTER DROP
F. Cartesian product	**L.** DROP CLUSTER

EXERCISES

1. Explain the difference between an Equi-JOIN and a Theta JOIN.
2. Explain the difference between an Equi-JOIN and an Outer JOIN.
3. Discuss what is meant by query optimization. When is it relevant?
4. Explain how clusters speed up retrieval in join queries.
5. Construct the necessary SELECT commands to satisfy the following queries.
   a. List each faculty member and the course titles that they teach.
   b. List each male faculty member and the courses that they teach.
   c. List the faculty members and the names of the students that they teach.
   d. List the female faculty members and the students that they teach.
6. Explain what the following SELECT command does.

```
SELECT FACULTY_NAME, STUDENT_NAME
FROM STUDENT S, COURSE C, FACULTY F
WHERE S.STU_ID = C.STU_ID
   AND C.FAC_ID = F.FAC_ID
   AND F.GENDER = 'FEMALE'
   AND S.GENDER = 'FEMALE'
ORDER BY FACULTY_NAME;
```

10

More Sophisticated Retrieval of Data

PURPOSE: The purpose of this chapter is to explore some of the more sophisticated retrieval techniques available in ORACLE. The subquery, group retrieval, and hierarchical retrieval are discussed.

We sometimes will want to retrieve tuples based on some previous query. For example, "Who are the faculty members who earn more money than Raymond J. Johnson?" To solve this query, we must first determine how much money Professor Johnson earns. Once this value is retrieved, we can then SELECT all the faculty members who earn more than this amount. This type query can be solved utilizing subqueries.

The second type of query concerns group retrieval of tuples. For example, "What is the total dollar value of salaries by department?" To solve this query we will have to aggregate the salaries after grouping the faculty members by departments.

The last type of query will make the relational structure of ORACLE behave like a tree structure. This consists of representing tuples in a hierarchical or tree structure and being able to retrieve them in a top-to-bottom or bottom-to-top order.

SUBQUERIES

In all the queries that we have illustrated up to this point, except for the second example in the "Joining a Table to Itself" section in the previous chapter, we always knew exactly what values we wanted to compare in our predicates. Here are some examples of simple predicates:

1. All the male students
2. All faculty members that earn more than $35,000
3. All the courses taught by Amy Dancer
4. All the male faculty members in the Computer Science Department who earn between $30,000 and $40,000

Suppose that we now wanted the names of the faculty members who earned more than Raymond J. Johnson. First, we would have to determine what salary Professor Johnson earns, then we could formulate a WHERE clause to retrieve the names of the faculty members who earn more than what ever salary Professor Johnson earns. This could be done as follows.

```
UFI> SELECT SALARY FROM FACULTY
   2   WHERE FACULTY-NAME = 'RAYMOND J. JOHNSON';

____SALARY
    40000


UFI> SELECT FACULTY-NAME, SALARY FROM FACULTY
   2   WHERE SALARY > 40000;

FACULTY-NAME__ ____SALARY
WENDY SWIMMER      45000
```

These two SELECT commands solve the query, but they are rather rustic. We could use a subquery to retrieve the data in one command. A subquery is a query within a query. We will let the subquery retrieve the salary of Raymond J. Johnson. Then we will use whatever value that the subquery returns as part of our main query's predicate.

```
UFI> SELECT FACULTY-NAME, SALARY FROM FACULTY
   2   WHERE SALARY >
   3        (SELECT SALARY FROM FACULTY
   4         WHERE FACULTY-NAME = 'RAYMOND J. JOHNSON');

FACULTY-NAME__ ____SALARY
WENDY SWIMMER      45000
```

There are several important concepts to note about this subquery. First, note that the subquery is placed in parentheses. Second, note that the subquery replaces the $40,000 in the predicate of our second SELECT command shown above. Third, note that the value retrieved from the subquery (SALARY) must come from the same domain as the value being tested. We are comparing the value of SALARY in each tuple in our FACULTY table to the value retrieved in the subquery. To do this efficiently, the subquery must be executed before the query. This is the reason that the subquery is placed in parentheses. What happens if the value of FACULTY-NAME does not appear in the FACULTY table?

```
UFI> SELECT FACULTY-NAME, SALARY FROM FACULTY
  2  WHERE SALARY > (SELECT SALARY FROM FACULTY
  3                        WHERE FACULTY-NAME = 'JOAN SMITH');

No records selected.
```

The value produced by the subquery is null, and the query compares SALARY to see if it is greater than null. It is not, so no tuples are generated for the resultant table.

Nesting Subqueries

Subqueries can be nested one inside the other. You can visualize this as follows.

```
SELECT . . . . .
FROM . . . . .
WHERE attribute1 <operator>
       (SELECT attribute1
        FROM . . . . .
        WHERE attribute2 <operator>
               (SELECT attribute2
                FROM . . . . .
                WHERE attribute3 <operator>
                       (SELECT attribute3
                        FROM . . . . .
                        WHERE attribute4 <operator>
                               (SELECT attribute4
                                FROM . . . . .
                                WHERE . . . . . . . . . .))));
```

There is no limit to the number of levels of nesting that can be specified for subqueries in ORACLE except for the amount of storage in the workspace. If the error "Workspace too small" occurs, simply use the SET WORKSIZE command to increase the size of the workspace.

The Use of Subqueries with Other SQL Commands

Subqueries are not restricted to use only in SELECT commands. They may be used in any data maintenance commands (DELETE, UPDATE, and/or INSERT). Here are some examples of subqueries in data maintenance commands.

1. Delete all the faculty members who are in the same department as Wendy Swimmer.

```
UFI> DELETE FROM FACULTY WHERE DEPARTMENT =
   2        (SELECT DEPARTMENT FROM FACULTY WHERE
   3         FACULTY-NAME = 'WENDY SWIMMER');

   3 Records deleted.
```

2. Give all faculty members who are the same gender as Amy Dancer a 30% raise.

```
UFI> UPDATE FACULTY SET SALARY = SALARY * 1.3
   2    WHERE GENDER = (SELECT GENDER FROM FACULTY
   3                    WHERE FACULTY-NAME = 'AMY DANCER');

   2 Records updated.
```

3. Assume that we have already created a table called KITCHEN (yes, that's right, the kitchen table) which we want to contain the IDs, names, and salaries of all the male faculty members who are in the same department as Wendy Swimmer. We will assume that the new table is structured as follows.

```
KITCHEN (FAC-ID, FAC-NAME, SALARY)

UFI> INSERT INTO KITCHEN (FAC-ID, FAC-NAME, SALARY)
   2    SELECT FAC-ID, FACULTY-NAME, SALARY FROM FACULTY
   3    WHERE GENDER = 'MALE'
   4      AND DEPARTMENT = (SELECT DEPARTMENT FROM FACULTY
   5                        WHERE FACULTY-NAME = 'WENDY SWIMMER');

1 Record created.
```

Subqueries with Multiple Values Retrieved

In all our previous subqueries, the subquery produced just one value; that is, Wendy Swimmer has only one department, Amy Dancer has only one gender, and so on. Suppose that we wanted to display the names of the faculty members who are either in the same department as Amy Dancer or Jack Nelson. Since each of these two faculty members resides in separate departments, the subquery will produce two values for DEPARTMENT.

```
UFI> SELECT FACULTY-NAME FROM FACULTY
  2   WHERE DEPARTMENT = (SELECT DEPARTMENT FROM FACULTY
  3                            WHERE FACULTY-NAME = 'AMY DANCER'
  4                            OR FACULTY-NAME = 'JACK NELSON');

WHERE DEPARTMENT = (SELECT DEPARTMENT FROM FACULTY
Error at line 2:1427   not a single row query block
```

The reason that this command produces an error is that more than one value is returned from the subquery. The way to solve this problem is by replacing the equal sign (=) after DEPARTMENT with the IN operator.

```
UFI> SELECT FACULTY-NAME FROM FACULTY
  2   WHERE DEPARTMENT IN (SELECT DEPARTMENT FROM FACULTY
  3                            WHERE FACULTY-NAME = 'AMY DANCER'
  4                            OR FACULTY-NAME = 'JACK NELSON');

FACULTY-NAME_____
RAYMOND J. JOHNSON
WENDY SWIMMER
AMY DANCER
JACK NELSON
```

Remember that the IN operator is used to place items in a list, for it is an implementation of multiple OR conditions. In this query, since Amy Dancer is affiliated with the Computer Science Department and Jack Nelson is affiliated with the History Department, two values will be placed into the IN list and the query will execute.

The ANY and ALL Operators

Consider the following query. What are the names of the faculty members who make more than anybody in the Accounting Department? To solve this query we would have do three things.

1. Find the salaries of all the faculty in the Accounting Department.
2. Determine the largest of these salaries.
3. Display the names of all of the faculty members who earn more than this maximum salary.

We can solve this type query very readily with the ALL operator.

```
UFI> SELECT * FROM FACULTY
  2   WHERE SALARY > ALL (SELECT SALARY FROM FACULTY
  3                            WHERE DEPARTMENT = 'ACCOUNTING');

FAC-ID FACULTY-NAME_____  DEPARTMENT GENDER SALARY
  J01    RAYMOND J. JOHNSON COMP SCI   MALE   40000
  S01    WENDY SWIMMER      COMP SCI   FEMALE 45000
```

Since there is only one person in the Accounting Department and he makes $35,000, we are looking for all the faculty members who make more than $35,000. If there were more than one member of the Accounting Department, the largest SALARY would be selected for comparison.

Let's use the ANY operator to display the data on all the faculty members who make more than the lowest-paid member of the Computer Science Department.

```
UFI> SELECT * FROM FACULTY
  2   WHERE SALARY > ANY (SELECT SALARY FROM FACULTY
  3                            WHERE DEPARTMENT = 'COMP SCI');

FAC-ID FACULTY-NAME_____   DEPARTMENT GENDER SALARY
  J01    RAYMOND J. JOHNSON COMP SCI   MALE   40000
  S01    WENDY SWIMMER      COMP SCI   FEMALE 45000
  J02    BOB JONES          ACCOUNTING MALE   35000
```

Since the lowest-paid faculty member of the Computer Science Department earns $34,500, we are looking for the faculty members who earn more than $34,500.

GROUPED RETRIEVAL

In all the examples that we have used so far, all our retrievals consisted of values extracted from single tuples. It is sometimes desirable to retrieve values from multiple tuples. Some examples of group queries are the following.

1. What is the total amount of salaries earned by faculty members?
2. What is the average salary earned by members of the Computer Science Department?
3. What faculty member earns the highest salary? the lowest salary?
4. How many students are females? males?
5. What is the average monthly salary of the faculty by department?
6. What is the average salary of faculty members in departments having more than one faculty member?

Group Functions

A function is a prewritten routine that produces a value. The format of the function is

```
function-name  (argument)
```

The "argument" is the value "passed" to the function. The argument is usually an attribute or an expression. Notice that the argument to the function is always placed in parentheses after the function name. There are eight group functions available in ORACLE:

AVG   Computes the average value of a numeric attribute.

SUM   Computes the sum of a numeric attribute.

MAX   Determines the largest value of an attribute.

MIN   Determines the smallest value of an attribute.

COUNT   Counts the number of values. COUNT DISTINCT Counts the unique number of values.

STDDEV   Computes the standard deviation of a numeric attribute.

VARIANCE   Computes the variance of a numeric attribute.

All the numeric functions exclude any null values within their computations.

Examples of Simple Group Functions

To illustrate these functions, let's use them to solve some of the queries proposed in the previous section.

```
UFI> REMARK . . .. What is the sum of all faculty salaries?
UFI> SELECT SUM(SALARY) FROM FACULTY;

SUM(SALARY)
     182500
```

Note that the function is used as the attribute heading. We can, of course, change this through the use of the COLUMN command.

```
UFI> COLUMN SUM(SALARY) HEADING TOTAL FORMAT $999,999
UFI> /

____TOTAL
 $182,500

UFI> REMARK . . .. What's the average salary in the CS Dept?
UFI> COLUMN AVG(SALARY) HEADING AVERAGE FORMAT $99,999.99
```

```
UFI>  SELECT AVG(SALARY) FROM FACULTY
   2   WHERE DEPARTMENT = 'COMP SCI';


____AVERAGE
 $39,833.33

UFI>  REMARK . . ., Who earns the highest salary?
UFI>  SELECT FACULTY-NAME, MAX(SALARY) FROM FACULTY;

SELECT FACULTY-NAME, MAX(SALARY) FROM FACULTY

Error at line 1: 937   not a single group set function
```

What happened? Group functions, such as MAX, can only be used with grouped retrieval, and an attribute, such as FACULTY-NAME, can only be used with tuple-at-a-time retrieval. *They can not be mixed in a SELECT list.* (We will get around this problem with the GROUP BY clause described shortly.) Does this mean that we cannot display the name of the person who makes the highest salary? Of course we can, but we will have to use a different approach to solve this query. Actually we will use a subquery.

```
UFI>  SELECT FACULTY-NAME, SALARY
   2   FROM FACULTY
   3   WHERE SALARY = (SELECT MAX(SALARY)
   4                     FROM FACULTY);


FACULTY-NAME___    ___SALARY
WENDY SWIMMER         45000
```

Note that the subquery retrieves the value of the maximum salary and this value is used to retrieve the tuple with the maximum salary.

```
UFI>  REMARK . . ..., Count the number of Male students
UFI>  SELECT COUNT(GENDER) FROM STUDENT WHERE GENDER = 'MALE';

COUNT(GENDER)
        5

UFI>  REMARK . . ..., Count the number of Female students
UFI>  SELECT COUNT(GENDER) FROM STUDENT WHERE GENDER = 'FEMALE';

COUNT(GENDER)
        5
```

The COUNT function is used to count the number of tuples that meet whatever condition(s) are specified in the WHERE clause. The COUNT function counts tuples, not attributes. If we specify the COUNT function with an attribute name, any tuple with a null value for that attribute is not counted. If we wanted to include null values in our count we would use the COUNT function with the asterisk as an argument. For example, if we wanted to count the number of tuples in the STUDENT table, we could use the following command.

```
UFI> SELECT COUNT(*) FROM STUDENT;

__COUNT(*)
        10
```

The GROUP BY Clause

In the previous example of counting the number of male and female students, we had to use two separate commands. We could have used the GROUP BY clause to reduce the number of commands to one. As the name implies, the GROUP BY clause groups tuples together by common attribute values. The GROUP BY clause is used exclusively with group functions. Only one line of output is produced for each group. We could have used the following SELECT command to count the number of male and female students.

```
UFI> SELECT GENDER, COUNT(*)
  2   FROM STUDENT
  3   GROUP BY GENDER;

GENDER __COUNT(*)
FEMALE          5
MALE            5
```

Note that the only values that can appear in the select list are group functions and the grouped by attribute.

We can apply multiple group functions to the same attribute in the same SELECT command.

```
UFI> SELECT DEPARTMENT, MAX(SALARY), MIN(SALARY),
  2   MAX(SALARY)-MIN(SALARY) RANGE
  3   FROM FACULTY
  4   GROUP BY DEPARTMENT;

DEPARTMENT MAX(SALARY) MIN(SALARY) _____RANGE
ACCOUNTING       35000       35000          0
COMP SCI         45000       34500      10500
HISTORY          28000       28000          0
```

We can even use WHERE clauses to filter out unwanted groups.

```
UFI> SELECT DEPARTMENT, MAX(SALARY), MIN(SALARY),
2    MAX(SALARY)-MIN(SALARY) RANGE
3    FROM FACULTY
4    WHERE DEPARTMENT = 'COMP SCI'
5    GROUP BY DEPARTMENT;
```

DEPARTMENT	MAX(SALARY)	MIN(SALARY)	RANGE
COMP SCI	45000	34500	10500

We are not limited to only one GROUP BY attribute. We may specify as many attributes as we desire. SQL will take each unique combination of the attributes to be a group. For example, if we wanted to count the number of faculty by gender by department, we could use the following SELECT command.

```
UFI> SELECT GENDER, DEPARTMENT, COUNT(*), AVG(SALARY)
2    FROM FACULTY
3    GROUP BY GENDER, DEPARTMENT;
```

GENDER	DEPARTMENT	COUNT(*)	AVG(SALARY)
FEMALE	COMP SCI	2	39750
MALE	ACCOUNTING	1	35000
MALE	COMP SCI	1	40000
MALE	HISTORY	1	28000

The HAVING Clause

The HAVING clause is analogous to the WHERE clause for GROUP BY items. The HAVING clause can be used to filter out unwanted tuples generated by GROUP BY clauses. The HAVING clause can only be used with grouped data. For example, suppose that we wanted to compute the average salary for each department at our university. However, we only want the average of those departments with more than one faculty member.

```
UFI> SELECT DEPARTMENT, COUNT(*), AVG(SALARY)
2    FROM FACULTY
3    GROUP BY DEPARTMENT
4    HAVING COUNT(DEPARTMENT) > 1;
```

DEPARTMENT	COUNT(*)	AVG(SALARY)
COMP SCI	3	39833

This query could not have been executed with the WHERE clause, for this condition, COUNT (DEPARTMENT) > 1, consists of a grouped attribute. The WHERE clause is used to exclude values *before* the GROUP BY clause is applied and the HAVING clause is used to exclude grouped values after they have been determined.

The operators available in the HAVING clause are the six standard relational operators, BETWEEN, IN, LIKE, IS NULL, and their NOT counterparts. Several conditions may be ANDed or ORed together.

Using the GROUP BY Clause to Load Tables

If GROUP BY data is to be used many times, perhaps it would benefit the user to create a separate table containing GROUP BY data.

```
UFI> CREATE TABLE SUMMARY (GENDER CHAR(6),
   2                       DEPARTMENT CHAR (10),
   3                       NO_OF_FAC NUMBER (2),
   4                       AVE_SAL NUMBER (10,2))
   5                       SPACE SCHOOL_SPACE;

Table created.

UFI> REMARK . . ... Let's use the SELECT command with the
UFI> REMARK . . ... INSERT command
UFI> REMARK . . ... to create tuples for the table
UFI> INSERT INTO SUMMARY
   2  (GENDER, DEPARTMENT, NO_OF_FAC, AVE_SAL)
   3  SELECT GENDER, DEPARTMENT, COUNT(*), AVG(SALARY)
   4  FROM FACULTY
   5  GROUP BY GENDER, DEPARTMENT;

4 Records created.
```

Since SUMMARY is now a table, we can use any SQL command to manipulate the data in the table.

```
UFI> SELECT*
   2  FROM SUMMARY
   3  WHERE NO_OF_FAC > 1;

GENDER DEPARTMENT _NO-OF-FAC ____AVE-SAL
FEMALE COMP SCI          2      39750.00
```

Note that this is the same query that we executed with the HAVING clause. Since SUMMARY is an actual table, we cannot use the HAVING clause to filter tuples. Remember that the HAVING clause can only be used with grouped data.

It is important to remember that if any data is changed in the underlying table, FACULTY, this change will not be reflected in the SUMMARY table. The reason for this is that SUMMARY has now become a base table. Perhaps a better method of implementing the SUMMARY table would be with a view. Views are described in Chapter 12.

Combining Subqueries with Grouped Retrieval

It is possible to combine subqueries with grouped retrieval to synergize very powerful queries. For example, let us display the three highest-paid faculty members. At first this might seem like a very simple query. We could probably use the virtual attribute ROWNUM to test against. The query could be formulated as follows.

```
UFI>  SELECT ROWNUM, FACULTY-NAME, SALARY
   2  FROM FACULTY
   3  WHERE ROWNUM <= 3
   4  ORDER BY SALARY DESC;

ROWNUM FACULTY-NAME_____  SALARY
     2 WENDY SWIMMER         45000
     1 RAYMOND J. JOHNSON    40000
     3 AMY DANCER            34500
```

As you can see, this is not the desired result. It gives us the first three tuples in the table (the ones where ROWNUM is <= 3), then sorts them. The reason is that the attribute ROWNUM is applied before the resultant table is sorted. We want the sort to be applied first, then the checking of ROWNUM for a value of less than or equal to three. The output is actually the first three tuples in the table in descending order by SALARY. The output that we desire should look as follows.

```
FACULTY-NAME_____  SALARY
WENDY SWIMMER         45000
RAYMOND J. JOHNSON    40000
HARMON D. RANGE       35000
```

Perhaps if we counted the number of salaries that were greater than each salary, and then tested to see which ones had a count greater than three, that would do the trick. To visualize this technique, let us consider the following query.

```
UFI>  SELECT A.SALARY, COUNT (*)
   2  FROM FACULTY A, FACULTY B
   3  WHERE A.SALARY > B.SALARY
   4  GROUP BY A.SALARY;

____SALARY __COUNT(*)
    34500         1
    35000         2
    40000         3
    45000         4
```

This query indicates that the salary $34,500 exceeds one other salary ($28,000), that the salary $35,000 exceeds two others ($28,000 and $34,500), and so forth.

We can use this grouped query in a subquery to solve our problem. There are a few permutations of the query to solve our problem. One of them is shown here.

```
UFI> SELECT FACULTY-NAME, SALARY
   2   FROM FACULTY F
   3   WHERE 3 > (SELECT COUNT(*)
   4                 FROM FACULTY
   5                 WHERE SALARY > F.SALARY)
   6   ORDER BY SALARY DESC;

FACULTY-NAME_____  SALARY
WENDY SWIMMER          45000
RAYMOND J. JOHNSON     40000
HARMON D. RANGE        35000
```

We still will not be able to get the sequential numbers displayed with ROWNUM, for these values are still generated before the sort is performed.

If we wanted the three-lowest paid faculty members, we would reverse the test of salaries within the subquery.

```
UFI> SELECT FACULTY-NAME, SALARY
   2   FROM FACULTY F
   3   WHERE 3 > (SELECT COUNT(*)
   4                 FROM FACULTY
   5                 WHERE SALARY < F.SALARY)
   6   ORDER BY SALARY;

FACULTY-NAME___  SALARY
JACK NELSON        28000
AMY DANCER         34500
BOB JONES          35000
```

If we wanted all the faculty members except the three-highest paid ones we would reverse the test operator in the query.

```
UFI> SELECT FACULTY-NAME, SALARY
   2   FROM FACULTY F
   3   WHERE 3 < (SELECT COUNT(*)
   4                 FROM FACULTY
   5                 WHERE SALARY > F.SALARY)
   6   ORDER BY SALARY DESC;

FACULTY-NAME___  SALARY
AMY DANCER         34500
JACK NELSON        28000
```

Finally, suppose that we wanted the faculty member who had the fourth highest salary? We could change the inequality in the outer query to an equality.

```
UFI> SELECT FACULTY-NAME, SALARY
  2    FROM FACULTY F
  3    WHERE 3 = (SELECT COUNT(*)
  4               FROM FACULTY
  5               WHERE SALARY > F.SALARY)


FACULTY-NAME___   SALARY
BOB JONES         35000
```

HIERARCHICAL RETRIEVAL

Even though ORACLE is an implementation of the relational model of data, it is sometimes useful to be able to retrieve data as if it was stored in a tree structure. To illustrate this concept, let us go back to the new PERSONNEL table that we introduced in the previous chapter.

TABLE NAME: PERSONNEL

FAC-ID	FACULTY-NAME	BOSS-ID	TITLE-OR-RANK	SALARY
D02	GREG DAVIS		PRESIDENT	$80,000
M01	SCOTT MIZE	D02	DEAN	$60,000
S02	LARRY SIMPSON	D02	DEAN	$44,000
N02	NICK NORMAN	S02	DEPARTMENT CHAIR	$50,000
C01	JAN CARNER	M01	DEPARTMENT CHAIR	$42,000
H01	BYRON HOGAN	S02	DEPARTMENT CHAIR	$43,000
F01	LEE FALDO	S02	DEPARTMENT CHAIR	$45,000
J01	RAYMOND J. JOHNSON	F01	PROFESSOR	$40,000
S01	WENDY SWIMMER	F01	PROFESSOR	$45,000
D01	AMY DANCER	F01	ASSOC PROFESSOR	$34,500
J02	BOB JONES	C01	ASSOC PROFESSOR	$35,000
N01	JACK NELSON	N02	INSTRUCTOR	$28,000
N03	BEN NELSON	H01	ASSIST PROFESSOR	$30,000
S03	MARK STEWART	H01	ASSIST PROFESSOR	$30,500
C02	PAT CARNER	H01	PROFESSOR	$44,000

The tree structure representing this data is shown in Figure 10.1. Notice that there is only one node at the top of the tree. This is called the root node, and it defines the start of the tree structure. The president is listed at the top of the tree; therefore, his record becomes the root node in the tree. The second level consists of all the deans; then come the department chairs, followed on the fourth level by the faculty members. As you can see by this diagram, there are two important aspects of defining a tree structure. The first is to define the root node, and the second is to specify how the nodes of the tree are linked together. In our example,

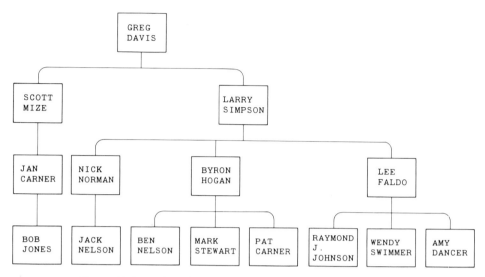

Figure 10.1 A Tree Structure Representation of the Personnel Table

we specified this linkage by including an attribute called BOSS-ID, which defined a link to the employee's boss (except for the president whose value of BOSS-ID was set to null). Without this linkage (attributes specified in each tuple), we cannot implement hierarchical retrieval.

To retrieve tuples in a hierarchy, we must include two additional clauses to our SELECT command. These two clauses are:

```
CONNECT BY [PRIOR] attribute1 = [PRIOR] attribute
START WITH attribute3 = value
```

The CONNECT BY clause defines the linkage between the tuples representing the nodes in the tree. The START WITH clause identifies the root node(s) in the tree structure. The word PRIOR is used to indicate which direction, top-to-bottom or bottom-to-top, the retrieval is to take place.

Top-to-Bottom and Bottom-to-Top Retrieval

To retrieve the tuples in a hierarchical manner, we could use the following SELECT command.

```
UFI> SELECT FACULTY-NAME, TITLE-OR-RANK
  2  FROM PERSONNEL
  3  CONNECT BY PRIOR FAC-ID = BOSS-ID
  4  START WITH FACULTY-NAME = 'GREG DAVIS';
```

```
FACULTY-NAME_____   TITLE-OR-RANK___
GREG DAVIS            PRESIDENT
SCOTT MIZE           DEAN
JAN CARNER           DEPARTMENT CHAIR
BOB JONES            ASSOC PROFESSOR
LARRY SIMPSON        DEAN
NICK NORMAN          DEPARTMENT CHAIR
JACK NELSON          INSTRUCTOR
BYRON HOGAN          DEPARTMENT CHAIR
BEN NELSON           ASSIST PROFESSOR
MARK STEWART         ASSIST PROFESSOR
PAT CARNER           ASSIST PROFESSOR
LEE FALDO            DEPARTMENT CHAIR
RAYMOND J. JOHNSON   PROFESSOR
WENDY SWIMMER        PROFESSOR
AMY DANCER           ASSOC PROFESSOR

15 Records selected.
```

Note that the tuples are displayed in top-to-bottom, left to right order. The top-to-bottom order (start with the root node and work to the bottom or leaf nodes) is determined by the placement of the word PRIOR in the CONNECT BY clause. The left-to-right order is the default order. The way that this clause is read is that BOSS-ID is PRIOR, or above, FAC-ID. This causes a top-to-bottom retrieval. If we wanted a bottom-to-top retrieval, we would have to move the position of the word PRIOR in the CONNECT BY clause, and we would have to designate one of the bottom nodes as the start node.

```
UFI> SELECT FACULTY-NAME, TITLE-OR-RANK
  2   FROM PERSONNEL
  3   CONNECT BY FAC-ID = PRIOR BOSS-ID
  4   START WITH FACULTY-NAME = 'AMY DANCER';

FACULTY-NAME____   TITLE-OR-RANK___
AMY DANCER         ASSOC PROFESSOR
LEE FALDO          DEPARTMENT CHAIR
LARRY SIMPSON      DEAN
GREG DAVIS         PRESIDENT
```

Note that only one branch of the tree is displayed when the PRIOR option is used to create bottom-to-top retrieval. The reason for this is that we only defined one path back to the top of the tree. If we wanted more tuples generated, we must specify more leaf or bottom nodes in the tree.

The left-to-right order is the default order. This can be changed with the ORDER BY clause.

Using Level Numbers

The level number in the tree structure of each tuple can be displayed with the use of the numeric system variable LEVEL. The root node is always level 1, the next level down is level 2, and so forth. LEVEL is a virtual value that is generated as the tree is being retrieved.

```
UFI> SELECT LEVEL, FACULTY-NAME, TITLE-OR-RANK
  2  FROM PERSONNEL
  3  CONNECT BY PRIOR FAC-ID = BOSS-ID
  4  START WITH FACULTY-NAME = 'GREG DAVIS';

__LEVEL FACULTY-NAME_____  TITLE-OR-RANK____
     1 GREG DAVIS           PRESIDENT
     2 SCOTT MIZE           DEAN
     3 JAN CARNER           DEPARTMENT CHAIR
     4 BOB JONES            ASSOC PROFESSOR
     2 LARRY SIMPSON        DEAN
     3 NICK NORMAN          DEPARTMENT CHAIR
     4 JACK NELSON          INSTRUCTOR
     3 BYRON HOGAN          DEPARTMENT CHAIR
     4 BEN NELSON           ASSIST PROFESSOR
     4 MARK STEWART         ASSIST PROFESSOR
     4 PAT CARNER           PROFESSOR
     3 LEE FALDO            DEPARTMENT CHAIR
     4 RAYMOND J. JOHNSON   PROFESSOR
     4 WENDY SWIMMER        PROFESSOR
     4 AMY DANCER           ASSOC PROFESSOR

15 Records selected.
```

Since the variable LEVEL is numeric, it can be used in various types of computations within the SELECT command.

Defining a New Root Node

Tree structures do not have to begin at the absolute root of the tree. We may define the root node to be some internal node in the tree. For retrieval purposes, that node becomes the root node. Defining a new root node is implemented through the START WITH clause. For example, suppose that we wanted to display all of the employees working for Dean Simpson. All we would have to change in our SELECT command is the value in the START WITH clause.

```
UFI> SELECT LEVEL, FACULTY-NAME, TITLE-OR-RANK
  2  FROM PERSONNEL
  3  CONNECT BY PRIOR FAC-ID = BOSS-ID
  4  START WITH FACULTY-NAME = 'LARRY SIMPSON';
```

```
__LEVEL FACULTY-NAME_____ TITLE-OR-RANK____
      1 LARRY SIMPSON         DEAN
      2 NICK NORMAN           DEPARTMENT CHAIR
      3 JACK NELSON           INSTRUCTOR
      2 BYRON HOGAN           DEPARTMENT CHAIR
      3 BEN NELSON            ASSIST PROFESSOR
      3 MARK STEWART          ASSIST PROFESSOR
      3 PAT CARNER            PROFESSOR
      2 LEE FALDO             DEPARTMENT CHAIR
      3 RAYMOND J. JOHNSON    PROFESSOR
      3 WENDY SWIMMER         PROFESSOR
      3 AMY DANCER            ASSOC PROFESSOR

   11 Records selected.
```

Note that the level numbers are relative level numbers. Whatever root node that we define becomes level 1.

We can even have multiple root nodes. Let's display the names of the employees who work for either Nick Norman or Byron Hogan.

```
UFI> SELECT LEVEL, FACULTY-NAME, TITLE-OR-RANK
   2 FROM PERSONNEL
   3 CONNECT BY PRIOR FAC-ID = BOSS-ID
   4 START WITH FACULTY-NAME IN
   5         ('NICK NORMAN', 'BYRON HOGAN');

__LEVEL FACULTY-NAME____ TITLE-OR-RANK____
      1 NICK NORMAN          DEPARTMENT CHAIR
      2 JACK NELSON          INSTRUCTOR
      1 BYRON HOGAN          DEPARTMENT CHAIR
      2 BEN NELSON           ASSIST PROFESSOR
      2 MARK STEWART         ASSIST PROFESSOR
      2 PAT CARNER           PROFESSOR

   6 Records selected.
```

Rearranging Output from Hierarchical Retrieval

We can use the ORDER BY clause to affect the order of the retrieved tuples.

```
UFI> SELECT LEVEL, FACULTY-NAME, TITLE-OR-RANK
   2 FROM PERSONNEL
   3 CONNECT BY PRIOR FAC-ID = BOSS-ID
   4 START WITH FACULTY-NAME IN
   5         ('NICK NORMAN', 'BYRON HOGAN')
   6 ORDER BY TITLE-OR-RANK;
```

```
__LEVEL FACULTY-NAME____  TITLE-OR-RANK____
     2 BEN NELSON         ASSIST PROFESSOR
     2 MARK STEWART       ASSIST PROFESSOR
     1 NICK NORMAN        DEPARTMENT CHAIR
     1 BYRON HOGAN        DEPARTMENT CHAIR
     2 JACK NELSON        INSTRUCTOR
     2 PAT CARNER         PROFESSOR

  6 Records selected.
```

Filtering Tuples from Tree Structures

The WHERE clause can be used to filter further the SELECT command output.

```
UFI> SELECT LEVEL, FACULTY-NAME, TITLE-OR-RANK
  2  FROM PERSONNEL
  3  CONNECT BY PRIOR FAC-ID = BOSS-ID
  4  START WITH FACULTY-NAME IN
  5          ('NICK NORMAN', 'BYRON HOGAN')
  6  WHERE FACULTY-NAME != 'BEN NELSON';

__LEVEL FACULTY-NAME____  TITLE-OR-RANK____
     1 NICK NORMAN        DEPARTMENT CHAIR
     2 JACK NELSON        INSTRUCTOR
     1 BYRON HOGAN        DEPARTMENT CHAIR
     2 MARK STEWART       ASSIST PROFESSOR
     2 PAT CARNER         PROFESSOR
```

Notice that the WHERE clause eliminated one tuple (Ben Nelson) from the resultant table. We can also eliminate entire branches on the tree by specifying conditions in the CONNECT BY clause. For example, let's eliminate all the personnel who work directly under Larry Simpson.

```
UFI> SELECT LEVEL, FACULTY-NAME, TITLE-OR-RANK
  2  FROM PERSONNEL
  3  CONNECT BY PRIOR FAC-ID = BOSS-ID
  4  AND FACULTY-NAME != 'LARRY SIMPSON'
  5  START WITH FACULTY-NAME = 'GREG DAVIS';

__LEVEL FACULTY-NAME____  TITLE-OR-RANK____
     1 GREG DAVIS         PRESIDENT
     2 SCOTT MIZE         DEAN
     3 JAN CARNER         DEPARTMENT CHAIR
     4 BOB JONES          ASSOC PROFESSOR
```

This operation is commonly called pruning branches on a tree. Pruning is illustrated in Figure 10.2.

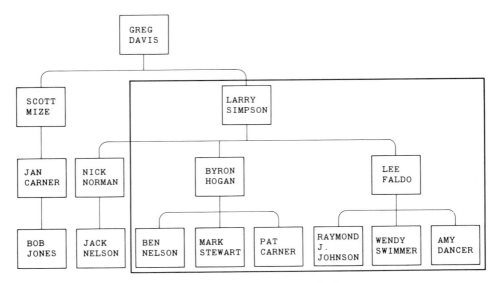

Figure 10.2   Pruning Branches of a Tree

SUMMARY

Three new retrieval methods were discussed in this chapter:

1. Subqueries, which allow the user to retrieve data based upon a previous retrieval
2. Grouped retrieval which gives the user the capability of retrieving data in sets
3. Hierarchical retrieval gives the user the capability to retrieve data in a tree structure

These methods allow the user to extract data in somewhat more sophisticated ways than what has previously been proposed.

After completion of this chapter, the reader should be familiar with the following commands, terms, and concepts.

A. Grouped retrieval
B. AVG
C. SUM
D. MAX
E. MIN
F. STDDEV
G. VARIANCE
H. COUNT (*)

I. COUNT (attribute)
J. Grouped retrieval
K. GROUP BY
L. HAVING
M. Hierarchical retrieval
N. CONNECT BY
O. START WITH
P. LEVEL

EXERCISES

1. Explain the difference in top-to-bottom and bottom-to-top retrieval in a simulated tree structure. Explain how this is accomplished in ORACLE.

2. Explain the difference between subqueries and JOIN queries.

3. Explain the difference between the ANY and ALL clauses of subqueries.

4. Explain the difference between the following two SELECT commands.

```
SELECT LEVEL, FACULTY-NAME, TITLE_OR_RANK
FROM PERSONNEL
CONNECT BY PRIOR FAC_ID = BOSS_ID
START WITH FACULTY_NAME = 'GREG DAVIS'
WHERE FACULTY_NAME != 'LARRY SIMPSON';

SELECT LEVEL, FACULTY_NAME, TITLE_OR_RANK
FROM PERSONNEL
CONNECT BY PRIOR FAC_ID = BOSS_ID
AND FACULTY_NAME != 'LARRY SIMPSON'
START WITH FACULTY_NAME = 'GREG DAVIS';
```

5. Using the table PERSONNEL, develop the SQL commands to satisfy the following queries.
   a. What are the names of the faculty members who earn less than the average salary?
   b. What are names of the faculty members who work for Lee Faldo and earn less than $38,000?
   c. What is the average, standard deviation, and variance of the salaries by department?
   d. What is the average salary of the employees in the same department as Amy Dancer?
   e. How many faculty members make less than the average salary plus $1,000?
   f. How many different bosses are there?
   g. How many different faculty members are at each professorial rank (professor, associate professor, or assistant professor)?
   h. What are the names of the three highest-paid employees?
   i. What are the names and salaries of the five lowest-paid employees? Display the results in ascending order.
   j. What are the names of the two highest paid associate professors?

11

Expressions and Functions

PURPOSE: This chapter is designed to describe how various types of arithmetic, character, and date expressions and functions can be used in ORACLE databases.

SQL commands are not limited to data that is stored in tables. Data can be transformed via expressions and/or functions. The transformations can apply to numeric, character, or date data. These expressions and functions are the primary focus of this chapter.

NUMERIC EXPRESSIONS

We introduced the arithmetic operators available in SQL in Chapter 6 of this text. These operators are:

Operator	Meaning
+	Addition
−	Subtraction
*	Multiplication
/	Division

These operators can be used with any numeric attribute. The multiplication and division operators have precedence over the addition and subtraction operators. If multiple operators on the same priority level are entered, the expression is evaluated in a left-to-right order. Parentheses may be used to adjust the priority of operators.

The operators are used to create numeric expressions. The values that these expressions produce can be displayed or used in a WHERE clause to filter tuples for the resultant table.

NUMERIC FUNCTIONS

ORACLE has a collection of numeric functions that can be used to transform data to some other form. A list of numeric functions and their meaning is shown in Table 11.1.

The arguments passed to these functions may be any of the following.

1. Constants: SQRT (10), ABS(-12), TRUNC (4.555, 2)
2. Attributes: ROUND (SALARY, 2)
3. Expressions: GREATEST (SALARY * 2, IQ * 5)
4. Other function calls: SQRT (ABS (INTELLIGENCE-QUOTIENT))

TABLE 11.1   ORACLE NUMERIC FUNCTIONS

Function Name	Syntax	Argument(s)	Results
Absolute value	ABS	number	Generates the absolute value of number.
Largest value	GREATEST	number1 [,number2. . .]	Determines the largest number from a list.
Smallest value	LEAST	number1 [,number2. . .]	Determines the smallest number from a list.
Modulo divide	MOD	number1, number2	Divides number1 by number2 and returns the remainder.
Exponentiation	POWER	number1, number2	Raises number1 to the number2 power.
Round	ROUND	number1 [,number2]	Rounds number1 to number2 or zero decimal places.
Signum	SIGN	number	Returns a +1 if number is positive, 0 if zero, or − 1 if negative.
Square root	SQRT	number	Returns the square root of number if it is positive or NULL if it is negative.
Truncation	TRUNC	number1 [,number2]	Truncates number1 at number2 decimal places.

Be aware that the GREATEST function considers null to be the *largest* value and the LEAST function considers null to be the *smallest* value.

To illustrate use of these numeric functions, we will use the following table.

TABLE NAME: WORKERS

NAME	HOURLY-PAY-RATE	NUMB-OF-DEP	IQ
NORMAN GREGG	8.750	3	113
WILLY MARTIN	6.625	0	98
DEE WILLIAMS	10.000	4	122
SID WILLIAMS	0.000	1	-25
MARY STEPHENS	4.000	0	0

1. What is the absolute value and signum of each worker's IQ?

```
UFI> SELECT NAME, IQ, ABS(IQ), SIGN(IQ) FROM WORKER;
```

NAME	IQ	ABS(IQ)	SIGN(IQ)
NORMAN GREGG	113	113	1
WILLY MARTIN	98	98	1
DEE WILLIAMS	122	122	1
SID WILLIAMS	-25	25	-1
MARY STEPHENS	0	0	0

2. Which is larger: a person's pay rate times 12, his IQ, or his number of dependents times 30? Select only those workers whose name contains an ''e.'' (This is a very common query!)

```
UFI> SELECT NAME, GREATEST (HOURLY-PAY-RATE*12, IQ,
  2                         NUMB-OF-DEP*30) BIGGEST
  3   FROM WORKER
  4   WHERE NAME LIKE '%E%';
```

NAME	BIGGEST
NORMAN GREGG	113
DEE WILLIAMS	122
SID WILLIAMS	30

3. Which is smaller: a person's pay rate times 12, his IQ, or his number of dependents times 30? Select only those workers whose name contains an ''e.''

```
UFI> SELECT NAME, LEAST (HOURLY_PAY_RATE*12, IQ,
  2                      NUMB_OF_DEP*30) SMALLEST
  3   FROM WORKERS
  4   WHERE NAME LIKE '%E%';
```

NAME	SMALLEST
NORMAN GREGG	90
DEE WILLIAMS	120
SID WILLIAMS	-25

4. Let's cube the number of dependents of each worker and also mod them by 3. (This again is a very useful query!)

```
UFI> SELECT NAME, POWER (NUMB_OF_DEP, 3) CUBE,
  2           MOD (NUMB_OF_DEP, 3) MODDING
  3   FROM WORKER;


NAME_____ CUBE MODDING
NORMAN GREGG        27       0
WILLY MARTIN         0       0
DEE WILLIAMS        64       1
SID WILLIAMS         1       1
MARY STEPHENS        0       0
```

5. What is the value of each worker's salary rounded to two decimal places? Truncated to two decimal places?

```
UFI> SELECT NAME, HOURLY_PAY_RATE,
  2           ROUND (HOURLY_PAY_RATE, 2) "RATE ROUNDED",
  3           TRUNC (HOURLY_PAY_RATE, 2) "RATE TRUNCED"
  4   FROM WORKER;

NAME_____ HOURLY_PAY_RATE RATE_ROUNDED RATE_TRUNCED
NORMAN GREGG               8.750         8.75         8.75
WILLY MARTIN               6.625         6.63         6.62
DEE WILLIAMS             10.000           10           10
SID WILLIAMS               .000            0            0
MARY STEPHENS             4.000            4            4
```

Note the difference in Willy Martin's pay rates when they are rounded and truncated.

6. What is the square root of each worker's IQ?

```
UFI> COLUMN "SQRTOFIQ" FORMAT 99.99

UFI> SELECT NAME, IQ, SQRT(ABS(IQ)) "SQRT OF IQ"
  2   FROM WORKERS;

NAME_____  __IQ SQRT_OF_IQ
NORMAN GREGG        113      10.63
WILLY MARTIN         98       9.90
DEE WILLIAMS        122      11.05
SID WILLIAMS        -25       5.00
MARY STEPHENS         0        .00
```

Note the use of the absolute value function within the square root function. The reason for this is that Sid William's IQ is a negative number. If we had not generated the absolute value of his IQ before passing it to the square root function, the value of the square root of his IQ would have displayed as a blank as the square root function generates a value of null for negative values.

CHARACTER STRINGS

Character strings can be defined in either of two different data types: CHAR or LONG.

The character manipulation functions and expressions that we will describe shortly are only applicable to the data type CHAR.

Displaying Literals

Literal strings can be displayed as part of the SELECT command's output by placing the literal in quotes. The following example illustrates the use of the literal.

```
UFI> SELECT 'The faculty member with the lowest salary is',
2          FACULTY_NAME
3   FROM FACULTY
4   WHERE SALARY = (SELECT MIN (SALARY) FROM FACULTY);

'THEFACULTYMEMBERWITHTHELOWEST_____ FACULTY-NAME
The faculty member with the lowest salary is JACK NELSON
```

Notice that the column heading is the first 30 characters of the literal string (including the opening quote). If we wished to remove these column headings, we could use the SET HEADING OFF command discussed in Chapter 6.

```
UFI> SET HEADING OFF
UFI> /
The faculty member with the lowest salary is JACK NELSON
```

The attribute heading on the literal can be removed as follows.

```
UFI> SELECT 'The faculty member with the lowest salary is' " ",
2          FACULTY_NAME
3   FROM FACULTY
4   WHERE SALARY = (SELECT MIN (SALARY) FROM FACULTY);


_____ FACULTY_NAME
The faculty member with the lowest salary is JACK NELSON
```

Note the double quote blank after the literal string which indicates that the temporary heading for the string is a blank.

Character Expressions

The only character string expression operation is concatenation. Concatenation joins two string values together to form one string. The character string operator is the double verticle bar (||). For example, if we wished to join the two strings "HOCKEY" and "PUCK" together to form one string, we could do the following.

```
"HOCKEY"||" "||"PUCK" ==> "HOCKEY PUCK"
```

Concatenated strings can be used in any place that a variable can be used in a SQL command.

Perhaps the most useful purpose of concatenation is in displaying names. For example, suppose that we had the students' first names and last names stored in separate attributes as follows.

```
UFI> SELECT FIRST_NAME, LAST_NAME FROM NAME_TABLE;
FIRST_NAME LAST_NAME
MADALINE    JONES
```

Suppose that we wanted to display the first name and the last name in reverse order separated by a comma. We could do this very easily with the concatenation operator.

```
UFI> SELECT LAST_NAME||', '||FIRST_NAME "FULL NAME"
  2  FROM NAME_TABLE;

FULL_NAME_____
JONES, MADALINE
```

Notice that we also changed the attribute heading. If we had neglected to do this, ORACLE would have used the entire expression as the attribute heading.

Character Functions

ORACLE has a collection of character-oriented functions that can be used to transform data to some other form. A list of numeric functions and their meanings is shown in Table 11.2.

Be aware that the GREATEST function considers null to be the *largest* value and the LEAST function considers null to be the *smallest* value. The GREATEST and the LEAST functions can be used with either numeric and/or character data. If a mixture of character and numeric data is specified as arguments to either function, ORACLE converts the numbers to character strings and executes the function.

TABLE 11.2   ORACLE CHARACTER FUNCTIONS

Function Name	Syntax	Argument(s)	Results
Largest value	GREATEST	string1 [, string2. . .]	Determines the largest string from a list.
Initial capital	INITCAP	string	Makes the first letter of the string an uppercase letter.
Substring search	INSTR	string,substring [, start [, n]]	Searches string for the Nth occurrence of substring, beginning in position *start*.
Smallest value	LEAST	string1 [, string2. . .]	Determines the smallest string from a list.
Length of string	LENGTH	string	Determines the length of string after deleting all trailing blanks.
Lowercase	LOWER	string	Converts string to lowercase.
Left pad	LPAD	string, length [, character]	Pads string from the left with length number of characters.
Right Pad	RPAD	string, length [, character]	Pads string from the right with length number of characters.
Trim characters from the left side of a string	LTRIM	string, charset	Trims the characters specified in *charset* from the left side of string.
Trim characters from the right side of a string	RTRIM	string, charset	Trims the characters specified in *charset* from the right side of string.
Matches strings on similar sounds	SOUNDEX	string	Matches strings that sound alike.
Substring	SUBSTR	string, start [, length]	Extracts substring from string beginning in position *start* for *length* characters.
Convert a string	TO_NUMBER	string	Converts a character string number to a numeric value.
Translates from one character set to another	TRANSLATE	string, from-set, to-set	Translates the characters in string from one set of characters to another.
Uppercase	UPPER	string	Converts all characters in string to uppercase.

We will use the STUDENT table to illustrate the use of character functions.

```
STU-ID STUDENT-NAME___  ADDRESS_____  BIRTHDATE GENDER
S001   WENDY JONES      125 MAPLE AVE   25-OCT-65 FEMALE
S002   SAM WALES        3006 NAVAJO CL  10-JAN-60 MALE
S003   CATHY SMITH      1600 PENN AVE   22-FEB-62 FEMALE
S004   DOTTIE STACY     10 DOWNING ST   31-MAR-67 FEMALE
S005   JAY LANGER       GOLF COURSE RD  19-APR-65 MALE
S006   AMY LOPEZ        123 SUN RAY RD  10-MAY-64 FEMALE
S007   SAM WATSON       225 TEST DRIVE  09-JUN-63 MALE
S008   TAMMY REDD       113 MANCHESTER  01-JUL-60 FEMALE
S009   TOMMY WADKINS    APPLE TREEE DR  24-AUG-67 MALE
S010   BEN TREVINO      BOWLING ALLEY   30-SEP-66 MALE
```

1. Which is the larger value: the student-identifier or S005? Which is the smaller?

```
UFI> SELECT STU_ID, GREATEST (STU_ID, 'S005') LARGEST,
  2            LEAST (STU_ID, 'S005') SMALLEST
  3  FROM STUDENT;

STU-ID GREATEST SMALLEST
S001   S005     S001
S002   S005     S002
S003   S005     S003
S004   S005     S004
S005   S005     S005
S006   S006     S005
S007   S007     S005
S008   S008     S005
S009   S009     S005
S010   S010     S005
```

2. Display the unique values of gender with only the first letter in uppercase, the entire string in uppercase, and the entire string in lowercase.

```
UFI> SELECT DISTINCT GENDER,
  2           INITCAP(GENDER) "FIRST LETTER",
  3           UPPER (GENDER) UPPER,
  4           LOWER (GENDER) LOWER
  5  FROM STUDENT;

GENDER FSTLET UPPER_ LOWER
FEMALE Female FEMALE female
MALE   Male   MALE   male
```

The INITCAP function is a very useful function to use when developing output from proper names. For example, we would not be able to produce the student's name (STUDENT-NAME) with uppercase letters in the proper places without some complex substringing. The reason for this is that the student's name is stored in one attribute. This is a good argument for keeping the student's first name and last name in separate attributes. When we need to display them together, we can always concatenate the first name to the last name or last name to the first name after using the INITCAP function to capitalize only the first letter of the first and last names.

3. How long is each student's name?

```
UFI> SELECT STUDENT_NAME, LENGTH(STUDENT_NAME) LENGTH
   2   FROM STUDENT;
```

STUDENT-NAME	LENGTH
WENDY JONES	11
SAM WALES	9
CATHY SMITH	11
DOTTIE STACY	12
JAY LANGER	10
AMY LOPEZ	9
SAM WATSON	10
TAMMY REDD	10
TOMMY WADKINS	13
BEN TREVINO	11

```
10 Records selected.
```

4. Search each student name to see if it contains the letter "e." If it does, display the position that the first "e" occurs in. If it does not, display a zero. Perform three searches. The first search will begin in position one of STUDENT-NAME, and the second will begin in position six. The third search will search for the second occurrence of an "e."

```
UFI> SELECT STUDENT_NAME,
   2        INSTR (STUDENT_NAME,'E') FIRST,
   3        INSTR (STUDENT_NAME,'E',5) "AFTER FIVE",
   4        INSTR (STUDENT_NAME,'E',1,2) SECOND
   5   FROM STUDENT;
```

STUDENT-NAME	FIRST	AFTER_FIVE	SECOND
WENDY JONES	2	10	10
SAM WALES	8	8	0
CATHY SMITH	0	0	0
DOTTIE STACY	6	6	0
JAY LANGER	9	9	0
AMY LOPEZ	8	8	0

```
SAM WATSON              0          0      0
TAMMY REDD              8          8      0
TOMMY WADKINS           0          0      0
BEN TREVINO             2          7      7
```

```
10 Records selected.
```

Note that even though we start the search in the sixth position, the position of the ''e'' is kept relative to the first position of the string.

5. Let's create a histogram of the number of letters in each student's name.

```
UFI> COLUMN HISTOGRAM FORMAT A25

UFI> SELECT STUDENT_NAME,
  2         LENGTH (STUDENT_NAME) LENGTH,
  3         LPAD (' ',LENGTH(STUDENT_NAME), '*') HISTOGRAM
  4   FROM STUDENT;

STUDENT-NAME_____ LENGTH HISTOGRAM_____
WENDY JONES          11  ***********
SAM WALES             9  *********
CATHY SMITH          11  ***********
DOTTIE STACY         12  ************
JAY LANGER           10  **********
AMY LOPEZ             9  *********
SAM WATSON           10  **********
TAMMY REDD           10  **********
TOMMY WADKINS        13  *************
BEN TREVINO          11  ***********
```

```
10 Records selected.
```

The LPAD command is interpreted as follows. It creates a virtual attribute of 25 blank characters (from the COLUMN command) and pad it with LENGTH (STUDENT-NAME) asterisks, starting at the left side of the attribute. Naturally, if we had used the right-pad function (RPAD), the asterisks would start on the right side of the histogram.

6. The left trim and right trim can be used to delete a group of characters that are specified in a set.

```
UFI> SELECT STUDENT_NAME,
  2         LTRIM (STUDENT_NAME, 'SA') "LEFT TRIM",
  3         RTRIM (STUDENT_NAME, 'S') "RIGHT TRIM"
  4   FROM STUDENT;
```

```
STUDENT-NAME_____   LEFT_TRIM_____   RIGHT_TRIM_____
WENDY JONES         WENDY JONES         WENDY JONE
SAM WALES           M WALES             SAM WALE
CATHY SMITH         CATHY SMITH         CATHY SMITH
DOTTIE STACY        DOTTIE STACY        DOTTIE STACY
JAY LANGER          JAY LANGER          JAY LANGER
AMY LOPEZ           AMY LOPEZ           AMY LOPEZ
SAM WATSON          M WATSON            SAM WATSON
TAMMY REDD          TAMMY REDD          TAMMY REDD
TOMMY WADKINS       TOMMY WADKINS       TOMMY WADKIN
BEN TREVINO         BEN TREVINO         BEN TREVINO
```

```
10 Records selected.
```

7. List all the names that sound like Cathi Smith.

```
UFI> SELECT STUDENT_NAME FROM STUDENT
  2   WHERE SOUNDEX (STUDENT_
  3   NAME) = SOUNDEX (`CATHI SMITH');
STUDENT_NAME
CATHY SMITH
```

The SOUNDEX function is designed primarily for people with a spelling handicap. It is also very useful for searching for multiple spellings of names, for example, Cathy, Cathi, or Cathey. The algorithm itself was developed by Margaret K. Odell and Robert C. Russell and is described in Knuth [1].

The algorithm is a five-step process.

1. Keep the first letter of the string.
2. Remove all spaces, vowels, and the letters ''h,'' ''w,'' and ''y'' from the string.
3. Assign the digits to the remainder of the letters in the string as per the following table.

Digit	Letters
1	b, f, p, v
2	c, g, j, k, q, s, x, z
3	d, t
4	l
5	m, n
6	r

4. If two or more letters with the same numeric code are adjacent in the original string before performing steps 1 and 2, delete the letters with the duplicate digits.

5. Convert the string to a quadruple consisting of the first letter of the string followed by three digits according to steps 3 and 4. If the string produces less than four characters, the quadruple is padded with zeros. If it is more than four characters, it is truncated.

To illustrate the use of the SOUNDEX function, let us compare the names Kathy, Kathi, Kathie, Cathy, Catherine and Kate.

Step #	KATHY	KATHI	KATHIE	CATHY	CATHERINE	KATE
1	K	K	K	C	C	K
2	KT	KT	KT	CT	CTRN	KT
3	K3	K3	K3	C3	C365	K3
4	K3	K3	K3	C3	C365	K3
5	K300	K300	K300	C300	C365	K300

As you can see from the quadruple generated by the SOUNDEX process Kathy, Kathi, and Kathie are equivalent; that is, SOUNDEX ('KATHY') = SOUNDEX ('KATHI') = SOUNDEX ('KATHIE'). You can also see that the process is not infallible, as Cathy and Kathie/Kathy/Kathi sound the same, but will not match. Also Kate will match Kathie/Kathy/Kathi (which does not sound right to me).

8. Let's assume that we wanted to extract the numeric part of each student's Id and add 1000 to it, to accomplish this we must use the SUBSTR function to extract positions 2–4 of each student's Id, then use the TO—NUMBER function to convert it to a number so that 1000 can be added to it.

```
UFI> SELECT STUDENT_NAME, STU_ID,
   2  'S' TO_NUMBER (SUBSTR (STU_ID,2,3))+1000 "NEW STU#"
   3  FROM STUDENT;

STUDENT-NAME_____  STU-ID  NEW_STU#
WENDY JONES         S001    S1001
SAM WALES           S002    S1002
CATHY SMITH         S003    S1003
DOTTIE STACY        S004    S1004
JAY LANGER          S005    S1005
AMY LOPEZ           S006    S1006
SAM WATSON          S007    S1007
TAMMY REDD          S008    S1008
TOMMY WADKINS       S009    S1009
BEN TREVINO         S010    S1010
```

9. Let's assume that we want to encrypt the names of our intrepid students. The encryption algorithm that we want to use is substituting one character for another. Our substitution matrix looks as follows:

```
Original Character -> ABCDEFGHIJKLMNOPQRSTUVWXYZ,
Substitute Character -> QWERTYUIOPASDFGHJKLZXCVBNM ,
```

This substitution matrix can be accomplished by using the TRANSLATE function.

```
TRANSLATE (STUDENT_NAME, 'ABCDEFGHIJKLMNOPQRSTUVWXYZ, ',
                        'QWERTYUIOPASDFGHJKLZXCVBNM ,')
```

The TRANSLATE substitutes a "Q" for each "A", a "W" for each "B", and so on. If a character does not appear in the "from set of characters," its value is deleted from the "to set of characters." For example, if we used the following TRANSLATE function

```
TRANSLATE (STUDENT_NAME, 'AB', 'YZ')
```

it would translate all A's to Y's and all B's to Z's. All other characters are removed from the output attribute.

The SELECT command to encrypt the name Wendy Jones is:

```
UFI> SELECT STUDENT_NAME,
   2    TRANSLATE (STUDENT_NAME, 'ABCDEFGHIJKLMNOPQRSTUVWXYZ, ',
   3                            'QWERTYUIOPASDFGHJKLZXCVBNM ,')
   4                            "ENCRYPTED NAME"
   5    FROM STUDENT
   6    WHERE STUDENT_NAME = 'WENDY JONES';
```

```
STUDENT_NAME          ENCRYPTED NAME
WENDY JONES           VTFRN,PGFTL
```

THE DECODE FUNCTION

The DECODE function is a special function that can be used with any data type. Its purpose is to convert a supplied "input" value to a specified "output" value. The format of the DECODE function is:

```
DECODE (input-attribute,
  [,input-attribute-value1, output-attribute-value1, . . .]
default-output-value)
```

To illustrate this function, let's suppose that we wanted to display the name and gender of each student in our student table. However, in lieu of ''male'' and ''female'', we wanted to list ''boy'' and ''girl''. In other words, we wanted to decode MALE into BOY and FEMALE into GIRL. Also, if we had inadvertently entered an invalid value (example: misspelled male or female), we want to display ERROR for the value of gender. Perhaps this can be easily understood if we utilize some generic conventional programming language syntax to illustrate the concept.

```
IF GENDER = 'MALE' THEN GENDER = 'BOY'
   ELSE IF GENDER = 'FEMALE' GENDER = 'GIRL'
        ELSE GENDER = 'ERROR'
```

Please be aware that these changes are not permanent; they are only in effect temporarily for the output of the SELECT command.

This task can be performed very easily with the DECODE function.

```
UFI> REMARK . . . Let's change a value so that we can illustrate

UFI> REMARK . . . an invalid value

UFI> UPDATE STUDENT SET GENDER = 'MAIL'
  2   WHERE STUDENT_NAME = 'SAM WALES';

1 Record updated.

UFI> SELECT STUDENT_NAME, GENDER,
  2          DECODE (GENDER,'MALE','BOY',
  3               'FEMALE','GIRL','ERROR') DECODE
  4   FROM STUDENT;

STUDENT_NAME_____  GENDER DECODE
WENDY JONES        FEMALE GIRL
SAM WALES          MAIL   ERROR
CATHY SMITH        FEMALE GIRL
DOTTIE STACY       FEMALE GIRL
JAY LANGER         MALE   BOY
AMY LOPEZ          FEMALE GIRL
SAM WATSON         MALE   BOY
TAMMY REDD         FEMALE GIRL
TOMMY WADKINS      MALE   BOY
BEN TREVINO        MALE   BOY

10 Records selected.


UFI> REMARK . . . Let's fix the error
```

```
UFI> UPDATE STUDENT SET GENDER = 'MALE'
  2  WHERE STUDENT_NAME = 'SAM WALES';

1 Record updated.
```

The DECODE function can also be used with numeric data. Let's use the COURSE table to illustrate the use of the DECODE function with numeric data. Let's spell out the section number for each course. We want to display ONE if the section number is 1, TWO if it is 2, and so on. If the section number is greater than 3, we want to display the message "TOO MANY."

```
UFI> SELECT COURSE-TITLE, SECTION_NO
  2         DECODE (SECTION_NO, 1, 'ONE',
  3                  2, 'TWO', 3, 'THREE',
  4                  'TOO MANY') "IN WORDS"
  5  FROM COURSE;

COURSE_TITLE_____ SECTION IN_WORDS
INTRODUCTION TO COMPUTING        1 ONE
INTRODUCTION TO COMPUTING        2 TWO
PASCAL PROGRAMMING               1 ONE
PASCAL PROGRAMMING               2 TWO
PRINCIPLES OF ACCOUNTING I       1 ONE
PRINCIPLES OF ACCOUNTING II      1 ONE
HISTORY OF PIROGUES              1 ONE
```

The output value specified in the DECODE function can even be an attribute name. To illustrate this concept, let's assume that for all section 1's of each course we want to display the faculty identifier of the faculty member teaching the class. However, for section 2's we want to display the name of the faculty member teaching the class. (We obviously will have to get this information through a JOIN.) If the section number is not equal to 1 or 2, we want the message "OOPS" displayed.

```
UFI> REMARK ... We must expand the field width in order to

UFI> REMARK ... be able to display the faculty members name

UFI> COLUMN OUTPUT FORMAT 999999999999999

UFI> SELECT COURSE_TITLE, SECTION_NO
  2         DECODE (SECTION_NO 1, COURSE.FAC_ID, 2, FACULTY_NAME,
  3                  'OOPS') OUTPUT
  4  FROM COURSE, FACULTY
  5  WHERE COURSE.FAC_ID=FACULTY.FAC_ID;
```

```
COURSE-TITLE_____ SECTION OUTPUT_____
INTRODUCTION TO COMPUTING        1  J01
INTRODUCTION TO COMPUTING        2  WENDY SWIMMER
PASCAL PROGRAMMING               2  WENDY SWIMMER
PASCAL PROGRAMMING               1  D01
PRINCIPLES OF ACCOUNTING I       1  J02
PRINCIPLES OF ACCOUNTING II      1  J02
HISTORY OF PIROGUES              1  N01
```

Note that even though the DECODed value is a character string, we had to specify the attribute with a numeric format (999999999999999) because the field used to determine (DECODE) the character string is numeric.

DATE DATA

The DATE data type is a very useful entity in the ORACLE database management system. Up to this point, all we know about the DATE data type is that it is input and output in the format DD-MON-YY, where DD represents a two-digit integer signifying the day of the month, MON represents a three-character uppercase abbreviation of the month, and YY represents the last two digits the year as in 19YY. We also know that the acceptable values of a DATE data type are between January 1, 4712 B.C. and December 31, 4711 A.D. We have only given the DATE data type cursory coverage up to this point, but this should not give any indication of its relative importance in constructing relational databases.

The DATE data type actually contains the date and time. The time part of the field is not displayed in the default output format. When any date is entered, and no time is specified, the default time of 12:00 A.M. is also entered in the date attribute. The default value of time can be changed via a special input formatting function.

We can also perform some date arithmetic on date attributes. These arithmetic operations include adding values to dates, subtracting values from dates, subtracting two dates from one another, and so forth.

Remember that the current date and time can be accessed with the system value SYSDATE.

Date Functions

ORACLE has a collection of date-oriented functions that can be used to manipulate date data. A list of the date functions and their meaning is shown in Table 11.3.

To illustrate the DATE functions we will use the STUDENT table.

TABLE 11.3   ORACLE DATE FUNCTIONS

Function Name	Syntax	Argument(s)	Results
Adds months to a date	ADD_MONTHS	Date, Integer number	Adds a number of months to a date. The number of months may be positive or negative.
How many months are between two dates	MONTHS_BETWEEN	Date1, Date2	Determines how many months are between date values.
Last day of the month	LAST_DAY	Date	Determines the last day of the month for the date specified.
Next dayname of of the week after the specified date	NEXT_DAY	Date, Dayname	Determines the next dayname day of the week.
Rounds the day	ROUND	Date	Rounds the date to 3 minutes past midnight.
Truncates the day	TRUNC	Date	Truncates the date to 3 minutes past midnight.
Formats a date	TO_CHAR	Date, 'Format mask'	Changes the default output format.
Formats a date	TO_DATE	Date, 'Format mask'	Changes the default input format.

The TO-CHAR function.   Since the TO-CHAR is so powerful and useful, we will dedicate a complete section to it. The purpose of the TO-CHAR function is to format date values for output. The format of the TO-CHAR function is:

```
TO-CHAR (DATE, 'FORMAT MASK')
```

There are three types of format masks that can be utilized with the TO—CHAR function. These masks are shown in Tables 11.4, 11.5, 11.6, and 11.7.

The default field width of the TO-CHAR function is A75. This value should be adjusted before you attempt any serious output using the TO-CHAR function.

Here are some examples of the TO-CHAR function.

1. What day of the week was each female student born?

```
UFI> REMARK ... Let's set up a field width for all dates

UFI> REMARK ... examples

UFI> COLUMN DATE_OUTPUT FORMAT A40

UFI> SELECT STUDENT_NAME,
  2    TO_CHAR (BIRTHDATE, 'DAY MONTH DD, YYYY')  DATE_OUTPUT
  3    FROM STUDENT
  4    WHERE GENDER = 'FEMALE';

STUDENT_NAME_____  DATE_OUTPUT_____
WENDY JONES         MONDAY      OCTOBER     25, 1965
CATHY SMITH         WEDNESDAY FEBRUARY      22, 1922
DOTTIE STACY        WEDNESDAY MARCH         22, 1967
AMY LOPEZ           SUNDAY      MAY         10, 1964
TAMMY REDD          FRIDAY      JULY        01, 1960
```

TABLE 11.4   NUMERIC FORMAT MASKS FOR DATES IN THE TO-CHAR FUNCTION

Format Mask	Meaning	Example(s)
CC	The first two digits of the century	19
SCC	Signed first two digits of the of the century	19, −19
Y,YYY	The year displayed with a comma between the first two digits	1,987
SY,YYY	The signed year displayed with a comma between the first two digits	-1,987
YYYY	Unsigned year	1987
YYY	The last three digits of the year	987
YY	The last two digits of the year	87
Y	The last digit of the year	7
Q	The quarter number of the year	1,2,3 or 4
WW	The week number of the year	1,2,. . .,52
W	The week number of the month	1,2,. . .,5
MM	The month number	1,2,. . .,12
DDD	The day of the year	1,2,. . .,365(6)
DD	The day of the month	1,2,. . .,31
D	The day of the week	1,2,. . .,7
J	The Julian date	Any Integer

TABLE 11.5   NUMERIC FORMAT MASKS FOR TIME IN THE TO-CHAR FUNCTION

Format Mask	Meaning	Example
HH or HH12	The hour of the day	1,2,. . .,12
HH24	The hour past midnight	0,1,. . .,23
MI	The minutes	0,1,. . .,59
SS	The seconds	0,1,. . .,59
SSSSS	The seconds past midnight	0,1,. . .,86399

2. What week of the year, Julian date, and quarter of the year were Ben Trevino and Sam Wales born?

```
UFI> SELECT STUDENT_NAME,
   2   TO_CHAR (BIRTHDATE,'"Week = "WW" Julian = "J" Quarter = " Q')
   3   DATE_OUTPUT
   4   FROM STUDENT
   5   WHERE STUDENT_NAME IN ('BEN TREVINO', 'SAM WALES');

STUDENT_NAME_____   DATE_OUTPUT_____
BEN TREVINO          Week = 02 Julian = 2436944 Quarter = 1
SAM WALES            Week = 39 Julian = 2439399 Quarter = 3
```

This example illustrates the use of inserted text into the format string. Inserted text must be enclosed in double quotes. Note that the ''J'' format mask (Julian date) actually computes the number of days between the first day that ORACLE can record (January 1, 4712 B.C.) and the date specified.

TABLE 11.6   CHARACTER FORMAT MASKS FOR THE TO-CHAR FUNCTION

Format Mask	Meaning	Example
YEAR	The year spelled out in English	Nineteen-hundred-eighty-seven
MONTH	The complete month name	OCTOBER
MON	The first three characters of the month name	OCT
DAY	The complete day name	WEDNESDAY
DY	The first three characters of the day name	WED
AM or PM	The meridian indicator.	AM, PM
A.M. or P.M.	The meridian indicator with periods	A.M. or P.M.
BC or AD	The BC/AD indicator on a date	BC, AD
B.C. or A.D.	The BC/AD indicator on a date	B.C. or A.D.

TABLE 11.7   FORMAT MASK SUFFIXES FOR THE TO-CHAR FUNCTION

Format Mask	Meaning	Example
TH	Suffixes the letters ST, ND, RD, or TH onto the day of the month.	1st, 2nd, 3rd
SP	Spells out the day of the month	TWENTY, FIFTEEN
SPTH or THSP	Spells out the day of the month and adds the ST, ND, RD, or TH suffixes	TWENTIETH, FIRST

Notice how in each of the above examples that the values are all aligned in columns. This sometimes can be a detriment to producing aesthetically pleasing output. This column alignment can be disregarded when specifying the ''fm'' option in the TO—CHAR format clause. Following are two examples illustrating the difference between column-aligned and non-column-aligned output.

3. Spell out the birthdays of all the female students.

```
UFI> COLUMN DATE_OUTPUT FORMAT A67


UFI> SELECT STUDENT_NAME,
   2    TO_CHAR (BIRTHDATE, '"The "DdSPTH" of "Month YyyySP')
   3    DATE_OUTPUT
   4    FROM STUDENT
   5    WHERE GENDER = 'FEMALE';
```

```
STUDENT-NAME       DATE-OUTPUT
------------       ------------------------------------------------------------
WENDY JONES        The Twenty-fifth of October One Thousand Nine Hundred Sixty-five
CATHY SMITH        The Twenty-second of February One Thousand Nine Hundred Twenty-two
DOTTIE STACY       The Twenty-second of March One Thousand Nine Hundred Sixty-seven
AMY LOPEZ          The Tenth of May One Thousand Nine Hundred Sixty-four
TAMMY REDD         The First of July One Thousand Nine Hundred Sixty
```

Notice that the output is aligned on columnar boundaries. The reason for this is that we have not used ''fm'' in the format mask string. Further notice that only the first letters of the months and years are capitalized. This is produced by capitalizing only the first D in Dd (for the day of the month) and the first Y in Yyyy (for the year).

The following is the same query with the ''fm'' inserted into the first two positions of the format mask.

```
UFI> COLUMN DATE_OUTPUT FORMAT A66
```

```
UFI> SELECT STUDENT_NAME,
   2   TO_CHAR (BIRTHDATE, `fm"The "DdSPTH" of "Month YyyySP')
   3   DATE-OUTPUT
   4   FROM STUDENT
   5   WHERE GENDER = `FEMALE';
```

```
STUDENT-NAME       DATE-OUTPUT
WENDY JONES        The Twenty-fifth of October One Thousand Nine Hundred Sixty-five
CATHY SMITH        The Twenty-second of February One Thousand Nine Hundred Twenty-two
DOTTIE STACY       The Twenty-second of March One Thousand Nine Hundred Sixty-seven
AMY LOPEZ          The Tenth of May One Thousand Nine Hundred Sixty-four
TAMMY REDD         The First of July One Thousand Nine Hundred Sixty
```

4. What time of day were each of the male students born? Actually this might not be the exact times when they were born; it is the time that was entered into the BIRTHDAY attribute when the tuple was inserted into the table.

```
UFI> COLUMN DATE_OUTPUT FORMAT A12
UFI> SELECT STUDENT_NAME,
   2   TO-CHAR (BIRTHDATE, `HH:MIPM')
   3   DATE-OUTPUT
   4   FROM STUDENT
   5   WHERE GENDER = `MALE';
```

```
STUDENT-NAME       DATE-OUTPUT
SAM WALES          12:00AM
JAY LANGER         12:00AM
SAM WATSON         12:00AM
TOMMY WADKINS      12:00AM
BEN TREVINO        12:00AM
```

These extensive formatting capabilities are very useful when interfacing ORACLE to word processors. We can use SQL commands to extract data from a database, format it as we like, write the output out to a file via the SPOOL command, and use this file as input to a word processor.

The TO-DATE function.   If the primary use of the TO—CHAR is to convert date data stored in tables to character strings for output, then the primary use of the TO-DATE function is to convert date data entered as character strings into internal date format. If you will remember that when we are entering date data as input, the default format is DD-MON-YY. If we use this default format, we are restricted to entering only dates in the twentieth century. We also cannot enter any dates that contain times. Remember the default time value for each date value is 12:00 noon.

The format for the TO-DATE is essentially the same as the TO-CHAR function.

```
TO-DATE (date-value, 'format mask')
```

Here are two examples of inserting new tuples in the STUDENT table utilizing the TO-DATE function.

1. Insert a new student named Charlie Palmer, whose birthday is 10/9/1967.

```
UFI> INSERT INTO STUDENT VALUES
  2  ('S099','CHARLIE PALMER', 'MADISON AVE',
  3  TO_DATE ('10/09/67','MM/DD/YY'), 'MALE');

1 Record created.
```

2. Insert another new student named Rose Simpson, who was born at 3:30 P.M. on the 300th day of 1968.

```
UFI> INSERT INTO STUDENT VALUES
  2  ('S098','ROSE SIMPSON', 'SMITH LANE',
  3  TO_DATE ('300 1968 15:30','DDD YYYY HH24:MI'), 'FEMALE');

1 Record created.
```

The TO-DATE function can also be used in updating activities.

We were mistaken on Rose Simpson's time of birth. It really was 3:30 A.M. instead of 3:30 P.M.

```
UFI> UPDATE STUDENT
  2  SET BIRTHDAY = TO_DATE ('300 1968 3:30','DDD YYYY HH:MI')
  3  WHERE STU_ID = 'S098';

1 Record changed.
```

Other date functions.   The remaining date-oriented functions (ADD-MONTHS, MONTHS-BETWEEN, LAST-DAY, NEXT-DAY, ROUND, and TRUNC) are illustrated with the following examples.

1. What was the date four months after each student was born?

```
UFI> COLUMN "PLUS FOURS" FORMAT A10

UFI> SELECT STUDENT_NAME, BIRTHDATE,
  2  ADD_MONTHS (BIRTHDATE, 4) "PLUS FOURS"
  3  FROM STUDENT;
```

```
STUDENT-NAME_____  BIRTHDATE PLUS_FOURS
WENDY JONES        25-OCT-65 25-FEB-66
SAM WALES          10-JAN-60 10-MAY-60
CATHY SMITH        22-FEB-22 22-JUN-22
DOTTIE STACY       22-MAR-67 22-JUL-67
JAY LANGER         19-APR-65 19-AUG-65
AMY LOPEZ          10-MAY-64 10-SEP-64
SAM WATSON         09-JUN-63 09-OCT-63
TAMMY REDD         01-JUL-60 01-NOV-60
TOMMY WADKINS      24-AUG-67 24-DEC-67
BEN TREVINO        30-SEP-66 31-JAN-67

10 Records selected.
```

2. How many months old is each male student?

```
UFI> REMARK . . . This query was run on April 21, 1986

UFI> SELECT STUDENT_NAME, BIRTHDATE,
   2   MONTHS_BETWEEN (SYSDATE, BIRTHDATE) "MONTHS OLD"
   3   FROM STUDENT
   4   WHERE GENDER = 'MALE';

STUDENT-NAME_____  BIRTHDATE MONTHS_OLD
SAM WALES          10-JAN-60 315.368142
JAY LANGER         19-APR-65 252.077819
SAM WATSON         09-JUN-63   2.744004
TOMMY WADKINS      24-AUG-67 223.916529
BEN TREVINO        30-SEP-66 234.722981
```

Notice that the months between the two days are not computed as strictly integer values. This is, of course, due to the time being stored in an attribute of type DATE.

3. What is the last day of the month of each month that the female students were born? For example, if Wendy Jones was born on October 25, 1965, what was the last day of the month of October in 1965? October 31, 1965, of course.

```
UFI> COLUMN "LAST DAY OF MONTH" FORMAT A17

UFI> SELECT STUDENT_NAME, BIRTHDATE,
   2   LAST_DAY (BIRTHDATE) "LAST DAY OF MONTH"
   3   FROM STUDENT
   4   WHERE GENDER = 'FEMALE';
```

```
STUDENT-NAME_____  BIRTHDATE LAST_DAY_OF_MONTH
WENDY JONES         25-OCT-65 31-OCT-65
CATHY SMITH         22-FEB-22 28-FEB-22
DOTTIE STACY        22-MAR-67 31-MAR-67
AMY LOPEZ           10-MAY-64 31-MAY-64
TAMMY REDD          01-JUL-60 31-JUL-60
```

4. What is the next Friday after each student was born?

```
UFI> COLUMN "NEXT FRIDAY" FORMAT A12
UFI> SELECT STUDENT-NAME, BIRTHDATE,
  2   TO-CHAR (NEXT-DAY (BIRTHDATE,'FRIDAY'), 'DY MM/DD/YY')
  3   "NEXT FRIDAY"
  4   FROM STUDENT;

STUDENT-NAME_____  BIRTHDATE NEXT_FRIDAY_
WENDY JONES          25-OCT-65 FRI 10/29/65
SAM WALES            10-JAN-60 FRI 01/15/60
CATHY SMITH          22-FEB-22 FRI 02/24/22
DOTTIE STACY         22-MAR-67 FRI 03/24/67
JAY LANGER           19-APR-65 FRI 04/23/65
AMY LOPEZ            10-MAY-64 FRI 05/15/64
SAM WATSON           09-JUN-63 FRI 06/14/63
TAMMY REDD           01-JUL-60 FRI 07/08/60
TOMMY WADKINS        24-AUG-67 FRI 08/25/67
BEN TREVINO          30-SEP-66 FRI 10/07/66
```

Date Arithmetic

Certain arithmetic operations can be performed on date data types. These operations include:

1. Adding or subtracting a number of days to or from a date.
2. Subtracting two dates from one another. If two dates are subtracted from each other, the result will be converted to a character string. Therefore, if you wish to format the result via a numeric format mask, you must use one of the numeric functions (TO_NUMBER, ROUND, TRUNC, etc.) to convert it to a number.

The following examples illustrate date arithmetic.

1. What day is/was 7000 days from each student's birthday.

```
UFI> COLUMN "THE FUTURE" FORMAT A10
```

```
UFI> SELECT STUDENT-NAME, BIRTHDATE,
  2           BIRTHDATE + 7000 "THE FUTURE"
  3  FROM STUDENT;

STUDENT_NAME_____ BIRTHDATE THE_FUTURE
WENDY JONES       25-OCT-65 24-DEC-84
SAM WALES         10-JAN-60 11-MAR-79
CATHY SMITH       22-FEB-22 23-APR-41
DOTTIE STACY      22-MAR-67 21-MAY-86
JAY LANGER        19-APR-65 18-JUN-84
AMY LOPEZ         10-MAY-64 10-JUL-83
SAM WATSON        09-JUN-63 08-AUG-82
TAMMY REDD        01-JUL-60 31-AUG-82
TOMMY WADKINS     24-AUG-67 23-OCT-86
BEN TREVINO       30-SEP-66 29-NOV-85

10 Records selected.
```

2. What was the next Monday, 2000 days before each female's birthdate.

```
UFI> COLUMN "-2000" FORMAT A17

UFI> COLUMN BIRTHDATE FORMAT A17

UFI> SELECT STUDENT_NAME,
  2  TO_CHAR (BIRTHDATE,'Dy, MON DD, YYYY') BIRTHDATE
  3  TO_CHAR (NEXT_DAY(BIRTHDATE - 2000,'MONDAY'),
  4          'DY, MON DD, YYYY') "-2000"
  5  FROM STUDENT
  6  WHERE GENDER = 'FEMALE';

STUDENT-NAME_____ BIRTHDATE_____ -2000_____
WENDY JONES       MON, OCT 25, 1965 SUN, MAY 08, 1960
CATHY SMITH       WED, FEB 22, 1922 MON, SEP 04, 1916
DOTTIE STACY      WED, MAR 22, 1967 MON, OCT 02, 1961
AMY LOPEZ         SUN, MAY 10, 1964 MON, NOV 24, 1958
TAMMY REDD        FRI, JUL 01, 1960 MON, JAN 10, 1955
```

3. How many days old is each student?

```
UFI> REMARK ... This query was run on April 21, 1986

UFI> COLUMN "DAYSOLD" FORMAT 99999.99999

UFI> SELECT STUDENT_NAME, BIRTHDATE,
  2          SYSDATE _ BIRTHDATE  "DAYS OLD"
  3  FROM STUDENT;
```

```
STUDENT_NAME_____  BIRTHDATE  ___DAYS_OLD
WENDY JONES        25-OCT-65  7483.41838
SAM WALES          10-JAN-60  9598.41838
CATHY SMITH        22-FEB-22  23434.41838
DOTTIE STACY       22-MAR-67  6970.41838
JAY LANGER         19-APR-65  7672.41838
AMY LOPEZ          10-MAY-64  8016.41838
SAM WATSON         09-JUN-63  8352.41838
TAMMY REDD         01-JUL-60  9425.41838
TOMMY WADKINS      24-AUG-67  6815.41838
BEN TREVINO        30-SEP-66  7143.41838

10 Records selected.
```

Notice that the number of days is not displayed as an integer value. The reason for this is that the time value is internally represented as fractions of days. The reason that all the fractions are the same is that each value of BIRTHDATE was entered with the default time of 12:00 A.M. What we must do to display the value in a more pleasing manner is to use either the ROUND or the TRUNC functions.

```
UFI> SELECT STUDENT_NAME, BIRTHDATE,
  2         ROUND (SYSDATE - BIRTHDATE) "DAYS OLD ROUNDED",
  3         TRUNC (SYSDATE - BIRTHDATE) "DAYS OLD TRUNCED"
  4    FROM STUDENT;

STUDENT_NAME_____  BIRTHDATE DAYS_OLD_ROUNDED DAYS_OLD_TRUNCED
WENDY JONES        25-OCT-65             7483             7483
SAM WALES          10-JAN-60             9598             9598
CATHY SMITH        22-FEB-22            23434            23434
DOTTIE STACY       22-MAR-67             6970             6970
JAY LANGER         19-APR-65             7672             7672
AMY LOPEZ          10-MAY-64             8016             8016
SAM WATSON         09-JUN-63             8352             8352
TAMMY REDD         01-JUL-60             9425             9425
TOMMY WADKINS      24-AUG-67             6815             6815
BEN TREVINO        30-SEP-66             7143             7143

10 Records selected.
```

4. How old is each student?

```
UFI> REMARK . . . This query was run on April 21, 1986
UFI> COLUMN AGE FORMAT 999
UFI> SELECT STUDENT_NAME, BIRTHDATE,
  2         TRUNC ((SYSDATE - BIRTHDATE) /365.25) AGE
  3    FROM STUDENT;
```

```
STUDENT-NAME_____   BIRTHDATE AGE
WENDY JONES         25-OCT-65  20
SAM WALES           10-JAN-60  26
CATHY SMITH         22-FEB-22  64
DOTTIE STACY        22-MAR-67  19
JAY LANGER          19-APR-65  21
AMY LOPEZ           10-MAY-64  21
SAM WATSON          09-JUN-63  22
TAMMY REDD          01-JUL-60  25
TOMMY WADKINS       24-AUG-67  18
BEN TREVINO         30-SEP-66  19
```

SUMMARY

This chapter was dedicated to the discussion of expressions and functions for the CHAR, NUMBER, and DATE data types. Various formatting options for the DATE data type were also introduced.

Now that you have completed this chapter, you should be familiar with the following terms, concepts, and commands.

A. Numeric functions	**T.** RPAD
B. ABS	**U.** LTRIM
C. GREATEST	**V.** RTRIM
D. LEAST	**W.** SOUNDEX
E. MOD	**X.** SUBSTR
F. POWER	**Y.** TO-NUMB
G. ROUND	**Z.** TRANSLATE
H. SIGN	**AA.** UPPER
I. SQRT	**BB.** Date functions
J. TRUNC	**CC.** ADD-MONTHS
K. Displaying literals	**DD.** MONTHS-BETWEEN
L. Character expressions	**EE.** LAST-DAY
M. Concatenation	**FF.** TO-CHAR
N. Character functions	**GG.** TO-DATE
O. INITCAP	**HH.** Numeric format masks for dates
P. INSTR	**II.** Numeric format masks for time
Q. LENGTH	**JJ.** Character format masks
R. LOWER	**KK.** Format mask suffixes
S. LPAD	**LL.** Date arithmetic

EXERCISES

1. Explain when you would use the ROUND and TRUNC functions with date data.

2. Explain the function of the ''fm'' clause when formatting date data.

3. Using the character string functions, create a histogram out of the STU-IDs. For example, display one asterisk for ''S001,'' two asterisks for ''S002,'' and so forth.

4. Using the PERSONNEL table create the following output:

```
GREG DAVIS - PRESIDENT
SCOTT MIZE - DEAN
   .           .              .
AMY DANCER - PROFESSOR
```

Please note that there are no headings on the output report.

5. Using the DECODE command, create a report using the PERSONNEL table. If the RANK-OR-TITLE is president, dean or department chair, list them as 'STAFF,' else list 'FACULTY.' The output should look something like the following.

```
FACULTY-NAME____    POSITION
GREG DAVIS          STAFF
SCOTT MIZE          STAFF
   .        .           .
AMY DANCER           FACULTY
```

REFERENCES

1. Knuth, Donald E. *The Art of Programming*, Vol. 3, *Sorting and Searching. Addison-Wesley, Reading, MA, 1975, pp. 391–392.*

12

Creating
and
Using Views

PURPOSE: This chapter is designed to acquaint the reader with the varied uses of the view construct. Topics covered in this chapter include reasons for using views, creation, and deletion and usage of views.

Views are often called virtual tables for actual data is not stored permanently in views. Views generate what appears to the user to be a table, when in actuality it is only attributes extracted from one or more tables or other views. An algorithm (actually a SQL SELECT command) is used to produce the view data. The algorithm for the view is permanently stored in the system's data dictionary. When data is needed from the view, the algorithm is applied to the specified "underlying" tables or views and the data is generated. Views can be used in essentially the same manner as any base table. They can be used for queries and, in some cases, data maintenance.

THE CREATE VIEW COMMAND

The command used to create a view is the CREATE VIEW command. It consists of the view name, optionally the naming of attributes in the view, and the SELECT command that defines the algorithm to create the view. The syntax of the CREATE VIEW command is

```
CREATE VIEW view-name [(attribute-name1, [attribute-name2,...])]
  AS SELECT [ | [attribute-name3 | expression1 | function1,
              [attribute-name4 | expression2 | function2,..]]
  FROM table-name1 | view-name1 [,table-name2 | view-name2...]
  [WHERE condition(s)]
  [GROUP BY attribute-name5 [,attribute-name6,...]
       HAVING conditions]
  [CONNECT BY [PRIOR] attribute-name7 = [PRIOR] attribute-name8
       [START WITH condition(s)]]
```

Notice that the only clause of the SELECT command that cannot be used to create a view is the ORDER BY clause. The reason for this is that the order of the tuples cannot be specified in the structure of the view (or in a base table either). The order in which the tuples are displayed is determined by the ORDER BY clause specified in the SELECT command used to extract data from the view.

Further note that a view can use either another base table or another view as its underlying table. This is shown in the syntax of the FROM subclause of the SELECT clause of the CREATE VIEW command. If one of these underlying tables is dropped, it renders the view invalid and unusable. The definition of the view, however, remains in the data dictionary.

To illustrate the creation of views, let's consider creating a view of the FACULTY table that contains all the attributes of FACULTY except SALARY.

```
UFI> CREATE VIEW TEACHERS
  2  AS SELECT FAC_ID, FACULTY_NAME, DEPARTMENT, GENDER
  3  FROM FACULTY;

View created.
```

If any change is made to the data stored in the underlying table (FACULTY), those changes are automatically reflected the next time that the view is accessed.

We may use the DESCRIBE command to view the structure of the view:

```
UFI> DESCRIBE TEACHERS
  #   size  csize  type              name
  1     6      6   2 CHARACTER       FAC_ID
  2    17     17   2 CHARACTER       FACULTY_NAME
  3    10     10   2 CHARACTER       DEPARTMENT
  4     6      6   2 CHARACTER       GENDER
```

Note the sizes of the attributes are exactly the same as the attribute sizes defined in the underlying table FACULTY.

Changing Attribute Names in Views

In the preceding example we did not specify the attribute names for attributes in the view. If the attribute names are not specified, the original attribute names are used. If we wish to change the attribute names in the view, we can specify the names in parentheses in a list after the view name.

```
UFI> CREATE VIEW TEACHERS2 (FID, NAME, DEPT, SEX)
  2   AS SELECT FAC_ID, FACULTY_NAME, DEPARTMENT, GENDER
  3   FROM FACULTY;

View created.
```

Specifying Computed Values in Views

It is sometimes cumbersome to specify computed values in a SELECT statement, particularly if the user is a novice computer user. Suppose, for example, that we wanted to look at the square root of double each faculty member's salary. (We realize that this is not a very complicated algorithm, but it will serve the purpose.) Normally we would have to specify the computation as follows.

```
UFI> COLUMN SQRT(SALARY*2) FORMAT 999.999999 HEADING SAL

UFI> SELECT FACULTY_NAME, SQRT(SALARY*2)
  2   FROM FACULTY;

FACULTY-NAME_____  _____SAL
RAYMOND J. JOHNSON   282.842712
WENDY SWIMMER        300.000000
AMY DANCER           262.678511
BOB JONES            264.575131
JACK NELSON          236.643191
```

Since the attribute "SAL" is a computed one, it would be convenient to store the algorithm as part of the table definition, so that we would not have to specify it each time that we wanted to retrieve it. This cannot be done in a base table definition in ORACLE. It can, however, be done in a view.

```
UFI> CREATE VIEW DOUBLE_SAL (NAME, SAL) AS
  2   SELECT FACULTY_NAME, SQRT(SALARY*2)
  3   FROM FACULTY;

View created.
```

Note that because there was a computed attribute in the SELECT statement, all attribute names must be specified in the view attribute list.

If we display the structure of the view via the DESCRIBE command, notice that the computed attribute's size is the default numeric attribute size.

```
UFI> DESCRIBE DOUBLE-SAL
  #   size  csize  type                name
  1    17    17    2 CHARACTER         NAME
  2    22    40    1 NUMERIC           SAL
```

Extracting Data from Views

Once the view is created, it can be used almost like any base table. The only thing that we cannot do to a view is delete tuples, but more on this later in the chapter.

We can use any type SELECT command that we wish on the view.

```
UFI> SELECT * FROM TEACHERS;

FAC-ID FACULTY-NAME_____ DEPARTMENT GENDER
J01    RAYMOND J. JOHNSON COMP SCI    MALE
S01    WENDY SWIMMER      COMP SCI    FEMALE
D01    AMY DANCER         COMP SCI    FEMALE
J02    BOB JONES          ACCOUNTING  MALE
N01    JACK NELSON        HISTORY     MALE

UFI> SELECT FACULTY-NAME, DEPARTMENT, GENDER
   2  FROM TEACHERS
   3  ORDER BY GENDER;

FACULTY-NAME_____ DEPARTMENT GENDER
WENDY SWIMMER      COMP SCI    FEMALE
AMY DANCER         COMP SCI    FEMALE
RAYMOND J. JOHNSON COMP SCI    MALE
BOB JONES          ACCOUNTING  MALE
JACK NELSON        HISTORY     MALE

UFI> SELECT FACULTY-NAME, DEPARTMENT, GENDER
   2  FROM TEACHERS
   3  WHERE DEPARTMENT LIKE 'COMP%'
   4  ORDER BY GENDER;

FACULTY-NAME_____ DEPARTMENT GENDER_
WENDY SWIMMER      COMP SCI    FEMALE
AMY DANCER         COMP SCI    FEMALE
RAYMOND J. JOHNSON COMP SCI    MALE
```

DROPPING VIEWS

The command used to eliminate a view from the data dictionary is the DROP VIEW command. The format of the command is

```
DROP VIEW view-name
```

If we wished to eliminate the view that we just created in the example, we could issue the following command.

```
UFI> DROP VIEW TEACHERS;

View dropped.
```

REASONS FOR USING VIEWS

Views are an interesting, useful, and powerful construct in the relational database repertoire of information management tools. There are many reasons for using views, and some of the more important ones are discussed in the paragraphs that follow.

Views Enhance Logical Data Independence

Logical data independence refers to insulating users from any changes in the data definition. If you will remember back to Chapter 1, this was one of the major goals of a database management system. For example, suppose that we wanted to break up the FACULTY table into two smaller tables as follows.

ORIGINAL TABLE:

```
FACULTY (FAC-ID, FACULTY-NAME, DEPARTMENT, GENDER, SALARY)
```

NEW TABLES:

```
FAC_TAB1 (FAC-ID, DEPARTMENT)
FAC_TAB2 (FAC-ID, FACULTY_NAME, GENDER, SALARY)
```

(The possible reasons for wanting to split the FACULTY table into these two tables are discussed in Chapter 15 under the topic of Normalization of Relations.) The FACULTY table could be split with the following commands.

```
UFI> CREATE TABLE FAC_TAB1 (FAC_ID CHAR (6) NOT NULL,
  2                          DEPARTMENT CHAR (10))
  3                          SPACE SCHOOL_SPACE;

Table created.
```

```
UFI> CREATE TABLE FAC_TAB2 (FAC_ID CHAR (6) NOT NULL,
   2                        FACULTY_NAME CHAR (17),
   3                        GENDER CHAR (6),
   4                        SALARY NUMBER (7))
   5                        SPACE SCHOOL_SPACE;

Table created,

UFI> CREATE UNIQUE INDEX PK_FAC_TAB2 ON FAC_TAB2 (FAC_ID);

Index created,

UFI> INSERT INTO FAC_TAB1 AS
   2 SELECT FAC_ID, DEPARTMENT FROM FACULTY;

5 Records created,

UFI> INSERT INTO FAC_TAB2 AS
   2 SELECT FAC_ID, FACULTY_NAME, GENDER, SALARY FROM FACULTY;

5 Records created,

UFI> REMARK , , , At this point we would want to display the

UFI> REMARK , , , data in the two new tables to ensure that we

UFI> REMARK , , , have created and loaded them correctly,

UFI> REMARK , , , After this is done we will eliminate the old

UFI> REMARK , , , FACULTY table,

UFI> DROP TABLE FACULTY;

Table dropped,
```

Now if the user wanted to access the old FACULTY table, we would have to use a JOIN in every SELECT command that accesses the attributes in the old table. We have made a change to the structure of our tables, and these changes now affect our access commands. This could be a problem if we had written a user's guide to assist novice users of our system in accessing the database. The user's guide would have to be altered to reflect the structure changes to our tables. (Some of the old queries would now have to be altered to incorporate the necessary joins to link the tables together.) Changing access commands for novice users can sometimes have a detrimental effect on their usage of the database. Also if we had some conventional language programs that accessed the database, these programs would have to be patched, recompiled, and relinked so as to reflect the table structure alterations.

To solve this problem, we could create a view, called FACULTY, that would contain the necessary JOIN condition to link the two tables together.

```
UFI> CREATE VIEW FACULTY AS
   2   SELECT FAC_TAB2.FAC_ID, FACULTY_NAME, DEPARTMENT,
   3          GENDER, SALARY
   4   FROM FAC_TAB1, FAC_TAB2
   5   WHERE FAC_TAB1.FAC_ID = FAC_TAB2.FAC_ID;

View created.
```

The user will now be able to use the same table, which is actually a view, to access the desired data without changing any of her SQL commands or patching our conventional language programs. In fact, the user need not even be aware of the structural changes that have been made to the tables. This is what is meant by logical data independence.

Views Give the User a Method of Restricting Access to Tables

Views give users a vehicle to restrict access to the rows and/or the columns in a table. The columns can be restricted by simply not listing them in the attribute list of the view. The rows can be restricted by using the WHERE clause in the SELECT algorithm used to create the view.

```
UFI> REMARK ... Create a view with restricted columns

UFI> CREATE VIEW TEACHERS2 (FID, NAME, DEPT, SEX)
   2   AS SELECT FAC_ID, FACULTY_NAME, DEPARTMENT, GENDER
   3   FROM FACULTY;

View created.

UFI> REMARK ... Create a view with restricted rows

UFI> CREATE VIEW COMPUTER_SCIENCE_INSTRUCTORS
   2   AS SELECT *
   3   FROM FACULTY
   4   WHERE DEPARTMENT = 'COMP SCI';

View created.

UFI> REMARK ... Create a view with restricted rows and

UFI> REMARK ... columns
```

```
UFI> CREATE VIEW MALE_CS_INSTRUCTORS (FID, NAME, SAL)
   2 AS SELECT FAC_ID, FACULTY_NAME, SALARY
   3 FROM FACULTY
   4 WHERE DEPARTMENT = 'COMP SCI' AND GENDER = 'MALE';

View created.
```

Views Are a Method of "Storing" Any Computed Value

This is especially helpful when the algorithm is rather long and complex.

```
UFI> CREATE VIEW AGES_OF_STUDENTS (NAME, AGE) AS
   2 SELECT STUDENT_NAME,
   3        TRUNC (BIRTHDATE_SYSDATE/365.25)
   4 FROM STUDENT;

View created.
```

Views Are an Efficient Method of Storing Complex and Frequently Used Subqueries and/or Joins

Complex queries that take several lines to type can be stored in views very readily.

```
UFI> CREATE VIEW FEMALES_WHO_TEACH_FEMALES
   2             (FAC_NAME, STU_NAME) AS
   3 SELECT FACULTY_NAME, STUDENT_NAME
   4 FROM FACULTY F, COURSE C, STUDENT S
   5 WHERE F.FAC_ID = C.FAC_ID
   6   AND S.STU_ID = C.STU_ID
   7   AND S.GENDER = 'FEMALE'
   8   AND F.GENDER = 'FEMALE';

View created.
```

Views Are an Efficient Method of Storing Grouped Data

Once grouped data type views are created, they can be accessed just like any other table.

```
UFI> CREATE VIEW HOW_MANY
   2    (DEPT, NUMB_OF_EMP, TOT_SAL, AVE_SAL) AS
   3 SELECT DEPARTMENT, COUNT(*), SUM(SALARY), AVG(SALARY)
   4 FROM FACULTY
   5 GROUP BY DEPARTMENT;

View created.
```

DISPLAYING VIEW INFORMATION

There is a data dictionary table (actually it is a view) that contains information on user-created views. The name of the table is VIEWS. The following command displays the names and other relevant information on all the views created by the user-name that the user is currently connected to.

```
UFI> COLUMN VIEWNAME FORMAT A8
UFI> COLUMN VCREATOR FORMAT A8
UFI> COLUMN VALID FORMAT A5
UFI> SET LONG 80
UFI> SELECT * FROM VIEWS;

VIEWNAME VCREATOR VALID
VIEWTEXT_____
--------------------
TEACHERS BOOK      Y
SELECT * FROM FACULTY
```

The attribute VIEWNAME contains the name of the view as per the CREATE VIEW command. VCREATOR contains the user-name of the user who created the view. VALID contains either "Y" or "N", indicating whether the view is valid or not. (If one or more of the underlying tables used to produce the view has been dropped, the view is invalid.) VIEWTEXT contains the SELECT command used to produce the data for the view. Notice that the attribute VIEWTEXT does not display on the same output line as the other attributes of the table VIEWS. The reason for this is that VIEWTEXT is defined as being of type LONG. Remember that the default output length for type LONG is 80 characters. Since the other attributes and VIEWTEXT will not fit on the default line length of 80 characters, ORACLE displays the results of the query on two lines. We could change the default output for the field VIEWTEXT with the SET LONG command.

```
UFI> SET LONG 25
UFI> /

VIEWNAME VCREATOR VALID VIEWTEXT_____
TEACHERS BOOK      Y      SELECT * FROM FACULTY
```

It should be noted that the algorithm stored in VIEWTEXT cannot be altered. If the algorithm must be changed, drop the view and create a new one.

Remember that if you perform an EXPORT command (see Chapter 8), views (actually VIEWTEXT) are copied out to the exported file and can be imported via the IMPORT command.

DATA MODIFICATION IN VIEWS

Even though a view is designed primarily to "view" data in base tables, certain data modification can be applied to views in ORACLE.

1. Under no circumstances can tuples be deleted from views.
2. Under certain circumstances view data can be updated or new tuples can be inserted into the view. In either case, even though we specify the view as being modified, it is the base table that is actually modified.
3. If the view algorithm does not contain a JOIN condition, new tuples can be inserted into the view. If the view that we are inserting the new tuple into does not contain all the attributes of the base table, those attributes not included in the view will receive null values. This assumes that the NOT NULL clause is not affixed to the attribute in the base table definition.
4. If the view algorithm does not contain a JOIN condition, attribute values can be modified through the view.

EXAMPLES OF THE USE OF A VIEW

In this section we will describe two different examples of the use of views. The first is a computational example using the grade computation problem introduced in Chapter 9 of this text. The second is a string-oriented example.

The Gradebook Problem Revisited

If you will remember back to our example of generating the student's grade with the use of joins in Chapter 9, we used a complex SELECT command to determine a student's letter grade based on his current class average.

To refresh your memory, the following table was created that contained the student's test scores for a certain class.

```
UFI> DESCRIBE GRADES
  # SIZE CSIZE TYPE            NAME
  1    6     6  2 CHARACTER    STU_ID
  2    3     3  1 NUMERIC      TEST1
  3    3     3  1 NUMERIC      TEST2
  4    3     3  1 NUMERIC      TEST3
  5    3     3  1 NUMERIC      FINAL_EXAM
```

After the GRADES table was loaded with values, it looked like this:

```
UFI> SELECT * FROM GRADES;
```

```
STU-ID  STUDENT-NAME        TEST1   TEST2   TEST3   FINAL-EXAM
S001    WENDY JONES         98      95      93      92
S002    SAM WALES           88      85      83      82
S003    CATHY SMITH         78      75      73      72
S004    DOTTIE STACY        68      65      63      62
S005    JAY LANGER          14      28      63      45
```

The algorithm to determine the student's grades was as follows.

```
AVERAGE = (TEST1 + TEST2 + TEST3 + (2*FINAL-EXAM)) / 5
```

We could have implemented this grade algorithm by using this formula in a SELECT command.

```
UFI> COLUMN TEST1 FORMAT 99999
UFI> COLUMN TEST2 LIKE TEST1
UFI> COLUMN TEST3 LIKE TEST1
UFI> COLUMN FINAL_EXAM LIKE TEST1
UFI> COLUMN (TEST1+TEST2+TEST3+(2*FINAL_EX HEADING AVE
UFI> COLUMN AVE FORMAT 999.99
UFI> SELECT GRADES.*, (TEST1+TEST2+TEST3+(2*FINAL-EXAM))/5
   2   FROM GRADES, STUDENT
   3   WHERE GRADES. STU_ID = STUDENT.STU_ID;

STUDENT-NAME        STU_ID  TEST1  TEST2  TEST3  FINAL_EXAM   AVE
WENDY JONES         S001    98     95     93     92      94.00
SAM WALES           S002    88     85     83     82      84.00
CATHY SMITH         S003    78     75     73     72      74.00
DOTTIE STACY        S004    68     65     63     62      64.00
JAY LANGER          S005    14     28     63     45      39.00
```

The above SELECT command can be incorporated into a view very easily.

```
UFI> CREATE VIEW CLASS_GRADES (SID, NAME, TEST1, TEST2,
   2                           TEST3, FINAL, AVE) AS
   3   SELECT STUDENT_NAMES GRADES.*, (TEST1+TEST2+TEST3+(2*FINAL_EXAM))/5
   4   FROM GRADES; STUDENT
   5   WHERE GRADES. STU_ID = STUDENT.STU_ID

View created.
```

We can now extract data from the CLASS-GRADES view without having to specify the grade computation algorithm each time we wanted to retrieve data.

We then expanded our example to include the assignment of a letter grade to each student based on the following table.

| | Letter |
Average	Grade
90 and above	A
89 to 80	B
79 to 70	C
69 to 60	D
59 and below	F

This was accomplished by creating and loading the following table, and then joining it to the GRADES table.

```
UFI> CREATE TABLE GRADE_SCALE (LOW_VALUE NUMBER (4,1),
   2                           HIGH_VALUE  NUMBER (4,1),
   3                           GRADE CHAR (1))
   4                           SPACE SCHOOL_SPACE;

Table created.
```

We could then join the GRADES table, the GRADE-SCALE table and the student table to produce our desired output.

```
UFI> SELECT GRADES.*, (TEST1+TEST2+TEST3+(2*FINAL_EXAM))/5,
   2  GRADE
   3  FROM GRADES, GRADE_SCALE
   4  WHERE (TEST1+TEST2+TEST3+(2*FINAL_EXAM))/5 BETWEEN
   5  LOW_VALUE AND HIGH_VALUE;

STUDENT-NAME__ STU_ID TEST1 TEST2 TEST3 FINAL-EXAM ___AVE GRADE
WENDY JONES    S001     98    95    93         92  94.00 A
SAM WALES      S002     88    85    83         82  84.00 B
CATHY SMITH    S003     78    75    73         72  74.00 C
DOTTIE STACY   S004     68    65    63         62  64.00 D
JAY LANGER     S005     14    28    63         45  39.00 F
```

Obviously, this is a complicated query to input each time we want to view a set of grades. One alternative would be to store the query in a START file, and each time that the output is needed, we could START the file containing the SELECT command. The second alternative would be to create a view to contain the desired algorithm.

```
UFI> CREATE VIEW CURRENT_GRADES (STU_ID, STUDENT_NAME,TEST1,TEST2,TEST3,
   2                             FINAL_EXAM,AVE,GRADE) AS
   3                             SELECT GRADES,STU_ID, STUDENT_NAME,
   4                                 TEST1,TEST2,TEST3,FINAL_EXAM,
   5                                 (TEST1+TEST2+TEST3+(2*FINAL_EXAM))/5,
   6                                 GRADE
```

```
 7                          FROM GRADES,GRADE_SCALE,STUDENT
 8                          WHERE (TEST1+TEST2+TEST3+(2*FINAL_EXAM))/5
 9                                BETWEEN LOW_VALUE AND HIGH_VALUE
10                          AND STUDENT.STU_ID = GRADES.STU_ID;

View created.

UFI> SELECT * FROM CURRENT_GRADES;

STU-ID STUDENT-NAME__ TEST1 TEST2 TEST3 FINAL-EXAM ___AVE GRADE
S001   WENDY JONES       98    95    93         92  94.00 A
S002   SAM WALES         88    85    83         82  84.00 B
S003   CATHY SMITH       78    75    73         72  74.00 C
S004   DOTTIE STACY      68    65    63         62  64.00 D
S005   JAY LANGER        14    28    63         45  39.00 F
```

We could use the CURRENT-GRADES view to extract whatever information that we need from our data.

```
UFI> SELECT * FROM CURRENT_GRADES WHERE GRADE < 'C';

STU_ID STUDENT_NAME__ TEST1 TEST2 TEST3 FINAL_EXAM ___AVE GRADE
S001   WENDY JONES       98    95    93         92  94.00 A
S002   SAM WALES         88    85    83         82  84.00 B
```

The only problem that may arise with this view is that the faculty member can only use this view at the end of the semester. Suppose that he wants to use the same view after he has given the first test. We could have to store values of zero for TEST2, TEST3, and the FINAL-EXAM. We could display the desired attributes by SELECTing only the students ID, name, first test score, the average, and the "current" grade.

```
UFI> SELECT STU_ID, STUDENT_NAME, TEST1, AVE, GRADE
  2  FROM CURRENT_GRADES;

STU-ID STUDENT-NAME__ TEST1 ___AVE GRADE
S001   WENDY JONES       98  19.60 F
S002   SAM WALES         88  17.60 F
S003   CATHY SMITH       78  15.50 F
S004   DOTTIE STACY      68  13.60 F
S005   JAY LANGER        14   2.80 F
```

Oops! What happened? Let's look at the VIEWTEXT of CURRENT-GRADES to see if we can determine what the problem is.

```
UFI> SET LONG 500
UFI> SELECT VIEWTEXT FROM VIEWS WHERE VIEWNAME = 'CURRENT-GRADES';
```

```
VIEWTEXT
--------------------------------------------------------------------
SELECT STU_ID, STUDENT_NAME, TEST1, TEST2, TEST3, FINAL_EXAM,(TEST1+TEST
2+TEST3+(2*FINAL_EXAM))/5,FROM GRADES, GRADE_SCALE, STUDENT WHERE (TEST1
+TEST2+TEST3+(2*FINAL_EXAM))/5 BETWEEN LOW_VALUE AND HIGH_VALUE AND STUD-
ENT.STU_ID = GRADES.STU_ID
```

The problem exists in the computation of the average grade. We are dividing by 5 in lieu of dividing by the 500 total points possible during the term, then multiplying the result by 100 to convert the result to a percentage. We should be dividing by only 1 (for the 100 total points for the first exam). We have a problem. View algorithms cannot be altered. What we will have to do is to delete this view and create another one that changes the average computation algorithm. What we really need to do is to generate one view that will compute the average after every exam. In other words, we have to find a method of changing the divisor in the average computation algorithm.

Why not incorporate a SQL variable into the view algorithm? Variables were introduced in Chapter 8 of this text. If you will remember back to Chapter 8, there are two types of SQL variables: long-term variables, which are preceded by two ampersands, and short-term variables, which are preceded by one ampersand. Short-term variables must be redefined each time a command containing the variable is executed. Once the values of long-term variables are defined, they remain in effect until they are changed or the user disconnects from ORACLE. Long-term variables are obviously what we need to use in our new view.

```
UFI> REMARK ... Let's drop the old CURRENT_GRADES view - again.

UFI> DROP VIEW CURRENT_GRADES;

View dropped.

UFI> CREATE VIEW CURRENT_GRADES (STU_ID, STUDENT_NAME, TEST1,
  2                              TEST2, TEST3, FINAL_EXAM, AVE,
  3                              GRADE) AS
  4  SELECT STU_ID, STUDENT_NAME, TEST1, TEST2, TEST3, FINAL_EXAM,
  5        (TEST1+TEST2+TEST3+(2*FINAL_EXAM))/&&DIV, GRADE
  6  FROM GRADES, GRADE_SCALE, STUDENT
  7  WHERE (TEST1+TEST2+TEST3+(2*FINAL_EXAM))/&&DIV BETWEEN
  8        LOW_VALUE AND HIGH_VALUE
  9    AND STUDENT.STU_ID = GRADES.STU_ID;

View Created.

UFI> REMARK ... Let's define a value for DIV
UFI> DEFINE DIV=1
UFI> SELECT STU-ID, STUDENT_NAME, TEST1, AVE, GRADE
  2  FROM CURRENT_GRADES;
```

```
STU_ID  STUDENT_NAME    TEST1   AVE GRADE
------  ------------    -----   --- -----
S001    WENDY JONES       98  98.00 A
S002    SAM WALES         88  88.00 B
S003    CATHY SMITH       78  78.00 C
S004    DOTTIE STACY      68  68.00 D
S005    JAY LANGER        14  14.00 F
```

We now have a very flexible view that can be used to compute the student's current average and assign the student a letter grade based on that average.

A Character String Example with Views

Let's assume that we wanted to produce a report that contained the student's name and birthday. We wanted the birthday spelled out in a format similar to the following.

```
WENDY JONES was born on Monday, October the Twenty-fifth, Nineteen Hundred Sixty-Five
SAM WALES was born on Sunday, January the Tenth, Nineteen Hundred Sixty
CATHY SMITH was born on Wednesday, February the Twenty-second, Nineteen Hundred Twenty-two
```

This type of output could be produced with the following SELECT command.

```
UFI> COLUMN DATE_OF_BIRTH FORMAT A90
UFI> SELECT STUDENT-NAME ||
  2          TO-CHAR (BIRTHDATE, 'fm" was born on ", Day, Month" the "DdSPTH,
  3                  YyyySP') DATE-OF-BIRTH
  4  FROM STUDENT;


DATE-OF-BIRTH
--------------------------------------------------------------------------------
WENDY JONES was born on Monday, October the Twenty-fifth, Nineteen Hundred Sixty-five
SAM WALES was born on Sunday, January the Tenth, Nineteen Hundred Sixty
CATHY SMITH was born on Wednesday, February the Twenty-second, Nineteen Hundred Twenty-two
DOTTIE STACY was born on Wednesday, March the Twenty-second, Nineteen Hundred Sixty-seven
JAY LANGER was born on Monday, April the Nineteenth, Nineteen Hundred Sixty-five
AMY LOPEZ was born on Sunday, May the Tenth, Nineteen Hundred Sixty-four
SAM WATSON was born on Sunday, June the Ninth, Nineteen Hundred Sixty-three
TAMMY REED was born on Friday, July the First, Nineteen Hundred Sixty
TOMMY WADKINS was born on Thursday, August the Twenty-fourth, Nineteen Hundred Sixty-seven
BEN TREVINO was born on Friday, September the Thirtieth, Nineteen Hundred Sixty-six

10 Records selected.
```

Even though the select-list of the above command contains a concatenated list of mixed data types (STUDENT-NAME is of type CHAR and BIRTHDATE is of type DATE), we can include this algorithm into a view.

```
                        UFI> COLUMN DOB FORMAT A65

UFI> CREATE VIEW HAPPY-BIRTHDAY (DOB) AS
  2  SELECT STUDENT_NAME ||
  3          TO_CHAR (BIRTHDATE, 'fm" was born on ", Day,
  4                  MonthSPTH" the "DdSPTH, YyyySP')
  5  FROM STUDENT;
```

```
View created.

UFI> SELECT * FROM HAPPY_BIRTHDAY
  2  WHERE DOB LIKE 'WENDY%';

DOB
------------------------------------------------------------------
WENDY JONES was born on Monday, October the Twenty-fifth, Nineteen Hundred Sixty-Five
```

SUMMARY

This chapter introduced a very valuable and useful concept available in ORA-CLE. The view has many advantages. It does not contain any data, only the algorithm (SELECT command) to generate the desired data. View are particularly useful when a complex algorithm must be used repeatedly in SELECT commands and/or selected tuples and/or attributes must be shielded from other users.

After you have completed this chapter, you should be familiar with the following terms, concepts, and commands.

A. Views

B. CREATE VIEW

C. DROP VIEW

D. Reasons for using views

E. Using defined variables in views

F. Displaying view information

G. VIEWTEXT

H. Valid and invalid views

EXERCISES

1. What is meant by an invalid view? How can you tell if a view is invalid?
2. Create a view based on the organization table presented in Chapter 10.
3. Should we be allowed to INSERT and UPDATE values in views with JOIN commands embedded in the views?
4. What is meant by logical data independence? How can views help preserve it?

13

Accessing Data from Other ORACLE User-names and Concurrent Processing

PURPOSE: This chapter is designed to show ORACLE users how to access data from other user-names. Methods of data protection and access are illustrated. The chapter also illustrates how ORACLE handles simultaneous users.

Up to this point in this text, we have created tables and views within a user-name and accessed them from within that user-name only. Data can be accessed from any user-name within the ORACLE system. The creator of the table may grant and revoke data access privileges for tables and views that he has created.

We have also assumed up to this point in this text that there would be only one user of tables at a time. This is probably the case in most academic environments, but it certainly is not true for most industrial or governmental environments. A database certainly would not be very useful if it did not handle simultaneous users.

ACCESSING DATA FROM OTHER USER-NAMES

There are two methods of accessing data from other user-names. The first method is to "transfer" or connect to the other account and access the tables and views directly. The second method is to access the tables and views by affixing the user-name to the table or view name in the FROM clause.

Connecting to Other User-names

Once you have successfully logged into ORACLE, you can transfer from one user-name to another with the CONNECT command. The format of the CONNECT command is:

```
CONNECT user-name/password
```

The CONNECT command is issued from the UFI prompt.

```
UFI> CONNECT NEW_USER_NAME/NEW_PASSWORD

Connected.
```

If you specify either an incorrect user-name or an incorrect password, you will still be in ORACLE, but you will no longer be connected to your original user-name. You should either reconnect to your original user-name, or if you realize what your error was, try to connect to the new user-name again.

```
UFI> CONNECT BAD_USER_NAME/BAD_PASSWORD

ERROR: 1017      Invalid username/password; logon denied.

Warning: You are no longer connected.
```

Please be aware that ORACLE user-names are not tied to computer system account numbers. You may connect to any ORACLE user-name from any computer system account number!

It is important to note that you can only reside in one user-name at any one instant of time. When you connect to one user-name, you are automatically disconnected from your previous user-name.

Accessing Tables and Views Directly from Other User-names

Tables and views may be accessed directly from other user-names by prefixing the table or view name with the user-name where the table or view resides. This is usually done in the FROM clause of the desired command. For example, assume that we had logged onto ORACLE under the user-name MY-USER-NAME. If we wished to access data from the faculty table that resides in the user-name YOUR-USER-NAME, as seen in Figure 13.1, we could issue the following command.

```
UFI> SELECT *
  2  FROM YOUR_USER_NAME.FACULTY;
```

FAC_ID	FACULTY_NAME	DEPARTMENT	GENDER	SALARY
J01	RAYMOND J. JOHNSON	COMP SCI	MALE	40000
S01	WENDY SWIMMER	COMP SCI	FEMALE	45000
D01	AMY DANCER	COMP SCI	FEMALE	34500
J02	BOB JONES	ACCOUNTING	MALE	35000
N01	JACK NELSON	HISTORY	MALE	28000

Note that the user-name where the table or view resides must prefix the table or view name. The user-name and table or view name are separated by a period.

Be aware that the user who originally created the table or view must give other users the ''privilege'' of accessing her table or view. More on this appears later in the chapter.

Joining Tables or Views from More than One User-Name

We can even join tables or views from different user-names. To illustrate, let's use our example of the grade assignment query. To complicate matters, let's further assume that the three tables that we need are all located in three different user-names as:

TABLE NAME	USER-NAME
STUDENT	BOOK
GRADES	CLASS-GRADES
GRADE-SCALE	ADMINISTRATIVE

We will assume that we are not logged into any one of the above three user-names. The query to extract our desired data would look as follows.

```
UFI> SELECT BOOK.STU_ID,BOOK.STUDENT_NAME GLASS_GRADES, TEST1,
   2        CLASS_GRADES.TEST2, CLASS_GRADES.TEST3,
   3        CLASS_GRADES.FINAL_EXAM,
   4        (CLASS_GRADES.TEST 1+CLASS_GRADES.TEST2+
   5        CLASS_GRADES.TEST3+(2*CLASS_GRADES.FINAL_EXAM))/5,
   6        ADMINISTRATIVE.GRADE
   7        FROM CLASS_GRADES.GRADES ADMINISTRATIVE.GRADE_SCALE,
   8        BOOK.STUDENT
   9        WHERE (CLASS_GRADES.TEST1+CLASS_GRADES.TEST2+
  10        CLASS_GRADES.TEST3+(2*CLASS_GRADES.FINAL_EXAM))/5
  11        BETWEEN ADMINISTRATIVE.LOW_VALUE AND
  12        ADMINISTRATIVE.HIGH_VALUE
  13        AND BOOK.STUDENT.STU-ID = CLASS_GRADES.GRADES.STU-ID;
```

STU-ID	STUDENT-NAME	TEST1	TEST2	TEST3	FINAL-EXAM	AVE	GRADE
S001	WENDY JONES	98	95	93	92	94.00	A
S002	SAM WALES	88	85	83	82	84.00	B
S003	CATHY SMITH	78	75	73	72	74.00	C
S004	DOTTIE STACY	68	65	63	62	64.00	D
S005	JAY LANGER	14	28	63	45	39.00	F

Figure 13.1   View of Two Oracle User-Names. User-names available to ORACLE users (for our example)

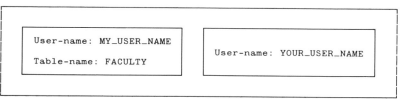

Creating and Using Synonyms

As you can see from the example, when data is extracted from multiple user-names, it becomes an arduous task to specify all the qualified table or view names. If we could shorten this process, it would be helpful. This can be done with the use of synonyms. ORACLE synonyms can only be created for tables in other user-names. Synonyms are created and stored in the data dictionary for system users to utilize.

Synonyms are created with the CREATE SYNONYM command, which is:

```
CREATE [PUBLIC] SYNONYM name FOR [user-name.]table | view-name
```

If a public synonym is created, it becomes valid for all users. Examples of public synonyms are all the data dictionary tables (DTAB, TAB, SESSIONS, VIEWS, etc.). All these tables (they are actually views) reside in a system account, but they do not have to be qualified as they are synonyms for the actual tables.

If the user-name is not specified, ORACLE prefixes the table or view name with the current user-name. If the table or view specified in the synonym does not exist, the appropriate error message is displayed and the synonym is not created.

Examples of the use of synonyms are:

```
UFI> CREATE SYNONYM STU FOR BOOK.STUDENT;

Synonym created.

UFI> CREATE PUBLIC SYNONYM GR_TAB FOR ADMINISTRATIVE.GRADE_SCALE;

Synonym created.

UFI> CONNECT CLASS-GRADES/WHAT_ME_WORRY

Connected.

UFI> CREATE SYNONYM MY_STUDENTS FOR GRADES;

Synonym created.
```

```
UFI> CREATE SYNONYM BAD_SYNONYM FOR NON_EXISTENT_TABLE;
                                         *
ERROR AT LINE 1:942      Table or view does not exist.
```

If you forget the names of the synonyms that you have created, they are stored in the data dictionary table TAB.

```
UFI> SELECT * FROM TAB WHERE TABTYPE = 'SYNONYM';

TNAME_____ TABTYPE _CLUSTERID
STU                                     SYNONYM
```

Notice that public synonyms are not listed in the TAB view. The use of synonyms would have made the grade assignment query much easier to create.

```
UFI> SELECT STU.STU_ID, STU.STUDENT_NAME, MY_STUDENTS.TEST1,
  2         MY_STUDENTS.TEST2, MY_STUDENTS.TEST3,
  3         MY_STUDENTS.FINAL_EXAM,
  4         (MY_STUDENTS.TEST1+MY_STUDENTS.TEST2+
  5          MY_STUDENTS.TEST3+(2*MY_STUDENTS.FINAL_EXAM))/5,
  6         GR_TAB.GRADES
  7  FROM MY_STUDENTS, STU, GR_TAB
  8  WHERE (MY_STUDENTS.TEST1+MY_STUDENTS.TEST2+
  9         MY_STUDENTS.TEST3+(2*MY_STUDENTS.FINAL_EXAM))/5
 10         BETWEEN GR_TAB.LOW_VALUE AND GR_TAB.HIGH_VALUE
 11     AND STU.STU_ID = STU.GRADES.STU_ID;


STU-ID STUDENT-NAME__  TEST1 TEST2 TEST3 FINAL-EXAM ___AVE GRADE
S001   WENDY JONES        98    95    93         92  94.00 A
S002   SAM WALES          88    85    83         82  84.00 B
S003   CATHY SMITH        78    75    73         72  74.00 C
S004   DOTTIE STACY       68    65    63         62  64.00 D
S005   JAY LANGER         14    28    63         45  39.00 F
```

Synonyms can be used as part of the view creation algorithm.

Dropping Synonyms

A synonym can be eliminated from the data dictionary with the DROP SYNONYM command. The syntax of the DROP SYNONYM command is:

```
DROP [PUBLIC] SYNONYM name
```

For example, if we wanted to drop the synonym MY-STUDENTS, we could use the command

```
UFI> DROP SYNONYM MY-STUDENTS;

Synonym dropped.

UFI> DROP PUBLIC SYNONYM GR-TAB;

Synonym dropped.
```

There are three basic reasons for dropping synonyms. First, we simply no longer want to use the synonym. Second, the user-name containing the table or view of the synonym has been eliminated. Third, the table or view that is the object of the synonym has been dropped.

GRANTING PRIVILEGES TO OTHER USERS

Allowing other users to access data in our user-name seems like a very handy concept to have in a database management system. However, think about what we are allowing. We are allowing other users to access and even modify data in tables that we have created **without even knowing our password**. This means that any user, if he knows our table name and user-name can access or alter any data that we have created. This does not appear to be very security conscientious.

There is a set of commands that allows us to restrict what other users can do to our tables. In reality when we create a table that table is restricted to operations performed only in our user-name. This means that no other system user can access or change our tables unless we specifically grant them the privilege to do so. The privileges that we can grant to other users include the following.

1. SELECT   Allows other users to display data from our tables or views.
2. UPDATE   Allows other users to change the values in our tables and possibly views (remember that we can not change values in views if they contain a join command).
3. INSERT   Allows other users to store new tuples in our tables and possibly views.
4. DELETE   Allows other users to delete tuples from our tables (remember that we cannot delete tuples from views).
5. INDEX   Allows other users to create indexes for the table (indexes cannot be generated on views).
6. ALTER   Allows other users to modify the structure of the table (the structure of views cannot be altered).
7. UPDATE   Allows other users to change only the values in (attribute(s)) specified attributes in a table and possibly views.

8. ALL   Allows other users to apply all of the first six privileges specified above.

The GRANT Command

These privileges are allocated through the GRANT command. Remember back to Chapter 6 that the GRANT command can also be used to create system user-names. We will now discuss the second function of the GRANT command, allocating table privileges to other system users. The syntax of this version of the GRANT command is

```
GRANT { ALL | privilege1 [,privilege2 , , ,] }
   ON [user-name,]table-name | view-name
   TO { PUBLIC | user-name1 [,user-name2 , , ,] }
   [WITH GRANT OPTION]
```

The privileges refer to one of the first seven specified. If the PUBLIC option is specified in the TO clause, then the privilege is extended to every user-name, current and future, on the system. The WITH GRANT OPTION allows the user-name granted the privilege(s) to pass those grants on to other system users.

Here are some examples of the use of the GRANT command.

```
UFI> GRANT SELECT ON FACULTY TO DEANS;

Grant succeeded,

UFI> GRANT SELECT , UPDATE ON STUDENT TO REGISTRAR;

Grant succeeded,

UFI> GRANT UPDATE (SALARY) ON FACULTY TO DOTTIE_BISLAND;

Grant succeeded,

UFI> GRANT ALL ON COURSE TO PUBLIC;

Grant succeeded,

UFI> GRANT SELECT ON STUDENT TO STUDENT_AID WITH GRANT OPTION;

Grant succeeded,
```

The REVOKE Command

Just as any of the seven privileges can be granted to any or all system users, the privileges can also be revoked. The only user-names that can revoke these privileges is the user-name who originally granted them or a user-name with DBA privilege.

The command used to revoke these privileges is the REVOKE command. The format of the command is:

```
REVOKE { ALL | privilege1 [,privilege2 . . . ] }
   ON [user-name,] {table-name | view-name}
   FROM { PUBLIC | user-name1 [,user-name2 . . .] }
```

Examples of the REVOKE command are:

```
UFI> REVOKE SELECT ON FACULTY FROM DEANS;

Revoke succeeded.

UFI> REVOKE ALL ON COURSE FROM PUBLIC;

Revoke succeeded.
```

If multiple users have granted a user-name a certain privilege on a particular table or view, they must all revoke this privilege before the privilege is lost.

If a user has granted a certain privilege(s) to another user and specified the WITH GRANT OPTION and the second user passes that privilege on to other users and the first users decides to revoke the original privilege(s), all the other users that have been passed that privilege have their privilege revoked.

AN EXAMPLE OF ACCESSING DATA FROM OTHER USER-NAMES

Let's use the gradebook example to illustrate the use of accessing data from other accounts. Let's assume that each student has his or her own ORACLE user-name and that their user-name have only CONNECT privilege. Remember that CONNECT privilege means that the user can only use other users' data; for he or she cannot create independent tables.

Remember that, in the previous chapter, we created a view called STUDENT—GRADES that contained each student's test scores, a computed average, and a letter grade. We will assume that this view resides in a user-name called DATA-BASE—GRADES. We would like to have each student be able to access (SELECT) tuples from the table but not be able to modify it. Data modification will be handled only by the class instructor who has access to the DATABASE—GRADES user-name via the proper password. To allow the students to access but not modify the data in the view (actually they could not modify it anyway for the view consists of a JOIN command), we will issue the following GRANT command.

```
UFI> GRANT SELECT ON STUDENT-GRADES TO PUBLIC;

Grant succeeded.
```

Now each student in the class will be able to access data from the view by using the proper SELECT command.

```
UFI> SELECT * FROM DATABASE-GRADES.STUDENT-GRADES;

STU-ID STUDENT-NAME__  TEST1 TEST2 TEST3 FINAL-EXAM ___AVE GRADE
S001   WENDY JONES        98    95    93         92  94.00 A
S002   SAM WALES          88    85    83         82  84.00 B
S003   CATHY SMITH        78    75    73         72  74.00 C
S004   DOTTIE STACY       68    65    63         62  64.00 D
S005   JAY LANGER         14    28    63         45  39.00 F
```

Although this is a good example of accessing data from other user-names, it is not very feasible for two reasons. The first is that even though our students will be able to access the data, so will every other user on the system. How will other users know that the STUDENT-GRADES view is available to them? If you will remember, the data dictionary table SYSTABS contains a list of all the tables to which each user has access. As soon as any user executes the command SELECT * FROM SYSTABS;, she will be aware of the table. This problem can be handled very easily. Instead of granting the SELECT privilege to PUBLIC, it would have been prudent simply to list the user-names of the students in our class in the grant command. The second problem is a bit more serious. Once we give each student access to the STUDENT-GRADES table, every student can now view her fellow classmates' grades. This would cause problems with the Buckley Amendment.

This problem can be solved by creating another view using the special system user-name variable USER. USER is the system variable that contains the user-name of the "current" user-name. If we created a view, in the user-name DATABASE-GRADES, using the view STUDENT-GRADES as follows, we could solve our problem.

```
UFI> CREATE VIEW STU-GRADES AS
   2  SELECT * FROM STUDENT-GRADES
   3  WHERE STUDENT-NAME = USER;

View created.

UFI> GRANT SELECT ON STU-GRADES TO PUBLIC;

Grant succeeded.
```

We would have to make one slight change to the data stored in our STUDENT-GRADES table. We would have to replace every internal blank in each student's name with an underline character, so as to make it a legal identifier. We would also have to make sure that each student's user-name was the same as the value of STUDENT-NAME. Our new STUDENT-NAMES (which is also a list of our user-names for our students) would look as follows.

```
UFI> SELECT STUDENT_NAME FROM STUDENT_GRADES;

STUDENT_NAME_____
WENDY_JONES
SAM_WALES
CATHY_SMITH
DOTTIE_STACY
JAY_LANGER
AMY_LOPEZ
SAM_WATSON
TAMMY_REDD
TOMMY_WADKINS
BEN_TREVINO

10 Records selected.
```

Now when the student, Sam Wales, executes the following command, he will only get access to his tuple, and we will not be invading anyone's privacy.

```
UFI> SELECT * FROM DATABASE_GRADES.STUDENT_GRADES;

STU_ID STUDENT_NAME__ TEST1 TEST2 TEST3 FINAL_EXAM ___AVE GRADE
S002   SAM WALES         88    85    83         82  84.00 B
```

Note that because Sam Wales was connected to his account (we assume), he can only view his tuple. This is due to the condition WHERE STUDENT-NAME = USER placed in the view. This is the technique that is used when accessing data dictionary tables (TAB, INDEXES, etc.) that you are presented with only the tables that pertain to your ORACLE user-name.

CONCURRENT PROCESSING

Concurrent processing refers to multiple simultaneous users of a database. Large database management systems would not be very useful if only one user at a time could be connected to the system. Concurrent processing is not a problem with microcomputers for only one user at a time can use the system (although some of the newer ones allow networking of users).

Problems with Concurrent Processing

The obvious problem that can occur with concurrent processing when two or more users attempt to access the same tuple, or attributes within a tuple simultaneously. Remembering that there are basically two types of access to a data table, retrieval and modification, let's see how concurrent processing affects data access.

If two users attempt simultaneously to retrieve data from the same tuple via a SELECT command, there is no problem. Both users are allowed to access the tuple(s) and utilize them in whatever manner they so desire. However, if one or more of the simultaneous users attempt to modify the data in any manner (add a tuple, delete a tuple, or modify an attribute value), there is an integrity problem.

To illustrate this problem, consider a database containing student's academic records. The table in question consists of the student's total quality points earned and total hours attempted. This table is used to keep track of the student's quality point average (or grade point average). The structure of the table is:

```
STU-RECS ( STU-ID, TOTAL-QPS, TOTAL-HOURS-ATTEMPTED)
```

Since the student's quality point average is computed by dividing TOTAL-QPS by TOTAL-HOURS-ATTEMPTED, the student's QPA is computed in view based on STU-RECS.

```
STU-RECS-VIEW (STU-ID, TOTAL-QPS, TOTAL-HOURS-ATTEMPTED, QPA)
```

Suppose that we had two simultaneous users of the student records system. We will assume that the database is running on some type of multiprogramming computer system where programs (actually they are SQL commands) are given some amount of time (usually called a time slice) to execute as much code as they can and if the program is not finished at the end of that time slice, the program is suspended and swapped out of the execution cycle. It will be swapped back into execution at some later time. This continues until the program completes execution.

The first user in our example, USER#1, has the job of updating the STU-RECS table at the end of each term at the university. This user would have to locate each student's tuple and update both the TOTAL-QPS and TOTAL-HOURS-ATTEMPTED for each student. This operation is what we have been calling a ''computed'' update, for the current values for these two attributes would have to be retrieved and the current term's values added to them, then both values would be restored in their proper places in the tuple. This job would probably be done through some host language program accessing the database. Notice that for the tuples in the database to be correct, both the TOTAL-QPS and TOTAL-HOURS-ATTEMPTED would have to be updated before we allow any other user to access the virtual attribute QPA through the view STU-RECS-VIEW. Therefore, we would want to make sure that both attributes are updated during the current computer execution cycle. What we do not want is for our program to update one of the attributes and be swapped out of execution before the other attribute is executed. This would cause our database to be in an inconsistent state (although temporarily).

The second user, USER#2, has the job of verifying quality point averages for various honor societies.

This person's job is to execute queries similar to the two SQL commands shown here.

```
SELECT *
FROM STU_REC_VIEW, STUDENT
WHERE STU_REC_VIEW.STU_ID = STUDENT.STU_ID
  AND STUDENT_NAME = 'RANDY WILSON';


SELECT *
FROM STU_REC_VIEW, STUDENT
WHERE STU_REC_VIEW.STU_ID = STUDENT.STU_ID
  AND QPA > 3.5;
```

Think about what would happen if USER#1 begins execution and during his time in execution is only able to update TOTAL—QPS for the student Randy Wilson before his program was swapped out of memory. Then USER#2 was swapped into memory and he uses the first query in an attempt to access Randy Wilson's QPA. Since only the attribute TOTAL-QPS is updated, this would make Randy's QPA artificially high, allowing him possibly to enter the fraternal order of I Ama Polymath honor society at the university.

This example is, of course, spurious one. However, think about an accounting transaction where the updates to the debits and credits of accounts have to balance. Also think about what would happen if the computer system crashed before the transaction is completed. We now would have a database that is not synchronized since only part of the transaction has been recorded. The system database administrator, it is hoped, could use the various journal files to return the database to a corrected state.

The example just described had only one of the users trying to update the database and the other user attempting simply to retrieve data. Think about the problems that could arise if USER#1 and USER#2 were both trying to update the same tuple simultaneously.

In summary, concurrent users are only a serious problem in database systems when one or more of the simultaneous users are performing updates to the database.

Solutions to Concurrent Updating

There are essentially four solutions to the problem of concurrent updating.

1. Only allow one update program to execute at a time. Since there is only one program accessing the database, there are no problems with concurrent processing. This is a very simplistic solution, and in most complex database environments, it is infeasible.

2. Adjust the program's execution time slice to ensure that the update transaction (both updates) is complete before the program is swapped out of memory. This solution requires adjustments be made to the computer's operating system.

3. When the update session begins, lock out all other users from accessing the tables that will be updated until all updating is complete. This is a useful

solution, assuming we can afford to lock the other users out of the system for a certain period of time. Our example system with the quality point average could be an example of this type solution to concurrent processing. Systems that are highly volatile (have many updates per period) will not be able to afford the luxury of locking out all other users for a period of time. Systems like airline reservation systems, stock exchange transaction systems, and so on are examples of highly volatile systems.

4. Just before a tuple or group of tuples are to be updated, lock only that tuple(s) from other user access. Once the update transaction is complete, release the tuples for access by any user. This is the solution that is used by highly volatile databases.

ORACLE's MECHANISMS FOR HANDLING CONCURRENT PROCESSING

When retrieving data via the SELECT command, neither tables nor tuples are locked. However, when using any of the data modification commands, INSERT, DELETE, or UPDATE, various types of locks can be applied to tables and/or tuples. These locks can be explicit or implicit.

The LOCK TABLE Command

The LOCK TABLE command is used to restrict access to tables. This can be done in either of two ways: it can temporarily lock other users from modifying data in a table, or it can prevent another user from locking a table in a conflicting locking mode (which is described shortly). The LOCK TABLE command remains in effect until a COMMIT, ROLLBACK, or EXIT command is executed.

The format of the LOCK TABLE command is:

```
LOCK TABLE [user-name1,]table-name1
           [,[user-name2,]table-name2 ...]
IN { SHARE | SHARE UPDATE | EXCLUSIVE } MODE [NOWAIT]
```

Examples of LOCK table commands are:

```
UFI> LOCK TABLE FACULTY IN SHARE MODE;

Table(s) locked.

UFI> LOCK TABLE STUDENT IN SHARE UPDATE MODE NOWAIT;

Table(s) locked.

UFI> LOCK TABLE COURSE IN EXCLUSIVE MODE NOWAIT;

Table(s) locked.
```

Locking modes.   As the LOCK COMMAND indicates, there are three locking modes available to ORACLE users.

1. *Exclusive*. In this mode, no other user can use the table for any purpose. The table is locked to all system users for any purpose.
2. *Share update*. In this mode, any other user can simultaneously update the table. Other users cannot try to lock the table in either SHARE or EXCLUSIVE mode. The only mode allowed for other users of the table is SHARE UPDATE.
3. *Share*. In this mode, any updates cannot be made to the table while this table is locked. It is used when a user is retrieving data for perhaps a large report and does not want changes to be made to the database while the report is being generated. The only mode allowed for other users of the table is SHARE.

When a user has a table locked in either SHARE or EXCLUSIVE modes, no other user can modify the table in any way. When a user has locked a table in SHARED UPDATE mode, other users can modify the table contents subject to certain restrictions discussed next.

What happens when a locking request fails.   Normally, when a locking request fails, the user requesting the lock is placed into an indefinite wait state until her request can be fulfilled. When the user is in this wait state, no other commands can be executed. If we have a long and complex update program executing that has captured the table in EXCLUSIVE mode, the lock requesting user may be in a wait state for several hours.

The safety valve to this condition is the NOWAIT clause of the LOCK TABLE command. If the user specifies NOWAIT on her LOCK TABLE command and the table cannot be locked, ORACLE generates the following error message and does not place the user in a wait state.

```
busy and nowait specified
```

It is obviously prudent always to specify the NOWAIT option.

Exclusive locks due to uncommitted changes.   If you will remember back to Chapter 9 when we discussed the various types of data modification, we said that unless we set the auto commit switch on (SET AUTOCOMMIT ON), all changes made to data tables were tentative. Data changes were not made permanent (they are written out to secondary storage) until the COMMIT command was executed. These tentative changes will automatically lock out all other users until a COMMIT is executed, even if other users have locked the table in SHARE UPDATE mode.

The question then becomes why use SHARE UPDATE if only one user can actually update the database at a time. The answer is that the other user's requests are queued up, and when the first user either commits or rolls back the changes or exits the system, the next user's changes become "active" until she commits or rolls back or exits.

In summary, even though the lock SHARE UPDATE connotes that multiple users can be updating the same table simultaneously, actually only one user can update the table and the other users' updates are queued up.

Implicit locking of tables.   In all the examples that we have presented thus far in this chapter, we have explicitly locked tables via the LOCK TABLE command. What happens if we do not lock a table and perform updates to it? How are other users affected? Any time that an UPDATE, INSERT, or DELETE command is executed and the table is not locked, an implicit exclusive lock is placed on the table until either a COMMIT, ROLLBACK, or EXIT is executed. This is a very nice feature that ORACLE provides for its users. The only detriment to implicit locking is that the NOWAIT feature is not implied. This could cause long delays in processing data.

Locking Select Tuples for Update

Individual tuples can be locked for update purposes via the FOR UPDATE clause that can be affixed to the SELECT command. When the SELECT command is executed, only those tuples that have been "marked" for update are locked, not the entire table or view. The format of this command is:

```
SELECT [ { table-name1 | view-name1 | table-label1 }, ]ROWID
       [ ,{ table-name2 | view-name2 | table-lable2 }, ]ROWID
       [ <select-list> ]
FROM [user-name1,] { table-name1 | view-name1 } table-label1
       [[,user-name2,] { table-name2 | view-name2 } table-label
       , , ,]
[WHERE conditions]
FOR UPDATE OF [ {table-name1 | view-name1 | table-label1},]
              attribute1
              [[, {table-name2 | view-name2 | table-label2},]
              attribute2 , , ,]
```

When the SELECT FOR UPDATE command is executed, the requested attributes are displayed, and the selected tuples are locked (if possible) in SHARE UPDATE mode. Note that the attributes that will be modified should be specified in the FOR UPDATE OF list. Once the command is executed, the user is free to UPDATE tuples in the table.

Please note that the ROWID (remember the ROWID is actually ORACLE's database key for each tuple) must be specified in the SELECT command. The reason for this is that by using the ROWID to locate the record, ORACLE can execute the accompanying UPDATE command as fast as it possibly can.

The following is an example of a SELECT FOR UPDATE command. Let's assume that we want to update Raymond J. Johnson's salary. (The ole boy has been working hard, and we want to reward him with a 10% raise.)

```
UFI> SELECT FACULTY_NAME, ROWID
  2  FROM FACULTY
  3  WHERE FACULTY_NAME = 'RAYMOND J. JOHNSON'
  4  FOR UPDATE OF SALARY;

FACULTY_NAME_____ ROWID_____
RAYMOND J. JOHNSON 00000270.0001.0002
```

Be aware that if you attempt to execute the command, the value that is displayed for ROWID might not be the same as the value shown, for your tuple might be in a different physical location on disk from our tuple.

Once this command is executed and we have the value for ROWID, we can use it to update the value of SALARY in Raymond J. Johnson's tuple.

```
UFI> UPDATE FACULTY
  2  SET SALARY = SALARY * 1.1
  3  WHERE ROWID = '00000270.0001.0002';

1 record updated.
```

This process might seem like a very tedious and clumsy one (using the SELECT command to lock the tuple and display the ROWID, then using that ROWID in the WHERE clause of the UPDATE command), but it is very efficient. Besides, if we were updating tuples in an industrial environment we would probably be executing these commands from within a conventional language program.

If the SELECT FOR UPDATE command cannot lock the tuples in a table, the user will be placed in a wait state. For this reason, the following sequence of commands is strongly advised.

```
UFI> LOCK TABLE FACULTY IN SHARE UPDATE MODE NOWAIT;

Table(s) locked.

UFI> SELECT FACULTY_NAME, ROWID
  2  FROM FACULTY
  3  WHERE FACULTY_NAME = 'RAYMOND J. JOHNSON'
  4  FOR UPDATE OF SALARY;

FACULTY_NAME_____ ROWID_____
RAYMOND J. JOHNSON 00000270.0001.0002

UFI> UPDATE FACULTY
  2  SET SALARY = SALARY * 1.1
  3  WHERE ROWID = '00000270.0001.0002';
```

```
1 record changed.

UFI> COMMIT

Commit complete.
```

Note that we committed the changes as soon as we made them. This is to release the changes to the user public and to unlock the table.

In summary, in a multiuser environment to ensure that the database is always in a consistent state, we must use locks when data altering takes place. These commands might seem to be rather tedious to execute, but remember that they will probably be executed from conventional programming language programs.

SUMMARY

This chapter illustrated how users can access data from other users' user-names. Methods of protecting data from unauthorized use and modification through the use of the GRANT and REVOKE commands were discussed. Problems and ORACLE's solutions to concurrent data modification via table and tuple locks were also extolled.

Upon completion of this chapter, you should now be familiar with the following terms, concepts, and commands.

A. CONNECT

B. Prefixing table and/or view names with other user-names

C. CREATE SYNONYM

D. CREATE PUBLIC SYNONYM

E. DROP SYNONYM

F. DROP PUBLIC SYNONYM

G. Granting access privileges to other users

H. Revoke access privileges

I. Concurrent processing

J. ORACLE's solutions to concurrent processing

K. LOCK TABLE

L. NOWAIT

M. EXCLUSIVE mode

N. SHARE UPDATE mode

O. SHARE mode

P. SELECT FOR UPDATE

EXERCISES

1. When are tables unlocked? Why are tables not locked for data retrieval? Why are they locked for data maintenance?

2. Explain the difference between table locking and tuple locking.

3. Create a synonym for one of the tables in your account.

4. Grant SELECT privilege to one of your classmates. Have them try to display the data in your table. Have them try to update an attribute in your table.

5. Try to lock one of your tables in exclusive mode. Have one of your classmates attempt to access the table. Type either COMMIT or ROLLBACK and then have your classmate attempt to access your data.

6. Try to SELECT FOR UPDATE one of the tuples in one of your tables. Update the tuple. Before you COMMIT the change, have one of your classmates attempt to access the locked table.

14

The
Internal Report Writer

PURPOSE: This chapter is designed to describe the ORACLE internal report writer capabilities of ORACLE. Control breaks, report headings, report footings, and control break totals are illustrated.

Even though the ORACLE system does have separate piece of software, the description of which is beyond the scope of this text, to generate reports, it also has a smaller version of a report writer through the use of SQL and UFI commands.

THE REPORT WRITER OVERVIEW

This chapter is entitled the "Internal Report Writer" to differentiate it from the separate "Report" processor that is also part of the ORACLE software package.

The internal report writer has the capabilities of a simple report writer. The following is a list of the basic capabilities of the internal report writer.

1. Places report titles atop each output page.
2. Places bottom titles at the bottom of each output page.
3. Handles spacing on control breaks.
4. Sums various numeric fields on control breaks.

5. Changes the number of output lines on an output page.

6. Changes the number of columns on an output page.

Issuing a set of UFI commands (TTITLE, BTITLE, etc.), activates features of the internal report writer. The user then executes a SQL SELECT command that extracts whatever data he wants and this data is formatted as per the currently active report writer commands. These commands remain in effect until the user disconnects from the system, clears the commands, or issues a new command of a similar type that replaces the current setting of the current command.

TOP AND BOTTOM TITLES

The UFI command TTITLE (Top TITLE) will place a user-defined title (page heading), a page number, and the current date and time atop each output page. The format of the TTITLE command is:

```
TTITLE 'page heading'
```

For example, if we wanted to generate the page heading "Faculty Salary Report" atop each SELECT command, we could issue the following command.

```
UFI> TTITLE 'FACULTY SALARY REPORT'
```

With the executing of this command, any SELECT command issued will have the page heading "Faculty Salary Report," the page number, and the system date atop each output page.

If we wanted to change the value of TTITLE, we could simply issue another TTITLE command and the new page heading would replace the current heading. If we wished to turn the TTITLE option off, we could issue the TTITLE OFF command. If we wanted to activate it again, we would use the TTITLE ON command. TTITLE OFF deactivates the TTITLE command, but it does not clear the current value of TTITLE. This can be done by setting the value of the heading to an empty string, that is, TTITLE '' (that's two consecutive single quotes).

If we wanted to view the current value of the page heading and determine whether TTITLE was active or not, we could issue the command TTITLE.

The command to place a bottom title (page footing) at the bottom of each output page is BTITLE (bottom title). BTITLE can not be activated without TTITLE first being activated.

Here are some examples of the use of top and bottom titles.

```
UFI> TTITLE 'FACULTY SALARY REPORT'
UFI> TTITLE
ttitle ON and is the following 21 characters:
FACULTY SALARY REPORT
UFI> SELECT * FROM FACULTY;
```

```
Mon Apr 21 10:09:27 1986                                        page 1
                        FACULTY SALARY REPORT

FAC_ID FACULTY_NAME_____ DEPARTMENT  GENDER SALARY
  J01    RAYMOND J. JOHNSON COMP SCI    MALE    40000
  S01    WENDY SWIMMER      COMP SCI    FEMALE  45000
  D01    AMY DANCER         COMP SCI    FEMALE  34500
  J02    BOB JONES          ACCOUNTING  MALE    35000
  N01    JACK NELSON        HISTORY     MALE    28000
```

Notice that the SELECT command retrieves the data that we want displayed, and since TTITLE is active, the page headings are displayed automatically. Also note that the title string is automatically centered on the page. (It is centered on the page, not on the output that is displayed.)

```
        UFI> REMARK . . . Let's turn TTITLE off
        UFI> TTITLE OFF
        UFI> /

        FAC_ID FACULTY_NAME_____ DEPARTMENT  GENDER SALARY
          J01    RAYMOND J. JOHNSON COMP SCI    MALE    40000
          S01    WENDY SWIMMER      COMP SCI    FEMALE  45000
          D01    AMY DANCER         COMP SCI    FEMALE  34500
          J02    BOB JONES          ACCOUNTING  MALE    35000
          N01    JACK NELSON        HISTORY     MALE    28000
```

Notice that now the headings do not appear.

```
UFI> REMARK . . . Let's turn TTITLE back on and try BTITLE
UFI> TTITLE ON
UFI> BTITLE 'DO NOT ALLOW ENEMY AGENTS TO VIEW THIS DATA'
UFI> /

Mon Apr 21 10:19:25 1986                                        page 1
                        FACULTY SALARY REPORT

FAC_ID FACULTY_NAME_____ DEPARTMENT  GENDER SALARY
  J01    RAYMOND J. JOHNSON COMP SCI    MALE    40000
  S01    WENDY SWIMMER      COMP SCI    FEMALE  45000
  D01    AMY DANCER         COMP SCI    FEMALE  34500
  J02    BOB JONES          ACCOUNTING  MALE    35000
  N01    JACK NELSON        HISTORY     MALE    28000
```

<10 Blank Lines>

```
        DO NOT ALLOW ENEMY AGENTS TO VIEW THIS DATA
```

Note that the BTITLE is also automatically centered on the output page.

Remember that we can create a stacked title by inserting the line separator character (|) into the header and/or footing strings wherever we want a new line to start.

```
UFI> TTITLE 'FACULTY | SALARY | REPORT'
UFI> /

Mon Apr 21 10:28:20 1986                              page 1
                        FACULTY
                        SALARY
                        REPORT

FAC_ID FACULTY_NAME_____   DEPARTMENT   GENDER SALARY
 J01    RAYMOND J. JOHNSON  COMP SCI      MALE    40000
 S01    WENDY SWIMMER       COMP SCI      FEMALE  45000
 D01    AMY DANCER          COMP SCI      FEMALE  34500
 J02    BOB JONES           ACCOUNTING    MALE    35000
 N01    JACK NELSON         HISTORY       MALE    28000
```

<10 Blank Lines>

```
           DO NOT ALLOW ENEMY AGENTS TO VIEW THIS DATA
UFI> REMARK . . . Turn off both titles

UFI> TTITLE OFF

UFI> BTITLE OFF
```

CONTROL BREAKS

Control breaks are formed by grouping tuples with like characteristics together. Every time there is a change in this characteristic, it is called a control break. The simplest method of grouping tuples with like characteristics is to sort the tuples by the characteristic attribute. For example, if we wanted to group the tuples in the FACULTY table by the characteristic GENDER, we could issue the following command.

```
UFI> SELECT * FROM FACULTY ORDER BY GENDER;

FAC_ID FACULTY_NAME_____   DEPARTMENT   GENDER SALARY
 S01    WENDY SWIMMER       COMP SCI      FEMALE  45000
 D01    AMY DANCER          COMP SCI      FEMALE  34500
 J01    RAYMOND J. JOHNSON  COMP SCI      MALE    40000
 J02    BOB JONES           ACCOUNTING    MALE    35000
 N01    JACK NELSON         HISTORY       MALE    28000
```

In this resultant table there would be one control break. It could come between the second and third tuple (when the value of GENDER changes). Anytime there is a change in the value of the characteristic (GENDER, in this case), it is considered a control break. If we had not sorted the resultant table, there would have been two control breaks.

```
UFI> SELECT * FROM FACULTY;

FAC_ID FACULTY_NAME_____ DEPARTMENT GENDER SALARY
 J01    RAYMOND J. JOHNSON COMP SCI   MALE   40000
 S01    WENDY SWIMMER      COMP SCI   FEMALE 45000
 D01    AMY DANCER         COMP SCI   FEMALE 34500
 J02    BOB JONES          ACCOUNTING MALE   35000
 N01    JACK NELSON        HISTORY    MALE   28000
```

The first control break occurs between the first and second tuple, and the second control break occurs between the third and fourth tuple.

It is also possible to have multiple control break attributes. For example, if we issued the following SELECT command, sorted on two different attributes, we could have two different control breaks.

```
UFI> SELECT * FROM FACULTY ORDER BY DEPARTMENT, GENDER;

FAC_ID FACULTY_NAME_____ DEPARTMENT GENDER SALARY
 J02    BOB JONES          ACCOUNTING MALE   35000
 S01    WENDY SWIMMER      COMP SCI   FEMALE 45000
 D01    AMY DANCER         COMP SCI   FEMALE 34500
 J01    RAYMOND J. JOHNSON COMP SCI   MALE   40000
 N01    JACK NELSON        HISTORY    MALE   28000
```

Since DEPARTMENT is the major sort field (it is listed first in the ORDER BY list), it is considered the major control break attribute. GENDER is considered the minor sort key (if there is a tie in the value of DEPARTMENT, the tie is broken by the corresponding value of GENDER) and therefore the minor control break item. Minor control breaks occur within major control breaks.

The BREAK ON Command

The BREAK ON command serves two basic purposes. The first is that it informs ORACLE that the user wants control break formatting to be activated. The second is that it tells ORACLE how to handle the line spacing at control breaks.

Control break formatting allows the user the option of suppressing the display of the value of the control break attribute after it is displayed for the first time. The user also has the option of spacing down *n* lines or advancing to the top of a fresh output page when a control break occurs.

The format of the BREAK ON command is:

```
BREAK ON attribute1 [SKIP {nn | PAGE] [DUP|NODUP]
       [ON attribute2 [SKIP {nn | PAGE] [DUP|NODUP]]
```

The following is an example of a simple control break report.

```
UFI> TTITLE 'SALARY REPORT BY GENDER'
UFI> BREAK ON GENDER
UFI> COLUMN SALARY FORMAT $99,999
UFI> SELECT GENDER, FACULTY_NAME, SALARY FROM FACULTY
  2   ORDER BY GENDER;

Mon Apr 21 10:48:20 1986                              page 1
                    SALARY REPORT BY GENDER


GENDER FACULTY_NAME_____  _SALARY
FEMALE WENDY SWIMMER       $45,000
       AMY DANCER          $34,500
MALE   RAYMOND J. JOHNSON  $40,000
       HARMON D. RANGE     $35,000
       FRANK FURTER        $28,000
```

Notice how the value of GENDER is only displayed the first time that it occurs. Further notice that the ORDER BY attribute is the same as the control break attribute. Let's change our example and place two blank lines at the control break.

```
UFI> BREAK ON GENDER SKIP 2
UFI> /

Mon Apr 21 10:49:45 1986                              page 1
                    SALARY REPORT BY GENDER


GENDER FACULTY_NAME_____  _SALARY
FEMALE WENDY SWIMMER       $45,000
       AMY DANCER          $34,500
MALE   RAYMOND J. JOHNSON  $40,000
       BOB JONES           $35,000
       JACK NELSON         $28,000
```

Let's print each new control break at the top of a new page.

```
UFI> BREAK ON GENDER SKIP PAGE
UFI> /

Mon Apr 21 10:51:29 1986                              page 1
                    SALARY REPORT BY GENDER
```

```
GENDER FACULTY_NAME_____ _SALARY
FEMALE WENDY SWIMMER        $45,000
       AMY DANCER           $34,500
```

<<<<<There will be 13 blank lines inserted here>>>>>

```
Mon Apr 21 10:51:29 1986                              Page 2
                   SALARY REPORT BY GENDER


GENDER FACULTY_NAME_____ _SALARY
MALE   RAYMOND J. JOHNSON $40,000
       BOB JONES           $35,000
       JACK NELSON         $28,000
```

The SKIP PAGE option caused each control break to begin on a fresh output page. The number of blank lines will be explained shortly.

We can also format multiple control breaks. Let's assume that we wanted our major control break to be DEPARTMENT and our minor control break to be GENDER. We will also assume that we want to display each major control break at the top of a new output page and double space the minor control break.

```
UFI> BREAK ON DEPARTMENT SKIP PAGE ON GENDER SKIP 1
UFI> SELECT DEPARTMENT, GENDER, FACULTY_NAME, SALARY
  2  FROM FACULTY ORDER BY DEPARTMENT, GENDER;

Mon Apr 21 10:52:45 1986                              Page 1
                   SALARY REPORT BY GENDER


DEPARTMENT GENDER FACULTY_NAME_____ _SALARY
ACCOUNTING MALE    JACK NELSON         $35,000

Mon Apr 21 10:52:45 1986                              Page 2
                   SALARY REPORT BY GENDER


DEPARTMENT GENDER FACULTY_NAME_____ _SALARY
COMP SCI   FEMALE WENDY SWIMMER        $45,000
                  AMY DANCER           $34,500

           MALE    RAYMOND J. JOHNSON $40,000

Mon Apr 21 10:52:45 1986                              Page 3
                   SALARY REPORT BY GENDER


DEPARTMENT GENDER FACULTY_NAME_____ _SALARY
HISTORY    MALE   BOB JONES            $28,000
```

The last option on the BREAK ON is the DUP/NODUP option. DUP allows duplicate values in a control break field to be displayed. NODUP allows only the first value of the duplicate value to be displayed. NODUP is the default option.

Control breaks remain in effect until we exit ORACLE, change the value or options with a new BREAK ON command, or clear the control break. The CLEAR BREAK command clears all control breaks currently in effect.

Computing Subtotals

In some cases the user desires subtotals by control breaks on certain numeric fields. This can be accomplished very readily via the COMPUTE SUM OF command. For the COMPUTE SUM OF command to be effective, the BREAK ON command should be activated, and the SELECT command should contain an ORDER BY clause referencing the control break attribute(s).

The format of the COMPUTE SUM OF command is:

```
COMPUTE SUM OF numeric-attribute1 [,numeric-attribute2, , ,]
         ON control-break-attribute1
            [,control-break-attribute2, , ,]
```

To illustrate the use of the COMPUTE SUM OF command, let's assume that we want to generate a control break on the attribute GENDER and produce subtotals of salaries.

```
UFI> BREAK ON GENDER SKIP 2
UFI> COLUMN SALARY FORMAT $999,999
UFI> COMPUTE SUM OF SALARY ON GENDER
UFI> SELECT GENDER, FACULTY_NAME, SALARY FROM FACULTY
   2  ORDER BY GENDER;

Mon Apr 21 10:54:43 1986                              page 1
                   SALARY REPORT BY GENDER


GENDER FACULTY-NAME_____  __SALARY
FEMALE WENDY SWIMMER         $45,000
       AMY DANCER            $34,500
******                       --------
                             $79,500


MALE   RAYMOND J. JOHNSON    $40,000
       BOB JONES             $35,000
       JACK NELSON           $28,000
******                       --------
                             $103,000
```

Note that ORACLE automatically inserts an extra line in the output to improve the readability of subtotals. The line consists of filling the control break field with asterisks and placing dashes below the attribute(s) to be subtotaled.

If we have multiple control breaks, subtotals will be generated for each subtotal.

```
UFI> BREAK ON DEPARTMENT SKIP PAGE ON GENDER SKIP 1
UFI> COMPUTE SUM OF SALARY ON DEPARTMENT, GENDER
UFI> SELECT DEPARTMENT, GENDER, FACULTY-NAME, SALARY
  2  FROM FACULTY ORDER BY DEPARTMENT, GENDER;


Mon Apr 21 10:55:00 1986                              Page 1
                    SALARY REPORT BY GENDER

DEPARTMENT GENDER FACULTY_NAME_____ _SALARY
ACCOUNTING MALE    JACK NELSON         $35,000
           ******                      -------
                                       $35,000
Mon Apr 21 10:55:00 1986                              Page 2
                    SALARY REPORT BY GENDER

DEPARTMENT GENDER FACULTY_NAME_____ _SALARY
COMP SCI   FEMALE WENDY SWIMMER        $45,000
                  AMY DANCER           $34,500
           ******                      $79,500

           MALE   RAYMOND J, JOHNSON  $40,000
           ******                      $40,000

                                       $40,000


Mon Apr 21 10:55:00 1986                              Page 3
                    SALARY REPORT BY GENDER

DEPARTMENT GENDER FACULTY_NAME_____ _SALARY
HISTORY    MALE   BOB JONES            $28,000
           ******                      $28,000
```

To deactivate the COMPUTE SUM OF command, we would use the CLEAR COMPUTE command.

CONTROLLING THE FORMATTING OF OUTPUT PAGES

We have previously discussed several formatting commands for arranging the display of output. Remember that these formats apply to output that is spooled to any file. Just to refresh your memory a bit, here are some of the formatting commands that we have previously introduced. They could be used in conjunction with the internal report writer.

The first is the COLUMN command that allows the user to do such formatting as changing the heading of attributes, placing format masks on various types of output, allowing either the wrapping or truncation for character fields too long to fit in the specified output format, and specifying output strings to display if the value of an attribute is null. Examples of the COLUMN command are:

```
COLUMN SALARY HEADING MONEY FORMAT $999,999.99
COLUMN STUDENT-NAME FORMAT A10 TRUNC
COLUMN SALARY NULL 'NONE'
```

The second command is the SET SPACE command that allows us to change the number of horizontal spaces between attributes. An example of the SET SPACE command follows.

```
SET SPACE 5
```

The third command is the SET LINESIZE command. This command allows the user to change the default line width. Remember that this value is set to 80 for terminals. The following SET LINESIZE command will change the linesize to 132 characters.

```
SET LINESIZE 132
```

The fourth command is the SET PAUSE command that will stop terminal screen scrolling. This command will freeze the terminal screen until the user presses the ENTER/RETURN key. At this point another screen is filled with output until the ENTER/RETURN is pressed again. Here are several examples of the SET PAUSE command.

```
SET PAUSE ON
SET PAUSE OFF
SET PAUSE "Press the ENTER key to view more data"
```

The SET PAGESIZE Command

The SET PAGESIZE command is used to define how many lines of output are to be used to display the lines of a report after the attribute headings are displayed. The command

```
SET PAGESIZE 5
```

allows a maximum of five detail lines to be displayed after the attribute headings are displayed.

The default value for PAGESIZE is 19.

The SET NEWPAGE Command

The SET NEWPAGE command is used to tell ORACLE how many blank lines are to be displayed when it reaches end-of-page as defined by the PAGESIZE command. The command

```
                    SET NEWPAGE 5
```

''prints'' five blank lines on each output page after the last line of output has been displayed.

The default value of NEWPAGE is 1. If the value of NEWPAGE is set to zero, ORACLE generates a formfeed immediately after the last output line of each page is displayed. The value of NEWPAGE does not affect BTITLE.

The following is an example of the use of NEWPAGE and PAGESIZE.

```
UFI> SET PAGESIZE 5
UFI> SET NEWPAGE 3
UFI> BREAK ON GENDER SKIP PAGE
UFI> TTITLE 'SALARY|REPORT|BY|GENDER'
UFI> BTITLE 'NOT FOR PUBLIC DISTRIBUTION'
UFI> COMPUTE SUM OF SALARY ON GENDER
UFI> COLUMN SALARY FORMAT $999,999
UFI> SELECT GENDER, FACULTY_NAME, SALARY FROM FACULTY
  2   ORDER BY GENDER;


Mon Apr 21 10:58:15 1986                                    Page 1
                              SALARY
                              REPORT
                                BY
                              GENDER

GENDER FACULTY_NAME_____    _SALARY
FEMALE WENDY SWIMMER         $45,000
       AMY DANCER            $34,500
******                       $79,500


Mon Apr 21 10:58:15 1986                                    Page 2
                              SALARY
                              REPORT
                                BY
                              GENDER

GENDER FACULTY_NAME_____    _SALARY
MALE   RAYMOND J. JOHNSON     $40,000
       BOB JONES              $35,000
       JACK NELSON           _$38,000
******                       $103,000
```

SUMMARY

This chapter was dedicated to a discussion of the various formatting aspects of the ORACLE internal report writer. Top and bottom titles, control breaks, control break sums, and formatting were introduced. Various page size options were also discussed.

Now that you have completed this chapter, you should be familiar with the following terms, concepts, and commands.

A. The internal report writer   **D.** COMPUTE SUM OF

B. TTITLE and BTITLE   **E.** SET PAGESIZE

C. BREAK ON   **F.** SET NEWPAGE

EXERCISES

1. Explain what is meant by control breaks. When would you want to use them?

2. Using the PERSONNEL table created in Chapter 11, create a report with control breaks on TITLE-OR-RANK. Double space all control break output. Compute the sum of salary by TITLE-OR-RANK. The report page heading should be as follows:

```
<Time  and  date>        PERSONNEL                              Page  n
                         SALARY
                         REPORT
```

15

Designing Relational Databases

PURPOSE: This chapter illustrates the concepts that the database designer will have to consider when attempting to design an actual database. Such things as recognizing entities, relationships, and characteristics as well as how to represent them in a database are presented. Various types of dependencies and the concept of normalization are also discussed. An overall design plan is presented at the end of the chapter.

Now that we have introduced all the ORACLE structural commands and illustrated how they can be used to build tables and views, it is now time to show how commands can be integrated to produce a viable database. It is easy to become enamored with a database management system and believe that just because it has some neat features, it will somehow produce well-designed databases. This simply is not true. A database management system will only allow us to utilize the data stored in the database and nothing else. To be able to use the data efficiently and effectively, we must produce a well-designed database.

This chapter is devoted to discussing the design of databases. If the previous chapters of this text have been rather specific (the syntax of the various commands is very specific), then this chapter will be very general. There is no one method (as evidenced by the number of books, chapters in books, and journal articles dedicated to the topic) that is "best" for designing databases. If there were one best method, it would be the only one described in books and articles and every designer would use it. Database designers use whatever technique(s) that work(s) for them. In this chapter we will focus on some concepts that we feel the database designer should consider when designing a database. Our examples will use the SQL commands, but this should not negate the idea that the same concepts could be used by the designers of databases utilizing any other database management system. Database design methods are basically generic, but since this book is oriented toward ORACLE, we will couch our discussion in terms of ORACLE concepts.

By design of databases, we are referring strictly to the logical design of databases. (Physical database design is a separate topic and, for the most part, is system dependent.) We will refer to the overall structure of the database as the schema. This includes all the tables, views, attributes, domains, integrity rules, and so on of the database. Remember that a database contains all the data that we wish to keep on one topic. A database may consist of only one table. (Think about a table that contains student test score data for the purpose of keeping track of student grades. Since this is the only information that an instructor would want to keep on a student, we could call this a database.) However, this small database would usually be considered a file management system, even though it was implemented through a database management system. When we refer to a database in this chapter, we are referring to something more complex than a one table database.

INTRODUCTION TO DESIGN

When a computer program is designed, the general approach that is usually taken to design the program is the so-called systems approach. This approach consists of viewing the program and all of its parts as a system. A common schematic of a system is presented in Figure 15.1.

In this approach, we would begin the design process by deciding what output was desired. The next step would be to decide what input we would need to produce the desired output. The final step would be to design some code to convert the input to the desired output. Note that the CONTROL function (error checking, integrity checking, etc.) was pervasive over the entire process.

This is a very simple design mechanism, and when used in conjunction with software engineering principles, such as abstraction, modularity, portability, and

Figure 15.1   A Schematic of a System

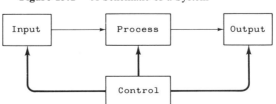

information hiding, it works very well in designing programs. However, the technique will not work in the design of databases, the reason being that we are not designing a process (program), we are designing the representation of data. Central to using the systems approach is that we know or can define the needed output very clearly. In designing a database, we really do not know what output all the current and future users of the database will desire. We have to be able to design a database that is flexible enough so that all users can utilize the database to its fullest. We also must consider that future users will want to use the database for purposes that have not been considered yet. Database designers cannot be expected to forecast accurately *all* future users' needs, although the better the designer can do this, the better overall database design they will (theoretically) produce. The only thing that the database designer can do is to design the database in a manner that considers access flexibility, potential update problems, and access speed constraints. Unfortunately, the solutions to these problems are not mutually exclusive. For example, if we design our database for maximum speed of access, we may generate some problems with updating tuples. This is illustrated in the section of this chaper on normalization.

Overview of the Design Process

The art of designing a database is an iterative one. Usually when a database is being designed, an initial design is developed and that design is implemented. After a period of time the original structure of the database will have to be altered. Reasons for these alterations include

1. **Changes in the information needs of the user community**. Consider the student database that we have been using as our example database. Suppose that the university decides that the data that we have currently stored in the attribute ADDRESS is no longer satisfactory. They decide that they need the hometown, state, and zip code stored for each student. We will now have to add these additional attributes somewhere in the database.

2. **Changes in the rules of the organization**. If we view the FACULTY table, we can see, by the structure of the table, that each faculty member can only be a member of one department:

FACULTY (FAC-ID, FACULTY-NAME, DEPARTMENT, GENDER, SALARY)

The very nature of the relational model prohibits us from storing more than one value in an attribute.

Suppose that the university changes its rules and allows faculty members to belong to more than one department. Perhaps our new table would look as follows:

```
FACULTY (FAC-ID, FACULTY-NAME, DEPT1, DEPT2, GENDER, SALARY)
```

What if a faculty member wanted to teach in three departments? Do we keep adding attributes to the tables? Probably not. We would now have to alter our design to create tables that would look like this:

```
FACULTY (FAC-ID, FACULTY-NAME, GENDER, SALARY)

MEMBER-OF (FAC-ID, DEPARTMENT)
```

3. **Changes in state or federal laws**. Suppose that the federal government decided that we could no longer record an employee's gender in his or her personnel records. To be in conformance with this new law, we would have to omit the attribute in the FACULTY table.

```
FACULTY (FAC-ID, FACULTY-NAME, DEPARTMENT, TITLE-OR-RANK, SALARY)
```

4. **Changes in the table structure due to the normalization procedure.** This will be illustrated later in the chapter.
5. **We have used incomplete and/or inaccurate information to develop the design of the database**. Our design will be only as good as the data we gather to assist us in the design. Design of database involves a lot of research work. Once we have acquired a piece of information concerning the design of the database, we should make every effort to verify its accuracy and validity. This seems like a very obvious thing to do, but because of time, cost, and other considerations sometimes is not done.
6. **We have come up with a bad initial design**. We hope that this will not happen, but maybe because of organizational politics, time constraints, cost constraints and/or incompetence of the designer(s), the initial database design is unusable. Unfortunately this might not be apparent until after the database has been put into production.

Changes to the structure of the database should be kept to an absolute minimum due to the tremendous overhead associated with restructuring databases. Think about what happens when we have to restructure. We must

1. Back up our current database via EXPORT commands.
2. Create the new tables with the necessary modifications.
3. Copy data (via INSERT/SELECT commands) into the new tables.
4. Possibly add data for the new attributes included in the new tables.
5. Drop the old tables.
6. Adjust any affected views accordingly.
7. Create new views to ensure data independence.

If changes do need to be made to the structure of the database, they should be made by the database administrator after careful consideration of the consequences. The database should naturally be closed to users while restructuring commands are being executed.

After a certain period of time the structure of most (but, unfortunately, not all) databases should stabilize and restructuring will become less and less a problem.

How Databases Are Designed

The design of a complex database is a very long and tedious task. Depending on the size of the database, the process could take anywhere from a few weeks to several years to complete. There have been several techniques developed to assist the database designer in constructing an acceptable database. No matter which technique is used, several basic steps must be followed. We will list those steps here and discuss them throughout the remainder of this chapter.

1. Determine what data is to be represented in the database.
2. Form some type logical model of the data to determine the relationships between the data.
3. Convert this logical model to the format of the database structure that you will be using.
4. Create the schema definition via CREATE TABLE, VIEW, CLUSTER, and INDEX commands.
5. Load the database.
6. Monitor usage of the database to determine if any tuning is needed.
7. Attempt to determine the validity of any user "suggested" changes to the overall structure of the database.

Even though the list is fairly short, it usually involves a tremendous amount of work and thought on the database designer's part if it is to be done correctly. Once the database is implemented, there is no guarantee that the designer has done it correctly. This is why we have referred to the design process as an iterative one. If the design does not work, it must be modified. This is usually a very difficult decision to make for it is time consuming, and costly, and the database designer(s) may have to admit that he made a mistake. One possible solution to this is to create a small version of the database, commonly called a prototype, and utilize it for a period of time to work the "bugs" out of the initial design. Once the prototype database seems to be acceptable, the production database can be created.

The Database Design Team

When we refer to designing a database, we are referring to some type of team effort. The design team usually consists of the following people:

1. *The database administrator.* This person's job is to lend technical database and database package expertise to the team.
2. *The system specialist.* Since databases are constructed to support systems, then a person(s) knowledgeable about that system should be included to lend system expertise.
3. *System users.* The database is being constructed to be used by these people, so some of them must be included on the design team to ensure that the system will produce what users want it to.
4. Systems analysts and programmers. These are the people that will design and implement the system around the database, so their input is needed.

Once this group is formed, a design leader is selected, probably the person representing database administration. This group will put in many long hard hours of work attempting to develop an acceptable and usable database design.

DETERMINING WHAT DATA IS TO BE REPRESENTED IN THE DATABASE

This first phase of database design is dedicated simply to getting familiar with the system that we are attempting to construct the database for. We will want to familiarize ourselves with such things as system terminology, system data, users of the system, and other relevant system matters. Remember that databases are constructed to supplement some type of information system. Databases are not built for the sake of building a database. Because of the time and financial investment they take, they must be economically useful for the organization.

In designing a database, there are two type of data scenarios that usually occur.

Converting an Existing System to a Database-Oriented System

The first scenario considered is one in which data associated with the system that currently exists, but in some nondatabase form. We want to convert it to a database so that we can get more usage and information from our current system. An example might be the university's payroll system that is currently implemented through a series of COBOL programs that manipulate a series of conventional master files.

Constructing a Database for a Completely New System

The second scenario is a new system that is not currently implemented. An example might be a traffic management system that keeps track of the students and faculty members who have cars registered on campus, which vehicles have unpaid vehicle fines, and so on. The first system, described in the preceding section, is more of a conversion and the second is a database that must be designed from scratch.

Determining which data is to be represented in the two scenarios is a bit different. In the system that must be converted, most of the data that will be represented in the database has already been gathered and defined. In the new system, the data that is to be represented must be determined.

The data gathering stage is sometimes referred to as "creating the data dictionary".

Sources of Data

There are many sources of data on data (usually referred to as metadata). If the database is a conversion from another system, then the currently existing system is probably the first source of metadata. System users can usually contribute useful data as to what information they need that is not being produced by the current system. System users can also indicate what information being produced by the current system is erroneous or is being produced in an unusable form. Sample reports produced by the system can give the designer an idea of what users will be using the current system. System specialists can also provide information on what data should be represented in the system. For example, if we were converting a university payroll, the university accountants would certainly be consulted concerning system data. System specialists can also direct the designer to other sources of data, such as the legal aspects of the system, feelings on any new organization policies that could affect the structure of the data, and so on.

Sources of data for new systems may not be quite so plentiful. The data for the new system probably has not been considered very much. The new system has probably been thought of in terms of what information it can provide for users, not in terms of what data is needed to produce this information. The best sources of data on new systems are system specialists, potential users of the system, and relevant literature. The system specialist can provide information as to what data is relevant to the system and how it can be represented. The user can provide data on what information they expect the new system to provide. Relevant literature can provide the designer with information as to how other similar databases were designed (assuming that databases similar to the one we are trying to design have been implemented).

DEVELOPING A LOGICAL MODEL OF THE DATA

Once we have become familiar with what data is needed in our database, we should then begin to ascertain the relationships that exist between our data. This step is called **creating the logical model of the data**. This task concerns itself with the semantics of the data. For this reason this process can also be called "semantic modeling." There have been several techniques developed to assist in performing this task.

The E-R Model (Entity-Relationship Model)[2] is a tool developed by Dr. Peter Chen to assist in creating the logical model of data. The E-R model is widely used as a tool for assisting database designers in determining the relationships between various system components. This model is described in several papers written by Dr. Chen. Once the E-R model is constructed, it must be converted into the relational schema.

The RM/T Model[3] developed by Dr. Codd is another tool developed to assist database designers. The T stands for Tasmania (really, it does) which is where Dr. Codd first presented a paper that encompassed his design ideas. This model was somewhat simplified by Date in his book A Guide to DB2[4]. The model is usually referred to as the *Extended Relational Model.*

It really doesn't make any difference which of these techniques or any other techniques that you use to develop the logical model of data as long as you understand the technique and it works for you. Creating the logical model of data for the system is an extremely important phase of database design and should not be taken lightly. It is a lot easier to correct errors at the design level than after the design has been implemented.

The Extended Relational Model

The technique that we have chosen to illustrate is the Extended Relational Model originally developed by Codd and simplified by Date.

Entities, Properties, and Relationships

To understand this model, we must understand some basic terminology associated with it. An entity is any distinguishable object. An entity may be something tangible such as a student, a faculty member, or a building, or it may be intangible such as a course, a degree, or a mood. Entities are essentially what databases contain. Each entity must be distinguished from all other entities of that type. For example, a student would have a student number or identifier, a faculty member would have a faculty number or identifier, a building would have a name or number, a degree would have a name, and so on. The unique identifiers naturally become the primary keys of the entities.

Each entity can have properties. Properties are single-valued facts about entities. A student has one gender, one major, one address, and so on. A faculty has one salary, teaches in one department, has one gender, and so on. Properties are determined by the semantics of the data. For example, if a student can have more than one major, then major would not be considered a property.

Entities do not exist in a vacuum. Therefore, a relationship is an association between two or more entities. These relationships take the form of 1:n or m:n. The faculty-student advisement process usually forms a 1:n relationship. We will assume that each faculty member advises N students. The 1:n indicates that a student is advised by only one faculty member. The m:n relationship is illustrated by the instructural relationship of students to faculty. A student can be taught by M faculty members and a faculty member can teach N students. Date refers to 1:n relationships as designations and m:n relationships as associations.

Designations are generally not considered entities in their own right although there is nothing wrong with doing so. Designations designate the existence of other entities. For example, if we have faculty members that exist in a Computer Science Department, then the existence of the department designates that there are (or will be) faculty members assigned in that department. Properties of the designation are generally regarded as properties of the designating entity. For example, the faculty member's salary can be considered a property of the relationship between department and faculty member, for the faculty member's salary is part of the department's wage budget.

Kernels, Associations, and Characteristics

Entities can be grouped into one of two classes. These classes are described in the paragraphs that follow.

Existence Independent Entities: Kernels.   Kernels are independent entities. This means that they can exist without any supporting data. Examples of kernels might be students and faculty. Kernels are the base unit of data in databases.

Existence Dependent Entities: Associations.   Existence-dependent entities depend on kernels for meaning. Associations are **m:n** relationships (or **m:n:o**) among entities. Since associations indicate relationships among entities, they are existence dependent on other entities. Since associations are entities, they may have properties and/or participate in other associations. Examples of an association might be the COURSE table that contains the **m:n** relationship between students and faculty. Note that each tuple in the COURSE table is existence dependent upon both the STUDENT table and the FACULTY table. Although we have not placed the attribute in the COURSE table, CURRENT-LETTER-GRADE would be considered a property of this association. If a student withdrew from a class, there would be no use for the tuple occurrence in the table.

```
COURSE (COURSE-ID, COURSE-TITLE, SECTION-NO, FAC-ID, STU-ID,
        CURRENT-LETTER-GRADE)
```

Describers of Entities; Characteristics.   Characteristics are used to describe or qualify entities. Characteristics are multivalued properties of entities. Characteristics are also existence dependent on other entities. An example of a characteristic might be a social club table. If we assumed that the powers that be of our university allow a student to be a member of only one club, then we would simply add an attribute to the table as the attribute would be considered a property.

```
STUDENT (STU-ID, STUDENT-NAME, ADDRESS, BIRTHDATE, GENDER, CLUB)
```

However, if a student could be a member of more than one social club, we would have to create a characteristic table as follows.

```
STUDENT (STU-ID, STUDENT-NAME, ADDRESS, BIRTHDATE, GENDER)

CLUBS (STU-ID, CLUB-NAME)
```

Note that CLUBS.STU-ID becomes a foreign key. The table CLUBS is existence dependent on the table student. If a student withdraws from the university, and we delete his tuple from the STUDENT table, there is no reason to keep his related tuples in the CLUBS table.

Perhaps it is easier to determine which entities are associations and which are characteristics and then by default whatever entities are left become kernels.

CONVERTING THE LOGICAL MODEL
TO THE PROPER DATABASE STRUCTURE

Once the composition of the database is understood, we must then convert this logical model to a database structure—the hierarchical, network, or relational models. However, since we feel that the relational model is the best model for implementing databases and this book is heavily oriented toward ORACLE, we will use the structure of the relational model.

To convert the logical model to the relational model, we will have to convert the kernels, associations, characteristics, properties, and so on to elements of the relational model.

All entities map directly into tables. Kernels become tables with the primary keys noted. Properties become attributes of tables. Associations become tables with the primary key(s) noted. Since associations represent **m:n** relationships between tables, they will also contain foreign keys to the kernel tables that they link together. Designations become tables with the primary keys and foreign key links back to the "owning" entity. Characteristics also become base tables with the appropriate primary keys. Characteristics will also contain foreign keys to other entities. When we get finished converting our logical model to the relational model, the tables should look like this:

KERNELS:

```
Table-Kernel-1 ( Primary Key, Property(s) )
Table-Kernel-2 ( Primary Key, Property(s) )
Table-Kernel-n ( Primary Key, Property(s) )
```

ASSOCIATIONS:

```
Table-Assoc-1  ( Primary Key, Foreign-Key-1, Foreign-Key-2,
                 [Property(s)] )
Table-Assoc-2  ( Primary Key, Foreign-Key-1, Foreign-Key-2,
                 [Property(s)] )
Table-Assoc-n  ( Primary Key, Foreign-Key-1, Foreign-Key-2,
                 [Property(s)] )
```

DESIGNATIONS:

```
Table-Desg-1   ( Primary Key/Foreign-Key *, Property(s) )
Table-Desg-2   ( Primary Key/Foreign-Key *, Property(s) )
Table-Desg-n   ( Primary Key/Foreign-Key *, Property(s) )
```

CHARACTERISTICS:

```
Table-Char-1   ( Primary Key/Foreign-Key *, Property(s) )
Table-Char-2   ( Primary Key/Foreign-Key *, Property(s) )
Table-Char-n   ( Primary Key/Foreign-Key *, Property(s) )
```

CREATING THE SCHEMA DEFINITION

Once all the tables and their associated attributes, including domains, have been discerned, they must be further defined. This can be done via some table definition form. One such format is

```
Domain-name1 Rules-for-domain
Domain-name2 Rules-for-domain
Domain-namen Rules-for-domain

Table name:
    Primary-Key:
    Foreign-Keys:           For table:

    Attribute1: Data-type Size Domain
    Attribute2: Data-type Size Domain
    Attributen: Data-type Size Domain
```

To illustrate this form, let us consider the STUDENT table and the COURSE table.

---

* The foreign key will be a subset of the primary key.

DOMAIN DEFINITIONS:

FACULTY-ID-DOMAIN	First letter of the faculty member's last name followed by a two digit integer.
STUDENT-ID-DOMAIN	First letter is an S followed by three digit integer.
STUDENT-NAME-DOMAIN	Any valid student name up to 17 characters in length.
ADDRESS-DOMAIN	Any valid street address up to 10 characters in length. It is assumed that all students live in the same town, so a city and state designation is not needed.
BD-DOMAIN	Any valid date of birth between January 1, 1900 and December 31, 1970. It is a school policy not to take anyone born before 1900 and no one born after 1970.
GENDER-DOMAIN	Either male or female.
COURSE-ID-DOMAIN	A 3-character departmental abbreviation followed by a three-digit positive integer followed by an optional ''L'' if the course is a laboratory course.
COURSE-NAME-DOMAIN	Any valid course name limited to 15 characters. A list of valid course titles is found in the table VALID-COURSES.
COURSE-SECTION-DOMAIN	Any positive integer between 1 and 99.

TABLE DEFINITIONS:

```
Table name: STUDENT
   Primary-Key: STU-ID
   Foreign-Keys: NONE


   Attribute___:_Type_&_Size_:_Domain_____
   STU-ID       : CHAR 4      : STUDENT-ID-DOMAIN
   STUDENT-NAME: CHAR 17      : STUDENT-NAME-DOMAIN
   ADDRESS      : CHAR 10     : ADDRESS-DOMAIN
   BIRTHDATE    : DATE        : BD-DOMAIN
   GENDER       : CHAR 6      : GENDER-DOMAIN

Table name: COURSE
   Primary-Key: COURSE-ID, FAC-ID, STU-ID
   Foreign-Keys: STU-ID  For Table: STUDENT
                 FAC-ID  For Table: FACULTY
```

```
Attribute___:_Type_&_Size_:_Domain_____
COURSE-ID    : CHAR 7      : COURSE-ID-DOMAIN
COURSE-NAME  : CHAR 15     : COURSE-NAME-DOMAIN
SECTION-NO   : NUMBER 2    : SECTION-DOMAIN
STU-ID       : CHAR 4      : STUDENT-ID-DOMAIN
FAC-ID       : CHAR 3      : FACULTY-ID-DOMAIN
```

CONVERTING THE SCHEMA DEFINITION TO ORACLE CONCEPTS

Once the tables have been designed, the base tables are fairly easy to construct. The ORACLE CREATE TABLE command is used to specify each table and attribute value. If the table contains a computed attribute, then an ORACLE view will have to be created. Since the tables that we will be creating are considered base tables, be sure to specify NOT NULL and create a unique index for each attribute in the primary key. Domains can not be specified directly in the ORACLE syntax.

LOADING THE TABLES

At first the initial loading of the data tables might seem like a simple thing. If the data for the tables currently exists on some type computer-readable medium, we can use the ORACLE bulk data loader (ODL) to bulk load our tables. Although this is a fairly fast and efficient method of initially loading our data tables, it can open the door for data contamination. There is no way to use ODL to perform domain checking or referential integrity checks on data. The NOT NULL clause specified on the attributes in the primary key will perform the entity integrity check. The unique index will ensure that the value of the primary key is unique.

There are two methods of handling domain checking. The first is to write a host language program to load the data tables and perform domain and integrity checks on the data as it is loaded into the tables from within the program. The second method is to write a host language program to pretest the "raw data file" that ODL uses as input, then use ODL to bulk load the data tables. The latter method has the basic disadvantage of processing the data twice, but the advantage of only tying up ORACLE for a minimum of time. The former method will allow us initially to load the majority of our raw data file records very quickly, but all rejected records must be run through the program again, after corrections are made. This process may unnecessarily tie up ORACLE for an unwanted period of time.

PERFORMANCE MONITORING

Once the database is placed into production, response times should be monitored very carefully so as to tune the database to its most efficient level. Some database management systems have monitoring mechanisms built into their systems, and all the database administrator has to do is turn them on. (The ORACLE Corporation has not implemented this feature into ORACLE.) Since performance monitoring requires the system to gather and record extra statistics, performance monitoring itself slows down system response time.

Suppose the database administrator monitors system performance and finds performance to be rather slow. He should then try to determine what is causing system performance to be slow. The ORACLE database administrator has two mechanisms at his disposal to speed up system response time.

The first is to create additional indexes on attributes. The first set of attributes to review for possible creation of indexes are those that are designated as foreign keys. Since foreign keys are used for join conditions and the join command is the slowest command to execute, if we could find a way to speed it up, we would naturally speed up our response time. However, remember that the creation of indexes creates B*-trees and they take up secondary storage space.

The second thing that we can do to speed up system response time is to use clusters. Remember that clusters are used primarily to speed up JOIN conditions. This feature places tuples with common values of an attribute on the same physical page if possible. This should have the system make less physical reads when attempting to retrieve data.

Tuning a database is a never ending task for database administrators. System performance should constantly be monitored in an attempt to tune system response to be as fast as it can be for users.

USER DESIRED CHANGES TO THE DATABASE

No matter how well a database is designed, as soon as it is put into production, some user(s) will be unhappy with the information that they are able to discern from it. This means that they will request that a change be made in the system. It is now up to the database administrator to evaluate the request(s) and honor, reject, or "put it on hold" for the time being. Once too many requests come in from users, the design team must begin to consider whether to restructure the database. In some cases the initial database design that is implemented becomes only a prototype for the actual database that finally evolves.

ADDITIONAL CONSIDERATIONS FOR FOREIGN KEYS

Since foreign keys are used to link associations and characteristics to kernels, if a change or a deletion is made to the target of a foreign key, that change must be reflected in the foreign key. For each foreign key, questions concerning the update and deletion of foreign keys must be answered during the design phase.

Deletion of the Target of a Foreign Key

To illustrate this condition, let's consider the association among the STUDENT, FACULTY, and COURSE tables.

```
STUDENT (STU-ID, STUDENT-NAME, ADDRESS, BIRTHDATE, GENDER)
FACULTY (FAC-ID, FACULTY-NAME, DEPARTMENT, GENDER, SALARY)
COURSE (COURSE-ID, COURSE-TITLE, SECTION-NO, STU-ID, FAC-ID)
```

Notice that COURSE.STU-ID and COURSE.FAC-ID are two foreign keys to the STUDENT and FACULTY tables.

Consider what would happen if we deleted student Wendy Jones from the university. What effect should that have on Wendy's tuples in the COURSE table? We have three options.

The first option is that we could set the value of STU-ID in each of Wendy's tuples to NULL (called the NULLIFIES option). This would only make sense if we wanted to maintain space in each of the three classes by keeping a "spot" in the class open by setting the student ID to NULL. In this case if we executed the following SQL SELECT command, we would get a count of the number of slots allocated to the class.

```
SELECT COURSE_TITLE, COUNT (*)
FROM COURSE GROUP BY COURSE_TITLE
```

If we wanted to determine a count of the number of students actually in the class, we could issue the following SQL command.

```
SELECT COURSE_TITLE, COUNT (STU-ID)
FROM COURSE GROUP BY COURSE_TITLE
```

If we wanted to determine how many empty slots there were in the courses, we could issue the following command.

```
SELECT COURSE_TITLE, COUNT(*)-COUNT(STU_ID)
FROM COURSE GROUP BY COURSE_TITLE
```

When another student wants to enter the class, all that would have to be done is to change the value of COURSE.STU-ID to that student's STU-ID in any tuple where COURSE.STU-ID was equal to NULL.

The second option would be not to allow the student to be deleted from the STUDENT table until she withdraws from all her classes. This is called the RESTRICTS option. If this option were selected, we could not delete the student tuple until all foreign key references to the student were first handled (either the tuple(s) containing the object of the foreign key would be deleted or changed to NULL). In effect we could only delete students who were not taking any classes or students who had withdrawn from all classes.

The third option would automatically cause tuples containing the object of foreign keys to be deleted. This is called the CASCADES option. This means that when the student Wendy Jones' tuple is deleted from the STUDENT table, some mechanism would automatically trigger the delete all the referenced tuples in the COURSE table.

In our school-oriented system only the RESTRICTS or CASCADES option makes sense to us. The NULLIFIES option would not be allowed because it would set part of the primary key of the COURSES table to NULL, and this breaks the entity integrity rule.

Updating the Primary Key of the Target of the Foreign Key

Using the same three tables, what would happen if we wanted to change Wendy Jones' STU-ID to S999? How would we handle the values of the updated foreign key in the COURSE table? Again we have three options.

In the NULLIFIES option, all the foreign key values of S001 (Wendy Jone's original STU-ID) would be set to NULL before the change is made in the STUDENT table. At this point, the value of COURSE.STU-ID could then be changed to S999 or left at NULL, whichever condition occurs in the actual system.

In the RESTRICTS option, the value of STUDENT.STU-ID cannot be changed unless there is no tuple in the COURSE.STU-ID that contains S001. All the tuples in the COURSE table where STU-ID was S001 would have to be deleted (the student would have to drop all her courses before a change could be made in her primary key value) or changed to some other fictitious value (possibly NULL) while the change is made.

In the CASCADES option, when the value so STU-ID is changed in the STUDENT table, it is automatically changed in all the related tuples in the COURSES table.

In our example, the CASCADES option makes the most sense to integrate into our database. Again the entity integrity constraint would not allow us to place a value of NULL into COURSE.STU-ID.

Null Values in Foreign Keys

In certain cases, a NULL value stored in a foreign key is acceptable, and some cases it is not. Consider a characteristic table representing the departments that a professor might be assigned to.

```
FACULTY (FAC-ID, FACULTY-NAME, GENDER, SALARY)

ASSIGNED-TO (FAC-ID, DEPARTMENT-NAME)
```

Notice that ASSIGNED-TO.FAC-ID is a foreign key to the FACULTY table. ASSIGNED-TO is a characteristic table. Let's look at some sample data for each table.

TABLE NAME: FACULTY

```
FAC-ID FACULTY-NAME_____  GENDER SALARY
G05    MIKE GREEN           MALE    43000
J04    AMY JOHNSON          FEMALE  43000
```

```
Table name: ASSIGNED-TO
```

```
FAC-ID DEPARTMENT_____
G05    MANAGEMENT INFO SYS
G05    COMPUTER SCIENCE
J04    MANAGEMENT INFO SYS
J04    COMPUTER SCIENCE
J04    WELDING
```

Does it make sense to have a null value for ASSIGNED-TO.FAC-ID? If we decided to change the value of FAC-ID in a tuple or delete a tuple from the FACULTY table, it would defy logical thinking to set the corresponding value of ASSIGNED-TO.FAC-ID to NULL. This will be true for any characteristic table. Also the only option for handling deletes and changes on characteristic tables that makes sense is CASCADES.

Additional Notation for Specifying Options on Foreign Keys

Date suggests that the method of handling the objects of foreign keys be added to the logical table definition[4]. This could be integrated into our table definition form in the following manner.

DOMAINS:

```
Domain-name1 Rules-for-domain
Domain-name2 Rules-for-domain
Domain-namen Rules-for-domain
```

```
Table Name:
   Primary-Key:
   Foreign-Keys:        For table:
                        NULLS ARE [NOT] ALLOWED
                        Delete (of target) option1 *
                        Update (of target primary key) option2 *
   Attribute1: Data-type Size Domain
   Attribute2: Data-type Size Domain
   Attributen: Data-type Size Domain
```

Using our same example with the COURSE table, our expanded notation would look like this:

* CASCADES, RESTRICTS or NULLIFIES

```
Table name: COURSE
    Primary-Key: COURSE-ID, FAC-ID, STU-ID
    Foreign-Keys: STU-ID  For Table: STUDENT
                         Nulls are not allowed
                         Delete of STU-ID CASCADES
                         Update of STU-ID CASCADES

                  FAC-ID  For Table: FACULTY
                         Nulls are not allowed
                         Delete of FAC-ID CASCADES
                         Update of FAC-ID CASCADES

    Attribute___:_Type_&_Size_:_Domain_____
    COURSE-ID   : CHAR 7      : COURSE-ID-DOMAIN
    COURSE-NAME : CHAR 15     : COURSE-NAME-DOMAIN
    SECTION     : NUMBER 2    : SECTION-DOMAIN
    STU-ID      : CHAR 4      : STUDENT-ID-DOMAIN
    FAC-ID      : CHAR 3      : FACULTY-ID-DOMAIN
```

In the foreign keys STU-ID and FAC-ID, it would be illegal to allow null values for these particular foreign keys because they are also part of the primary key of the COURSE table. Also if the values of STUDENT.STU-ID or FAC-ID are changed or the tuple is deleted, we want these changes cascaded over the STUDENT table and the FACULTY table.

How to Implement These Additional Constraints on Foreign Keys

If we have decided that the value of a foreign key cannot be null, we can simply use the NOT NULL clause in the attribute definition of the CREATE TABLE command.

The CASCADES/RESTRICTS/NULLIFIES options on updates and deletes of targets of foreign keys cannot be directly implemented in ORACLE. The only method of implementing these options is to incorporate them into a data entry/data maintenance program written in a conventional language.

DEPENDENCIES

A dependency is a relationship among attributes. The attributes may be in the same table or different tables. There are several different types of dependencies: functional dependencies, transitive dependencies, multivalued dependencies, and so on. It is important to understand the concept of dependencies for they affect the various normal forms discussed later in this chapter. For this reason, we are presenting them before our discussion of normal forms.

Functional Dependency

The dependency that probably occurs the most times when developing a database design is the functional dependency. The term "functional dependency" has its genesis in the mathematical theory of sets. Functional dependency is concerned with the relationship between two groups of attributes. Let's call the two groups of attributes A and B. Either or both of these sets of attributes can be single valued or multivalued. We say that B is functionally dependent on A if for a given value of A, a unique value of B can be determined. The notation for this functionally dependency is A --> B. This notation is read "A determines B" or "B is functionally dependent on A." A is called the determinant because it determines the value of B. B is called the object of the determinant.

To illustrate functional dependencies further, let's consider our faithful tables.

```
STUDENT (STU-ID, STUDENT-NAME, ADDRESS, BIRTHDATE, GENDER)
```

TABLE NAME: STUDENT

STU-ID	STUDENT-NAME	ADDRESS	BIRTHDATE	GENDER
S001	WENDY JONES	125 MAPLE AVE	25-OCT-65	FEMALE
S002	SAM WALES	3006 NAVAJO CL	10-JAN-60	MALE
S003	CATHY SMITH	1600 PENN AVE	22-FEB-22	FEMALE
S004	DOTTIE STACY	10 DOWNING ST	31-MAR-67	FEMALE
S005	JAY LANGER	4 GOLF COURSE RD	19-APR-65	MALE
S006	AMY LOPEZ	123 SUN RAY RD	10-MAY-64	FEMALE
S007	SAM WATSON	225 TEST DRIVE	09-JUN-63	MALE
S008	TAMMY REDD	113 MANCHESTER	01-JUL-60	FEMALE
S009	TOMMY WADKINS	93 APPLE TREE DR	24-AUG-67	MALE
S010	BEN TREVINO	300 BOWLING ALLEY	30-SEP-66	MALE

As we look over the STUDENT table, we can see many apparent functional dependencies. Since STU-ID is the primary key of the table, by definition it must uniquely identify all other attributes in the table. S001 uniquely identifies the student whose name is WENDY JONES, who lives at 125 MAPLE AVE, was born on October 25, 1967, and is a FEMALE. STU-ID S009 uniquely identifies the student whose name is TOMMY WADKINS, who lives on 93 APPLE TREE DR, was born on August 24, 1967, and is a MALE. Therefore, we can say that STUDENT-NAME, ADDRESS, BIRTHDATE, and GENDER are all functionally dependent upon STU-ID or that STU-ID determines STUDENT-NAME, ADDRESS, BIRTH-DATE, and GENDER. These functional dependencies are noted as follows.

```
STU-ID --> STUDENT-NAME
STU-ID --> ADDRESS
STU-ID --> BIRTHDATE
STU-ID --> GENDER
```

or

```
STU-ID --> STUDENT-NAME, ADDRESS, BIRTHDATE, GENDER
```

If we look a little more closely, we notice that all of the students have unique names and, therefore, all attributes appear to be functionally dependent on STUDENT-NAME. However, common sense tells us that sooner or later, we will get two students with the same name. When this happens, STUDENT-NAME will not uniquely identify the other table attributes. The same could be said about the attribute AD-DRESS. Even though the current tuples in our table appear to indicate that each student resides at a unique address, intuition tells us that this will probably not always be the case (think about a married couple going to school). Even though everyone appears to have a unique birthday, that will not always be the case.

In considering our simple example, it becomes obvious that functional dependency is a semantic concept. We must be able to recognize not only the current state of the database but future states of the database when determining functional dependency.

The foregoing example illustrated a single-value attribute being functionally dependent on another single-value attribute. This does not have to always be true. Consider the situation where ADDRESS would consist of the attributes STREET-ADDRESS, CITY, STATE, and ZIP-CODE. We would have functional dependency between STU-ID and the multiple attributes STREET-ADDRESS, CITY, STATE, and ZIP-CODE.

```
STU-ID --> STREET-ADDRESS, CITY, STATE, ZIP-CODE
```

Note that even though STREET-ADDRESS, CITY, STATE, and ZIP-CODE are individual attributes, they can be considered as a group attributes.

The determinant can also be a composite of several attributes.

```
COURSE  (COURSE-ID, COURSE-TITLE, SECTION-NO, STU-ID, FAC-ID)
```

TABLE NAME: COURSE

COURSE-ID	COURSE-TITLE	SECTION	STU-ID	FAC-ID
CSC100	INTRODUCTION TO COMPUTING	1	S001	J01
CSC100	INTRODUCTION TO COMPUTING	2	S002	S01
CSC200	PASCAL PROGRAMMING	1	S001	D01
CSC200	PASCAL PROGRAMMING	2	S003	S01
ACC200	PRINCIPLES OF ACCOUNTING I	1	S001	J02
ACC201	PRINCIPLES OF ACCOUNTING II	1	S004	J02
HIS200	HISTORY OF PIROGUES	1	S005	N01

Note that the composite determinant COURSE-ID + STU-ID + FAC-ID uniquely determines the value of SECTION.

```
COURSE-ID, STU-ID, FAC-ID --> SECTION
```

Full Functional Dependence

Full functional dependence is only relevant with composite determinants. If we must use all the attributes of the composite determinant to identify its object uniquely, we have full functional dependency. Let us consider the COURSE table. It has a composite determinant of COURSE-ID+STU-ID+FAC-ID. Notice that we only need the attribute COURSE-ID to determine the value of COURSE-TITLE. Therefore, we do not need the complete composite determinant to determine the value of COURSE-TITLE. (Note: This will cause a problem that we will identify and solve later in this chapter.)

Transitive Dependency

Transitive dependency exists when we have intermediate dependency. For example, assume that we have three attributes or groups of attributes called A, B, and C. Let us further assume that we have recognized the following functional dependencies (A determines B and B determines C).

$$A \rightarrow B$$
$$B \rightarrow C$$

This means that we have the following transitive dependency.

$$A \rightarrow B \rightarrow C$$

To illustrate the concept of transitive dependency, we will have to add two new rules to the hiring practices at our university:

1. There are only two departments allowed in our university: Computer Science and Accounting.
2. Only female faculty members can teach in the Computer Science Department, and only male faculty members can teach in the Accounting Department.

These new rules are reflected in our FACULTY table.

```
FACULTY (FAC-ID, FACULTY-NAME, DEPARTMENT, GENDER, SALARY)
```

TABLE NAME: FACULTY

FAC-ID	FACULTY-NAME	DEPARTMENT	GENDER	SALARY
W01	EMMA D. GREG	COMP SCI	FEMALE	40000
S01	WENDY SWIMMER	COMP SCI	FEMALE	45000
D01	AMY DANCER	COMP SCI	FEMALE	34500
J02	BOB JONES	ACCOUNTING	MALE	35000
N01	BOB WHALES	ACCOUNTING	MALE	28000

We now have the following functional dependencies.

```
        FAC-ID --> DEPARTMENT
        DEPARTMENT --> GENDER
```

These functional dependencies yield the following transitive dependency.

```
    FAC-ID --> DEPARTMENT --> GENDER
```

We used just two departments in our illustration to keep it simple. Actually, we could have allowed many different departments in the example. We would still have transitive dependencies as long as the two functional dependencies,

```
        FAC-ID --> DEPARTMENT
        DEPARTMENT --> GENDER
```

hold true.

(Note: This type dependency also generates problems for database designers. These problems and their solutions are explored later in this chapter.)

Multivalued Dependency

Multivalued dependencies are concerned with attempting to represent many-to-many relationships (m:n) in tables. Remember that many-to-many relationships are also called *associations*. For example, if our university allowed professors to teach in more than one department, we would have an m:n relationship between department and faculty member. A department can have many faculty members, and a faculty member can "belong" to many departments. Multivalued dependencies are denoted as follows.

```
            A -->-> B
```

To illustrate this type relationship, our original FACULTY table

```
FACULTY (FAC-ID, FACULTY-NAME, DEPARTMENT, GENDER, SALARY)
```

TABLE NAME: FACULTY

```
FAC-ID  FACULTY-NAME_____  DEPARTMENT  GENDER  SALARY
 J01    RAYMOND J. JOHNSON  COMP SCI    MALE    40000
 S01    WENDY SWIMMER       COMP SCI    FEMALE  45000
 D01    AMY DANCER          COMP SCI    FEMALE  34500
 J02    BOB JONES           ACCOUNTING  MALE    35000
 N01    JACK NELSON         HISTORY     MALE    28000
```

would have to be decomposed (restructured) into two tables as follows.

```
FACULTY (FAC-ID, FACULTY-NAME, GENDER, SALARY)
FAC-ASGN (FAC-ID, DEPARTMENT)
```

Note that the FAC-ASGN table represents an association. The attribute DE-PARTMENT is a foreign key to another table completing the association relationship. The reader should be aware that in associations the primary key of the association table is usually composed of foreign keys to other tables. However since that other table is not relevant to this example, we do not show it.

TABLE NAME: FACULTY

FAC-ID	FACULTY-NAME	GENDER	SALARY
J01	RAYMOND J. JOHNSON	MALE	40000
S01	WENDY SWIMMER	FEMALE	45000
D01	AMY DANCER	FEMALE	34500
J02	BOB JONES	MALE	35000
N01	JACK NELSON	MALE	28000

TABLE NAME: FAC-ASGN

FAC-ID	DEPARTMENT
J01	COMP SCI
J01	PSYCHOLOGY
S01	COMP SCI
S01	ENGLISH
S01	PHYSICS
S01	PHYS ED
D01	COMP SCI
J02	ACCOUNTING
N01	HISTORY
N01	BIOLOGY

FAC-ID -->-> DEPARTMENT

Note that if we wanted to display the names of the faculty and which departments they were assigned to, we would have to join the FACULTY table to the FAC-ASGN table.

Join Dependency

Join dependency is a concept related to decomposing a table into smaller tables. To illustrate this let us consider a table called ORIGINAL1 that consists of three attributes X, Y, and Z. The values x1, x2, x3, x4, y1, y2, z1, z2, z3, and z4 represent occurrences of the three attributes.

TABLE NAME: ORIGINAL1

_X_	_Y_	_Z_
x1	y1	z1
x2	y2	z3
x3	y1	z2
x4	y2	z4

Functional dependencies: X --> Y
                         Z --> Y

Let us now assume that we decompose the table ORIGINAL1 into two tables called FIRST (X,Y) and SECOND (Y,Z).

```
FIRST <- PROJECT ORIGINAL1 OVER X, Y
SECOND <- PROJECT ORIGINAL1 OVER Y, Z
```

TABLE NAME: FIRST   **TABLE NAME: SECOND**

_X_	_Y_		_Y_	_Z_
x1	y1		y1	z1
x2	y2		y2	z3
x3	y1		y1	z2
x4	y2		y2	z4

Functional Dependencies
Table: FIRST   X --> Y
Table: SECOND   Z --> Y

If the table ORIGINAL1 is deleted, can we use the tables FIRST and SECOND to reproduce it? If we join the two tables over the common attribute Y, we get the following result.

```
NEW-ORIGINAL1 <- JOIN FIRST, SECOND OVER Y
```

TABLE NAME: NEW-ORIGINAL1

_X_	_Y_	_Z_	
x1	y1	z1	
x1	y1	z2	*
x2	y2	z4	*
x2	y2	z3	
x3	y1	z1	*
x3	y1	z2	
x4	y2	z3	*
x4	y2	z4	

Notice that four spurious tuples are generated (denoted by asterisks) by the JOIN command. Obviously we did not reproduce the ORIGINAL1 table. This is called a "lossy join." Even though we produced four unwanted tuples, the original information content stored in the original table is lost, hence the name lossy. Notice that the JOIN attribute was not the determinant in the ORIGINAL1 table.

Let us consider another table called ORIGINAL2, which also has the same three attributes X, Y, and Z, but different functional dependencies.

TABLE NAME: ORIGINAL2

_X_	_Y_	_Z_	Functional dependencies: $X \longrightarrow Y$
x1	y1	z1	$X \longrightarrow Z$
x2	y2	z2	
x3	y2	z1	
x4	y1	z2	

Let us decompose the table ORIGINAL2 into two tables called FIRST (X,Y) and SECOND (X,Z).

```
FIRST  <- PROJECT ORIGINAL2 OVER X, Y
SECOND <- PROJECT ORIGINAL2 OVER X, Z
```

TABLE NAME: FIRST   **TABLE NAME: SECOND**

_X_	_Y_		_X_	_Z_	Functional Dependencies
x1	y1		x1	z1	Table: FIRST $X \longrightarrow Y$
x2	y2		x2	z2	Table: SECOND $X \longrightarrow Z$
x3	y2		x3	z1	
x4	y1		x4	z2	

If we try to reproduce the ORIGINAL2 table through the use of a JOIN command, we would get the following:

```
NEW-ORIGINAL2 <- JOIN FIRST, SECOND OVER X
```

TABLE NAME: NEW-ORIGINAL2

_X_	_Y_	_Z_
x1	y1	z1
x2	y2	z2
x3	y2	z1
x4	y1	z2

This JOIN command does reproduce the original table. This is called a lossless join, for no information is lost due to the decomposition of the original table. The reason for this is that the JOIN attribute and the determinant attribute were the same.

What does all this mean? It means that the first table (ORIGINAL1) should not have been decomposed into two tables because the JOIN attribute will not be the determinant, and, therefore, there is a join dependency. The second table (ORIGINAL2) could be decomposed for the join dependency does not exist.

Trivial Dependency

Trivial dependencies exist when we have composite attributes as determinants. Assume that we have the attributes X, Y, and Z that are found to be a determinant. The following trivial dependencies then exist.

$$X,Y,Z \rightarrow X$$
$$X,Y,Z \rightarrow Y$$
$$X,Y,Z \rightarrow Z$$
$$X,Y,Z \rightarrow X,Y$$
$$X,Y,Z \rightarrow Y,Z$$
$$X,Y,Z \rightarrow X,Z$$
$$X,Y,Z \rightarrow X,Y,Z$$

Trivial dependencies mean that a set of attributes in a determinant determines all of its subsets.

NORMALIZATION OF RELATIONS

In some cases, database designers must choose between efficiency of either maintaining a database or retrieving data from a database. Relations that are not in the proper normal form could encounter problems (called anomalies) during data maintenance. (Notice that we are using the term "relations" instead of "tables" to discuss normalization. The reason for this is that normalization is considered a theoretical concept and relations are considered more theoretical than tables. In our discussion of normalization we will use the term "relation" when referring to the theoretical aspects of normalization and "table" when illustrating the process of normalization.) The process of converting relations to the proper normal form is called normalization. Normalization usually involves decomposing relations into two or more relations with fewer attributes. When relations are in the proper normal form, anomalies should not occur. The basic problem with converting relations to normal forms is that the decomposed tables will have to utilize joins to retrieve data that we could have retrieved from the one original table. **When normalizing relations, we are generally sacrificing retrieval speed to prevent data maintenance problems**.

Normalization of relations is a database design aspect dealing with the semantics of the data. Because of the semantic nature of the process, it is usually considered heuristic in nature, although Ceri and Gottlob have developed a Prolog program to normalize relations stemming from academic exercises.[2]

Dr. Codd in his flagship article on relational databases outlined three normal forms. Since this time, many new normal forms have been developed. The newer normal forms assist in solving more and more obscure (but in some cases very important) problems in data maintenance.

Normal forms build on each other. For example, if we conclude that a relation is in the third normal form, in the first and second normal forms.

Anomalies

Anomalies are undesirable side effects that can occur if relations are not in the proper normal form. Anomalies fall into three categories:

1. Insertion anomalies
2. Deletion anomalies
3. Update anomalies

Insertion anomalies occur when we cannot insert a tuple occurrence into a table. This usually occurs because the value of the primary key is unknown when the tuple occurrence is inserted into the table. There are two methods of handling this situation. The first is to insert the value of NULL for the primary key. This violates the entity integrity rule and, of course, is unacceptable. The second method is to insert a fictitious value for the primary key. This violates any common sense rule that exists (we now have to keep track of which primary key values are real and which are fake!!!). What happens is that we have a tuple that should be inserted into a table, but we cannot insert it.

Deletion anomalies occur when three circumstances exist.

1. We delete a tuple from a table
2. The tuple that we delete contains an important piece of information
3. This tuple is the last one in the table that contains this piece of information.

The deletion of the tuple causes the inadvertent deletion of this important piece of information.

Update anomalies occur when we have unnecessary redundancy in our data. If we have to update one attribute value, we must then search for every occurrence of that value to change it.

All three anomalies are illustrated in the discussion of the various normal forms that follows.

The First Normal Form

The first normal form, commonly abbreviated 1NF, states that all relations must be flat. There can be no repeat groups in relations. All attributes can only contain one value per tuple. Another method of defining this property is to state that attributes can only be scalar values, not arrays. This is sometimes called a structural constraint. The 1NF is, of course, one of the basic tenants of the relational model as described in Chapter 2.

The Second Normal Form

The second normal form (2NF) pertains only to relations with composite primary keys. If a relation is in the 1NF and has a single-attribute primary key, it is automatically in the 2NF. If a relation has a composite primary key, the 2NF criterion states that each nonkey attribute must be fully functionally dependent on the primary key.

Illustration of the 2NF.   To illustrate the 2NF, let us consider our COURSE table.

```
COURSE (COURSE-ID, COURSE-TITLE, SECTION, STU-ID, FAC-ID)
```

TABLE NAME: COURSE

COURSE-ID	COURSE-TITLE	SECTION-NO	STU-ID	FAC-ID
CSC100	INTRODUCTION TO COMPUTING	1	S001	J01
CSC100	INTRODUCTION TO COMPUTING	2	S002	S01
CSC200	PASCAL PROGRAMMING	1	S001	D01
CSC200	PASCAL PROGRAMMING	2	S003	S01
ACC200	PRINCIPLES OF ACCOUNTING I	1	S001	J02
ACC201	PRINCIPLES OF ACCOUNTING II	1	S004	J02
HIS200	HISTORY OF PIROGUES	1	S005	N01

Notice that the COURSE table has a composite primary key of COURSE-ID + STU-ID + FAC-ID. For this table to be in the 2NF, the following functional dependencies must hold true.

```
COURSE-ID, STU-ID, FAC-ID --> COURSE-TITLE
COURSE-ID, STU-ID, FAC-ID --> SECTION-NO
```

These functional dependencies mean that we must know the COURSE-ID, the STU-ID, and the FAC-ID to determine uniquely the COURSE-TITLE and the SECTION-NO. If we look at the table very closely, we should be able to determine that the only attribute that we need to determine uniquely the COURSE-TITLE is COURSE-ID. The functional dependencies in the COURSE table are

```
COURSE-ID --> COURSE-TITLE
COURSE-ID, STU-ID, FAC-ID --> SECTION-NO
```

This means that COURSE-TITLE is not fully functionally dependent upon the primary key. Therefore, the COURSE table is not in the 2NF. What can we do to correct this condition? We must decompose the COURSE table into two tables as follows.

```
COURSE  (COURSE-ID, SECTION-NO, STU-ID, FAC-ID)
COU-TITLE (COURSE-ID, COURSE-TITLE)
```

TABLE NAME: COURSE

COURSE-ID	SECTION	STU-ID	FAC-ID
CSC100	1	S001	D01
CSC100	2	S002	D02
CSC200	1	S001	L01
CSC200	2	S003	D02
ACC200	1	S001	M01
ACC201	1	S004	M01
HIS200	1	S005	D03

TABLE NAME: COU-TITLE

COURSE-ID	COURSE-TITLE
CSC100	INTRODUCTION TO COMPUTING
CSC200	PASCAL PROGRAMMING
ACC200	PRINCIPLES OF ACCOUNTING I
ACC201	PRINCIPLES OF ACCOUNTING II
HIS200	HISTORY OF PIROGUES

The new table was formed by extracting the attribute that caused the table to not be in the 2NF along with its determinant.

2NF Anomalies.   To illustrate the three types of anomalies, we consider the original COURSE table that is not in the 2NF.

COURSE (COURSE-ID, COURSE-TITLE, SECTION-NO, STU-ID, FAC-ID)

Insertion Anomalies.   Suppose we had just received approval for a new course, CSC 400—Fertilization of B-Trees. We have no students currently taking the course and no instructor currently teaching the course. We would like to add the fact that this new course exists into our database. However, we have no value for STU-ID or FAC-ID. We have two options. We could place either null values or fictitious values into these attributes.

TABLE NAME: COURSE (WITH NULL VALUES)

COURSE-ID	COURSE-TITLE	SECTION-NO	STU-ID	FAC-ID
CSC100	INTRODUCTION TO COMPUTING	1	S001	J01
CSC100	INTRODUCTION TO COMPUTING	2	S002	S01
CSC200	PASCAL PROGRAMMING	1	S001	D01
CSC200	PASCAL PROGRAMMING	2	S003	S01
ACC200	PRINCIPLES OF ACCOUNTING I	1	S001	J02
ACC201	PRINCIPLES OF ACCOUNTING II	1	S004	J02
HIS200	HISTORY OF PIROGUES	1	S005	N01
CSC400	FERTILIZATION OF B-TREES	NULL	NULL	NULL

TABLE NAME: COURSE (WITH FICTITIOUS VALUES)

COURSE-ID	COURSE-TITLE	SECTION-NO	STU-ID	FAC-ID
CSC100	INTRODUCTION TO COMPUTING	1	S001	D01
CSC100	INTRODUCTION TO COMPUTING	2	S002	D02
CSC200	PASCAL PROGRAMMING	1	S001	L01
CSC200	PASCAL PROGRAMMING	2	S003	D02
ACC200	PRINCIPLES OF ACCOUNTING I	1	S001	M01
ACC201	PRINCIPLES OF ACCOUNTING II	1	S004	M01
HIS200	HISTORY OF PIROGUES	1	S005	D03
CSC400	FERTILIZATION OF B-TREES	NULL	S999	X99

The null value would violate the entity integrity guideline. If we placed fictitious values into the attributes, they would have to be changed when the ''actual'' values are determined.

Deliberate falsification of data is certainly not good practice. (We would now have to keep track of which data is real and which is not!) Neither of these alternatives is acceptable. With the normalized form of the two tables, we would have no difficulty inserting the fact that we have a new course into the COU-TITLE table.

TABLE NAME: COU-TITLE

COURSE-ID	COURSE-TITLE
CSC100	INTRODUCTION TO COMPUTING
CSC200	PASCAL PROGRAMMING
ACC200	PRINCIPLES OF ACCOUNTING I
ACC201	PRINCIPLES OF ACCOUNTING II
HIS200	HISTORY OF PIROGUES
CSC400	FERTILIZATION OF B-TREES

Deletion Anomalies.   Student Dottie Stacy (S004) has decided to drop the course ACC201—Principles of Accounting II.

TABLE NAME: COURSE (BEFORE TUPLE DELETION)

COURSE-ID	COURSE-TITLE	SECTION-NO	STU-ID	FAC-ID
CSC100	INTRODUCTION TO COMPUTING	1	S001	J01
CSC100	INTRODUCTION TO COMPUTING	2	S002	S01
CSC200	PASCAL PROGRAMMING	1	S001	D01
CSC200	PASCAL PROGRAMMING	2	S003	S01
ACC200	PRINCIPLES OF ACCOUNTING I	1	S001	J02
ACC201	PRINCIPLES OF ACCOUNTING II	1	S004	J02
HIS200	HISTORY OF PIROGUES	1	S005	N01

Since Dottie is the only student in the class, when we delete the tuple, we have no evidence that the course ACC201 exists at our university.

TABLE NAME: COURSE (AFTER TUPLE DELETION)

COURSE-ID	COURSE-TITLE	SECTION-NO	STU-ID	FAC-ID
CSC100	INTRODUCTION TO COMPUTING	1	S001	J01
CSC100	INTRODUCTION TO COMPUTING	2	S002	S01
CSC200	PASCAL PROGRAMMING	1	S001	D01
CSC200	PASCAL PROGRAMMING	2	S003	S01
ACC200	PRINCIPLES OF ACCOUNTING I	1	S001	J02
HIS200	HISTORY OF PIROGUES	1	S005	N01

However, if the tables were properly normalized, we could simply delete the tuple and the information that the course ACC201 exists would be stored in the COU-TITLE table.

TABLE NAME: COURSE

COURSE-ID	SECTION	STU-ID	FAC-ID
CSC100	1	S001	J01
CSC100	2	S002	S01
CSC200	1	S001	D01
CSC200	2	S003	S01
ACC200	1	S001	J02
HIS200	1	S005	N01

TABLE NAME: COU-TITLE

COURSE-ID	COURSE-TITLE
CSC100	INTRODUCTION TO COMPUTING
CSC200	PASCAL PROGRAMMING
ACC200	PRINCIPLES OF ACCOUNTING I
ACC201	PRINCIPLES OF ACCOUNTING II
HIS200	HISTORY OF PIROGUES

These two normalized tables indicate that the course exists (by its being in the COU-TITLE table), but it is not currently being offered (no tuple with COURSE-ID = ACC201 exists in the normalized COURSE table).

Update Anomalies.   In considering the unnormalized COURSE table again, suppose that we wish to change the title of the course CSC200 from Pascal Programming to Ada Programming.

TABLE NAME: COURSE (BEFORE CHANGE)

COURSE-ID	COURSE-TITLE	SECTION-NO	STU-ID	FAC-ID	
CSC100	INTRODUCTION TO COMPUTING	1	S001	J01	
CSC100	INTRODUCTION TO COMPUTING	2	S002	S01	
CSC200	PASCAL PROGRAMMING	1	S001	D01	<--
CSC200	PASCAL PROGRAMMING	2	S003	S01	<--
ACC200	PRINCIPLES OF ACCOUNTING I	1	S001	J02	
ACC201	PRINCIPLES OF ACCOUNTING II	1	S004	J02	
HIS200	HISTORY OF PIROGUES	1	S005	N01	

TABLE NAME: COURSE (AFTER CHANGE)

COURSE-ID	COURSE-TITLE	SECTION-NO	STU-ID	FAC-ID
CSC100	INTRODUCTION TO COMPUTING	1	S001	J01
CSC100	INTRODUCTION TO COMPUTING	2	S002	S01
CSC200	ADA PROGRAMMING	1	S001	D01	<--
CSC200	ADA PROGRAMMING	2	S003	S01	<--
ACC200	PRINCIPLES OF ACCOUNTING I	1	S001	J02
ACC201	PRINCIPLES OF ACCOUNTING II	1	S004	J02
HIS200	HISTORY OF PIROGUES	1	S005	N01

Since two students (S001 and S003) are currently taking CSC200, we would have to change two tuples when we really should only have to change one if the tables were normalized.

TABLE NAME: COU-TITLE

COURSE-ID	COURSE-TITLE	
CSC100	INTRODUCTION TO COMPUTING	
CSC200	ADA PROGRAMMING	<-- only one change made here
ACC200	PRINCIPLES OF ACCOUNTING I	
ACC201	PRINCIPLES OF ACCOUNTING II	
HIS200	HISTORY OF PIROGUES	

This may not seem like a significant problem to you—updating 2 tuples versus 1 tuple, but consider an industrial strength database where the trade-offs might be updating 5000 tuples versus only 1 tuple. When taken in this perspective, update anomalies could cost an enterprise a significant amount of computer time. We must also consider which tuples get updated and which do not if a system failure occurs during the update process.

The Third Normal Form

The third normal form (3NF) is probably the most important normal form for database designers. The reason for this is that the 3NF is where most of the potential anomalies occur. It is also where most of our decisions must be made as to leaving deliberate redundancy for the sake of retrieval convenience. The 3NF is concerned with the removal of transitive dependencies from tables.

An illustration of the 3NF. Let's assume that we have added an additional attribute called OFFICE that contains the name of the building where each faculty member has his office. Let's further assume that all the faculty members of one department have their offices in one building, that is, all the Computer Science faculty have their offices in one building, all of the Accounting faculty are housed in one building, and so on.

FACULTY (FAC-ID, FACULTY-NAME, DEPARTMENT, GENDER, SALARY, OFFICE)

TABLE NAME: FACULTY

```
FAC-ID FACULTY-NAME_____ DEPARTMENT GENDER SALARY OFFICE____
 J01   RAYMOND J. JOHNSON COMP SCI   MALE   40000  BYTE HALL
 S01   WENDY SWIMMER      COMP SCI   FEMALE 45000  BYTE HALL
 D01   AMY DANCER         COMP SCI   FEMALE 34500  BYTE HALL
 J02   BOB JONES          ACCOUNTING MALE   35000  DEBIT HALL
 N01   JACK NELSON        HISTORY    MALE   28000  WAR HALL
 C01   POLLY CARTER       MATH       FEMALE 35000  WAR HALL
```

This table has the following functional dependencies.

```
        FAC-ID --> FACULTY-NAME
        FAC-ID --> DEPARTMENT
        FAC-ID --> GENDER
        FAC-ID --> OFFICE
        DEPARTMENT --> OFFICE
```

Two of the functional dependencies shown form a transitive dependency.

```
    FAC-ID --> DEPARTMENT --> OFFICE
```

This transitive dependency states that FAC-ID determines DEPARTMENT and DEPARTMENT determines OFFICE.

This means that this table is not in the 3NF. To rectify this, we must decompose the faculty table into two smaller tables.

```
FACULTY (FAC-ID, FACULTY-NAME, DEPARTMENT, GENDER, SALARY)
WHERE-OFFICE (DEPARTMENT, OFFICE)
```

TABLE NAME: FACULTY

```
    FAC-ID FACULTY-NAME_____ DEPARTMENT GENDER SALARY
     J01   RAYMOND J. JOHNSON COMP SCI   MALE   40000
     S01   WENDY SWIMMER      COMP SCI   FEMALE 45000
     D01   AMY DANCER         COMP SCI   FEMALE 34500
     J02   BOB JONES          ACCOUNTING MALE   35000
     N01   JACK NELSON        HISTORY    MALE   28000
     C01   POLLY CARTER       MATH       FEMALE 35000
```

TABLE NAME: WHERE-OFFICE

```
        DEPARTMENT OFFICE____
        COMP SCI   BYTE HALL
        ACCOUNTING DEBIT HALL
        HISTORY    WAR HALL
        MATH       WAR HALL
```

Again the new table was formed by extracting the attribute that caused the transitive dependency (OFFICE) along with its determinant (DEPARTMENT).

3NF Anomalies.   To illustrate the three types of anomalies, which could occur if a table is not in the 3NF, we will utilize the new augmented FACULTY table, which is not in the 3NF.

```
FACULTY (FAC-ID, FACULTY-NAME, DEPARTMENT, GENDER, SALARY, OFFICE)
```

Insertion Anomalies.   Let us assume that our university has just created a new department called English, but it has not hired any faculty members for this new department. We would like to insert the fact that we have a new department into our FACULTY table. Just as with the 2NF, we will not be able to do this, for we do not have a value for the primary key of the FACULTY table, FAC-ID. It would be unacceptable to place either a null or a fictitious value into the FAC-ID attribute of the new tuple. However, if the FACULTY table were decomposed, purging it of the transitive dependency, we could very easily enter the new information into the WHERE-OFFICE table.

TABLE NAME: WHERE-OFFICE

```
DEPARTMENT OFFICE____
COMP SCI    BYTE HALL
ACCOUNTING  DEBIT HALL
HISTORY     WAR HALL
MATH        WAR HALL
ENGLISH     <null>
```

Notice that we would not even have to know what building the members of the ENGLISH faculty (as evidenced by the null value in the attribute OFFICE) will be located to make the entry into the WHERE-OFFICE table.

Deletion Anomalies.   Suppose that Professor Nelson decided to leave our university. As you can see by the following FACULTY table, Professor Nelson is the only member of the History faculty. When we delete his tuple we have no record that there is a History Department. In actuality we have a History Department, but we have no current faculty members assigned to it.

TABLE NAME: FACULTY (BEFORE DELETION)

```
FAC-ID FACULTY-NAME_____ DEPARTMENT GENDER SALARY OFFICE____
 J01   RAYMOND J. JOHNSON COMP SCI   MALE   40000  BYTE HALL
 S01   WENDY SWIMMER      COMP SCI   FEMALE 45000  BYTE HALL
 D01   AMY DANCER         COMP SCI   FEMALE 34500  BYTE HALL
 J02   BOB JONES          ACCOUNTING MALE   35000  DEBIT HALL
 N01   JACK NELSON        HISTORY    MALE   28000  WAR HALL
 C01   POLLY CARTER       MATH       FEMALE 35000  WAR HALL
```

TABLE NAME: FACULTY (AFTER DELETION)

FAC-ID	FACULTY-NAME	DEPARTMENT	GENDER	SALARY	OFFICE
J01	RAYMOND J. JOHNSON	COMP SCI	MALE	40000	BYTE HALL
S01	WENDY SWIMMER	COMP SCI	FEMALE	45000	BYTE HALL
D01	AMY DANCER	COMP SCI	FEMALE	34500	BYTE HALL
J02	BOB JONES	ACCOUNTING	MALE	35000	DEBIT HALL
C01	POLLY CARTER	MATH	FEMALE	35000	WAR HALL

The normalized tables will allow us to perform our deletion very cleanly.

TABLE NAME: FACULTY (BEFORE DELETION)

FAC-ID	FACULTY-NAME	DEPARTMENT	GENDER	SALARY
J01	RAYMOND J. JOHNSON	COMP SCI	MALE	40000
S01	WENDY SWIMMER	COMP SCI	FEMALE	45000
D01	AMY DANCER	COMP SCI	FEMALE	34500
J02	BOB JONES	ACCOUNTING	MALE	35000
N01	JACK NELSON	HISTORY	MALE	28000
C01	POLLY CARTER	MATH	FEMALE	35000

TABLE NAME: FACULTY (AFTER DELETION)

FAC-ID	FACULTY-NAME	DEPARTMENT	GENDER	SALARY
J01	RAYMOND J. JOHNSON	COMP SCI	MALE	40000
S01	WENDY SWIMMER	COMP SCI	FEMALE	45000
D01	AMY DANCER	COMP SCI	FEMALE	34500
J02	BOB JONES	ACCOUNTING	MALE	35000
C01	POLLY CARTER	MATH	FEMALE	35000

TABLE NAME: WHERE-OFFICE

DEPARTMENT	OFFICE
COMP SCI	BYTE HALL
ACCOUNTING	DEBIT HALL
HISTORY	WAR HALL
MATH	WAR HALL

The normalized tables reflect the current condition at our university: Professor Nelson no longer works in the History Department, but we still have a History Department as shown in the WHERE-OFFICE table.

Update Anomalies. If the Computer Science Department moves its offices from Byte Hall to Bit Hall, we would have to make changes in three tuples in the unnormalized FACULTY table, whereas we would only have to change one value in the normalized WHERE–OFFICE table.

TABLE NAME: FACULTY (BEFORE CHANGE)

FAC-ID	FACULTY-NAME	DEPARTMENT	GENDER	SALARY	OFFICE	
J01	RAYMOND J. JOHNSON	COMP SCI	MALE	40000	BYTE HALL	<--
S01	WENDY SWIMMER	COMP SCI	FEMALE	45000	BYTE HALL	<--
D01	AMY DANCER	COMP SCI	FEMALE	34500	BYTE HALL	<--
J02	BOB JONES	ACCOUNTING	MALE	35000	DEBIT HALL	
N01	JACK NELSON	HISTORY	MALE	28000	WAR HALL	
C01	POLLY CARTER	MATH	FEMALE	35000	WAR HALL	

TABLE NAME: FACULTY (AFTER CHANGE)

FAC-ID	FACULTY-NAME	DEPARTMENT	GENDER	SALARY	OFFICE	
J01	RAYMOND J. JOHNSON	COMP SCI	MALE	40000	BIT HALL	<--
S01	WENDY SWIMMER	COMP SCI	FEMALE	45000	BIT HALL	<--
D01	AMY DANCER	COMP SCI	FEMALE	34500	BIT HALL	<--
J02	BOB JONES	ACCOUNTING	MALE	35000	DEBIT HALL	
N01	JACK NELSON	HISTORY	MALE	28000	WAR HALL	
C01	POLLY CARTER	MATH	FEMALE	35000	WAR HALL	

TABLE NAME: WHERE-OFFICE (BEFORE CHANGE)

DEPARTMENT	OFFICE
COMP SCI	BYTE HALL
ACCOUNTING	DEBIT HALL
HISTORY	WAR HALL
MATH	WAR HALL

TABLE NAME: WHERE-OFFICE (AFTER CHANGE)

DEPARTMENT	OFFICE
COMP SCI	BIT HALL
ACCOUNTING	DEBIT HALL
HISTORY	WAR HALL
MATH	WAR HALL

The Boyce-Codd Normal Form

There is an extension to the 3NF called the Boyce-Codd normal form (BCNF).
The BCNF concerns itself with a somewhat rare situation that consists of three
circumstances.

1. There are at least two candidate keys in the table.

2. All the candidate keys are composite keys.

3. There is an overlapping attribute in the candidate keys.

Some authors consider the BCNF as simply a more powerful form of the 3NF. We will consider it a separate normal form. Remember that before we consider the BCNF, the table should already be in the 3NF.

An illustration of the BCNF.   To illustrate the BCNF, we will create a table called STU-COURSES that consists of STU-ID, TELEPHONE#, COURSE-ID, and CURRENT-GRADE.

```
STU-COURSES (STU-ID, TELEPHONE#, COURSE-ID, CURRENT-GRADE)
```

TABLE NAME: STU-COURSES

STU-ID	TELEPHONE#	COURSE-ID	CURRENT-GRADE
S001	555-1234	CSC100	A
S001	555-1234	CSC200	B
S001	555-1234	ACC200	A
S002	555-2345	CSC100	B
S002	555-2345	CSC200	C
S003	555-3456	CSC100	C
S003	555-3456	ACC200	B
S003	555-3456	HIS100	A

The university has implemented a rule that each student will have one and only one telephone with a unique telephone number.

If we look at the STU-COURSES table very closely we notice that we have two candidate keys.

```
STU-ID+COURSE-ID
```

and

```
TELEPHONE#+COURSE-ID
```

Either one of these combinations could be used as the primary key of the table, which makes them candidate keys. Also notice that the attribute COURSE-ID participates in both candidate keys. Since this table has only one field (CURRENT-GRADE) that does not participate in the candidate keys, the table is in the 3NF.

The functional dependencies for this table include the following.

```
        STU-ID, COURSE-ID --> CURRENT-GRADE
    TELEPHONE#, COURSE-ID --> CURRENT-GRADE
                   STU-ID --> TELEPHONE#
```

For a table to be in the BCNF, every key must be a determinant. To convert the STU-COURSES table to the BCNF, we must decompose the table as follows.

```
STU-COURSES (STU-ID, COURSE-ID, CURRENT-GRADE)
      PHONE# (STU-ID, TELEPHONE#)
```

TABLE NAME: STU-COURSES

```
STU-ID_  COURSE-ID  CURRENT-GRADE
S01      CSC100     A
S01      CSC200     B
S01      ACC200     A
S02      CSC100     B
S02      CSC200     C
S03      CSC100     C
S03      ACC200     B
S03      HIS100     A
```

TABLE NAME: PHONE#

```
STU-ID_  TELEPHONE#
S01      555-1234
S02      555-2345
S03      555-3456
```

The two tables are now in the BCNF because each key (STU-COURSES.STU-ID+STU-COURSES.COURSE-ID and PHONE#.STU-ID) is a determinant.

```
STU-COURSES.STU-ID, STU-COURSES.COURSE-ID --> CURRENT-GRADE
PHONE#.STU-ID --> TELEPHONE#
```

BCNF Anomalies.   To illustrate the potential anomalies that could occur when a table is not in the BCNF, we will use our new STU-COURSES table.

```
STU-COURSES (STU-ID, TELEPHONE#, COURSE-ID, CURRENT-GRADE)
```

Insertion Anomalies.   If we wanted to store the student's telephone number, we could not do it until he takes a class (unless we inserted a null or fictitious value for COURSE-ID). However, if the STU-COURSE table was normalized to the BCNF, we could insert the student's telephone number very easily into the PHONE# table.

```
STU-ID_  TELEPHONE#
S01      555-1234
S02      555-2345
S03      555-3456
S99      BR549
```

Also note that if we use the unnormalized table, a student cannot register for a class until a telephone number has been assigned to him.

Deletion Anomalies.   Suppose student S01 withdraws from school for this term. We inadvertently lose her telephone number.

TABLE NAME: STU-COURSES (BEFORE DELETION)

STU-ID	TELEPHONE#	COURSE-ID	CURRENT-GRADE
S01	555-1234	CSC100	A
S01	555-1234	CSC200	B
S01	555-1234	ACC200	A
S02	555-2345	CSC100	B
S02	555-2345	CSC200	C
S03	555-3456	CSC100	C
S03	555-3456	ACC200	B
S03	555-3456	HIS100	A

TABLE NAME: STU-COURSES (AFTER DELETION)

STU-ID	TELEPHONE#	COURSE-ID	CURRENT-GRADE
S02	555-2345	CSC100	B
S02	555-2345	CSC200	C
S03	555-3456	CSC100	C
S03	555-3456	ACC200	B
S03	555-3456	HIS100	A

Update Anomalies.   If a student changes telephone numbers, we would have to update multiple tuples. If the student is currently taking three courses, we would have to update three tuples. For example if we wanted to change student S01's telephone number to 555–9999, we would have to change three tuples as follows.

TABLE NAME: STU-COURSES (BEFORE UPDATE)

STU-ID	TELEPHONE#	COURSE-ID	CURRENT-GRADE	
S01	555-1234	CSC100	A	<----
S01	555-1234	CSC200	B	<----
S01	555-1234	ACC200	A	<----
S02	555-2345	CSC100	B	
S02	555-2345	CSC200	C	
S03	555-3456	CSC100	C	
S03	555-3456	ACC200	B	
S03	555-3456	HIS100	A	

TABLE NAME: STU-COURSES (AFTER UPDATE)

STU-ID	TELEPHONE#	COURSE-ID	CURRENT-GRADE	
S01	555-9999	CSC100	A	<----
S01	555-9999	CSC200	B	<----
S01	555-9999	ACC200	A	<----
S02	555-2345	CSC100	B	
S02	555-2345	CSC200	C	
S03	555-3456	CSC100	C	
S03	555-3456	ACC200	B	
S03	555-3456	HIS100	A	

The Fourth Normal Form

The fourth normal form (4NF) is concerned with multivalued dependencies. For a table to be in the 4NF, there can be only one multivalued dependency per table.

An Illustration of the Fourth Normal Form.   Let us assume that a student at our university is allowed to have more than one academic major. This means that there is an m:n relationship between student and academic major, for a student can have N majors and a major can have M students. Let us further assume that each student is taught several different programming languages. There is also an m:n relationship between student and programming languages. A student can know several different programming languages, and a programming language can be known by several students. We will assume that knowledge of a programming language is independent of academic major. The table that we use to represent these multivalued dependencies is

$$\text{STU-MAJ-LAN (\underline{STU-ID}, \underline{MAJOR}, \underline{LANGUAGE})}$$

TABLE NAME: STU-MAJ-LAN

STU-ID	MAJOR	LANGUAGE
S01	COMP SCI	PASCAL
S01	MATH	COBOL
S01	HISTORY	ADA
S01	MATH	FORTRAN
S02	COMP SCI	ADA
S02	MGMT SCI	APL
S03	HISTORY	PASCAL
S03	MGMT SCI	APL
S04	COMP SCI	PASCAL
S04	MGMT SCI	PASCAL

Note that all the attributes in the STU-MAJ-LAN table form the primary key of the table. Without even considering the 4NF, this table contains very confusing information, such as

1. Does student S01 do her Computer Science work in Pascal?
2. Does she do her math work in COBOL? (We would suspect that there is a problem here.)
3. Do History majors only know Pascal and ADA? Management Science majors only APL?
4. Do History majors have to know ADA or Pascal or both languages?
5. Just because student S01 knows four programming languages and has ''only'' three academic majors, we had to duplicate the fact that she is a math major so that we can indicate that she knows more programming languages than she has majors.

6. Student S04 knows only one programming language, but has two academic majors. We must duplicate the fact that he knows Pascal so that we can record the fact that he has two academic majors.

How should we represent these two sets of independent multivalued dependencies? Perhaps we could place null values where relationships do not exist.

TABLE NAME: STU-MAJ-LAN

STU-ID	MAJOR	LANGUAGE
S01	COMP SCI	null
S01	null	PASCAL
S01	MATH	null
S01	null	COBOL
S01	HISTORY	null
S01	null	ADA
S01	null	FORTRAN
S02	COMP SCI	null
S02	null	ADA
S02	MGMT SCI	null
S02	null	APL
S03	HISTORY	null
S03	null	PASCAL
S03	MGMT SCI	null
S03	null	APL
S04	COMP SCI	null
S04	MGMT SCI	null
S04	null	PASCAL

This configuration will not work, for we would have to place null values in attributes that make up the primary key, and this would violate the entity integrity rule. There are other configurations, equally invalid, to store these facts that we will not even go into. The obvious solution to this problem is to decompose the table into two tables. The first table contains the relationships between student and academic major, and the second contains the relationships between student and programming language known.

```
ACADEMIC-MAJOR   (STU-ID, MAJOR)
PROG-LANG-KNOW   (STU-ID, LANGUAGE)
```

TABLE NAME: ACADEMIC-MAJOR

STU-ID	MAJOR
S01	COMP SCI
S01	MATH
S01	HISTORY
S02	COMP SCI
S02	MGMT SCI

```
                          S03        HISTORY
                          S03        MGMT SCI
                          S04        COMP SCI
                          S04        MGMT SCI
```

TABLE NAME: PROG-LANG-KNOW

```
                   STU-ID    LANGUAGE
                   S01       PASCAL
                   S01       COBOL
                   S01       ADA
                   S01       FORTRAN
                   S02       ADA
                   S02       APL
                   S03       PASCAL
                   S03       APL
                   S04       PASCAL
```

4NF Anomalies.   To illustrate the three types of anomalies that can occur if a table is not in the 4NF, we will use the STU-MAJ-LANG table.

Insertion Anomalies.   With all attributes in the table participating in the primary key, a student cannot learn a new programming language without acquiring a new academic major or having the fact that he has a certain major duplicated. How about, ''A student cannot select another academic major without learning a new programming language or having the fact that he knows a particular programming language duplicated?'' For example, suppose that student S04 has decided to learn the Prolog language. The only way that we can insert this tuple into the STU-MAJ-LAN table is for S04 to either acquire a new academic major (example: Sociology) or duplicate the fact that he is a Computer Science (or Management Science) major.

TABLE NAME: STU-MAJ-LAN

```
      STU-ID    MAJOR         LANGUAGE
      S01       COMP SCI      PASCAL
      S01       MATH          COBOL
      S01       HISTORY       ADA
      S01       MATH          FORTRAN
      S02       COMP SCI      ADA
      S02       MGMT SCI      APL
      S03       HISTORY       PASCAL
      S03       MGMT SCI      APL
      S04       COMP SCI      PASCAL
      S04       MGMT SCI      PASCAL

      S04       SOCIOLOGY     PROLOG ⎫  One of the three tuples must
      S04       COMP SCI      PROLOG ⎬  be inserted into the table
      S04       MGMT SCI      PROLOG ⎭
```

If the STU-MAJ-LAN table were normalized, this would not be a problem.

TABLE NAME: ACADEMIC MAJOR (NO CHANGES NEEDED)

STU-ID	MAJOR____
S01	COMP SCI
S01	MATH
S01	HISTORY
S02	COMP SCI
S02	MGMT SCI
S03	HISTORY
S03	MGMT SCI
S04	COMP SCI
S04	MGMT SCI

TABLE NAME: PROG-LANG-KNOW (BEFORE)

STU-ID	LANGUAGE_
S01	PASCAL
S01	COBOL
S01	ADA
S01	FORTRAN
S02	ADA
S02	APL
S03	PASCAL
S03	APL
S04	PASCAL

TABLE NAME: PROG-LANG-KNOW (AFTER)

STU-ID	LANGUAGE_
S01	PASCAL
S01	COBOL
S01	ADA
S01	FORTRAN
S02	ADA
S02	APL
S03	PASCAL
S03	APL
S04	PASCAL
S04	PROLOG

Deletion Anomalies.   If a student decides not to pursue an academic major that he has previously declared, must he then disclaim knowledge of a programming language? Or if a student fails a programming language proficiency examination, this means that the student can not claim proficiency in that language and will therefore, have to drop one academic major. For example, if student S02 decided to drop his academic major in Management Science, he must give up his proficiency in the APL programming language. (He could actually give up his proficiency in the Ada programming language, but this would entail some additional updating.)

TABLE NAME: STU-MAJ-LAN (BEFORE S02 DROPS MANAGEMENT SCIENCE AS AN ACADEMIC MAJOR)

STU-ID	MAJOR___	LANGUAGE_	
S01	COMP SCI	PASCAL	
S01	MATH	COBOL	
S01	HISTORY	ADA	
S01	MATH	FORTRAN	
S02	COMP SCI	ADA	
S02	MGMT SCI	APL	<-----

```
S03    HISTORY     PASCAL
S03    MGMT SCI    APL
S04    COMP SCI    PASCAL
S04    MGMT SCI    PASCAL
```

TABLE NAME: STU-MAJ-LAN (AFTER S02 DROPS MANAGEMENT SCIENCE AS AN ACADEMIC MAJOR)

```
STU-ID  MAJOR___    LANGUAGE_
S01     COMP SCI    PASCAL
S01     MATH        COBOL
S01     HISTORY     ADA
S01     MATH        FORTRAN
S02     COMP SCI    ADA
S03     HISTORY     PASCAL
S03     MGMT SCI    APL
S04     COMP SCI    PASCAL
S04     MGMT SCI    PASCAL
```

Note that there is no evidence that student S02 is proficient in the APL programming language.

If the tables were normalized and student S02 decided to drop his Management Science major, it would not cause problems.

TABLE NAME: ACADEMIC MAJOR (BEFORE)   **TABLE NAME: ACADEMIC MAJOR (AFTER)**

```
STU-ID  MAJOR___              STU-ID  MAJOR___
S01     COMP SCI              S01     COMP SCI
S01     MATH                  S01     MATH
S01     HISTORY               S01     HISTORY
S02     COMP SCI              S02     COMP SCI
S02     MGMT SCI              S03     HISTORY
S03     HISTORY               S03     MGMT SCI
S03     MGMT SCI              S04     COMP SCI
S04     COMP SCI              S04     MGMT SCI
S04     MGMT SCI
```

TABLE NAME: PROG-LANG-KNOW (NO CHANGES NECESSARY)

```
STU-ID  LANGUAGE_
S01     PASCAL
S01     COBOL
S01     ADA
S01     FORTRAN
S02     ADA
S02     APL
S03     PASCAL
S03     APL
S04     PASCAL
```

Update Anomalies.   If the name of an academic major is changed, several tuples might have to be changed. For example, if we decided to change the name of the academic major Mathematics to Numbers, the two tuples belonging to S01 would have to be changed.

TABLE NAME: STU-MAJ-LAN (BEFORE CHANGE)

STU-ID	MAJOR___	LANGUAGE_	
S01	COMP SCI	PASCAL	
S01	MATH	COBOL	< - - - - -
S01	HISTORY	ADA	
S01	MATH	FORTRAN	< - - - - -
S02	COMP SCI	ADA	
S02	MGMT SCI	APL	
S03	HISTORY	PASCAL	
S03	MGMT SCI	APL	
S04	COMP SCI	PASCAL	
S04	MGMT SCI	PASCAL	

TABLE NAME: STU-MAJ-LAN (AFTER CHANGE)

STU-ID	MAJOR___	LANGUAGE_	
S01	COMP SCI	PASCAL	
S01	NUMBERS	COBOL	< - - - - -
S01	HISTORY	ADA	
S01	NUMBERS	FORTRAN	< - - - - -
S02	COMP SCI	ADA	
S02	MGMT SCI	APL	
S03	HISTORY	PASCAL	
S03	MGMT SCI	APL	
S04	COMP SCI	PASCAL	
S04	MGMT SCI	PASCAL	

With a normalized table we would only have to make one change in the table.

TABLE NAME: ACADEMIC MAJOR (BEFORE CHANGE)

STU-ID	MAJOR___
S01	COMP SCI
S01	MATH
S01	HISTORY
S02	COMP SCI
S02	MGMT SCI
S03	HISTORY
S03	MGMT SCI
S04	COMP SCI
S04	MGMT SCI

TABLE NAME: ACADEMIC MAJOR (AFTER CHANGE)

STU-ID	MAJOR
S01	COMP SCI
S01	NUMBERS
S01	HISTORY
S02	COMP SCI
S02	MGMT SCI
S03	HISTORY
S03	MGMT SCI
S04	COMP SCI
S04	MGMT SCI

The Fifth Normal Form

The fifth normal form (5NF) is sometimes called the project join normal form (PJNF), for it is concerned with join dependencies. The reason that it is sometimes called the PJNF, because for a table to be in this normal form, we must be able to join the projections (decompositions) of an original table and be able to reconstruct the original table. If we cannot reconstruct the original table from its projections, we have join dependencies. If we have join dependencies, we should not have decomposed the table in the first place.

An Illustration of the Fifth Normal Form. To illustrate the 5NF, we will assume the existence of a table called LANG-IN-COURSE that contains the attributes STU-ID, COURSE, and PROG- LANG.

LANG-IN-COURSE (STU-ID, COURSE, PROG-LANG)

TABLE NAME: LANG-IN-COURSE

STU-ID	COURSE	PROG-LANG
S01	CSC100	BASIC
S01	CSC100	PASCAL
S01	CSC200	PASCAL
S01	CSC200	ADA
S02	CSC200	PASCAL
S03	CSC100	BASIC

This table contains information about the relationship between programming languages needed by students in various courses. We will assume that each student is "assigned" a programming language to know for a particular class. We will also assume that there is no functional dependency between course and programming language.

Let us assume that for whatever reason, we decide to decompose the ternary table LANG-IN-COURSE into three binary tables as follows.

```
IN-COURSE (STU-ID, COURSE)
LANG-KNOW (STU-ID, PROG-LANG)
COUR-LANG (COURSE, PROG-LANG)
```

TABLE NAME: IN-COURSE COUR-LANG		TABLE NAME: LANG-KNOW		TABLE NAME:	
STU-ID	COURSE	STU-ID	PROG-LANG	COURSE	PROG-LANG
S01	CSC100	S01	BASIC	CSC100	BASIC
S01	CSC200	S01	PASCAL	CSC100	PASCAL
S02	CSC200	S01	ADA	CSC200	PASCAL
S03	CSC100	S02	PASCAL	CSC200	ADA
		S03	BASIC		

This all seems very innocent and very legal (the tables are in the 4NF) until we try to reproduce the original table through the use of natural joins.

```
JOIN IN-COURSE, LANG-KNOWN OVER STU-ID
```

STU-ID	COURSE	PROG-LANG	
S01	CSC100	BASIC	
S01	CSC100	PASCAL	
S01	CSC100	ADA	<----
S01	CSC200	BASIC	<----
S01	CSC200	PASCAL	
S01	CSC200	ADA	
S02	CSC200	PASCAL	
S03	CSC100	BASIC	

Note the generation of two spurious tuples (indicated by the arrows).
    Let's try another permutation of a JOIN.

```
JOIN IN-COURSE, COUR-LANG OVER COURSE
```

STU-ID	COURSE	PROG-LANG	
S01	CSC100	BASIC	
S01	CSC100	PASCAL	
S01	CSC200	PASCAL	
S01	CSC200	ADA	
S02	CSC200	PASCAL	
S02	CSC200	ADA	<-----
S03	CSC100	BASIC	
S03	CSC100	PASCAL	<-----

Note that there are also two spurious tuples generated from this JOIN. They are not the same two spurious tuples generated from the first JOIN.
    The final permutation of the join is:

```
JOIN LANG-KNOW, COUR-LANG OVER LANGUAGE

STU-ID      COURSE       PROG-LANG____
S01         CSC100       BASIC
S01         CSC100       PASCAL
S01         CSC200       PASCAL
S01         CSC200       ADA
S02         CSC100       PASCAL         <-----
S02         CSC200       PASCAL
S03         CSC100       BASIC
```

This permutation generates only one spurious tuple. This one is different from the two generated in the first JOIN and the two generated by the second JOIN.

Note that the reason that we cannot reproduce the original table is because we have join dependencies in the table. Since the LANG-IN-COURSE table has join dependencies, it cannot be decomposed into three binary tables. This problem was recognized by Dr. Codd in his early writings. He referred to the problem as the "connection trap."

5NF Anomalies.   To illustrate the various types of anomalies possible in the 5NF we will use our three decomposed tables: IN-COURSE, LANG-KNOW, and COURS-LANG.

Insertion Anomalies.   If we wanted to insert the fact that student S05 must know the APL language when taking the course CSC200, this information would have to be inserted into three different tables.

TABLE NAME: IN-COURSE		TABLE NAME: LANG-KNOW		TABLE NAME: COUR-LANG	
STU-ID	COURSE	STU-ID	PROG-LANG____	COURSE	PROG-LANG____
S01	CSC100	S01	BASIC	CSC100	BASIC
S01	CSC200	S01	PASCAL	CSC100	PASCAL
S02	CSC200	S01	ADA	CSC200	PASCAL
S03	CSC100	S02	PASCAL	CSC200	ADA
*S05	CSC200	S03	BASIC	*CSC200	APL
		*S05	APL		

The new tuples are shown with asterisks (*).

If these tables were in the 5NF, we would only have to insert one tuple into one table to store the information into the database.

TABLE NAME: LANG-IN-COURSE

```
STU-ID      COURSE       PROG-LANG____
S01         CSC100       BASIC
S01         CSC100       PASCAL
S01         CSC200       PASCAL
```

                        S01   CSC200   ADA
                        S02   CSC200   PASCAL
                        S03   CSC100   BASIC
                        S05   CSC200   APL

    Deletion Anomalies.   If we wanted to delete the fact that student S05 was to know the APL programming language for the course CSC200, we would have to delete tuples from three different tables.

TABLE NAME: IN-COURSE   **TABLE NAME: LANG-KNOW**   **TABLE NAME:**
COUR-LANG

STU-ID	COURSE	STU-ID	PROG-LANG	COURSE	PROG-LANG
S01	CSC100	S01	BASIC	CSC100	BASIC
S01	CSC200	S01	PASCAL	CSC100	PASCAL
S02	CSC200	S01	ADA	CSC200	PASCAL
S03	CSC100	S02	PASCAL	CSC200	ADA
*S05	CSC200	S03	BASIC	*CSC200	APL
		*S05	APL		

    The tuples that would have to be deleted are shown with asterisks (*).
    If the tables were in the 5NF, we would only have to delete one tuple from the normalized table.

TABLE NAME: LANG-IN-COURSE (BEFORE DELETION)

STU-ID	COURSE	PROG-LANG
S01	CSC100	BASIC
S01	CSC100	PASCAL
S01	CSC200	PASCAL
S01	CSC200	ADA
S02	CSC200	PASCAL
S03	CSC100	BASIC
S05	CSC200	APL

TABLE NAME: LANG-IN-COURSE (AFTER DELETION)

STU-ID	COURSE	PROG-LANG
S01	CSC100	BASIC
S01	CSC100	PASCAL
S01	CSC200	PASCAL
S01	CSC200	ADA
S02	CSC200	PASCAL
S03	CSC100	BASIC

    Update Anomalies.   If there is to be a change in any fact (STU-ID, PROG-LANG, or COURSE), that change will have to be made in two of the three unnormalized tables. For example, if we wanted to change student S01's identifier from

S01 to S99, we would have to change tuples in both the IN-COURSE and the LANG-KNOW tables.

TABLES BEFORE CHANGES ARE MADE

TABLE NAME: IN-COURSE   **TABLE NAME: LANG-KNOW**

STU-ID	COURSE		STU-ID	PROG-LANG
S01	CSC100		S01	BASIC
S01	CSC200		S01	PASCAL
S02	CSC200		S01	ADA
S03	CSC100		S02	PASCAL
			S03	BASIC

TABLES AFTER CHANGES ARE MADE

TABLE NAME: IN-COURSE   **TABLE NAME: LANG-KNOW**

STU-ID	COURSE		STU-ID	PROG-LANG
S99	CSC100		S99	BASIC
S99	CSC200		S99	PASCAL
S02	CSC200		S99	ADA
S03	CSC100		S02	PASCAL
			S03	BASIC

Again if the tables were in the 5NF, the minimum number of tuples would have to be changed within only one table.

TABLE NAME: LANG-IN-COURSE (BEFORE CHANGE)

STU-ID	COURSE	PROG-LANG
S01	CSC100	BASIC
S01	CSC100	PASCAL
S01	CSC200	PASCAL
S01	CSC200	ADA
S02	CSC200	PASCAL
S03	CSC100	BASIC

TABLE NAME: LANG-IN-COURSE (AFTER CHANGE)

STU-ID	COURSE	PROG-LANG
S99	CSC100	BASIC
S99	CSC100	PASCAL
S99	CSC200	PASCAL
S99	CSC200	ADA
S02	CSC200	PASCAL
S03	CSC100	BASIC

The Domain Key Normal Form

Up to this point we have discussed five or six normal forms (five if you count the BCNF as an extension of the 3NF and six if you do not). Where will this end? Will we have the 43NF before the turn of the century?

A definition of the domain key normal form.   Ronald Fagin has proposed what he calls the highest normal form, the domain key normal form (DK/NF). The definition of the DK/NF is as follows:

> a relation is in the DK/NF if every constraint can be inferred by simply knowing the set of attribute names and their underlying domains, along with their set of keys. [4, p. 387]

By constraints, Fagin is referring to any restrictions that are placed on a table. We have discussed two types of constraints thus far in this chapter: domain constraints and key constraints. A domain constraint is any constraint that restricts the values in a domain: that is, AGE must be an integer value between 21 and 65; CLASSIFICA-TION must be FRESHMAN, SOPHOMORE, JUNIOR, SENIOR, or GRAD; and so on. The key constraints refer to the fact that a certain attribute(s) is (are) a primary key. We know that the primary key must a unique identifier of each tuple in the relation. We are also aware that the value of the primary key of a relation cannot be null. As the definition of the DK/NF implies, these are the only two types of constraints allowed in tables.

Other constraints can be similar to functional dependencies. An example of a nondomain key constraint would be the relationship between COURSE-ID and COURSE-TITLE in our original COURSE table. We have already showed that the original COURSE table was not in the 2NF because functional dependencies existed between a part of the primary key (COURSE-ID of COURSE-ID + STU-ID + FAC-ID) and COURSE-TITLE.

```
COURSE (COURSE-ID, COURSE-TITLE, SECTION, STU-ID, FAC-ID)
```

Using the DK/NF terminology, we would say that there is a constraint on COURSE-TITLE. This constraint says that COURSE-TITLE is dependent upon COURSE-ID since every tuple where the COURSE-ID CSC100 occurs, the corresponding value of COURSE-TITLE must be Introduction to Computing. We must remove this additional constraint from the table by decomposing it into two smaller tables as follows.

```
COURSE (COURSE-ID, SECTION, STU-ID, FAC-ID)

COU-TITLE (COURSE-ID, COURSE-TITLE)
```

This is no different from what we did in converting the original COURSE table to the 2NF. We did use some different terminology to attain the same results.

DK/NF Insertion Anomalies.   Another more exotic constraint would be that our university policy dictates that no member of the Accounting Department can make over $50,000. This is a domain constraint that has a range constraint.

```
$0 <= SALARY (where FACULTY.DEPARTMENT = ACCOUNTING) <= $50,000
```

This means that if we attempt to insert a tuple of a new member of the Accounting faculty, the value of SALARY cannot be above $50,000. If it is, then an insertion anomaly is produced. (Be aware that the DK/NF definition of an anomaly is slightly different from Codd's definition of an anomaly.) This condition is not covered in our previous normal forms.

DK/NF deletion anomalies.   To illustrate a DK/NF deletion anomaly, let us look at our PERSONNEL table.

TABLE NAME: PERSONNEL

FAC-ID	FACULTY-NAME	BOSS-ID	TITLE-OR-RANK	SALARY
D02	GREG DAVIS		PRESIDENT	$80,000
M01	SCOTT MIZE	D02	DEAN	$60,000
S02	LARRY SIMPSON	D02	DEAN	$44,000
N02	NICK NORMAN	S02	DEPARTMENT CHAIR	$50,000
C01	JAN CARNER	M01	DEPARTMENT CHAIR	$42,000
H01	BYRON HOGAN	S02	DEPARTMENT CHAIR	$43,000
F01	LEE FALDO	S02	DEPARTMENT CHAIR	$45,000
J01	RAYMOND J. JOHNSON	F01	PROFESSOR	$40,000
S01	WENDY SWIMMER	F01	PROFESSOR	$45,000
D01	AMY DANCER	F01	ASSOC PROFESSOR	$34,500
J02	BOB JONES	C01	ASSOC PROFESSOR	$35,000
N01	JACK NELSON	N02	INSTRUCTOR	$28,000
N03	BEN NELSON	H01	ASSIST PROFESSOR	$30,000
S03	MARK STEWART	H01	ASSIST PROFESSOR	$30,500
C02	PAT CARNER	H01	PROFESSOR	$44,000

If we view the hierarchical structure that is represented in the PERSONNEL table, it would look like Figure 15.2.

The relationship of the FAC-ID and EMP-ID attributes indicates that each boss is also a faculty member. If we deleted faculty member Nick Norman (who is also a boss), we would have the following table.

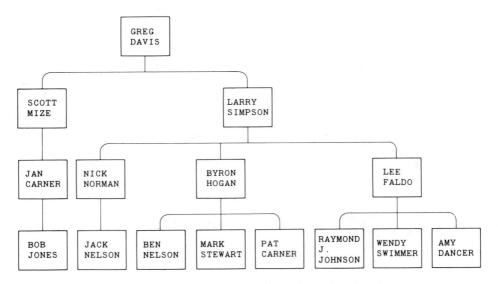

Figure 15.2   A Hierarchical View of the Personnel Table

TABLE NAME: PERSONNEL (AFTER DELETION)

FAC-ID	FACULTY-NAME	BOSS-ID	TITLE-OR-RANK	SALARY
D02	GREG DAVIS		PRESIDENT	$80,000
M01	SCOTT MIZE	D02	DEAN	$60,000
S02	LARRY SIMPSON	D02	DEAN	$44,000
C01	JAN CARNER	M01	DEPARTMENT CHAIR	$42,000
H01	BYRON HOGAN	S02	DEPARTMENT CHAIR	$43,000
F01	LEE FALDO	S02	DEPARTMENT CHAIR	$45,000
J01	RAYMOND J. JOHNSON	F01	PROFESSOR	$40,000
S01	WENDY SWIMMER	F01	PROFESSOR	$45,000
D01	AMY DANCER	F01	ASSOC PROFESSOR	$34,500
J02	BOB JONES	C01	ASSOC PROFESSOR	$35,000
N01	JACK NELSON	N02	INSTRUCTOR	$28,000
N03	BEN NELSON	H01	ASSIST PROFESSOR	$30,000
S03	MARK STEWART	H01	ASSIST PROFESSOR	$30,500
C02	PAT CARNER	H01	PROFESSOR	$44,000

Notice that faculty member Jack Nelson is managed by BOSS-ID N02 who no longer exists. This voids the constraint that a boss must also be a faculty member. This situation is similar to deleting the object of a foreign key, which we have previously discussed. Because this constraint can be voided, this table is not in the DK/NF.

Converting Tables to the DK/NF.   Fagin states that the purpose of his article is to illustrate the problems that could occur if a table is not in the DK/NF and not to show how to convert tables to the DK/NF. It is certainly more difficult to convert tables to the DK/NF. For example it is not very obvious how to remove the insertion anomaly from the FACULTY table. Perhaps we can create two tables each with the same set of attributes:

```
FACULTY (FAC-ID, FACULTY-NAME, DEPARTMENT, SALARY, GENDER)

ACC-FACULTY (FAC-ID, FACULTY-NAME, DEPARTMENT, SALARY, GENDER)
```

The only difference between the two tables would be that FACULTY.SALARY would be defined over a different domain from ACC-FACULTY.SALARY. ACC-FACULTY.SALARY would probably be a subset of FACULTY.SALARY. You might be wondering why we left the attribute DEPARTMENT in the ACC-FACULTY table, as every occurrence would certainly be ACCOUNTING. Suppose we wanted to do a global search over all faculty members for some condition. The easiest method of doing this would be to union the two tables together and make them one logical table. This could possibly be a view.

DK/NF Summary.   Fagin contends that if the domain and key constraints are fully enforced and all the other constraints (dependencies) are removed, the table(s) will automatically be devoid of any anomalies. This means that no anomalies can occur if the table(s) are in the DK/NK. Conversely, if the table(s) are arranged in such a manner that no anomalies can occur, the table(s) must be in the DK/NF.

Again the enforcement of these constraints can either be done through conventional language programs and/or embedded as "rules" with in the database schema definition.

The basic problem with the DK/NF is that there is no recipe for transforming tables into this normal form. The process is still a heuristic one. Some of the constraints are very obvious (such as the dependency between COURSE-ID and COURSE-TITLE) and can be removed very readily. However, some constraints are very subtle and require very detailed knowledge of the data to be represented in the database.

Summary of Normal Forms

Normal forms are an interesting aspect of database design. Let's summarize the seven normal forms that we have introduced.

First normal form	All attributes must contain only one value per tuple. All relations must be flat.
Second normal form	All non-key attributes must be fully- functionally dependent on the primary key.

Third normal form	There can be no transitive dependencies between non-key attributes. Boyce-Codd normal form All keys must be determinants.
Fourth normal form	There can be no more than one multi- valued dependency can be represented per relation.
Fifth normal form	There can be no join dependencies represented in decomposed tables. Domain key normal form Every constraint is either a domain constraint or a key constraint.

These normal forms are designed to reduce the various types of anomalies that can occur in database maintenance. As we have previously discussed, the usual method of converting a relation to a normal form (except for the 5NF) is to decompose a relation into several subsidiary relations. This action eliminates the various anomalies, but also decreases the retrieval speed in the database. The reason for this is that the decomposition directs some of the information that was previously stored in one relation into several relations. Now to retrieve the same information we must execute JOIN commands to reconstruct the original table so that the information can be retrieved. We can make this task easier on the user by utilizing views that contain the JOIN algorithm(s), but the JOIN operation must be executed regardless.

SHOULD WE NORMALIZE?

Normalization exchanges retrieval speed for the reduction of possible data maintenance anomalies. In attempting to answer the question posed, we must decide what the most important criterion in our database is: retrieval speed or data accuracy. The obvious answer is that we want them both. However, in this situation it is very rare where we can maximize both criteria. It seems to us that whenever we have this decision to make, we should always opt for data accuracy. We would certainly not want members of our organization to have rapid retrieval of inaccurate data. With speed advances being made in specialized database hardware, we will be able to buy faster retrieval, but we will not be able to buy more accurate data.

If we accept the choice of data accuracy over data retrieval speed, the question becomes: How far do we normalize? In to how many normal forms do we try to get our tables? As you can see from our examples, the BCNF, 4NF, and 5NF occur in somewhat obscure situations. For this reason, we feel that the third normal form is the most important normal form, for it should occur the most times in attempting to design a database. This does not mean that we feel that the higher normal forms are unimportant!!! It just means that we feel that their circumstances will not occur as much as the circumstances concerning the 3NF. What this means is that unless your database has some of the obscure situations, you will not have to worry as much about the "upper" normal forms anyway.

A DESIGN PROCESS

Now that we have introduced all the concepts involved with the logical design of database, we will attempt to put them together into what we think is a useful design procedure. This procedure consists of nine steps:

1. Determine the entities of the data that you are trying to represent. Classify these entities as kernels, associations, designations, or characteristics.
2. Determine the properties that are associated with each entity.
3. Determine the unique identifier of each entity.
4. Create a base table to represent each kernel entity. The properties of the kernel become the attributes of the table. Select the attribute(s) representing the unique identifiers as the primary keys of the table. When creating the table, specify NOT NULL for each attribute in the primary key. Create a UNIQUE index over the primary key. Create the index before the table is loaded.
5. Create a base table for each association entity. The properties of the kernel become the attributes of the table. Be sure to include the foreign keys so that linkage can be made to the proper kernel entities. Specify the primary key of the table.
6. Create a base table for each designation entity. The properties of the association become attributes of the table. Select an attribute(s) to be the primary key of the table. Part of the primary key will be an attribute that is used as the foreign key to the kernel table that this table designates.
7. Create a base table for each characteristic entity. Be sure to include the foreign keys so that linkage can be made to the proper entity tables. Specify the primary key of the table.
8. Determine all the dependencies (functional, transitive, multivalued, and join) necessary for normalization.
9. Apply the necessary decompositions to place the base tables into the desired normal form.

Once the logical design process is complete and we feel that we have developed the best logical schema that we possibly can, we can then transform this schema into ORACLE tables and views. This "ultimate" schema is sometimes called the canonical schema.

SUMMARY

This chapter discussed the various aspects of logical database design. We described a method of formulating the logical database model: the RM/T model. We suggested the necessary enterprise personnel who could comprise the design team. The various types of dependencies: functional, transitive, multivalued, and join were introduced. These dependencies and their relationship to the various normal forms were explored. The chapter concluded with a nine point design procedure.

Now that you have finished this chapter, you should be familiar with the following design terms and concepts.

A. Logical design of databases	**N.** Transitive dependency
B. Semantic modeling	**O.** Multivalued dependency
C. RM/T model	**P.** Join dependency
D. Entity	**Q.** Normalization
E. Property	**R.** 1NF
F. Relationship	**S.** 2NF
G. Association	**T.** 3NF
H. Designation	**U.** BCNF
I. Kernel	**V.** 4NF
J. Characteristic	**W.** 5NF, PJNF
K. Performance monitoring	**X.** DK/NF
L. Functional dependency	**Y.** Anomalies
M. Determinant	

EXERCISES

1. Explain why the same methodology that is used to design computer programs cannot be used to design databases.

2. Explain why database designs change over time.

3. Explain the three circumstances that could occur if we attempt to delete the object of a foreign key.

4. Explain the three circumstances that could occur if we attempt to modify the object of a foreign key.

5. Explain the difference between the 3NF and the BCNF.

6. Explain the difference between Codd's concept of anomalies and Fagin's concept of anomalies.

7. Select an environment and, using the techniques described in this chapter, develop a logical design for a database encompassing that environment. Here are some suggestions.

    (a) A university environment. We have tried to utilize the university environment as a database environment in this text. There are some other aspects of the university environment that could be represented in a database. How about a departmentalized record keeping system?

    (b) A local epicurean directory. Assume that you have started a company whose function is to evaluate the various eateries and taverns in your town. You could include such things as what is served at the various establishments, prices per item, quality of food, service, and so on and other interesting things about these establishments.

(c) A car brokerage firm. Assume that customers would come to your company with an idea of what type car (new or used) they would like to purchase. They might have some criteria (price range, color, horsepower, manufacturer, model, etc.) as to what type car they would like to see. Your firm would run the requests through your database and direct the customers to the car dealers that have cars that meet their criteria.

(d) A fraternity/sorority directory. Develop a database to keep records of graduated students. We could keep track of where these former students are, who they are working for, and so on. This could be used for future employment contacts.

(e) A sports league record book. Take any professional or amateur sports league or conference and design a database to keep track of team and player records. For example, with the professional baseball leagues, you could record batting, pitching, and team statistics for the leagues' players and teams. We could assume that every day we would want to generate such statistics as team standings, batting, and pitching leaders, and so on.

Make sure that the environment you select is complex enough to contain enough relationships that you can utilize the various types of entities and relationships described in this chapter.

REFERENCES

1. Ceri, S. and G. Gottlob "Normalization of Relations and Prolog," *Communications of the ACM*, 29, no. 6, (June 1986), 524–544.

2. Chen, Peter "The Entity-Relationship Model—Towards a Unified View of Data," *ACM Transactions on Database Systems"*, 1, 1, (March 1976), 9–36.

3. Codd, E.F. "Extending the Database Relational Model to Capture More Meaning," *Transactions on Database Systems*, 4, 4, (December 1979) 397–434.

4. Date, C. J. *A Guide to DB2*, Addison-Wesley, Reading, MA, 1984.

5. Date, C. J. *An Introduction to Database Systems*, (4th ed), Addison-Wesley, Reading, MA, 1986.

6. Fagin, Ronald, "A Normal Form for Relational Databases That Is Based on Domains and Keys," *ACM Transactions on Database Systems*, VOL. 6, NO. 3, (September 1981), 387–415.

7. Hawryszkiewycz, I. T. *Database Analysis and Design*, Science Research Associates, Chicago, 1984.

8. Kent, William "A Simple Guide to Five Normal Forms in Relational Database Theory," *Communications of the ACM*, VOL. 26, NO. 2, (February 1983), 120–125.

A

Appendix:
Summary
of UFI Commands

UFI commands are used to do such things as manage the SQL command buffer, manage the interface to certain external files, format data retrieved from ORACLE tables, and so on. UFI commands are executed from the UFI> prompt. UFI commands are usually differentiated from SQL commands in that UFI commands do not end with a semicolon (;) whereas most SQL commands do. UFI commands do not span more than one line.

I. SQL Buffer Management Commands

   Description: These commands are used to manage the SQL command currently residing in the SQL command buffer. Each of these commands can be abbreviated to the first letter of the command.

   A. LIST

      Syntax: LIST [n]

      Purpose: To display a single line or all of the lines in the SQL command buffer. It determines the current line in the buffer. The current line is designated with an asterisk (*) beside the line number.

      Examples: LIST
                 L
                 LIST 4

B. RUN

Syntax: RUN

Purpose: To display and then execute the command stored in the command
buffer.

Examples: RUN
           R

C. /

Syntax: /

Purpose: To execute the command stored in the buffer.

Example: /

D. DEL

Syntax: DEL

Purpose: To delete the current line in the command buffer.

Examples: DEL
           D

E. INPUT

Syntax: INPUT

Purpose: To insert a new line after the current line in the buffer. After
the command is typed and the RETURN/ENTER key is pressed,
UFI prompts the user for the new line.

Examples: INPUT
           I

F. APPEND

Syntax: APPEND

Purpose: To append a string onto the end of the current line in the
command buffer. There must be one space between the command and the string to be appended.

Examples: `APPEND additional text to be appended`
          `A new text`

G. CHANGE

Syntax: `CHANGE/old string/new string/`

Purpose: To substitute the first occurrence of one string for another in the current line of the command buffer.

Examples: `CHANGE/sname/student-name/`
          `C/sname/student-name/`

II. SQL Buffer/External File Commands

Description: These three commands allow the user to either copy the contents of the SQL buffer to an external file, retrieve the contents of an external file into the SQL command buffer, or retrieve and execute the contents of an external file.

A. SAVE

Syntax: `SAVE filename [APPEND]`

Purpose: To write the contents of the SQL buffer out to an external file. If the APPEND option is not specified, a new file is created and the contents of the SQL command buffer are written to the file. If the file currently exists and the APPEND option is not specified, its current contents are overwritten. If APPEND is specified, the contents of the SQL command buffer are appended to the end of the file. Check with your specific ORACLE manual for file naming conventions.

Examples: `SAVE file1`
          `SAVE file1 APPEND`

B. GET

Syntax: `GET filename`

Purpose: To copy the contents of an external file into the SQL command buffer. Once the command resides in the buffer it can be executed, modified, or saved to another file. The external file can only contain a single SQL command.

Example: `GET file1`

C. START

Syntax: `START filename [parameters]`

Purpose: To copy the contents of an external file into the SQL command buffer and execute the command(s). This external file may contain either SQL or UFI commands. If the command(s) in the external file contain short–term variables (variables preceded by a single ampersand (&)) parameters for the variables can be specified in the START command.

Examples: `START file1`
`START file1 parm1 parm2`

III. Set Commands

Description: Set commands give the user the ability to do such things as change the SQL terminator character, change the spacing between output columns, and set the number of lines on an output page. The commands listed next are <u>not an exhaustive list</u>. Your version of ORACLE may have additional <u>SET commands</u>.

A. AUTOCOMMIT

Syntax: `SET AUTOCOMMIT {OFF | IMM}`

Purpose: To inform ORACLE whether data maintenance changes are to be committed immediately or when the COMMIT command is executed.

Examples: `SET AUTOCOMMIT OFF`
`SET AUTOCOMMIT IMM`

Default Setting: `SET AUTOCOMMIT OFF`

B. Command Separator

Syntax: `SET CMDSEP {character | OFF}`

Purpose: To allow the user to place multiple UFI commands on one input line. The character specified becomes the UFI command separator.

Examples: `SET CMDSEP *`
`SET CMDSEP OFF`

Default Setting: `SET CMDSEP OFF`

C. Define Short-Term Variables

Syntax: `SET DEFINE character`

Purpose: To define the character that is to precede all short-term variables.

Examples: `SET DEFINE %`
`SET DEFINE *`

Default Setting: `SET DEFINE &`

D. Display Error Numbers

Syntax: `SET ERRORFLAG {ON | OFF}`

Purpose: To allow the user to see the ORACLE error message number.

Examples: `SET ERRORFLAG ON`
`SET ERRORFLAG OFF`

Default Setting: `SET ERRORFLAG OFF`

E. Display Column Headings

Syntax: `SET HEADING {ON | OFF}`

Purpose: To allow the user to control whether he or she wants all column headings displayed or not.

Examples: `SET HEADING ON`
`SET HEADING OFF`

Default Setting: `SET HEADING ON`

F. Heading Separator

Syntax: `SET HEADSEP character`

Purpose: To define the character that signifies end-of-line in stacked headings.

Example: `SET HEADSEP "*"`

Default Setting: `SET HEADSEP "|"`

G. Display Length for LONG Data Types

Syntax: `SET LONG integer-number`

Purpose: To set the display width per output line for attributes of data type LONG.

Examples: `SET LONG 25`
          `SET LONG 100`

Default Setting: `SET LONG 80`

H. Maximum Length of a Tuple

Syntax: `SET MAXDATA number`

Purpose: To establish the maximum number of bytes for a tuple.

Example: `SET MAXDATA 1000`

Default Setting: `SET MAXDATA 5000`

I. Display Characters for Null Values

Syntax: `SET NULL "string"`

Purpose: To establish the default value that is to be displayed for all null values.

Examples: `SET NULL "none"`
          `SET NULL "N/A"`

Default Setting: `SET NULL " "`

J. Disregard String Substitutions in Variables

Syntax: `SET SCAN {ON | OFF}`

Purpose: To turn the substitution of characters in both long term and short term variables.

Examples: `SET SCAN ON`
          `SET SCAN OFF`

Default Setting: `SET SCAN ON`

K. Display Old and New Settings of SET Commands

Syntax: `SET SHOWMODE {ON | OFF}`

Purpose: To give the user the option to display both the old and new settings each time a SET command is entered.

Examples: `SET SHOWMODE ON`
          `SET SHOWMODE OFF`

Default Setting: `SET SHOWMODE OFF`

L. Numbering of Multiline SQL Commands

Syntax: `SET SQLNUMBER {ON | OFF}`

Purpose: To allow the user to turn off the numbering of multiline SQL commands. If this option is turned off, lines 2 - N are prefixed with the current value of SQLPROMPT.

Examples: `SET SQLNUMBER ON`
          `SET SQLNUMBER OFF`

Default Setting: `SET SQLNUMBER ON`

M. The SQL Terminator Character

Syntax: `SET SQLTERM "character"`

Purpose: To allow the user to change the character that begins execution of each SQL command.

Examples: `SET SQLTERM "*"`
          `SET SQLTERM "#"`

Default Setting: `SET SQLTERM ";"`

N. The SQL Prompt

Syntax: `SET SQLPROMPT "string"`

Purpose: To specify the value of the prompt that is displayed on multiline SQL commands. The value of ''string'' is used as a prompt on lines 2 through N of the SQL command buffer. This command is used in conjunction with the SQLNUMBER command.

Examples: SET SQLPROMPT "RBB:"
          SET SQLPROMPT "Have a nice day ->"

Default Setting: SET SQLPROMPT "SQL>"

O. Hardware Tabbing

Syntax: SET TAB {ON | OFF}

Purpose: To allow the user to change the value of the hardware tab
         setting. This affects the display of the results of a SQL SELECT
         command.

Examples: SET TAB ON
          SET TAB OFF

P. Termination Display to the Terminal

Syntax: SET TERMOUT {ON | OFF}

Purpose: To terminate temporarily the display of ORACLE commands
         to the terminal. This command is very useful when we are
         SPOOLing the results of large queries that do not need to be
         displayed on terminal screens.

Examples: SET TERMOUT ON
          SET TERMOUT OFF

Default Setting: SET TERMOUT ON

Q. UFI Prefix

Syntax: SET UFIPREFIX "character"

Purpose: To specify the character that indicates that a UFI command is
         embedded within a SQL command.

Examples: SET UFIPREFIX "*"
          SET UFIPREFIX "&"

Default Setting: SET UFIPREFIX "#"

R. The UFI Prompt

Syntax: SET UFIPROMPT "string"

Purpose: To allow the user to tailor the UFI prompt.

Examples: `SET UFIPROMPT "RBB>"`
          `SET UFIPROMPT ". . .---. . ."`

Default Setting: `SET UFIPROMPT "UFI>"`

S. Prefixing the UFI Prompt with the Time

Syntax: `SET TIME {ON | OFF}`

Purpose: To allow the user the option of prefixing the UFI prompt with the current time.

Examples: `SET TIME ON`
          `SET TIME OFF`

Default Setting: `SET TIME OFF`

T. The Underline Character

Syntax: `SET UNDERLINE "character"`

Purpose: To give the user the option of changing the character used to separate the attribute headings from the attribute values. Normally this is the underline character.

Examples: `SET UNDERLINE "*"`
          `SET UNDERLINE "_"`

Default Setting: `SET UNDERLINE "_"`

U. Display the Old and New Values of Variables

Syntax: `SET VERIFY {ON | OFF}`

Purpose: To allow the user the option of displaying the old and new values of substitution variables in SQL commands.

Examples: `SET VERIFY ON`
          `SET VERIFY OFF`

Default Setting: `SET VERIFY ON`

V. Setting the Value ORACLE's Workspace Size

Syntax: `SET WORKSPACE number`

Purpose: To allow the user to change the number of bytes allocated to the current workspace.

Examples: `SET WORKSIZE 10000`
`SET WORKSIZE 50000`

Default Setting: `SET WORKSIZE 8000`

W. Displaying the SQL Command Before It Is Executed

Syntax: `SET ECHO {ON | OFF}`

Purpose: To give the user the option of displaying the text of commands (both SQL and UFI) before they are executed. This command is very useful when executing commands stored in external files.

Examples: `SET ECHO ON`
`SET ECHO OFF`

Default Setting: `SET ECHO ON`

X. Specifying How Many Tuples Were Retrieved

Syntax: `SET FEEDBACK integer-number`

Purpose: To allow the user to change the number of tuples retrieved to get the message

`n rows selected`

displayed. If the value is set to zero, the feedback message is never displayed.

Examples: `SET FEEDBACK 20`
`SET FEEDBACK 0`

Default Setting: `SET FEEDBACK 6`

Y. The Maximum Line Size

Syntax: `SET LINESIZE integer-number`

Purpose: To establish the maximum output line size.

Examples: `SET LINESIZE 120`
`SET LINESIZE  50`

Default Setting: `SET LINESIZE 80`

Z. The Number of Blank Lines from the Top of an Output Page

Syntax: `SET NEWPAGE integer-number`

Purpose: To establish the number of blank lines from the top of each new output page.

Example: `SET NEWPAGE 3`

Default Setting: `SET NEWPAGE 1`

AA. The Number of Numeric Digits Displayed

Syntax: `SET NUMWIDTH integer-number`

Purpose: To establish the default number of positions allocated to the output of each numeric value.

Example: `SET NUMWIDTH 7`

Default Setting: `SET NUMWIDTH 10`

BB. The Number of Output Lines per Page

Syntax: `SET PAGESIZE integer-number`

Purpose: To specify the number of output lines per page.

Example: `SET PAGESIZE 30`

Default Setting: `SET PAGESIZE 19`

CC. Pausing After N Lines of Output

Syntax: `SET PAUSE {ON | OFF}`
or `SET PAUSE "string"`

Purpose: To allow page at a time scrolling of output. ORACLE will display a screen or page of data, then wait for the user to press the RETURN key to display another screen or page of data. If the ''string'' option is used, ORACLE displays the value of the string after it displays each screen or page of data.

Examples: `SET PAUSE ON`
`SET PAUSE OFF`
`SET PAUSE "To see another screen, press RETURN"`

Default Setting: `SET PAUSE OFF`

DD. Spacing Between Columns

Syntax: `SET SPACE integer-number`

Purpose: To allow the user to specify the spacing between attributes. The number specified must be between 1 and 10.

Example: `SET SPACE 3`

Default Setting: `SET SPACE 1`

IV. Column Commands
Description: Column commands are used to assist in the formatting of columns (attributes) of data. The column command may be specified with the word COLUMN or the shortened form COL. The columns whose settings have been altered during the current ORACLE session are kept in an ''active settings list.'' If we want to display the names of the columns whose formats have been altered, we may enter the command

COLUMN

If we want to see the current settings for one particular setting, we may enter the command

COLUMN column-name

Through out this section of this appendix we will use the term column-name to refer to any of the following:

1. An attribute or column name
2. An expression
3. A table label

A. What's Available?

Syntax: `COLUMN ?`

Purpose: To display to the user a list of possible column commands.

Example: `COLUMN ?`

B. Column Headings

Syntax: `COLUMN column-name HEADING string`

Purpose: To allow the user the flexibility of specifying different column headings.

Examples: `COLUMN SNAME STUDENT-NAME`
`COL SNAME 'STUDENT NAME'`
`COL SNAME 'STUDENT | NAME'`

Default Value: The attribute name specified in the CREATE TABLE command.

C. Formatting Attribute Values

Syntax: `COLUMN column-name FORMAT format-mask`

Purpose: To allow the user to alter the default display format for a particular column. The format masks are described in Chapter 6 of this text.

Examples: `COLUMN SNAME FORMAT A20`
`COLUMN SALARY FORMAT 999.99`
`COL SALARY FORMAT $9,999.99`

Default Values: The value specified in NUMWIDTH for numeric values. The size of the field specified in the CREATE TABLE

command for character data. The standard date format
(dd-MON-yy) for date data.

D. Wrapping Character Data

Syntax: `COLUMN column-name {WRAP | TRUNC}`

Purpose: To specify what happens when a character attribute is too large
to fit in the allocated output field size. The options available
are to wrap the extra text around to the next output line or to
truncate the text at the end of the specified attribute width.

Examples: `COLUMN BIOGRAPHY WRAP`
`COLUMN NAME-OF-PARENT TRUNC`

Default Setting: `WRAP`

E. Defining an Alias

Syntax: `COLUMN column-name ALIAS alias-name`

Purpose: Allows the user to rename a column. This is particularly useful
when we have long arithmetic expressions.

Examples: `COLUMN STUDENT-NAME ALIAS SN`
`COL A+B-C/D+E-F*G ALIAS Z`

F. Clearing Column Settings

Syntax: `COLUMN column-name CLEAR`

Purpose: To return all the column's altered column settings back to their
default values and remove the column name from the ''active
settings list.''

Example: `COLUMN SNAME CLEAR`

G. Return to Default Settings

Syntax: `COLUMN column-name DEFAULT`

Purpose: To return all the column's altered column settings back to their
default values. The column remains on the ''active setting list.''

Example: `COLUMN SNAME DEFAULT`

H. Justifying Column Headings

Syntax: COLUMN column-name JUSTIFY {LEFT | CENTER
        | RIGHT}

Purpose: To allow the user to specify column heading justification. Only the heading is justified, not the actual data.

Example: COLUMN SNAME JUSTIFY CENTER
         COLUMN SALARY JUSTIFY LEFT

Default Values: Headings on character and date are left justified, and headings on numeric data are right justified.

I. Duplicating Column Specifications

Syntax: COLUMN column-name-1 LIKE column-name-2

Purpose: To allow the user to duplicate column formatting specifications of a previously formatted column.

Example: COLUMN SPOUSE_NAME LIKE EMPLOYEE-NAME

J. Specifying New Lines

Syntax: COLUMN column-name NEWLINE

Purpose: To force the displaying of a specified column on a new output line.

Example: COLUMN SNAME NEWLINE

K. Displaying Column Specific Values for Null Values

Syntax: COLUMN column-name NULL 'string'

Purpose: To allow the user to customize the display for null values for a particular column. The SET NULL 'string' command specifies what is to be displayed for all null values, whereas the COLUMN NULL specifies what is to be displayed for null values in a specific column. The COLUMN NULL takes precedence over the SET NULL command.

Examples: COLUMN SALARY NULL '----'
          COLUMN SNAME NULL '** ERROR **'

L. Displaying Columns or Not

Syntax: `COLUMN column-name {PRINT | NOPRINT}`

Purpose: To allow the user the flexibility of displaying a column or not. This command is very useful with tables that contain many columns. If we want to display all but one or two of the columns, we can turn the ones we do not wish to display off and still execute the

```
        SELECT *
        FROM table
```

command. The attributes designated with NOPRINT will no display.

Example: `COLUMN SALARY NOPRINT`

Default Setting: `PRINT`

M. Temporary Format Settings

Syntax: `COLUMN column-name TEMPORARY`

Purpose: To allow the user to specify column formatting command that are in effect only for the next SQL SELECT command.

Example: `COLUMN SNAME TEMPORARY`

N. Temporarily Restore Default Format Settings For Columns

Syntax: `COLUMN column-name {ON | OFF}`

Purpose: To suspend temporarily altered format settings for a column.

Examples: `COLUMN SALARY OFF`
          `COLUMN SALARY ON`

V. Miscellaneous UFI Commands
    A. Exiting ORACLE

Syntax: `EXIT`

Purpose: To exit the UFI processor. All uncommitted file maintenance changes are automatically committed upon exit.

Example: EXIT

B. Connecting to Other ORACLE User-names

Syntax: CONNECT user-name/password

Purpose: To transfer to another ORACLE user–name.

Example: CONNECT THEIR-USER-NAME/THEIR-PASSWORD

C. Accessing the HELP Facility

Syntax: HELP [SQL command | UFI command]

Purpose: To enter the ORACLE HELP facility.

Eamples: HELP
         HELP SELECT
         HELP COLUMN

D. Spooling Output to External Files

Syntax: SPOOL {filename | OUT | OFF}

Purpose: To open a spool file so that the ORACLE output can be written
         out to the external file. The name of the file (filename) must
         be valid for the computer system that ORACLE is being run
         on. The OUT option closes the spool file and directs it to the
         system printer. The OFF option merely closes the file. There
         can be only one spool file open at any instant of time.

Examples: SPOOL FILE1
          SPOOL OUT
          SPOOL OFF

E. Displaying the Current Settings of the SET or UFI Commands

Syntax: SHOW {set-command | UFI Command | ALL}

Purpose: To allow the user to view the current settings of either UFI
         or SET commands.

Examples: SHOW ALL
          SHOW NUMWIDTH

F. Description of Tables

Syntax: `DESC[RIBE] user-name,table`

Purpose: To allow the user to get a quick description of the attributes
that make up a table.

Example: `DESC STUDENT-TABLE`

G. Designate Control Breaks

Syntax: `BREAK ON column-name1 [ON column-name2]`
`[SKIP n] [PAGE] [DUP | NODUP]`

Purpose: To inform ORACLE what to do on control breaks. This command is associated with the ORACLE internal report writer.

Examples: `BREAK ON DEPARTMENT SKIP 2`
`BREAK ON DEPARTMENT PAGE`
`BREAK ON DEPARTMENT SKIP 5 NODUP`

H. Computing the Sum of Values on Control Breaks

Syntax: `COMPUTE SUM OF numeric-column-name1`
`[numeric-column-name2]`
`ON column-name`

Purpose: To compute the sum of a numeric column-name on a control
break. This command is associated with the ORACLE internal
report writer.

Example: `COMPUTE SUM OF SALARY ON DEPARTMENT`

B

Appendix:
Summary
of SQL Commands

I. The CREATE Command

Description: To make ORACLE aware of the existence of such entities as tables, views, synonyms, indexes, space definitions, clusters, and partitions.

A. Creating Tables

Syntax: `CREATE TABLE table-name (attribute-definitions)`
`[SPACE space-definition]`

Purpose: To define the structure of a table. The attribute definitions consist of the following:

`Attribute-name {NUMBER | CHAR | DATE | LONG}`
`[NOT NULL]`

If no space definition is specified, the table data and indexes are placed in the SYSTEM partition.

Examples: `CREATE TABLE MY_TABLE (ATTRIBUTE-1 NUMBER,`
`                            ATTRIBUTE_2 CHAR (10),`
`                            ATTRIBUTE_3 DATE,`
`                            ATTRIBUTE_4 LONG);`

`        CREATE TABLE MY_TABLE_1 (ATTRIBUTE_1 NUMBER (5)`
`                            NOT NULL,`
`                            ATTRIBUTE_2 NUMBER (10,3),`
`                            ATTRIBUTE_3 NUMBER)`
`                            SPACE MY_SPACE;`

B. Creating Views

Syntax: `CREATE VIEW view-name [attribute-names] AS`
`        select command`

Purpose: To create a virtual table. The view SELECT command can contain any optional clause of the SELECT command except the ORDER BY clause. The SELECT clause may contain attributes, constants, or expressions.

Examples: `CREATE VIEW MY_VIEW AS`
`        SELECT * FROM MY_TABLE`
`        WHERE ATTRIBUTE_1 = 'abcd';`
`        CREATE VIEW MY_VIEW-2 (FLD1, FLD2, FLD3) AS`
`        SELECT ATTRIBUTE_1, ATTRIBUTE_2/5,`
`          SQRT (ATTRIBUTE_3)`
`        FROM MY_TABLE_2;`

C. Creating Indexes

Syntax: `CREATE [UNIQUE] INDEX index-name ON`
`        table-name (column-name(s))`
`        [SYSSORT | NOSYSSORT] [PCTFREE integer-number]`
`        [COMPRESS | NOCOMPRESS]`
`        [ROWS = integer-number]`

Purpose: To create indexes over a column(s) in a table. Indexes generally speed up retrieval and slow down data maintenance. Indexes are maintained through B* trees.

Examples: `CREATE INDEX MY_INDEX ON MY_TABLE_`
`        1 (ATTRIBUTE_1);`
`        CREATE UNIQUE INDEX PK_MY_TABLE_1`
`          ON MY_TABLE_2 (ATTRIBUTE_1);`

D. Creating Partitions

Syntax: `CREATE PARTITION partition-name;`

Purpose: To allow the system DBA to create partition names. This command can only be executed by a user with DBA privilege. This command only creates the partition name. The partition must be altered (through the ALTER PARTITION command) to allocate the space for the partition.

Example: `CREATE PARTITION MY-PARTITION;`

E. Creating Space Definitions

Syntax:
```
CREATE SPACE [DEFINITION] space-definition-name
   [DATAPAGES ( [INITIAL page-allocation ]
                [,INCREMENT page-allocation ]
                [,MAXEXTENTS number-of-extents ]
                [, PCTFREE percent ])
    [INDEXPAGES ( [INITIAL page-allocation ]
                [,INCREMENT page-allocation ]
                [,MAXEXTENTS number-of-extents ] )
    [PARTITION    partition-name ]
```

Purpose: To create templates for table data and index space and to direct the data and indexes into a specific partition. If the PARTITION clause is omitted, the data and indexes are placed into the SYSTEM partition.

Examples:
```
CREATE SPACE DEFINITION MY_SPACE;
CREATE SPACE YOUR_SPACE PARTITION
   YOUR_PARTITION;
CREATE SPACE DEFINITION OUR_SPACE
   DATAPAGES (INITIAL 3, INCREMENT 10,
              MAXEXTENTS 10, PCTFREE 25)
   INDEXPAGES (INITIAL 4, INCREMENT 8,
              MAXEXTENTS 10)
   PARTITION MY_PARTITION;
```

Default Values:
```
INITIAL = 5
INCREMENT = 25
MAXEXTENTS = 16
PCTFREE = 20
```

F. Creating Synonyms

Syntax: `CREATE [PUBLIC] SYNONYM synonym-name FOR`
`[user-name.] {table-name | view-name }`

Purpose: To create an unqualified name for a table or view. Normally when accessing a table or view from another user-name, the table or view name must be prefixed with the user-name where the table or view is located:

`MY-ACCOUNT.MY-TABLE`

The creation of a synonym allows the user of the table or view to create a shortened (by removing the qualifier) name for the table or view. Only the creator or the synonym can use the synonym. Database administrators can create PUBLIC synonyms so that all system users can use the synonyms.

Examples: `CREATE SYNONYM FRED FOR`
`YOUR_USER_NAME.YOUR_TABLE;`
`CREATE PUBLIC SYNONYM FOR MY_USER_NAME.MY_TABLE;`

G. Creating Clusters

Syntax: `CREATE CLUSTER cluster-name (column-name(s) type(s))`
`[SPACE definition-name]`
`[SIZE page-allocation]`
`[ {COMPRESS | NOCOMPRESS} ]`

Purpose: To place tuples from different tables with the same value of the JOIN key on the same physical page. Cluster are used to speed up join operations. Once the cluster is created, it must be altered (via the ALTER CLUSTER command) to add the necessary tables.

Example: `CREATE CLUSTER MY-CLUSTER (STUDENT-`
`ID CHAR(3));`

II. The DROP Command

Description: To remove the existence of an entity that was created via the CREATE command. To remove any entity that was CREATEd (except partitions), we must execute the drop command.

A. Dropping Tables

Syntax: `DROP TABLE table-name`

Purpose: To remove the table description from the data dictionary and all its associated data from the system.

Example: `DROP TABLE MY_TABLE;`

B. Dropping Views

Syntax: `DROP VIEW view-name`

Purpose: To remove the view description from the data dictionary.

Example: `DROP VIEW MY_VIEW;`

C. Dropping Indexes

Syntax: `DROP INDEX index-name`

Purpose: To remove an index from a table. Removing an index does not affect the data stored in the table in any way.

Example: `DROP INDEX PK_MY_TABLE;`

D. Dropping Storage Spaces

Syntax: `DROP SPACE space-name;`

Purpose: To make the space definition template unusable. This command does not affect any of the existing tables that used the dropped storage space to allocate data and index storage. That storage space definition is still in effect for them.

Example: `DROP SPACE MY_SPACE;`

E. Dropping Synonyms

Syntax: `DROP [PUBLIC] SYNONYM synonym-name`

Purpose: To remove the synonym for the data dictionary.

Examples: `DROP SYNONYM FRED;`
`DROP PUBLIC SYNONYM ALBERT;`

F. Dropping Clusters

Syntax: `DROP CLUSTER cluster-name`

Purpose: To uncluster all tables stored in the cluster. Dropping clusters does not affect the data stored in clusters.

Example: `DROP CLUSTER MY_CLUSTER;`

III. The ALTER Command

Description: To allow the user to modify table descriptions, partitions, and clusters.

A. Altering Tables

Syntaxes:
```
ALTER TABLE table-name
ADD{column-name data-type |
     (column-name1 data-type1,
      column-name2 data-type2, . . .)}

ALTER TABLE table-name
MODIFY {column-name data-type |
        (column-name1 data-type1,
         column-name2 data-type2, . . .)}
```

Purpose: To allow the user to either add additional attributes to the right side of a table and/or modify attributes currently in a table.

Examples:
```
ALTER TABLE MY_TABLE
ADD NEW-COLUMN CHAR (5);
ALTER TABLE MY_TABLE
ADD (NEW_COLUMN2 NUMBER (5), NEW_COLUMN3 DATE);
ALTER TABLE MY_TABLE
MODIFY NEW_COLUMN CHAR (8);
ALTER TABLE MY_TABLE
MODIFY (NEW_COLUMN2 CHAR (5),
        NEW_COLUMN CHAR (20));
```

B. Altering Partitions

Syntax:
```
ALTER PARTITION partition-name
ADD FILE 'file-name';
```

Purpose: To increase the size of a currently existing partition by conjoining a new file to the partition. This command can only be executed by a user with DBA privilege.

Example: `ALTER PARTITION MY_PARTITION ADD FILE 'MY_FILE';`

C. Altering Clusters

Syntaxes: ```
ALTER CLUSTER cluster-name
    ADD TABLE table-name
    WHERE [cluster-name,]clusterkey-column1 =
        [table-name,]column1
    [AND [cluster-name,]clusterkey-column2 =
        [table-name,]column2] , , ,

ALTER CLUSTER cluster-name
    DROP TABLE table-name
```

Purpose: To either add tables to clusters or remove tables from clusters. The **WHERE** clause should be the forecasted equi-JOIN keys. The DROP TABLE clause does not delete the tuples in the table, it merely unclusters the table.

Examples: ```
ALTER CLUSTER MY_CLUSTER
    ADD TABLE MY_TABLE
    WHERE MY_CLUSTER.STUDENT_ID = MY_TABLE.SID;
ALTER CLUSTER MY_CLUSTER
    ADD TABLE YOUR_TABLE
    WHERE MY_CLUSTER.STUDENT.ID = YOUR_TABLE.SID;
ALTER CLUSTER MY_CLUSTER
    DROP TABLE MY_TABLE;
```

IV. The SELECT Command

Description: To retrieve tuples from ORACLE tables.

A. The Simple SELECT Command

Syntax: ```
SELECT [DISTINCT] select-list
FROM table-name [table-label]
[WHERE theta-condition(s)]
[ORDER BY {attribute-name | expression} [DESC] , , ,]
```

Purpose: To extract tuples from ORACLE tables for display. The value for the select list can be either an asterisk (*), which means that all attributes of the table will be displayed, or individual attributes, constants, or expressions. The DISTINCT clause removes duplicate tuples.

Examples: ```
SELECT * FROM MY_TABLE;
SELECT NAME, AGE, GPA FROM STUDENT_TABLE;
SELECT * FROM STUDENT_TABLE WHERE GENDER = 'MALE';
SELECT NAME, AGE, GPA/3
FROM STUDENT
```

```
                    WHERE GENDER = 'FEMALE'
                      AND GPA > 3.0
                    ORDER BY AGE DESC;
```

B. Inner JOIN Commands

Syntax:
```
SELECT [DISTINCT] select-list
FROM table1 [table-label1], table2 [table-label2] . . .
WHERE Join-condition
[AND theta-conditions]
[ORDER BY {attribute-name | expression} [DESC] . . .]
```

Purpose: To extract related data from two or more tables. Only tuples whose JOIN keys match the JOIN condition(s) will produce an output tuple. If the JOIN condition(s) are omitted, the command functions like a Cartesian product.

Examples:
```
SELECT STUDENT_NAME,COURSE_TITLE,*
FROM STUDENT, COURSES
WHERE STUDENT.SID = COURSE.SID;

SELECT NAME, AGE, COURSE_TITLE
FROM STUDENT S, COURSE C
WHERE S.SID = C.SID
  AND AGE BETWEEN 19 AND 22;

SELECT FACULTY_NAME, STUDENT_NAME
FROM FACULTY F, COURSE C, STUDENT S
WHERE F.FID = C.FID
  AND C.SID = S.SID
  AND F.GENDER = 'MALE'
  AND S.GENDER = 'FEMALE'
  AND S.AGE BETWEEN 25 AND 40
  AND S.GPA > 2.75
ORDER BY GPA;

SELECT FACULTY_NAME, STUDENT_NAME
FROM FACULTY F,  STUDENT S
WHERE F.AGE , C.AGE;
```

C. Outer JOIN Commands

Syntax:
```
SELECT [DISTINCT] select-list
FROM table1 [table-label1], table2 [table-label2] . . .
WHERE {Join-key1 (+) = Join-key2 |
       Join-key1     = Join-key2 (+)}
[AND theta-conditions]
[ORDER BY {attribute-name | expression} [DESC] . . .]
```

Purpose: To extract related data from two or more tables. Tuples will be created whether the JOIN keys match or not. If the JOIN key does not match in the table with the plus sign, a tuple will be created with null values placed in that tables attributes.

Example:
```
SELECT STUDENT_NAME,COURSES_TITLE,*
FROM STUDENT, COURSES
WHERE STUDENT.SID (+) = COURSE.SID;
```

D. Subqueries

Syntax:
```
SELECT [DISTINCT] select-list
FROM table-name [table-label]
WHERE attribute relational-operator
      (SELECT attribute
       FROM table-name [table-label]
       [WHERE theta-condition(s)) . . .
[AND theta-condition(s)]
[ORDER BY {attribute-name | expression} [DESC] . . .]
```

Purpose: To retrieve tuples based and values retrieved through embedded SELECT commands. The SELECT command placed in parentheses within the WHERE clause is the subquery and is executed before the outer SELECT command is executed.

Examples:
```
SELECT *
FROM STUDENT
WHERE AGE = (SELECT AGE
             FROM STUDENT
             WHERE NAME = 'MIKE SMITH');
```

E. Grouped Retrieval

Syntax:
```
SELECT [DISTINCT] select-list
FROM table [table-label]
[WHERE theta-condition(s)]
GROUP BY column-name(s)
    [HAVING theta-condition(s)]
```

Purpose: To retrieve data that has been grouped by a specified attribute(s). Also allows the user to use the special group functions of AVG, SUM, MAX, MIN, COUNT, VARIANCE, and STDDEV. The optional HAVING clause allows the user to filter out unwanted groups.

Examples: `SELECT DEPARTMENT_NAME, SUM (SALARY), AVG(SALARY)`
`FROM DEPT_TABLE`
`GROUP BY DEPARTMENT_NAME;`

`SELECT DEPARTMENT_NAME, COUNT(*), MAX (SALARY)`
`FROM DEPT_TABLE`
`GROUP BY DEPARTMENT_NAME`
`HAVING COUNT(*) > 1;`

F. Hierarchical Retrieval

Syntax: `SELECT [LEVEL] select-list`
`FROM table`
`[WHERE theta-condition(s)]`
`CONNECT BY {column-name1 = PRIOR column-name2 |`
`            PRIOR column-name1 = column-name2}`
`START WITH theta-condition(s)`
`[GROUP BY column-name(S)`
`    [(HAVING theta-condition(s)]]`

Purpose: To allow ORACLE the capability to perform hierarchical retrieval.
The placement of the PRIOR clause determines if the retrieval
path is top-to-bottom or bottom-to-top in the tree structure. The
START WITH clause defines the root node(s) in the tree. The
columns specified in the CONNECT BY clause determine the
relationship(s).

Example: `SELECT *`
`FROM PERSONNEL`
`CONNECT BY BOSS_ID = PRIOR EMPLOYEE_ID`
`START WITH EMPLOYEE_NAME = 'JOE SMITH';`

V. The File Maintenance Commands
Description: To give the user the capability of adding new record occurrences,
deleting old occurrences, or modifying the values currently stored
in attributes.

A. The INSERT Command

Syntaxes: `INSERT INTO table-name [attribute-list]`
`VALUES (value-list)`

`INSERT INTO table-name [attribute-list]`
`select-command`

Purpose: To store new tuple occurrences into a table. The first format is
used to insert one tuple at a time into the table. Variables can

be used for values in the value-list. The second format is used
to copy data from one table to another. If the attribute-list option
is utilized, any attributes not specified are given null values.

Examples:
```
INSERT INTO STUDENT_TABLE VALUES
('S55', 'TELLY VYSION', 'COMP SCIENCE',
'12-DEC-67');
INSERT INTO STUDENT (SID, SNAME) VALUES
('S56', 'PARRY SHOOT');
INSERT INTO STU-TAB
  SELECT * FROM STUDENT_TABLE WHERE AGE > 20;
INSERT INTO SUMMARY_TABLE (DEPT, NUMB, AVE_SAL)
  SELECT DEPARTMENT, COUNT(*), AVG(SALARY)
  FROM FACULTY
  GROUP BY DEPARTMENT;
```

B. The DELETE Command

Syntax: `DELETE FROM table-name [WHERE theta-condition(s)]`

Purpose: To remove tuple occurrences from tables.

Examples:
```
DELETE FROM STUDENT;
DELETE FROM STUDENT WHERE GENDER = 'MALE';
```

C. The UPDATE Command

Syntax:
```
UPDATE table-name
   SET attribute-name1 = {constant1 | expression1}
     [attribute-name2 = {constant2 | expression2} . . .
   [WHERE theta-condition(s)]
```

Purpose: To change the value of attributes.

Examples:
```
UPDATE STUDENT
SET CLASS = 'SENIOR';

UPDATE STUDENT
SET TOTAL_QPS = TOTAL_QPS + 45
    TOTAL_HRS = TOTAL_HRS + 15
    GPA = TOTAL_QPS / TOTAL_HRS
WHERE SNAME = 'CAL N. DAR';
```

VI. Locking Commands
Description: To prevent other users from simultaneously accessing tables or
individual tuples from tables.

A. The SELECT FOR UPDATE Command

Syntax:
```
SELECT {* | attribute-name1
       [,attribute-name2 ...]}, ROWID
FROM table-name
WHERE theta-condition(s)
FOR UPDATE OF attribute-name-n
```

Purpose: To lock individual tuples temporarily within a table so that they can be updated. Locked tuples can be SELECTed by other users, but they cannot be modified. Locked tuples are modified by the UPDATE command. These tuples must be accessed via their ROWID. Locked tuples are unlocked by committing or rolling-back the changes to the tables.

Example:
```
SELECT SNAME, TOTAL_QPS, ROWID
FROM STUDENT
WHERE SNAME = 'MISS KEETO'
FOR UPDATE OF TOTAL_QPS;
```

B. The LOCK Command

Syntax:
```
LOCK TABLE table-name1 [,table-name2 ...]
IN { SHARE | SHARED UPDATE | EXCLUSIVE } MODE
[ NOWAIT ]
```

Purpose: To lock all the tuples temporarily in a table. The table is unlocked when the changes are committed or rolled back.

Examples:
```
LOCK TABLE STUDENT IN SHARE MODE NOWAIT;
LOCK TABLE FACULTY IN SHARED UPDATE MODE;
```

VI. Granting and Revoking Table Privileges
   Description: To allow the creator of a table or view to pass certain privileges on these tables to other users.
A. The GRANT Command

Syntax:
```
GRANT {ALL | [ALTER, DELETE, INDEX, INSERT,
                SELECT, UPDATE,
                UPDATE (attribute-name)]}
ON {table-name | view-name}
TO {PUBLIC | user-name1 [, user-name2 , , ,]}
[WITH GRANT OPTION]
```

Purpose: To grant to all or selected system users all or specified privileges on specified tables or views. The grantor also has the power to pass the granted privilege(s) on to other users. The only privilege that cannot be passed to other users is DROP.

Example: `GRANT ALL ON MY_TABLE TO PUBLIC;`

```
GRANT SELECT
ON STUDENT
TO DEANS_OFFICE, REGISTRAR;

GRANT SELECT, UPDATE
ON FACULTY
TO PRESIDENT
WITH GRANT OPTIONS;

GRANT SELECT, INSERT, DELETE, UPDATE (SALARY)
ON FACULTY
TO PERSONNEL;
```

B. The REVOKE Command

Syntax:
```
REVOKE {ALL | [ALTER, DELETE, INDEX, INSERT,
               SELECT, UPDATE,
               UPDATE (attribute-name)]}
ON {table-name | view-name}
FROM {PUBLIC | user-name1 [,user-name2 . . .]}
```

Purpose: To take away privileges on tables or views that have been previously granted.

Examples:
```
REVOKE ALL ON MY_TABLE FROM PUBLIC;
REVOKE SELECT ON STUDENT FROM REGISTRAR;
```

VII. Creating and Deleting ORACLE User-names

Description: To create and delete ORACLE user-names. Only users with DBA privilege can execute these verions of the GRANT and REVOKE commands. User-names can be created with three privileges.

CONNECT   Allows user to log on to user-name. This privilege does not allow the user to use a version of the CREATE command. These type users can only use tables and views that other users have given them the privilege of using.

RESOURCE   Allows the user to use the CREATE command.

DBA   Allows the user to do anything that can be done in ORACLE. DBA privilege implies both CONNECT and RESOURCE privileges.

A. The GRANT Command

Syntaxes: GRANT {CONNECT | DBA}
         TO user-name1 [, user-name2 , , ,]
         IDENTIFIED BY password1 [,password2 , , ,]

         GRANT RESOURCE
         TO user-name1 [,user-name2 , , ,]

Purpose: To create user-names/passwords with their associated privileges.

Examples: GRANT CONNECT TO USER1 IDENTIFIED BY PASS1;
          GRANT RESOURCE TO USER1;
          GRANT DBA TO USER2 IDENTIFIED BY PASS2;

B. The REVOKE Command

Syntax: REVOKE [DBA | CONNECT | RESOURCE]
        FROM user-name1[, user-name2 ,,,]

Purpose: To rescind the privileges previously granted.

Examples: REVOKE RESOURCE FROM USER1;
          REVOKE CONNECT, RESOURCE FROM USER2;
          REVOKE CONNECT FROM USER1, USER2;

VIII. Making Data Maintenance Changes Permanent
    Description: ORACLE has two UFI commands that determine when and if
                data maintenance changes are to be made permanently. The com-
                mands are only relevant when the UFI command

                    SET AUTOCOMMIT OFF

        has be previously executed. If the

                    SET AUTOCOMMIT IMM

        command has been executed, file maintenance changes are made
        permanent when the DELETE, INPUT, or UPDATE command
        is executed.
    A. The COMMIT Command

        Syntax: COMMIT [WORK]

Purpose: To cause queued–up changes to be committed to the ORACLE
tables. A COMMIT command is automatically executed when
the ORACLE processor has be exited.

Example: `COMMIT`

B. The ROLLBACK Command

Syntax: `ROLLBACK [WORK]`

Purpose: Backs out all file maintenance changes made to ORACLE tables
since the last commit point.

Example: `ROLLBACK`

IX. Validating Indexes
Description: To ensure the integrity of an index.
A. The VALIDATE INDEX Command

Syntax: `VALIDATE INDEX index-name`

Purpose: To ensure that an index has not been corrupted. If any other message
than ''Index validated.'' appears, the index should be dropped and
recreated. Note that even though the VALIDATE INDEX command
is considered a SQL command, it is not terminated with a semicolon.

Example: `VALIDATE INDEX MY_INDEX`

C

APPENDIX:
ORACLE Reserved Words

These reserved words cannot be used as identifiers in ORACLE. Not all of the commands, concepts, and so forth that are identified by these reserved words have been implemented.

ADD	ALL	ALTER	AND
ANY	AS	ASC	ASSERT
ASSIGN	BETWEEN	BY	CHAR
CLUSTER	COLUMN	COMPRESS	CONNECT
CONTAIN	CONTAINS	CRASH	CREATE
CURRENT	DATAPAGES	DATE	DBA
DECIMAL	DEFINITION	DELETE	DESC
DISTINCT	DOES	DROP	EACH
ELSE	EVALUATE	EXCLUSIVE	FILE
FLOAT	FOR	FROM	GRANT
GRAPHIC	GROUP	HAVING	IDENTIFIED
IF	IMAGE	IMMEDIATE	IN
INCREMENT	INDEX	INDEXED	INDEXPAGES
INITIAL	INSERT	INTEGER	INTERSECT
INTO	IS	LEVEL	LIKE
LIST	LOCK	LONG	MAXEXTENTS
MINUS	MODE	MODIFY	MOVE
NEW	NOCOMPRESS	NOSYSSORT	NOT
NOWAIT	NULL	NUMBER	OF
OLD	ON	OPTOMIZE	OPTION
OR	ORDER	PARTITION	PCTFREE
PRIOR	PRIVILEGES	PUBLIC	RESOURCE
REVOKE	ROW	ROWID	ROWNUM
ROWS	RUN	SELECT	SET
SHARE	SIZE	SMALLINT	SPACE
START	SYNONYM	SYSDATE	SYSSORT
TABLE	THEN	TO	TRIGGER
UID	UNION	UNIQUE	UPDATE
USER	USING	VALIDATE	VALUES
VARCHAR	VARGRAPHIC	VIEW	WHERE
WITH			

Source: *ORACLE SQL/UFI Reference Manual Version 4.0*, ORACLE Corporation, Menlo Park, CA, 1984, p. 53.

Index